STERLING HAYDEN'S WARS

HOLLYWOOD LEGENDS SERIES
CARL ROLLYSON, GENERAL EDITOR

Sterling Hayden's Wars

LEE MANDEL

UNIVERSITY PRESS OF MISSISSIPPI • JACKSON

www.upress.state.ms.us

Designed by Peter D. Halverson

The University Press of Mississippi is a member of the
Association of University Presses.

Frontispiece from the Sterling Hayden Collection, Howard Gotlieb Archival
Research Center at Boston University.

Manufactured in the United States

First printing 2018
∞

Library of Congress Cataloging-in-Publication Data

Names: Mandel, Lee author.
Title: Sterling Hayden's wars / Lee Mandel.
Description: Jackson : University Press of Mississippi, 2018. | Series:
Hollywood legends | Includes bibliographical references and index. |
Identifiers: LCCN 2017048919 (print) | LCCN 2017053197 (ebook) | ISBN
9781496816986 (epub single) | ISBN 9781496816993 (epub institutional) |
ISBN 9781496817006 (pdf single) | ISBN 9781496817013 (pdf institutional) |
ISBN 9781496816979 (cloth : alk. paper)
Subjects: LCSH: Hayden, Sterling, 1916–1986. | Actors—United
States—Biography.
Classification: LCC PN2287.H34 (ebook) | LCC PN2287.H34 M36 2018 (print)
| DDC 791.4302/8092 [B] —dc23
LC record available at https://lccn.loc.gov/2017048919

British Library Cataloging-in-Publication Data available

THIS BOOK IS DEDICATED TO CATHERINE "KITTY" HAYDEN,
THE LOVE OF STERLING HAYDEN'S LIFE.

CONTENTS

ACKNOWLEDGMENTS IX

PROLOGUE XI

INTRODUCTION 3

PART ONE: PREPARING TO ENGAGE 7

CHAPTER ONE: Beginnings 9

CHAPTER TWO: The Lure of the Sea 14

CHAPTER THREE: Mentors 30

CHAPTER FOUR: Youngest Captain 40

CHAPTER FIVE: Inventing a Hollywood Star 48

PART TWO: THE FIRST WAR 57

CHAPTER SIX: Walking Out on Hollywood 59

CHAPTER SEVEN: Joining the OSS 82

CHAPTER EIGHT: Yugoslavia 90

CHAPTER NINE: Bravery, Chaos, and a Rescue Mission 104

CHAPTER TEN: Missions to Albania and an Effort in Filmmaking . . 117

CHAPTER ELEVEN: Air Crew Rescue Unit and a Loss of Faith 131

CHAPTER TWELVE: European Theater 150

PART THREE: THE SECOND WAR 157

CHAPTER THIRTEEN: Joining the Communist Party in Hollywood . . 159

CHAPTER FOURTEEN: Searching for Subversives in Hollywood. . . . 171

CHAPTER FIFTEEN: Naming Names 192

PART FOUR: LATER BATTLES 233

CHAPTER SIXTEEN: Divorce and Escape 235

CHAPTER SEVENTEEN: *Wanderer* to Tahiti and Back 247

CHAPTER EIGHTEEN: A New Bride and Literary Acclaim 259

CHAPTER NINETEEN: Radical Redux 269

CHAPTER TWENTY: Return to Film 274

CHAPTER TWENTY-ONE: Alcohol, Hashish, and River Barges 278

CHAPTER TWENTY-TWO: A Literary Triumph and Final Years 288

EPILOGUE 311

NOTES 312

BIBLIOGRAPHY AND SOURCES 335

INDEX 339

ACKNOWLEDGMENTS

THERE ARE SEVERAL PEOPLE THAT I WOULD LIKE TO ACKNOWLEDGE FOR their invaluable assistance in writing this book. I was fortunate enough to be able to speak with two of Sterling Hayden's friends who shared recollections of their times together with him. Through the efforts of film archivist Susan Strange, I spoke on several occasions with Norm Hatch, Hayden's friend and colleague since they were teenagers. I also was able to interview film producer Dennis Powers, who was the youngest member of the crew of the *Wanderer* when Hayden captained the schooner to Tahiti in 1959. Their insights into the mind and character of Sterling Hayden were invaluable.

The behind-the-scenes staff at the National Archives in College Park, Maryland, provided excellent service during my research into Hayden's World War II exploits, as did the staff at the Dwight D. Eisenhower Presidential Library. I was fortunate to be able to spend several days examining the Sterling Hayden Collection, the repository of his personal papers that are housed at the Howard Gotlieb Archival Research Center at Boston University. I am especially indebted to archivist Sarah Pratt for her assistance, as well as to Manager of Public Service Laura Russo.

Journalist Scott McConnell, Sterling Hayden's stepson, graciously responded to my inquiries about his stepfather, and his daughter-in-law, Sarah Hayden, provided me encouragement throughout the writing of the book.

My greatest debt is to Catherine "Kitty" Hayden, Sterling Hayden's widow, and to David Hayden, Sterling and Kitty's youngest son. I originally took a chance and wrote them a letter explaining my interest in Sterling Hayden and attached the original draft of my manuscript. To my good fortune, they responded positively to my efforts and invited me to meet with them to discuss the various aspects of Sterling's life. Their candor was impressive—they helped flesh out the story of this remarkable man, warts and all. In addition, they shared photographs and documents with me that greatly enhanced my original manuscript. After our initial meetings, they authorized me to have access to the Sterling Hayden Collection at Boston University, and I became the only researcher ever granted such access. Over the ensuing months, they have put up with multiple phone calls from me and we have become close friends. As much as I enjoyed researching and writing this book, the greatest source of gratification for me has been my friendship with Kitty and David Hayden.

Lastly, I have to acknowledge my number one assistant and supporter, my wife Ann. She helped me through the entire process of writing this book, by proofreading, critiquing, and recommending changes in the manuscript. For over thirty years, she has been my partner and my greatest inspiration.

PROLOGUE

ADRIATIC SEA
DECEMBER 1943

THE CREW COULD SEE THAT THEIR CAPTAIN WAS IN THE FOULEST OF moods. Up to this point the mission had gone well. Making the transit across the Adriatic Sea to Yugoslavia, the mission was, as always, twofold. First, they had brought much needed supplies across the sea for the Yugoslav Partisans, led by Josef Broz, better known by his nom de guerre of Tito. The other purpose of the mission was to pick up Allied airmen who had bailed out over Yugoslavian territory, many of whom were wounded or injured. In addition, wounded Partisan combatants would also be evacuated back to the Allied base at Monopoli, Italy.

Departing from Monopoli in the evening, the boat operated by the Office of Strategic Services, commonly known as the OSS, had transited throughout the night and tied up in the morning in a hidden cove on the Dalmatian coast of Yugoslavia. Under the cover of the following night, they unloaded their cargo and departed back to Monopoli the following night. The transit was made perilous not only because of the Allied minefields off the Italian coast, but by the patrolling German boats. The Yugoslavian coast was patrolled by German E-boats, swift 108-foot vessels capable of speeds up to forty knots. The OSS fleet, comprised largely of armed fishing vessels, was no match for these boats, relying instead on stealth and superior seamanship. It was superior seamanship that the OSS boat captain brought to the mission, along with an almost reckless obsession for mission completion. His crew greatly admired his courage and leadership.

The captain was a huge man at six foot five and over two hundred pounds of muscle. He was a second lieutenant in the United States Marine Corps who had been accepted into the OSS and was in charge of all maritime operations at Monopoli. The strikingly handsome officer was named John Hamilton. Less than two years before, he had been known as Sterling Hayden, the star of two major Hollywood movies, *Virginia* and *Bahama Passage*, before he abruptly quit the film industry. After enlisting in the Marine Corps and then receiving an officer's commission, he legally changed his name so he would not be tied to his previous persona. Although the men serving under him knew who he really was, woe to any of them who dared to address him by any name other than Capt. Hamilton. His men knew him as a no-nonsense, hard-drinking, mission-driven leader.

Hamilton had become increasingly frustrated with the British, who continued to treat the OSS as stepchildren. As a result of previous agreements reached between the two countries, the British Special Operations Executive, or SOE, was the senior partner in the Mediterranean theater of operations and in the Balkans. OSS personnel continually chafed under British restrictions and incidents that they perceived as British interference with their missions. Hamilton's patience with the British was nearing an end. His crew had already witnessed a display of Hamilton's mercurial temper on a prior mission.

On that previous mission they had rescued four American airmen from Yugoslavia and after departing the coast they were attacked by several German E-boats. Their vessel was shot up badly and they now had three seriously wounded airmen aboard. Unbeknownst to Hamilton, his glamorous wife, movie star Madeleine Carroll, had been brought to the pier back in Monopoli in a publicity stunt arranged by the Army and the Red Cross. Arriving at the pier, the livid Hamilton began screaming obscenities as he worked to evacuate his wounded passengers and inspect his damaged ship. He then turned to the Fifteenth Air Force public relations officer who had arranged the affair, Maj. Bernal Clark, and proceeded to grab him and throw him into the harbor.

On their current mission as they departed the Yugoslavian coast, they came under attack by two German E-boats. As Hamilton furiously attempted to maneuver out of harm's way and their boat returned machine-gun fire at their attackers, he called the British for help, pleading for them to send air support. Finally screaming for help over open radio transmissions, he was stunned to hear his British allies respond: "Negative, negative. Can't help you, old chap." Hamilton and his crew finally were able to evade the Germans, nearly losing their boat, but it was the last straw for John Hamilton.

As they approached their home harbor, they saw a British PT boat nearby. Speeding alongside, Hamilton ordered his forward gunner to open fire on the British boat. The stunned crew hesitated; they knew what Hamilton was capable of when he was furious and they, too, feared that they would get tossed over the side by their captain.

After a short pause, they aimed their guns, and opened fire. . . .

STERLING HAYDEN'S WARS

Introduction

HE WAS THE MOST ICONOCLASTIC OF ACTORS. IN AN INDUSTRY where it is very fashionable to claim that you care nothing about money and don't really enjoy acting, he truly didn't care about either. He had a dysfunctional upbringing during the Depression and left home at the age of sixteen to go to sea. By the time he was twenty years old, he had sailed around the world as first mate on a schooner. Despite having no professional training as an actor, he successfully marketed his handsome looks and impressive physique, and in a matter of months, he was starring in a major Hollywood production, titled *Virginia*. After his second movie, *Bahama Passage*, he simply walked away from the film industry.

He considered himself a coward, yet he volunteered for commando training in Europe before the United States entered the Second World War. He turned down a commission from the United States Navy, but shortly thereafter enlisted in the United States Marine Corps. Feeling constrained by rigid military discipline, he appealed to America's spymaster, Gen. William J. Donovan, and was accepted into the Office of Strategic Services, better known as the OSS. He would distinguish himself in combat alongside the Yugoslavian and Albanian Partisans and fall under the spell of their communist philosophy. He was an idealistic young man looking for a cause in which to believe.

Sterling Hayden's brief membership in the Communist Party of the United States would come back to haunt him, and he would become enmeshed in the battle between Hollywood and the House Un-American Activities Committee in public testimony. He would be the first Hollywood star to name names and would hate himself for the rest of his life for this. He would emerge with his career thriving and would soon engage in other battles: a vicious battle for the custody of his children with his second wife, with alcoholism and substance abuse, and the persistent battle against his self-doubt and self-hatred.

With only a tenth-grade education and no formal training as a writer, he would publish his first book, his autobiography *Wanderer*, at the age of forty-seven and it would be a critically acclaimed bestseller. His second book, a novel called *Voyage: A Novel of 1896*, was published when he was sixty years old and it, too, was a critically acclaimed international bestseller.

Although remembered today primarily as a "B-actor" with occasional flashes of brilliance, such a description does not tell the real story. Novelist and film scholar Jake Hinkson has offered a richer, more nuanced assessment of his acting skills: "His voice, a kind of rapid-fire bellow, is made for the clipped dialogue of a suspicious cop or a surly thug. His shopworn good looks and imposing physical presence make him a natural to play men stalking darkened city streets at three in the morning. What he lacks in nuance, he makes up for in essence. In crime films, he's as natural as cheap carpet and cigarette smoke. No, he couldn't act, he could only *be*. And that *being* is the key to why he was a great actor. Among noir heroes, he may well be the most intrinsically existential."[1]

Despite a lucrative film career, followed by a successful writing career, he was frequently broke and in debt. He never invested a penny of his earnings as he didn't believe in accepting money that he didn't actually earn with his own labor. He could be gregarious around family and friends yet he continually sought solitude. Perhaps the best description of Sterling Hayden was offered by his stepson Scott McConnell, who wrote shortly after his death: "He was the natural center of any room he occupied. Curious, kind, capable of mordant self-mockery, he was blessed with the ability to make those in his company feel that they were close to the center of all that was interesting in the world. None of these gifts, it would seem, ever brought him a fair portion of satisfaction."[2]

It would be a mistake to dismiss Sterling Hayden as just another eccentric Hollywood personality. In *Sterling Hayden's Wars*, I explore in detail this complex man who was full of self-doubt and proved to be an adept nonconformist who was able to accomplish a great deal in various fields in spite of himself. His wartime records, which are examined in detail for the first time, and an in-depth investigation of the HUAC hearings, provide the framework on which to attain a true understanding of this unique man. Helping to flesh out the narrative are interviews conducted with members of the Hayden family, as well as material from Hayden's personal papers that are maintained in the Sterling Hayden Collection at the Howard Gotlieb Archival Research Center at Boston University. The adjective "unique" is the key—Hayden was always too much of an individualist to truly belong to any one organization or to fit into conventional society. Whether it was his dysfunctional childhood, battling Hollywood, the Nazis, the HUAC, his ex-wife, alcoholism and substance abuse, his life was a series of wars that he was engaged in, including the most difficult one of them all—the war that Sterling Hayden fought with himself.

PART ONE

PREPARING TO ENGAGE

"I started from the top and worked my way down."

STERLING HAYDEN

"Of course he can act. I can act, you can act,
anybody can act if he feels like actin',
what's so tough about actin'?"

LAWRENCE "LARRY" O'TOOLE

CHAPTER ONE

Beginnings

HE WAS BORN STERLING RELYEA WALTER ON MARCH 26, 1916. THE only child of George and Frances Walter of Upper Montclair, New Jersey, they had originally planned to name him Montaigu but his godfather, Mont Sterling, convinced them to name his godson after him. Growing up in the suburbs of New York City in the years before the Depression, Sterling Hayden would recall an unremarkable childhood. Life, he recalled, was quiet. He would also describe it as peaceful. "We lived a peaceful life," he would recall, "so peaceful, in fact, that it made me restless."[1] Even at that young age, the lure of adventure and restlessness was beginning to shape his personality.

His father George was a tall, thin man. He appeared to his son to be in poor health. Hayden would describe him as a distant, humorless man. He never played with his son or talked to him, except to scold or discipline him.[2] His preferred method of disciplining his son was to take a thin piece of wood dipped in water and apply it to his son's backside while he was bent over his lap. Although he was not around him much, young Sterling much preferred being with his Uncle Mont, who was also tall but strongly built. Mont was much more interesting to his nephew than his own father. He was a successful businessman, a boxer, and an expert pistol marksman who taught handgun shooting to the state police. This Renaissance man had a much greater appeal to young Sterling as a role model than his rather bland, humorless father.

George Walter worked selling advertising for the *New York World*, a daily newspaper in Manhattan. His wife Frances, a homemaker, showered her affection on her young son, something that her husband was unable to do. She, too, was a large woman, weighing more than her husband. Hayden would acknowledge his deep love for his mother, who was much more outgoing than his father. She was also a very disciplined pianist and would delight her son with her musical talents. She never called her son "Sterling"; rather, she preferred calling him "Buzz" or "Buzzy."

Life for the Walter family revolved around routines. Every morning George would take the 7:18 a.m. train into the city and he would arrive back in Upper Montclair on the 6:53 p.m. train. This was his routine six days a week, every week with the exception of two weeks a year every summer. The annual summer retreat for the family was to a cabin at Lake Minnewaska in the Catskills. Perhaps it was inevitable that their restless son would become bored and inattentive, even at an early age.

He was a lazy and indifferent student. He had failed the third grade, and even in his second time around in that grade, he made little effort to apply himself to his studies. In addition, he was prone to mischief, culminating in a rock-throwing incident directed towards his teacher. Towards the end of his second stint in the third grade, his teachers had had enough of his antics and decided to both expel him from school and to personally call his mother to report on his unacceptable behavior. Knowing he was capable of much more, Frances was heartbroken over the news. Not being a disciplinarian, she made him wait in his room until his father came home to handle the situation. With dread, young Sterling waited up in his room in the attic, fearing he was in for another backside lashing from his father. However, his father had a different form of "punishment" in mind, one that would inadvertently change his son's life, although not in a way that he had intended.

George Walter entered the room, minus the wooden switch that his son expected him to be holding and quietly sat down on the edge of the bed. "Son," he began, "I don't know what to do with you."

"Why don't you go ahead and wallop me?" Sterling challenged him.

"No," shot back his father. "You're too old for spanking. I'm going to try something different this time. There's a man I know who has a son who has been a good deal of trouble. When this man's son was your age, he was expelled from school, too. And do you know where he is today?"

"No, Father, where is he?"

"He is in prison, in Sing Sing."[3] George proceeded to outline his plan. He would take Sterling into the city with him the following morning to meet his friend so he could relate to him his son's terrible life experiences. The idea was for Sterling to be "scared straight" by the encounter and begin to apply himself in his studies. That night, young Sterling had a nightmare about being in a reformatory with a gang of vicious thugs.

Upon awakening that morning, he took solace in his favorite book, *The Wonder Book of Ships*, and got dressed to prepare for his trip into New York City.

Sitting obediently with his father, Sterling watched the towns go by as the commuter train wound its way north towards New York. The last part of the commute required the passengers to transfer to a ferry to cross the Hudson River, and as they walked along the wharf to the ferry, a magical feeling swept over the boy. Hayden recalled, "A cold, clean wave of salt air broke like magic over my head . . . I felt so excited I laughed and turned to my father, for I thought he might feel the same. No sign that he did."[4]

The young boy was virtually intoxicated by his first real experience on the water. He would recall in his autobiography the absolute joy he felt as the ferryboat sliced through the water towards Manhattan. "The skyscrapers of Lower Manhattan loom toward us, but I wish they were far away. I wish I could ride back and forth for days and months and live in a lifeboat or up in the pilothouse."[5] Although he couldn't possibly know it at the time, at the age of nine, Sterling Hayden had discovered his life's passion.

Hayden never described in his writings the meeting with his father's friend. His relationship with George Walter continued to be distant and often strained. The dysfunctional relationship reached its culmination around Thanksgiving of 1925. Once again, the confrontation centered around mischief that Sterling had gotten into. This time, he and a friend had bought slingshots and were determined to shoot at passing cars. Sterling was attempting to fire a staple at the tires of a Maxwell Roadster going by, but the sling slipped and instead he managed to hit his friend. As his friend screamed out in pain, the driver screeched to a halt and seeing Sterling attempting to flee the scene, ran after him. After a short chase, he caught the boy and dragged him by his ear to his home. Just as they arrived at his home, George and Frances drove up in the driveway.

The motorist explained what George and Frances's son and his friend had done. In addition to the injury suffered by his friend, the motorist's wife had received a gash along her cheek as a result of the boys' antics. This time, George was livid and determined to deliver some serious punishment to his ne'er-do-well son. He dragged him down to the basement and sought out his punishment stick. Soaking the end in water to increase the stinging, he threw his son across his lap. Sterling started to cry as his father raised the stick to begin. His mother, upstairs in the kitchen, could hear him screaming as each blow was delivered to his bare buttocks. "Then suddenly," Hayden recalled, "his body froze and the stick slipped out of his hand."

George Walter, who had congenital heart disease, was suddenly struggling for breath and began calling his wife's name. She ran down the stairs to her husband's side while her son ran over to some neighbors who came to render assistance. They helped to carry George up to his room. "That night the doctor came. And every week all winter long he came back, but it never occurred to me that my father was sick enough to die."

George Walter survived until the following February, when he passed away. Because he was only nine years old, Sterling was not allowed to attend the funeral. He and his mother arrived at an understanding: from that point on, they would never mention his father again.[6]

• • •

To make ends meet, Frances went to work for *Good Housekeeping* magazine, earning a salary of thirty dollars a week. About three years after George died, she announced to her son and mother that she was bringing home a man for them to meet. His name was James Hayden. As Sterling soon found out from his mother, he was married but was seeking a divorce from his wife. At first, Sterling was happy for his mother, feeling that she certainly deserved happiness and companionship, and it was obvious to him that marriage was in the plans for the couple. After meeting Jim Hayden, however, he was less than impressed.

There was something phony about the man with whom his mother was smitten. He was a sharp dresser who seemed to have many grandiose business plans. By that time, Sterling and Frances's mother had already heard about his business ventures. He had supposedly run a boys' camp in New Hampshire, of which he was also a part-owner. He was going to enter the hotel-resort business and bragged that he had a large deal already lined up in that regard.[7] As Frances and Sterling would find out to their dismay, Jim Hayden was a schemer and a talker, always on the verge of the big deal that he never was able to achieve, and always fleeing town one step ahead of his creditors. Before the end of the year, he was forced out by the owners of the boys' camp and his big resort deal also fell through. He quickly came up with a new business deal that collapsed just as quickly as the previous one.

Still residing in Upper Montclair by 1929, Sterling was called into the room by his mother and Jim. They had an announcement—they were going to be married and asked how the young boy felt about that prospect. Sterling paused, then he responded enthusiastically. His mother's happiness was his paramount concern. Also adding to his enthusiasm, he realized: "At least we'll get out of this place, we'll travel and maybe live in a better house, and I'll go to a different school." Shortly after, reality set in as he noted: "We hit the road. The road to Nowhere Sure."[8]

After Jim and Frances married, Jim adopted Sterling, and his parents had his name legally changed to Sterling Walter Hayden. It didn't take long for "Daddy Jim," as Sterling called him, to show his true colors. Life for the Hayden family became a series of constant moves, as Daddy Jim, or J. Watson Hayden (as he liked to be called), pursued one big deal after another. They moved to an island on a lake in New Hampshire, to Boston, to Washington, DC, and back to New Hampshire. Sterling realized that Daddy Jim was continually creating a house of cards and false grandeur, confirming his initial suspicions. As they departed each location, they left behind multiple unpaid creditors. After borrowing money from Frances's wealthy sister, they were on the road again—this time headed for the shore and another "deal." The next destination would change Sterling Hayden's life forever.

CHAPTER TWO

The Lure of the Sea

THEY DROVE UP TO MAINE AND HEADED FOR THE COASTAL SEAPORT OF Boothbay Harbor. As they drove into town, young Hayden would describe his first viewing of the harbor: "I caught a glimpse of the harbor. The glow inside me turned to a dancing flame. At the end of a sun-swept wharf lay a ship with two high masts. She was gone in a flash but I knew I'd be back, and I shivered. This was an enchanted village, compared to the places we'd been."[1] The sensation that had come over him several years back on that first ferry ride returned with a vengeance. He knew then that the sea was calling to him.

The family found lodging at a rooming house called Tinker Tavern, and although his tiny bedroom was barely bigger than a closet, Sterling was delighted. The room featured a huge window that looked out over the harbor. As soon as they checked into their new living quarters, he announced to his parents that he was going to take a walk. He had several hours before suppertime, and he headed straight for the docks.

Walking along the wharfs, he was absolutely mesmerized by the maritime environment. The ship's chandler shop, the smell of the ocean, the ships tied to the pier—it was magic for him. Watching a schooner pull into the harbor, he knew he had to get closer, to become, even if only for a short while, a part of the seaman's world. As the sun started to set, he looked back as he returned to the boarding house. He knew he had to return, and soon. The next morning, he headed for the waterfront again.

He found an old man on the pier who appeared to him what a sea captain should look like. Would it be possible to rent a rowboat for the day? he inquired. For fifty cents, the older man led him to his first vessel. Although he had been in rowboats before, it had always been on lakes or rivers. Now he would be in a harbor, an entrance to the open sea. As he rowed out, the feeling was exhilarating. With his collie Laird as his companion, he headed towards a group of three abandoned derelict sailing ships that were tied up next to each other at the end of the pier. Feeling both inquisitive and adventurous, he boarded one named *Josiah B. Chase*. Exploring the entire ship, he envisioned himself as an adventurous pirate, roaming the high seas. After spending the entire afternoon aboard the rotting vessel, it was time to head back. As he rowed away, he relaxed and then laid on his back on the floor of the boat, staring up at the sky until he dozed off. He couldn't help but think: "What could be more wonderful than a year or two on a schooner?"[2] That thought would stay with him his entire life.

The little boat began to drift into the edge of one of the many tiny islands that dotted the entrance to the harbor. Once again, the urge to explore came over him and he noticed the solitary home on this island that was no bigger than one hundred yards long. It appeared to be unoccupied and to his surprise, as he pulled up to the small dock there was a sign announcing: FOR SALE. It immediately hit him—this solitary home overlooking the ocean would be an ideal place to live. He had to let his mother and Daddy Jim know about it.

Arriving back at the boarding house, he told his parents of his discovery, and to his delight, they were very interested in the isolated home. Visiting the sales agent, they learned that tiny Tumbler Island was indeed for sale. The price, $3,000, was too rich for J. Watson Hayden's blood. The agent then countered that the property was also for rent. For $100, they could rent it through the fall. Daddy Jim jumped at the opportunity, asking if they could rent it for the entire winter. After pointing out that the house was not heated, the surprised agent agreed and the lease was signed. Young Sterling Hayden, who had grown to distrust his stepfather, would admit: "A surge of affection went through me for this man who had gone through such a run of bad luck. He closed the deal, and out on the street I wanted to tell him how much I loved him but all I could do was smile."[3] Shortly after, the three Haydens and their pet dog became the sole residents of Tumbler Island.

Young Sterling enjoyed leading a solitary life on the family's private island. The teenager would continue to fantasize about a life at sea, and the island's location provided a nonstop panorama of sailing ships of all sizes. On occasion, he would take a small catboat into Boothbay Harbor and wander through the town. The town, crowded with tourists throughout the summer, began to thin by the end of August, and by September, it was only sparsely populated by the town's permanent residents. Walking through the town, he discovered the Boothbay Harbor Memorial Library and he also noticed that one of the drugstores had a book rental library. Once again, he experienced a sense of euphoria over what would become his other life's passion.

"Books and the sea, I discovered, had more than a little in common," he recalled in his autobiography *Wanderer*. "Both were distilled of silence and solitude. I was an islander now, so what could be more fitting than that my places of refuge on the mainland should be the sail loft and the public library, for these were islands too—in the turbulent social seas." He went on to embellish this mantra by stating: "Silence and solitude, books and the sea, sail loft and library. World enough for any man. Yet how few of them knew it."[4]

Throughout the winter of 1931–32, the Haydens lived on Tumbler Island, as Daddy Jim's deals, as always, amounted to nothing. In addition, his Packard had been repossessed. Relations between his stepfather and the teenaged Sterling continued to slowly but surely worsen. Sterling's secret passion was always that of an escape to sea. He read voraciously about ships and the sea and, in his mind, he would pretend that he was part of a great sea venture aboard a three-masted sailing ship. On one of his visits to the mainland, he received the advice and inspiration that would goad him into action to fulfill his dream.

Walking on the wharf, he saw a sign that read "JOHN HOWELL—SAILMAKER." The title seemed to lure him into the shop where he saw several men working. Fearing that they might throw him out, he began to initiate a conversation. To his relief, one of the men came up to him, offered his hand and introduced himself. It was the owner, John Howell. As Sterling began to introduce himself and explain that he lived on Tumbler Island, the old man interrupted him, exclaiming: "I know where you live, you live on the island out by the buoy; and you're spending the winter 'cause your daddy didn't pay his bills and they came and took his beautiful car and—"

"He's not really my father at all." Hayden countered.

"He's your stepfather, I know that too. And you don't go to school and you sail all the time except when it blows too hard, then you go for rows in your dory." Howell took a swig of rum before he continued speaking to his young guest, who was smiling back at him. "You're sea-struck, boy, that's what you are," declared the old man. "All you care for is ships, old ships, sailing ships, am I right? Of course I'm right, don't tell me any different."

Shaking his head, Hayden asked him how he could tell that. It was, Howell explained, because he was the very same way when he was Sterling's age. The lure of the sea was too great for him and he had run away and shipped out on a clipper ship. "Now you're ready to go to sea," declared John Howell. "You go, boy, you go, no matter what they say, you go, understand?"[5] It was the start of a memorable mentor-student relationship. Every day, Hayden would return to spend time with the old sailor. He knew that it was just a matter of time before he would follow in John Howell's footsteps.

• • •

By the fall of 1932, sixteen-year-old Sterling Hayden's idyllic life on Tumbler Island and Boothbay Harbor was coming to a close. As usual, it was Daddy Jim's business failures that compelled them to move on. This time, they traveled to Hallowell, near the capital city of Augusta. It was ninety miles from his beloved sea. Shortly after arrival, they moved into a seedy boarding house. Due to their financial straits, Frances Hayden was forced to go to work as a door-to-door cosmetics saleswoman. Once again, James Hayden came up with a money-making plan that was going to lift them out of poverty.

To facilitate this latest dream plan, Daddy Jim bought two cars: a convertible for his wife and a roadster for himself. They enrolled Sterling in what he described as the most expensive preparatory school in the country—the Wassookeag School in Dexter, Maine.[6] To complete the plan, the Haydens moved into a local upscale hotel. The only thing missing, as usual, was the necessary ingredient of money. For his needed capital, Daddy Jim had to turn to his stepson. Claiming to have fought off the thought for months, he announced: "We can, if Buzz here is willing, use his three thousand dollars to tide us over and give Dad Jim the money he needs to close the deal."[7]

The money, they explained was in a trust fund that Sterling's Uncle Mont had set up for him after he was born. The money was intended to be used for his nephew's college education or for him to use to start a business. This was the first that Sterling had ever heard of such an arrangement. In his sweetest and most convincing fatherly terms, Daddy Jim told him: "It's up to you, son; if you want to release that money, I know your Uncle Mont will oblige." Sterling readily agreed to the request.[8]

Daddy Jim was ecstatic, promising Sterling that he would pay him back multiple times over in a matter of months. As Jim rushed out the door, he realized he didn't even have enough money to wire the request from the Western Union office, and would have to send the wire to Mont Sterling collect.

The big business deal never materialized, and Sterling Hayden would never see a penny of the money his uncle had put aside in a trust for him.

• • •

It had been three years since Hayden had been in school when he enrolled for the fall 1932 semester. The transition to the Wassookeag School proved to be very difficult for him. He enjoyed the company of his fellow students, although he clearly didn't fit in with the wealthy young boys. He again proved to be an indifferent student who wasn't interested in his schoolwork. In his letters home to his mother, he admitted how badly he was doing with his studies, but pledged to try and improve his academics. By November, he was convinced that the teachers were ganging up on him. In addition, he expressed dismay that his mother was still working as a door-to-door cosmetics saleswoman. Referring to Daddy Jim, he asked: "Why do you work when he has so much money? . . . Is the deal closed yet? I trust so."[9] To add to his troubles, he had been called in by the headmaster for a very strident counseling session.

The headmaster berated him for his academic failures and his apparent lack of effort. After comparing his own story of his excellent work ethic to that of the young man sitting in front of him, he informed Hayden that he wasn't going to allow anyone to interfere with the school's fine record and excellent reputation. It then came down to dollars and cents. "When you write your stepfather," he instructed Hayden, "tell him he owes me quite a good deal of money. He said he would pay last month and I haven't received a cent. This is not a charitable institution."[10]

The only joy that Hayden derived from his experience at the prep school was the fact that he had a girlfriend. Her name was Debbie, and in his letters to his mother, he wrote glowingly of her, quite sure that his mother would approve of this girl who came from a fine family in Bangor. On November 21, 1932, Hayden wrote to Debbie and confided a secret to her—he had decided to run away from the school. "You may remember I told you how much I loved the sea," he explained. "Well, I have decided to beat my way (as they say) to Portland this weekend and land a job on a ship going to South America or the South Seas or around the world." His plan was to ride the railroads into Portland that weekend. He asked his girlfriend if she would come to the railroad yard so he could say goodbye to her in person. The sixteen-year-old prospective wanderer then asked if she would bring with her a full length picture of herself so he could remember her. Preferably, he requested, one taken of her in a bathing suit.[11]

Shortly after sending the letter, he packed some clothing early one evening, said goodbye to his roommates, and left on the first of his many life adventures. Heading out on the road, he flagged down a passing truck and hitched a ride to Bangor where he planned to board a train to Portland. From there, he would begin his sea odyssey. Other than pictures of his mother and his dog Laird, his wallet contained only two dollars. Arriving in Bangor around midnight, he headed to the train depot to meet with his beloved Debbie one last time. Much to his disappointment, she never showed up. In anger and frustration, he briefly considered heading back to the school before he was missed, but then resolved to push on with his plan. In due time, he heard the sound of a locomotive beginning to leave the station. He quickly pulled himself on to a flatcar and settled in.

As dawn broke the following morning, Hayden watched as the train pulled into Bath, Maine, not far from his beloved Boothbay Harbor. As snow flurries began to fall, he could see several sailing ships along the waterfront and once again, his fantasies of a life aboard sailing ships came alive within him. After traveling all day, the train finally pulled into the Portland train yards. Disembarking from the gondola, he had already formulated a plan. "I hope to find one of the fishing schooners I'd known in Boothbay. There I'd surely have a place to sleep while I search for a berth in a deep-water ship."[12]

The streets were deserted as he began his search. Walking to the end of the first dock he saw no schooners. He pressed on to the fish pier and there he found what he had been looking for. Half a dozen schooners were tied up to the pier. And he knew every one of them. At the very end of the dock, he spied a schooner that he was very familiar with. She was named *Restless*, and Hayden had befriended one of the crewmembers, Albert Powers. This was the opportunity he was looking for. Just as he stood there looking at the ship, two crewmembers arrived by his side, obviously intoxicated. "Hey you, sonny boy, watcha want who ya lookin' fer hay what?" one of them blurted out.

"Albert," he replied. "I'm trying to find my friend Albert Powers."

"Albie's home wit' the wife an' kids. Come down though, boy, come down out of it up there now, boy."[13] Hayden gladly accepted their invitation and went aboard with the sailors.

Going below to the crew's quarters, Hayden spied about a dozen bunks and couldn't help but notice the obvious stench. Other crewmembers were sitting around eating; upon seeing the young boy enter their quarters, they offered him a mug of coffee and a slice of pie. Find a bunk, they told him. He would be their guest for the night. After selecting a bunk near the bow that looked clean, he threw back the blanket, and saw "oily black bugs" crawl out.

It didn't matter to him. He wasn't hungry any more after the snack offered by the crewmembers. He was ecstatic, lying in the bunk with his new acquaintances around him. "Here I am," he would recall, "in an honest-to-God fo'c'sle in the plumb-stemmed schooner *Restless* which has been fishing out of Portland since 1888—how about that? Sterling Walter Hayden, born Montaigu Relyea Walter, alias Buzzy—in a fo'c'sle bunk full of bugs, with a northeast gale lashing the water front and the rigging cased in ice. Wouldn't John Howell be proud if he came down that ladder just now?"[14]

The following morning, as Hayden enjoyed breakfast with his newly found friends, Albert Powers arrived back aboard *Restless*. Surprised at seeing his young acquaintance from Boothbay Harbor, he asked him if he was lost. "Albert," began the young boy, "I'm running away from school."

"Oh? What the hell for?" shot back Powers. "Knock up a girl or something?"

"No, I'm going to get a job on a ship going to Africa or South America or someplace."

Hayden studied his older friend as several other crewmembers watched them. After a few moments, Powers asked him if he had any money. After hearing the boy's reply, he got down to business. "Now you listen to me, kid. Go home, see? If you ain't got a home, go back to that school. Stay there. Learn a trade or learn how to dance or play ball, but whatever you do don't come messing around with vessels." Hayden tried to say something, but the older man abruptly cut him off. "Shut up. Stay out of sight of the water except if you're on vacation. Make your dough and salt it away, then do your traveling around."[15]

It was over. Just as John Howell had planted the dream in young Sterling Hayden's mind, Albert Powers had abruptly quashed it. He now had no money and nowhere else to go to pursue his dream. He couldn't return to school. Even if his academic record hadn't been so thoroughly dismal, his parents couldn't afford it. He came to the sad realization that he would have to go back to his parents in Hallowell. His grandiose plans for a life at sea had crumbled.

But only temporarily.

• • •

After returning to his mother and stepfather, Hayden learned that once more it was time to move again. This time, they headed once again for Boston. Their cars having been repossessed, the Haydens traveled by bus to their new home. Relations between Daddy Jim and Frances had become tenuous; at times, being around them was like walking on eggshells. The tension always centered around money and her husband's seeming unwillingness to get a job instead of cooking up new financial deals.

They moved to Cambridge and stayed in the rooming house run by Daddy Jim's sister Emma. It was another residence in keeping with the line of seedy, borderline-slum boarding houses that the Haydens had lived in. While Daddy Jim worked on his deals, Frances continued her cosmetics sales, and young Sterling began looking for work. The relationship between Sterling and his stepfather had deteriorated badly and he was glad to leave the house to look for work. Taunted by Daddy Jim because he hadn't found a job, Sterling would return the taunts, pointing out the fact that that his stepfather didn't have a job either. Jokingly, the teenager told him that he couldn't decide which among the "plentiful" jobs he should accept. Daddy Jim just glared at him. By now, Sterling was nearing his adult height and was well over six feet tall, powerfully built, and also strikingly handsome. With disgust, Jim informed him: "You know something, young man? You're going to be a big man when you grow up; you're gonna grow up and have a 46-inch chest and a size-three hat."[16]

With the country in the midst of the Great Depression, there were no jobs to be had. Especially for an unskilled sixteen-year-old boy. Walking in the cold, snowy winter winds after a couple of months of fruitless searching, he decided one morning to inquire along the waterfront for any available work. Spotting the masts of a schooner over the roof of a waterfront warehouse, he walked towards it. It was a beautiful ship named *Wander Bird*. With curiosity and hope, he went aboard and knocked on the hatch. "Hello!" he heard from inside the ship. "Come down, whoever you are." He entered the hatch, closing it behind him and stomped the snow off of his boots.

A man appeared and to Hayden's surprise and delight, he was a friendly and gracious host. He offered his young guest hot chocolate and an invitation to stay and visit as long as he wanted. As they struck up a conversation, Hayden looked around and marveled at the beauty of this opulent, well-maintained schooner. The vessel was powered only by sail; it had no engines. The captain and his wife would host a trip to Europe every year aboard the *Wander Bird* for groups of college students. Hayden was mesmerized by his host, the ship, and the tales of life at sea aboard *Wander Bird*. This was the life of which he was dreaming. Once again, the dreams and the incentive planted by John Howell were coming to life. After a while, it was time for him to leave and continue his search for a job. He thanked his host profusely, who invited him to return again, indicating that he was always welcome to visit.

The captain's name was Warwick Tompkins. Although there was no way to possibly know at the time, Sterling Hayden had just met one of the most important people he would ever know, a person who would affect his entire life. Their relationship, one that evolved out of genuine friendship and affection, would result years later in public betrayal, bitterness, and lifelong regret.

The visit aboard *Wander Bird* buoyed the teenager's spirits. As he walked down the pier he made a decision: he would only look for shipboard jobs. And he was determined to find one that very day. Traveling up every pier and going aboard ship after ship, he was greeted with hostility and outright rejection. All along Rowe's Wharf, T Wharf, and Long Wharf, he ambled until there were no more ships in which to inquire, so he turned his attention to the seedier side of the waterfront in East Boston, where the fishing piers were located. Walking along the piers, he noticed the pawn shops, the trash, and the people like himself. Desperate people, victims of the Depression, all looking for jobs that didn't exist.

He was scared at the thought of becoming a fisherman, one whose life was a nonstop repetitive journey back and forth from the coast to the fishing waters of the North Atlantic. He wanted to voyage south to the tropical climes. Self-doubt began to creep into his mind. "Something must be wrong after all," he thought to himself. "I'm not of the sea and I'm not of the land . . . I'm sworn and anxious to go, yet scared to go, so all I do is tramp the water front."[17] He walked the length of the fishing piers but to no avail. There were no schooners moored there. The day was growing late and it was time for him to head back home after another unsuccessful day of job-hunting. Leaving the waterfront, he headed up State Street towards uptown.

A few blocks up State Street was a store that young Hayden had frequented ever since his family had arrived in Boston. It was the nautical instrument shop of Kelvin & Wilfred O. White. The shop had existed on State Street since 1918, and its front window attracted many pedestrians who enjoyed looking at the gleaming brass sextants, nautical flags, and ship's bell clocks. One of the owners had befriended the tall, strapping teenager and was accustomed to seeing him stop at the front window, as well as his occasional forays into the shop. As was his habit, that afternoon after leaving the waterfront, Hayden paused at the front window to gaze at the nautical treasures within.

As he looked at the various instruments, he noticed Wilfred White motioning to him to enter. After looking around to be sure that he was the one being beckoned, Hayden entered the shop and the owner pulled him over to speak to him. Had he been able to find any shipboard jobs? inquired the owner. When he replied that he hadn't, White then asked him: "How would you like to work on a big schooner sailing from New London to California?" Hayden was too stunned to respond.

"The captain was in for his charts this afternoon," explained White. "I told him you were a good lad. He sails in ten days and he'll sign you on as the ship's boy and give you ten dollars a month. How does that sound?" Hayden could only stammer in response and finally promised that he would leave for New London as soon as he packed a bag and then he would ride the rails back again to get to the pier.

As the clerk began to lock up the store, White smiled at the teenager and reached into his pocket. Handing him the cash, he said: "Here, this will buy a bus ticket, anyway. Pay me back if you wish—when you get a ship of your own."[18]

It was finally happening. Sterling Hayden was going to begin living his dream. The sixteen-year-old dreamer was finally going to sea.

• • •

He didn't use the money for a bus ticket. Instead, he again rode the rails to New London. Leaping from the boxcar upon arrival, he hit the ground and tumbled into a ditch, jarring his lower back. Emerging from the ditch, he began his trek towards the waterfront. Wearing a wool cap and with his sea bag slung over his shoulder, he was beginning to feel the part of a seafaring man. It was midday, March 21, 1933.

At the dock, he spied his objective: the two-masted schooner *Puritan*. Arriving alongside the ship, he saw two sailors working aboard. After ascertaining which one was the ship's mate, he handed him a note given to him back in Boston. "Sir," he announced, "this is for you, I believe." Reading the note and then looking at the young stranger, the man exclaimed, "Jesus Christ. The new man. Fresh from kindergarten." The unimpressed seaman grabbed Hayden's hands and inspected them. As he suspected, they were soft and un-callused. That was Hayden's official welcome to a life at sea.[19]

Sterling Hayden began his lifelong habit of writing and documenting once he reported aboard the *Puritan*. He had decided to keep a journal in a spiral notebook, and in the first entry, dated March 23, he expressed much dismay. Although he was only aboard for two days, he wondered if he had made a mistake coming to the ship. He was lonely and disillusioned his first week aboard as the ship made preparations to get underway. His bunk was small and the crew's quarters were cramped and dirty. What really bothered the idealistic teenager, someone who had never spent a day at sea, was the attitude of the other crewmembers. "These men don't understand anything about the sea," he wrote. "To them this is just a job." Expressing disgust with his choice to leave home and come to the ship, he recorded: "I hope nobody ever sees these words. I would never write them down but I want them to serve as a reminder if I ever do anything stupid like this again!!! Never again!! I wonder if these men are good sailors? The ship is okay I guess."[20]

The *Puritan* was to set sail on March 30. The day before, Hayden was the only crewmember aboard as the others were spending some last moments with families and loved ones. That day, he wrote to his mother. He described the crew to her—there were seven crewmembers other than himself. At the age of seventeen (his birthday was March 26), he was the youngest man aboard. His best friend among the crew was the cook, Harvey, a powerfully built and affable man who took the young boy under his wing. In spite of his first journal entry, the letter expressed no regrets about having come to the ship. Instead, as a dutiful son, he let his mother know how much he missed her, assuring her that he would conduct himself as a gentleman at all times. Someday, he promised, they would have a little home in Maine or Gloucester and the three of them—Sterling, his mother, and his dog Laird—would live together. He did not mention Daddy Jim.

That night, in his spiral notebook, he wrote entry number seven. He had made up his mind. "Have decided to stick it out. I will think of Von Luckner and Jack London and the men in the Cape Horners and in the Grain Races and then this will not perhaps seem quite so bad."[21]

• • •

Sterling Hayden's first sea voyage lasted four months, traveling from New London, to San Pedro harbor in Los Angeles via the Panama Canal. In his autobiography *Wanderer*, he wrote little about the journey, other than to describe some of the crew's antics while they were in the American Zone of the Panama Canal. There, the older crewmembers took their young colleague on a tour of strip clubs and pornographic movie houses. Arriving in Los Angeles in early August, the new owner of the crew arranged to have a small delegation come aboard for the final leg of the journey to their mooring site. The well-dressed young guests contrasted with the rough-and-tumble crew, and Hayden noted that he felt a little awkward; he couldn't decide which of the groups he really belonged to. He was a member of the crew, yet given the clothes and the money, he could fit in just as well with the guests, even though he could never truly be a part of their crowd. He observed, with disdain, their way of not looking at things, but rather, through them.[22]

It had been a learning experience for the aspiring sailor and now it was time for him and the crew to muster out. He had performed his duties as a seaman admirably. As he prepared to leave the schooner for the last time, Capt. Howard T. Horton handed him a pair of ten-dollar bills and a piece of paper. It read: "This is to certify that the bearer, S. Hayden, served for four months as ordinary seaman in the schooner yacht PURITAN. He is very strong and at all times willing and it gives me pleasure to give him this recommendation."[23] With his pay and recommendation in his pocket, Hayden left the ship with his friend Harvey, uncertain what their next move would be.

The two sailors stayed in the Los Angeles area for several days before deciding that their futures were on the East Coast. Once again, young Hayden, accompanied by his mentor, rode the rails east back across the country, finally arriving in New Jersey. Riding the ferry across to Manhattan, Hayden realized that he was on the very same vessel that he had ridden with his father nearly a decade before. Once in Manhattan, he found that his options were extremely limited, if nonexistent. There were still no jobs for someone like him. He had to head back home to his mother and Daddy Jim.

The two friends parted company at the midtown bus depot. As they shook hands and promised to keep in touch, Harvey offered a final piece of advice and encouragement. "You're gonna make it, kid, don't ever forget it neither. You ain't like the rest of us chumps."[24]

• • •

Back in Boston at his Aunt Emma's boarding house, Hayden learned that his mother and stepfather had moved to Woonsocket, Rhode Island, near Providence. As he departed, his aunt yelled after him, telling him to remind Frances that she still owed her money.

Frances was overjoyed to see her son, and Daddy Jim pretended that he was, too. The feeling towards his stepfather was mutual. For Sterling, it was as if he had never left. His mother still worked selling cosmetics door-to-door, and Daddy Jim was allegedly looking for work, all the while planning his next big financial deal. His parents fought constantly over their financial straits and things only got worse. What's more, the teenager realized how much he missed being at sea. The home situation continued to deteriorate.

Just after New Year's Day 1934, the Hayden family once again skipped town without paying their bills and returned to Boston. Once again, Daddy Jim was just steps away from closing a huge deal on a resort. Once again, to keep up appearances for all of his important financial connections, they needed to have an impressive address, so they arrived at Beacon Hill to check into a fancy hotel. Later they smuggled in the cartons that contained all of their possessions. Shortly thereafter, and to the surprise of no one, Jim's "deal" fell through and they were again on the verge of starvation. More fighting erupted between Daddy Jim and Frances, and their ignominy culminated in the confiscation by the hotel management all of their possessions, including Sterling's sea bag. More importantly, they also took Frances's cosmetics sales bag, which provided their only means of support.

In *Wanderer*, Hayden stated that shortly after the confiscation of their possessions, Daddy Jim went out to buy cigarettes and never returned. In reality, Frances had become increasingly disgusted with the chronically unemployed Jim Hayden and his never-ending money-making schemes. Her anger finally boiled over one night at dinner. After helping himself to several extra portions of meat, all put on the table as a result of Frances's work, she finally exploded and ordered him out of their lives.[25] Fifty years later, Sterling Hayden would describe his stepfather thusly: "My stepfather was a barnstormer, a promoter, and he was as full of shit as a Christmas turkey. We were always broke."[26]

Sterling desperately argued with the hotel manager to get his mother's cosmetics bag back, but his pleas fell on deaf ears. They needed money and the only thing young Hayden could think of was the kindness shown to him at the nautical instrument shop. Explaining his situation to Mr. White, the older man was very sympathetic to their plight and loaned him ten dollars. Returning to the hotel he found his mother stuffing cardboard into her shoes to cover the holes. They decided to move on. Mapping out their strategy together, one place that they agreed they'd like to live was Gloucester, Massachusetts. So, on an icy winter morning,

Frances and Sterling Hayden, along with Laird, walked over to North Station and boarded a train to Gloucester. It would prove to be another life-changing decision.

Arriving in Gloucester, Hayden was immediately exhilarated, noting, "As we pulled into Gloucester, my heart soared at the sight of sail in the distance."[27] Finding a decent room at a clean house, they were delighted to discover that the owner was both friendly and sympathetic to their plight. Unloading what few possessions they had, Sterling immediately headed out for the docks. It didn't take long for him to extend his lucky streak. Walking along the docks and inhaling the salty air that he loved, he came upon a nautical shop called Atlantic Supply Company. Its owner was Capt. Ben Pine. Looking in through the door, Hayden was transfixed by the nautical gear and pictures, much like he was at White's nautical shop on State Street.

In short order, a man walked up to him; to his surprise, it was Capt. Ben Pine himself. The captain invited the boy to come in and chat. They ended up talking for over two hours.

Ben Pine was deeply impressed with the tall, handsome teenager, who told him in detail about his experiences aboard the *Puritan*, as well as his desires to make a life at sea a reality. When Hayden left the shop, he had fifty dollars in his pocket, along with a letter addressed to several sea captains from Pine. It read: "This boy is all right. He wants to go dory-trawling from a schooner but I think he should start off in the beam trawlers first. Give him a job if you can. Ben Pine."[28]

The buoyant Sterling Hayden rushed home, and finding his mother asleep, he did not disturb her. Instead, he tucked some of the money into a hastily written note and departed for the train depot. He was headed back to Boston.

• • •

Strolling the fishing piers, Hayden spotted a trawler that seemed to call to him and he went aboard. Although his ultimate goal was to sail on schooners to the southern hemisphere, he needed to establish his bona fides, as well as learn and refine the requisite seamanship that he had begun to master aboard the *Puritan*. To accomplish this, he would follow Ben Pine's recommendation and become a fisherman, starting out on beam trawlers. Seeking out the captain, he introduced himself and produced the recommendation from Ben Pine.

The rough-looking captain read the note and looked at the strapping, six-foot-five-inch teenager and noticed that he didn't have any gear. Not a problem, the boy responded. He had the funds to acquire gear. The captain pondered for a few minutes and then made a decision. "All right, son, I'll give you a chance, if you're willing to make a couple of trips for nothing."

"Yes, sir; I am, sir," Hayden eagerly responded.

"We'll haul-ass out of here around ten tomorrow morning. Find yourself a bunk, and never mind saying 'sir' all the time, this is a dragger, not a yacht."[29]

And so commenced the year where Sterling Hayden became a fisherman. Out to sea went the various fishing trawlers that he served on, fishing until their holds were filled, and then they returned to Boston to sell off their catch. It was tedious, repetitive, and back-breaking work. There was no such thing as a day off while at sea, and the fishermen worked around the clock—six hours on and then six hours off. During the frigid winter of 1934–35, Hayden made a detached observation of his fellow fisherman as he watched and took part in their rituals in the sub-freezing weather, often covered with ice. They were thick in the legs, thick in the chest, thick in the skull, and thick in the ways of the world. How else could they stand such a life? he wondered.[30]

The beam trawlers that Hayden served on were sturdy boats that cast large nets called trawls behind them, and traveled the fishing lanes off the Atlantic coast. The fish would be scooped up in the trawl and hauled aboard so the catch could be stored in the boat's refrigerated hold. Dory trawlers, on the other hand, were fishing vessels that carried smaller two-man dories designed to be lowered into the water at the fishing sites. The dories were tied to the mother trawler and multiple fishing lines were cast over its sides. It was considerably more dangerous, but also paid much higher wages. In either event, the life of a New England fisherman was fraught with danger, as the Gloucester Fishermen's Memorial will attest to even to this day.

All throughout 1934, Hayden continued to work on beam trawlers, honing his seamanship skills and also saving money. He would dutifully give half of his earnings to his mother to pay off whatever debts she owed. But all along, he knew he was different from his fellow fisherman; he had bigger plans. His ultimate plan was to sail a schooner to the southern hemisphere, not freeze his butt off every year hauling fish. By Christmastime 1934, he found that he had had his fill of the life of a New England fisherman. He decided that he needed to try a shore-based job with regular hours. He needed a change of pace from the life he had been living for the past year.

Somewhat improbably, he got hired as a sales clerk at Filene's Basement Department Store in downtown Boston. He quickly learned that he was not cut out for this type of life. Every day on his lunch break, he would head down to the waterfront to sit, read, and contemplate his future. He clearly was unhappy with his life and his restlessness gnawed away at him. He had to make a decision. Either he threw himself wholeheartedly into the work of commerce, or he would go back to sea and try to resist the brutalizing process that seemed to go with it. There must be a better way, he reasoned. There had to be some sort of middle passage between these extremes.[31]

The answer came to him as a result of his voracious reading habits. In the last week of the busy Christmas season, he received his revelation while reading Rockwell Kent's 1930 book *N by E*. Kent, a writer, sailor, painter and adventurer, had sailed from New York to Greenland in a thirty-three-foot boat in 1929 and described his solitary journey in his book. Sitting on the waterfront during his lunch break from his totally boring and unfulfilling job at Filene's, Hayden suddenly realized what he had to do, what his life's work should be. He had to return to the sea.

This time, though, it would be different. He was not going to spend the rest of his life as a fisherman. After the New Year, he would return to the waterfront to fish, but only through April. He would save all of the money he earned and combine it with the more than $400 he had saved. To bring in even more money, he would graduate to the more lucrative (and dangerous) world of dory-trawler fishing. After April, he planned to scour the New England coast for a small boat to buy, spending the summer outfitting her to his own specifications. In the fall, he would sail his boat, already named in his mind as *Horizon*, to the South Seas and possibly around the world and earn his living by writing. Like Rockwell Kent, he would sail alone.[32]

CHAPTER THREE

Mentors

FROM JANUARY THROUGH APRIL 1935, STERLING HAYDEN WENT TO sea aboard the fishing schooner *Gertrude L. Thebaud* out of Gloucester. The 132-foot ship carried six dories on either side of her deck. Each dory was sixteen-feet long and manned by two fishermen. In the dead of the freezing winter and amidst the most treacherous sea states, twelve dories would be put in the water. Rowing the dories about a mile from the schooner to the likeliest fishing spot, the sailors would toss overboard the barrel buoy and feed out about a mile of fishing line.[1] Two thousand hooks spaced at intervals of six feet were attached to the line of the trawl. One end was anchored, the other made fast to the dory. In his autobiography, Hayden would describe the terror he felt with such experiences. He tried to make light of it, stating: "Well, he thought, here I am; all my life I'll be able to say: When I was a kid hauling trawl in a dory down on the Banks in the dead of wintertime . . ."[2] The life of a dory-trawler fisherman was succinctly summarized by his fellow dory-mate, a sailor named Jack Hackett. As Hackett told his young colleague: "Boy, lemme tell you, this is a poor fuckin' way to get rich."[3]

He persevered. By April, he had achieved his goal and had $500 deposited in a savings account at the bank. Withdrawing the money, he rented a bicycle and began pedaling up to Maine, a distance of 185 miles. When he finally reached Camden, he scoured the waterfront in search of a boat—what would be his boat. It didn't take long before a thirty-foot sloop caught his eye. In the ships rigging was a sign announcing: FOR SALE—$450. Renting a small skiff, he paddled around the boat several times, inspecting the hull with a critical eye. Satisfied with what he saw on the outside, he went aboard to inspect the inside. After giving the boat the "third degree," he liked what he saw. The next day he bought it boat for $400.

At age nineteen, Sterling Hayden owned his very own boat. The sloop was a start, a step in the right direction as he tried to pursue his dream. The boat featured two bunks, a rusty engine, a small wood-burning stove, and new sails. As he had envisioned while sitting at the waterfront on his lunch break from Filene's the previous Christmas, he named his boat *Horizon*. Living aboard his new castle, he did what refurbishing he could in preparation for sailing *Horizon* to her new home—Gloucester. Getting underway in late spring, he headed south for Massachusetts.

About a week later, he approached the port of Gloucester, navigating for the wharves at Rocky Neck. As he pulled into a berth, he noted two schooners docked near him. One was familiar to him—it was the *Wander Bird*. The other was named *Yankee*. He would spend the summer sailing, doing more rehab on his boat, and making money by taking tourists on sailing parties. By the end of the summer, however, reality had set in. He was questioning the wisdom of attempting to sail around the world in his little sloop. In addition, he was having problems with the *Horizon*. He had known that her many of her frames were rotten when he bought the boat, and she leaked like a sieve. It would be insanity to try a long voyage at sea.

• • •

Shortly after he returned to Gloucester, Hayden was working aboard the *Horizon* when he heard a young man inquire, "How are you?" Looking up, he saw fourteen-year-old Norman Hatch smiling at him. "I'm OK," he replied. They immediately struck up a conversation. Although Hayden was five years older than Hatch, they had an instant rapport, and their friendship would last their entire lifetimes. Hayden usually stayed aboard the boat at night, and he often invited Norm to stay with him. They would often take groups of women out for cruises.

Impressed with the man who became like a brother to him, Hatch would later describe Sterling Hayden as "the somewhat bashful, restrained and nice guy that I sailed with out of Gloucester for two years."[4] Despite his later status as a Hollywood leading man, he would always retain a certain degree of decorum around women, never being vulgar or boastful around them.[5] Hatch laughed as he recalled that when Hayden's mother would come looking for him, she would stand on the pier next to the *Horizon* and yell out, "Steeerrrllinng!" bringing peals of laughter to all of the sailors within earshot and much embarrassment to her son.[6]

Hayden and Hatch would remain close friends until Hatch enlisted in the United States Marine Corps when he was eighteen years old. As the years went by, Sterling would often contact his friend, seeking his counsel at times of crisis. Their high regard for each other would never diminish.

• • •

One afternoon in September, Hayden was asleep in his bunk when he was awakened by the approach of a squall. Leaping up and running on deck, he saw that the anchored *Horizon* was being driven by the storm directly into the side of the schooner *Yankee*. He worked feverishly to get his boat's engine to come alive, but it was to no avail. He worked his mainsail as a group of spectators watched from the dock in the driving rain. The collision appeared imminent when suddenly, "the schooner's master, stripped to the waist, came flying over the rail to land like a cat on my deck."[7] Without speaking a word, the two men worked together to bring *Horizon* out of danger and into the open water of the harbor. Then, almost as a bonding ritual, the two sailed for about an hour. After the storm had passed, they brought the sloop back to its mooring. Climbing back aboard his schooner, the master turned to Hayden and invited the young man to have dinner with him and his wife aboard their ship. Hayden gladly accepted the invitation.

Hayden was about to meet another key influence in his life. The master of the *Yankee* was Irving Johnson. As Hayden described Johnson in *Wanderer*, "They broke the mold when they made him . . . He was commonly regarded as the finest all-around schooner master on the face of the earth."[8] He was a former merchant seaman, author, filmmaker, and adventurer. He had met his wife Electra, known as Exy, aboard the *Wander Bird* in 1932 when he sailed as mate under Capt. Warwick Tompkins, and the couple married shortly after that. They became inseparable. They had already sailed around the world, and during their life together, he and Exy would circumnavigate the globe multiple times, often taking well-to-do students with them on the eighteen-month voyages. Each student paid the going rate of nearly $5,000. In 1957, at Pitcairn Island, one of their favorite ports of call, they recovered the anchor of the legendary HMS *Bounty* from its watery grave, where it had rested for nearly two hundred years.[9]

Young Hayden was mesmerized by the Johnsons. Irving was a physically fit specimen of a man, and neither smoked nor drank, making him quite an anomaly among the seamen that Hayden had known. He and Exy were gracious hosts, taking their guest on a tour of their ship. *Yankee* had been built in 1896 in Holland and the Johnsons bought it in 1933. It was immaculately maintained. The schooner's main cabin had fourteen bunks and was painted in ivory colors and trimmed with varnished teak. One side of the berthing area contained a wall of solid books. To Hayden, "my eyes were full of a ship that was really a ship."[10] After the tour, the trio sat down to dinner. The Johnsons were impressed not only with the handsome teenager's knowledge of sailing but with his manners. As the evening progressed, Johnson started to sense the young man's potential to be an outstanding sailor.

The conversation continued after dinner and Johnson told his wife about Hayden's plans to sail solo around the world. Eventually, Johnson leaned forward and made a proposition to his young guest. "A year from now," he explained, "we start on our second voyage around the world. I'll be needing a mate . . . to join the ship in the spring . . . I can't pay much; maybe a hundred a month during the summer cruises along the coast . . . nothing at all on the voyage around the world.

"Now," Johnson continued, "this isn't a promise—only a thought, or maybe a hunch. But if you worked for the winter down in the West Indies . . . picked up some more schooner experience; then you might come on board here in March, and if things worked out all around . . . you could mate around the world."[11]

Hayden could only stammer in response. He had just been offered an opportunity of a lifetime, from the premier schooner master in the world. How could he not pursue this offer, even if it was not a guaranteed job offer? He was so euphoric at the prospect that Johnson had dangled in front of him that he forgot to thank his hosts for the wonderful dinner when he departed the *Yankee*. Returning to his world aboard his little sloop, Hayden looked around the dismal cabin and compared it to the world he had left minutes before. He had just spent an evening aboard a real sailing ship with a real sailor who was also a real gentleman and whose wife was another fine sailor and a real lady. He knew what he had to do. The next morning, he put up a "For Sale" sign on the mast of the *Horizon*.

He was heading south.

• • •

His odyssey began immediately and he never took his eye off of the prize. He wanted to sail with Irving Johnson and, as his mentor instructed, he was going to attain the requisite experience that he needed to measure up in Johnson's eyes. He promptly signed on as a crewmember of the fishing schooner *Blue Lagoon*, which was departing from Gloucester and heading to Palm Beach, Florida, where her new owner awaited delivery. He arrived in Palm Beach in mid-November, after a storm-wracked passage, and left the ship fifty dollars richer for his efforts. Hitchhiking down to Miami, he settled at Biscayne Park, which had been transformed largely into a vagrant's camp, crowded with unemployed men, all seeking jobs in the midst of the Depression.

He haunted the riverfront in Miami, seeking a job aboard anything that sailed, but there were almost none to be had. After working various odd jobs, he was able to get a series of short-lived jobs on various ships sailing out of Miami. His skills as a seaman having been noted, he was hired as the captain of a sixty-foot schooner sailing from Miami. On the last day of February, one of the owners approached him, clutching a piece of paper in his hand. It was a telegram from the United States. It read: "LOOKING FORWARD YOUR ARRIVAL SCHOONER YANKEE AS MATE VESSEL LAID UP AT RUDDOCK'S SHIPYARD GREENWICH REGARDS JOHNSON."[12] It was the moment that he had worked so hard for all of the previous months. He was going to go around the world in a first-class schooner, captained by a world-class sailor. He was going to be first mate. The dream was coming true.

The next day Sterling Hayden was once again riding the rails, heading north.

. . .

He arrived at the pier, sea bag slung over his shoulder, on March 26, 1936—his twentieth birthday. At the end of the pier, the *Yankee* was moored, looking all the more majestic to its new mate. He described his excitement in his autobiography: "An idyll was in the making. For thirty months I dwelled in a land so bathed in golden sunshine, so placid, so laden with charms and new sensations, that I was all but entranced."[13] He promptly reported aboard to the captain, Irving Johnson, a man for whom his admiration knew no bounds.

As mate, he was second in command and ran the ship for the captain, carrying out his orders and policies. It was a daunting responsibility for a twenty-year-old, yet Hayden chose to downplay his role to a degree, noting that Johnson supplied the driving force, the crew supplied the cash and whatever muscle was needed, and he was a go-between, an interpreter in the ways of the sea for the assortment of "well-heeled vagabonds."[14] The vagabonds—the wealthy young people who actually comprised the paying crew—consisted of twelve young men and two young women, each of whom had paid several thousand dollars to be part of the adventure. Other than a paid cook, Johnson's only other crewmembers were his wife Exy and their baby son.

One of the "well-heeled vagabonds" that comprised the crew was a young man who was a year younger than Hayden. His name was David Donovan and he was listed on the crew roster as the engineer.[15] The friendship that developed between Hayden and Donovan would have a significant impact on Sterling Hayden's life over the next few years. Donovan was the son of legendary World War I hero and Medal of Honor recipient William J. "Wild Bill" Donovan. William Donovan was now a highly successful Wall Street lawyer and international traveler, and a troubleshooter for President Franklin D. Roosevelt. He had run unsuccessfully for the governorship of New York in 1932 and, despite the fact he was a Republican, he and Roosevelt were kindred spirits. David Donovan had dropped out of Harvard after two years and was scheduled to enroll in Cornell University for the 1939 fall semester after returning from *Yankee*'s voyage.[16]

Throughout the summer, they trained aboard the *Yankee*. Taking charter crews all along the New England coast, they would return to Gloucester, their base of operations, for restocking provisions and refueling. By the fall, they were ready. Johnson had decided that they would get underway for *Yankee*'s second around-the-world voyage on November 1, 1936.

Yankee departed on schedule and headed south. It was a new experience for Hayden, his first time at sea that he would describe as tranquil. Traversing the Panama Canal, they explored the Galapagos Islands and, by February 1937, they arrived at Easter Island, the remote island famous for its mysterious statues, called moai. From there they sailed westward 1,300 a to Pitcairn Island, the famous final destination of the HMS *Bounty* mutineers. By the time they arrived at Tahiti, Hayden was already envisioning the perfect ship for his own purposes, one that would be very much like *Yankee*.

In spite of the success that the expedition was having and his fine performance as mate, the self-doubt that would plague Sterling Hayden for the rest of his life had already begun to set in. Was he more suited to be a mate than a ship's master? he wondered. Was it the inspiring leadership of Irving Johnson that was actually responsible for any success that the expedition was enjoying? Johnson's skillset differed greatly from his own. Johnson was knowledgeable about matters of finance, organization, and interpersonal skills—all qualities Hayden knew he lacked. In contrast to the pragmatic Johnson, Hayden was a free spirit, a romantic, a man who couldn't even balance a checkbook. Johnson was a disciplined teetotaler who avoided tobacco and alcohol, two vices that Hayden vowed that he, too, would try to resist. He also saw that Johnson was tolerant of others, even people he didn't respect. In contrast, Hayden lacked this quality. He became determined to try and emulate his mentor as much as he could, and he decided to pursue his dream to become the master of a schooner.[17]

When the *Yankee* moored at Bali, Indonesia, on September 1, 1937, it picked up two additional crewmembers for the final leg back to the United States and Gloucester. David Donovan's mother Ruth and sister Patricia joined the crew, with Ruth officially listed as "blacksmith" and Patricia listed as "cooper."[18]

Yankee completed its successful circumnavigation of the globe on May 1, 1938, when it arrived back at its homeport of Gloucester. During the eighteen-month voyage, Hayden had only spent one night ashore, when the ship was anchored at Pitcairn Island. He knew he had performed creditably as mate and had tremendously burnished his seagoing resume. The highest praise of Hayden's performance was offered by Irving Johnson himself. Writing about his voyage in his 1939 book *Sailing to See: Picture Cruise in the Schooner Yankee,* Johnson described his mate thusly: "Sterling Hayden of Gloucester, the first mate, was that rare find, a born sailor, a 'natural.' This is the greatest quality a man can hope to find in a man to whom he will at times have to entrust the command of his ship. In addition, he had the ability to assume authority, and apparently that too was innate. He gave orders easily and they were followed unquestioningly, though most of those under him were older than this twenty-year-old mate."[19]

...

After their return, Hayden stayed on as mate aboard the *Yankee*. The schooner would continue to work the New England coast throughout the spring and summer. It was on a trip from Penobscot Bay in Maine in July that a very special passenger came aboard. Hayden saw the launch approaching the schooner with a dozen Girl Scouts aboard, and also one distinctive looking passenger. The launch pulled alongside and the passengers boarded the schooner. At that moment, Sterling Hayden got the first close look at another man who would have a great impact on his life. He was a rugged, handsome man who looked like he belonged on a ship. His name was Lincoln Colcord, and the *Yankee* would be taking him to his hometown of Searsport, Maine.

Just as Irving Johnson was a superb sailor with a multitude of talents, Lincoln Colcord was another Renaissance man. He had literally been born at sea on August 14, 1883, aboard the sailing ship *Charlotte A. Littlefield* in the midst of a raging storm as the ship rounded Cape Horn in the middle of winter. His father was the ship's captain and his mother had already given birth to Lincoln's sister at sea during a previous voyage. At the age of twenty-six, the journey aboard the *Charlotte A. Littlefield* from Valparaiso to New York City was his father's first command.

Colcord attended the University of Maine, majoring in civil engineering. He first achieved fame in 1904 when he wrote the lyrics to the university's fight song, entitled "The Stein Song."[20] In 1930, crooner Rudy Vallee would record a version of the song that stayed at the number one hit spot in the United States for eight weeks.[21] After graduation, he worked for a while on the railroad, but shortly after that began publishing short stories and poems, most of which had a nautical theme. In 1912, he published his first major novel, *The Drifting Diamond*, and he followed it up in 1915 with a book-length poem in free verse entitled *Vision of War*. Both were literary successes. For a while, he worked as a newspaper correspondent and for a year served as associate editor of the leftist journal *The Nation*.[22]

In 1927, Colcord convinced Norwegian writer Ole Rolvaag to translate his classic book *Giants in the Earth* from Norwegian into English. Colcord took the crude translation and rewrote the book into a cogent version of the novel for English-speaking audiences. During the 1930s, he continued to dedicate his efforts to two endeavors: going to sea in sailing ships, and writing about the sea.

Once aboard *Yankee*, Johnson offered his distinguished guest the opportunity to take the helm for a while. Colcord declined, instead requesting a tankard of rum. Johnson informed him that his was a dry ship, explaining that it was better that way, considering the long distance voyaging that was their routine. The astonished Colcord blurted out, "No! You don't say. A dry ship. Well, I'll be goddamned!"[23] This was Sterling Hayden's first exposure to the famous Lincoln Colcord. Both Johnson and Colcord were superb sea captains, but they represented the opposite ends of the spectrum as far as personal discipline and temperament were concerned. Hayden now had two role models to emulate, but he would be unable to follow the example of the self-disciplined Johnson. Instead, in many ways his life would mirror that of the free-spirited Lincoln Colcord.

During the short trip to Searsport, Colcord took a liking to the ship's young mate despite their thirty-three-year age difference. After docking, he invited Hayden to stroll with him through the streets of the town. Detecting real potential in his new young friend, he invited him home to have dinner with him and his wife Frances. Hayden gratefully accepted. Upon entering the famous man's house, he was immediately struck with its maritime beauty. Gazing at the multiple paintings of ships and exotic ports of call on the walls, and the huge collection of books that were located all over the house, he was, in his own words, awed. "This is a home," he recalled. "This is what people mean when they talk about home, not the houses in the suburbs like we used to have, not the hotels and the fancy apartments and all that—just an old white house by the water—feeling its way into the life of the village."[24]

As they relaxed, Colcord offered his young guest a glass of rum. To his surprise, Hayden told him that he did not drink. When asked why, Hayden replied that he thought he just didn't care for it. "Nonsense," shot back his new mentor. "You don't drink because you've been taught it was wrong." Taking a swipe at Irving Johnson, he continued: "You don't drink because that goddamn Boy Scout of a skipper—he's a good seaman, understand—he doesn't drink, right?" Upon further questioning, Hayden also admitted to Colcord that he didn't smoke. Throughout the conversation, Hayden always addressed the Colcords as "sir" or "ma'am."

"Don't call me Mister and don't call me sir, . . . you and I are going to have a talk," lectured Colcord. "I've had my eye on you all afternoon. Johnson tells me you're the best mate he ever had. That may be. But you're all tensed up. That's bad."[25]

As his new mentor continued on, Hayden began to reflect on this lifestyle. He had just spent two and a half years aboard the *Yankee*, reading journals and books, not smoking or drinking. In his own words, he was skimming the world, looking at it from a distance. He suddenly made a decision right then and there—he asked his host for some of the rum. It was his first taste of alcohol and he enjoyed it.

Colcord pressed on. What did the crew do when they reached Tahiti? Did they all get stinking drunk? No, Hayden replied, they had all gone ashore for ice cream and milk. The astonished host exploded. "Ice cream and milk! Frances! Did you hear that? Hayden here says when they were in Tahiti there wasn't any drinking. Instead they went for ice cream. Good God!"[26]

The topic shifted to politics, with Colcord asking what he thought of President Roosevelt. Hayden was ignorant about the politics of the time, but Colcord vented on the evils of FDR and railed that he was leading the country to war. Hayden shifted the conversation to ships, asking for advice about which type of sailing ship would be the best with which to circumnavigate the globe. Colcord then expressed his disgust at Irving Johnson's business of "farting around the world with a group of spoiled kids fresh from school in search of pleasure. Gawd!" Be your own man, he advised Hayden. "You say you'd like to write. Well, damn it, son, go ahead. Write."[27]

Towards the end of the evening, Colcord inquired about Hayden's sexual experience, much to the embarrassment of his wife who tried to caution him about such talk. "Well, I'm worried about our young friend here," Colcord explained. "I'm very much afraid he's a hell of a good mate but he's long overdue when it comes to discovering life. Wouldn't you say?" Frances countered by asking what Colcord was doing when he was Hayden's age other than going to the university. Colcord replied in detail. "Sure I was," he agreed. "Writing songs and making socialist speeches and screwing girls and getting drunk and laughing like hell and getting mad. That's good. That's life. This boy has been working his ass off since he was fifteen and he's still just a child inside."[28]

The hour grew late and it was time for Hayden to leave. As they traveled through the village toward the wharf, Colcord told Hayden that he hoped he hadn't made him feel bad about anything that had been discussed. An intoxicated Hayden assured him that he was fine. Good, the older man replied. Paying Hayden the ultimate compliment, Colcord declared, he was "a damn good sailorman."

As he lay in his bunk aboard the *Yankee* that night, Colcord's words no doubt reverberated in his thoughts. Here, almost simultaneously, he had been exposed to two highly different influences, both of whom were examples of the sailor he hoped to become. They had totally opposite approaches to life, but shared a passion for sailing. Johnson was the disciplined, pragmatic man who lived life on his own terms, wrote several books, and would ultimately make nine around-the-world voyages. Colcord, too, was a master sailor, and his life at sea was combined with his passion for writing as well. But whereas Johnson, the teetotaler, was pristine in his personal habits, Colcord's life was intertwined with alcohol, tobacco, whoring, and a hedonistic approach to life. It's unlikely that twenty-two-year-old Sterling Hayden made a conscious decision that night, but as his life progressed, when it came to smoking and alcohol, it would in many ways mirror the life of his latest mentor—Lincoln Colcord.

CHAPTER FOUR

Youngest Captain

IN THE FALL OF 1938, STERLING HAYDEN WAS PREPARING FOR ANOTHer sea adventure. This time, he was involved in competitive racing—the annual International Fisherman's Cup competition. Started in 1920, the 1938 races would turn out to be the last competition held. The races pitted longtime rival schooners against each other: Gloucester's own *Gertrude L. Thebaud*, captained by Ben Pine, versus Canada's *Bluenose*, captained by his personal rival Angus Walters. The series of five races would originate out of Gloucester harbor. Hayden would be part of Ben Pine's forty-man crew.

Hayden's job in the crew was that of masthead man on the ship's main mast. The foremast would be manned by his old shipmate Jack Hackett. Virtually all of Gloucester turned out for the races to witness the contest between the *Bluenose* and the *Thebaud*. The *Thebaud* was victorious in the first race, while *Bluenose* won the second race four days later. During the second race the weather conditions had deteriorated due to the high winds and *Thebaud*'s outer peak halyard block became loose during the middle of the race. Capt. Pine ordered Hayden to jury-rig the block, an extremely dangerous and potentially suicidal task considering the winds and the sea state. Much to the disbelief of virtually all of the race's observers, Hayden didn't hesitate to carry out his captain's order.[1] The third race was delayed for ten days because of weather conditions, but that wasn't the only reason for the delay. Adding to the delay was the extreme animosity between Ben Pine and Angus Walters.

Although Hayden didn't mention it in his autobiography, the main reason for a hiatus of several days was a fight over the sight of the next race. Walters wanted it to be off of Nahant Bay so that more Bostonians could observe the race. He had already sailed the *Bluenose* there, assuming the site was approved by the racing officials. Pine exploded, insisting that the races remain off of Gloucester.[2] The officials agreed with Pine and the *Bluenose* was forced to return to Gloucester, causing the race's delay. *Bluenose* was victorious in the third race.

Just before the fourth race, disaster nearly struck the *Thebaud*. As the dawn of the day of the fourth race broke, Hayden was nervous. The previous day, Capt. Pine had informed him that he was going to have Hayden serve as navigator for the upcoming fourth race. Pine had fired his navigator (who had gotten lost in the last race). Pine felt that Hayden would be an excellent replacement. As if this wasn't enough pressure, the day of the race Pine suffered a severe sinus attack and had to be hospitalized. Capt. Cecil Mouton replaced him.[3]

On the day of the race, Hayden performed his navigation duties admirably. The *Thebaud* was victorious, but their glory was fleeting. When the competition ended with the fifth and final race two days later, it was *Bluenose* that emerged victorious and was declared the winner of the International Fisherman's Cup. Interestingly, several details and the timing of the events during the races described by Hayden in *Wanderer* differ from more authoritative accounts of the races.[4] One particular event that Hayden described as occurring after the end of the races actually occurred on October 12, just before the second race. The occasion was the dedication of the Gloucester Community Fish Pier.

Moored to the dock were the two great rivals, the *Bluenose* and the *Thebaud*. While the politicians and admiring public gathered on the dock for speeches and celebrations, the crews of the two schooners were gathered in the fish hold of the *Bluenose* for a private party. Arriving with an invitation to the private party down below was Associated Press correspondent Tom Horgan. Handed a cup of rum, he was proposing a toast to the host ship *Bluenose* when a drunken arm slapped him across his back in welcome.

The arm belonged to a Boston celebrity named Lawrence Patrick Joseph O'Toole, a man Hayden described as a "legend" who hung out on T Wharf with the likes of Horgan or with "any one of a thousand friends. People like to have him around because he makes them happy. He doesn't drive a car and he is always broke, and the worse things are, the more he laughs, painting away at his pictures of people and ships, or carving a figurehead." Hayden liked him at once.[5] The nearly one hundred sailors, including Hayden, drank themselves into a semi-stupor, eventually stumbling onto the dock for the formal dedication ceremonies. At the conclusion of the National Anthem, Hayden noted that three new friends were sitting together: Tom Horgan, Larry O'Toole, and Sterling Hayden.

The Internationals Fisherman's Cup competition also marked the first time that Hayden received national recognition. During the races, he was spotted by the crowds daily. The ruggedly handsome sailor attracted many admirers, primarily women, to the docks to watch his displays of fine seamanship aloft and to admire his handsome good looks.[6] On a national level, the October 24, 1938, issue of the *Boston Post*, in addition to the local *Gloucester Daily Times*, featured stories about him. On the second page of the *Post* was a photograph of Sterling Hayden with the headline: THEBAUD SAILOR LIKE MOVIE IDOL. As the paper reported, "Gloucester youth, 22, Born Sea Rover . . . Fine masculine specimen . . . Neat seamanship may decide the victor of the fishermen's races, but when it comes to masculine pulchritude, Sterling W. Hayden, tall, blond, and lithe, wins by 100 fathoms over fellow members of both crews. He stands straight as a ramrod and is six foot five inches tall . . . More than a few of the scores of women who viewed the vessels yesterday at the fish pier inquired as to his identity."[7]

• • •

Hayden's growing reputation was enhanced with his fine performance aboard the *Thebaud* in the 1938 International Fisherman's Cup races. Days after the competition ended, he stopped into Ben Pine's Atlantic Supply Company and the receptionist handed him an urgent message: call Mr. William A. Robinson over in Ipswich. She explained the urgency of the call as Hayden listened in stunned silence. Robinson had been very impressed with the young man and had received glowing recommendations about him from both Ben Pine and Irving Johnson. He wanted Hayden to take command of the brigantine *Florence C. Robinson* and deliver her out to Tahiti. Minutes later he returned the call, and at the age of twenty-two, Sterling Hayden had his first command at sea.

The *Robinson* had been built in Ceylon and was intended for use in the Indian rice trade. At eighty-nine-feet long, it was about the same size as *Yankee*, and Robinson's plan was to convert it to a yacht. That summer and fall of 1938, a crew of Hindus worked to prepare the ship. Meeting the crewmembers already aboard, he was immediately unimpressed and told Robinson that he needed to pick his own crew or he would not take the command. Robinson immediately agreed to his demand. The new captain was free to pick his crew, so he headed for Boston's T Wharf without delay.

His first recruit was his new drinking buddy Larry O'Toole, who was both surprised and delighted by the invitation. As he recruited nine other crewmembers, publicity for the upcoming voyage was generated in the Associated Press by Tom Horgan, his other new friend. The final crew was an eclectic bunch. The average age was twenty-six, and Hayden, the captain, was the youngest of them. There was only one other experienced seaman besides the captain.[8] By late November, they were ready to sail.

On November 22, a crowd of well-wishers assembled on the pier to witness the departure of the *Florence C. Robinson*. Due to the publicity generated for the voyage, the young crew had become local celebrities. Among the spectators was Norm Hatch. He had wanted to go on the voyage as part of the crew, but as he was not quite seventeen years old, his mother would not grant him permission to do so. That afternoon, the ship was towed out of the harbor by a motor diesel tow boat named *Dorothy*. Once let loose by their tow, under direction of their young captain the *Florence C. Robinson* set its sails to begin the voyage. Hatch recalled the moment seventy-seven years later: "As the sails were set, all of the experienced sailors in the crowd stood at attention in tribute to Sterling. That's how highly he was regarded. You have to remember, he was only twenty-two years old."[9]

Tom Horgan reported the event for the Associated Press on November 22, 1938. Under the title of "Adventurers Sail from Gloucester for Tahiti in 89-Foot Brigantine," he wrote: "At sunset today 11 young adventurers sailed into the dusk, bound on a 7,000 mile voyage to the South Sea Islands and Tahiti. They are the crew of the awkward, antiquated little brig FLORENCE C. ROBINSON and they traveled in a style little different than seamen a century ago. Youngest and biggest of the ship's company is her skipper, Sterling Hayden, 22, taking his first command. Oldest of the crew is Lawrence O'Toole, Boston artist, and he is only 30 . . . Her skipper believes she should reach her destination in time for him to catch a steamer for home April 6 next spring."[10]

The *Boston Herald* featured an editorial two days later that, on first blush, seemed critical of the voyagers, calling the crew of eleven "ill-advised young men," citing the dangers of the long voyage in the old ship. Continuing on however, the editor transformed the article into an adventurer's compliment, stating, "But always—just beyond the horizon—there lies a vision or an experience worth a king's ransom . . . Eleven visionary young men, without question. But what young men would not be with them?"[11]

The voyage nearly ended in disaster three days after getting underway. On November 25, the *Florence C. Robinson* was fighting for her life, wracked by hurricane winds of seventy-five miles an hour. For fifty hours, the *Robinson* was lashed by the hurricane and nearly foundered. As the seas raged around them, Hayden experienced fear like he had never felt before. Why did this have to happen during his very first command? He sought escape from the pressures of command in the form of sleep. As it had in the past, his self-doubt began to overtake him. "Why must I go on playing this game, why not give up the sea and live as others do?" he asked himself. "Why not, once this voyage is done, take a fling at Hollywood? Take the dough and fool around with the starlets and read your name in the papers."[12]

As the hurricane-force winds continued to batter the ship along with the forty-foot seas, the crew heard a loud popping sound above roar of the wind. It was the sound of the topsail breaking free of its gaskets and rapidly being torn to shreds. Next, the horrified crew watched the foresail starting to unravel. Crewmember Donald Langley watched as Hayden and another crewmember began to climb the rigging. "Hand over hand, barely able to see thru the salt spray pelting their faces, they climbed the rigging to reach the wayward sail. Precariously balancing on the foot ropes they worked with the gaskets to contain the flapping canvas."[13]

Just as they secured the sail, the crew heard another loud popping sound as the sail broke loose and began flapping wildly. To Langley, the terrifying scene seemed to play out in slow motion as he watched Hayden and his partner being blown backward into the rigging. They miraculously were able to grab a back stay as they fell and were able to slide down safely to the deck. Luckily, neither man was injured. The damage to the sails, as well as the resultant contamination of their fresh water supply, required that *Florence C. Robinson* pull into Jamaica for several days for repairs and provisioning.

After leaving Jamaica, the remainder of the voyage was routine. When transiting the Panama Canal, Hayden spotted a ship laid up for repairs on the Gatun Lake. He also saw that it was for sale. The 161-foot luxury yacht, the *Aldebaran*, had been launched in 1902 as the *Meteor III* for Kaiser Wilhelm. Originally christened by Alice Roosevelt, it had changed hands (and names) many times since, finally ending up in the possession of an American, Frances Taylor.[14] The luxurious yacht featured a dozen staterooms, and the young captain spent a day going over her, taking pictures and "measuring, scheming, and dreaming." The future possibilities for the ship intrigued him.

On February 15, 1939, *Florence C. Robinson* sailed into the Tahitian capital of Papeete, ahead of their projected schedule. Once again, the media sang the praises of the young crew. The *Boston Herald* reported: "The good ship FLORENCE C. ROBINSON got safely to Tahiti because intelligent men of self-discipline cooperated with intelligent leadership, for the common good. All eleven did not try simultaneously to steer the ship."[15] Hayden was individually lauded in *Boys' Life* magazine in their "News in the News" section. Accompanying a photograph of the handsome young sailor, they reported: "Only 22 years old, Sterling Hayden is skipper of the crew of eleven on the little brigantine *Florence C. Robinson* which sailed a short while ago on a 7,700-mile voyage to Tahiti."[16]

In 1998, crewmember Donald J. Langley Jr., writing with Holly J. Blake, published his memoir of their epic journey titled *Tahiti Bound*, in which he wrote glowingly of their young skipper. "I thought about our captain and the way he made navigation seem almost easy. He was the best, and the entire crew had the utmost confidence in him. Nothing was left to chance. Sterling certainly loved boats and the sea! His cabin was covered with snapshots of the *Gertrude L. Thebaud*. A large chart of Cape Ann was the focus of the cabin and back issues of *Yachting* and *Motor Boating* were all over the place. As I reflect over his later 'accomplishments,' I can see where they might have been a double edged sword after his life at sea. When I knew him he was a young man full of life and enthusiasm. He didn't drink and seemed a happy go lucky sort."[17]

Having arrived in their paradise-like environment, for the next two months Hayden and his crew relaxed and enjoyed the carefree life on Tahiti. One night, over free-flowing liquor, his admiring colleagues came up with a plan for him to start a business. Get your hands on a big fast schooner, they advised, and bring it back to Papeete. They advised him to open up a packet service between Papeete and Honolulu. There would be, they predicted, more business than he could handle. His thoughts immediately turned to the Kaiser's old yacht. Maybe this was the opportunity he was looking for to fulfill his dreams of becoming a legitimate sea captain with a regal ship of his own.

During his time on Tahiti, he fell in love for the first time with a half-Tahitian, half-American girl named Marno Meersman, the daughter of Scudder Meersman, the American vice-consul to Tahiti. They got engaged in April, just before he departed for the States. Prior to his departure, her parents threw an engagement party for them at *Mahina*, their plantation seventeen miles from Papeete. Even then, Hayden harbored doubts about the marriage, knowing among other things that his mother would not approve. The same fear he felt in the hurricane off of the Atlantic coast seemed to return that night. He knew that the marriage couldn't work. He promised her he would buy a ship—the *Aldebaran*—and return to start the business that his colleagues had proposed. When he returned they would marry, he reassured her.

He would not keep that promise.

• • •

Hayden arrived back in the United States, the lone passenger on a Danish freighter. Once again, the feelings of uncertainty and hopelessness seemed to engulf him as he went to meet his mother at a Manhattan hotel. As he walked towards Times Square, he saw a movie marquee announcing the main feature—*Mutiny on the Bounty*. Although he had already seen the film, he needed an escape, a boost, so he bought a ticket, "to study the actors at work, and imagine myself in their place."[18]

As he wandered around Manhattan, he felt depressed and uneasy. He made tepid attempts to raise capital for his ship purchase project, but to no avail. He endured a severe lecture from his Uncle Mont, earnestly trying to coerce him into joining his business firm. Still, he went through the motions. That summer he obtained a job captaining a fifty-foot sailing yacht of a wealthy manufacturer, but the job didn't work out satisfactorily.

That fall, he was back in Boston, making a last-ditch effort to make the *Aldebaran* project a reality. Larry O'Toole had a wealthy friend named Herb Talbot, who was interested in the project, but if he were to finance the deal, he wanted a degree of operational control. In order for Hayden to buy the ship with Talbot's financing, he agreed to operate the *Aldebaran* out of Boston and Gloucester for a year before he sailed to Tahiti to establish their Papeete-Honolulu connection. That November, a council of Hayden's colleagues and business partners met with Talbot to finalize the deal. It would cost $15,000 to purchase the ship. While the rum flowed, they agreed to form a partnership to sail the ship back to Boston and for Talbot to provide the financing. Talbot interrupted the reverie, outlining his terms: "No money down. Not a penny changes hands till we get her back here to Boston, where we can put her in dry dock and have her surveyed."[19]

Fourteen fellow sailors joined Hayden on the trip down to Panama with the intention of sailing the *Aldebaran* immediately back to Boston. Problems started the moment they boarded the ship. The ship's caretaker informed them they would have to put the ship in dry dock immediately before departing. Hayden responded to the man by telling him: "The hell I will!" The caretaker proceeded to show him several holes in the hull that Hayden had not detected during his last visit. Hayden was undaunted—they would patch the holes and fortify them with cement to shore them up. They would not put the ship in dry dock until they arrived in Boston. On December 10, the *Aldebaran* departed Panama.

Things progressed satisfactorily for the first ten days before it all began to unravel. It began with engine difficulty and constant leaking that had the young captain concerned. But the structural problems of the ship were only a minor part of the impending fiasco. Once again, the weather proved to be Sterling Hayden's main antagonist. By Christmas Eve, major squalls engulfed the ship, overwhelming the structural flaws of the ship. Within a short while, they had four feet of water in the bilge and three pumps were working nonstop to evacuate the water over the sides. Soon two of the pumps shorted out. Large walls of water pounded the ship and the ship's masts sustained major damage. For nearly twenty-four hours, the fifteen men battled to keep the ship afloat. The ship's engine was inoperable, rendering the ship incapable of proceeding under its own power.

The crippled ship headed towards Charleston, South Carolina. Its upside-down flag was an unmistakable maritime distress signal. For four more days, the ship drifted until it was spotted by a Coast Guard cutter. Attaching a towline, the cutter towed the *Aldebaran* into Charleston Harbor where tugboats guided the crippled ship to a pier. Talbot had transferred to the cutter while on the open seas, promptly heading back to Boston once the cutter docked. Unfortunately for Hayden, the bad luck that plagued the disastrous voyage was not over.

Pumps were placed by a salvage company to purge the water from the crippled ship. As Hayden was overseeing the process, he received a telegram from Herb Talbot in Boston. The message was devastating. "FIND I CAN DEVOTE NO MORE TIME OR MONEY TO VENTURE—GOOD LUCK—HERB."[20] Hayden and the rest of the partners would have to foot the bill for the repairs. They had no insurance on the boat. Working with a surveyor, they inspected all the damage that needed to be fixed before the ship could get underway. The estimate came to a staggering $18,000 at a minimum. The ship's value purely as scrap iron was estimated at perhaps $10,000. Stacked up against these estimates, Hayden ruefully noted that his net worth was $45.[21] With the withdrawal of Herb Talbot's financing, the project was no longer feasible.

It was over. Hayden had no other options left, except to return to Boston.

CHAPTER FIVE

Inventing a Hollywood Star

THE WHOLE PROCESS STARTED SO IMPROBABLY THAT IT WOULD ALMOST seem to have been the plot of a Hollywood movie. Sterling Hayden was unemployed, back at Boston's T Wharf with his friends and drinking buddies Larry O'Toole and Tom Horgan. It was almost Christmas 1940, and the three had just finished dinner. It was Horgan who brought up the subject once again, pointing out to his young friend that he really didn't have any other options left. To his surprise and delight, Hayden finally agreed. He would try and break into Hollywood. It was O'Toole who burst out with: "Now you're talkin' some sense."[1]

Horgan had several connections in the entertainment industry. A key contact was his friend Virginia Hawks. A year earlier, she had married influential Hollywood agent William Hawks. Among Hawks's prestigious clients was novelist William Faulkner. Grabbing another drink, Horgan dictated a letter to Virginia Hawks while O'Toole wrote down his message. Addressing it to Virginia care of the William Hawks Agency, he began to rattle off his message. "Dear Virginia: This is important. There's a young fellow here named Hayden who, if the Boston newspapers are any judge, is made to order for Hollywood. He is twenty-four years old, six feet four inches tall, weighs 220. I'll enclose some pictures and clippings to show you what he looks like. Also he is the youngest Master Mariner in this part of the world . . . Now tell that agent husband of yours to come back and take a look at this Viking and sign him up, before somebody else does." He closed by adding: "Also, he is broke."[2] Finishing his dictation, Horgan raised his glass and the three friends toasted to the future. The booze kept flowing.

It started just as improbably as that.

Throughout January 1940, they waited for an answer from Hawks. O'Toole planned to give the agent three weeks and then they would travel to New York City. The three weeks passed without a reply from the agent. There was another slight issue complicating their plans—both Hayden and O'Toole were broke. Hayden was forced to take a job making a run on the schooner *Ethel B. Penney* to raise money for their New York trip. After a wild, alcohol-filled farewell party, the duo jumped on a steamer to New York and upon arrival, checked into the Edison Hotel on Times Square. Immediately requesting that the bellhop bring up a bottle of rum, O'Toole got to work. His Irish rascal charm was in full force as he picked up the phone and called across the street to Harry Goufrain, a theatrical agent with whom he was acquainted. Within a minute, he secured an appointment for them with Goufrain.

As the pair approached the agent's office, O'Toole offered Hayden advice that was likely never endorsed by Stanislavski. "Keep your hands outa your pockets, stand up straight, look this guy square in the eye and keep thinkin' over and over: 'Go fuck yourself, Harry, go fuck yourself Harry'—like that—over an' over, got it?"[3] Before entering the office, O'Toole assured Hayden that he and Goufrain were good buddies and if the agent liked him, "then you're as good as a star right now."[4]

The buoyant O'Toole made the introductions and Hayden shook the agent's hand so firmly that the man grimaced in pain. Goufrain proceeded to question the handsome young man in front of him, trying to ascertain his theatrical background, which Hayden assured him was nonexistent. Finally, the agent asked Hayden what made him think he could act. Before he could even answer, O'Toole emphatically interjected: "Harry, the kid's modest, that's what. Of course he can act. I can act, you can act, anybody can act if he feels like actin', what's so tough about actin'?"[5] Convinced of the young man's potential, the agent signed him to a standard New York agency contract. He also insisted that O'Toole sign it, to keep his investment straight.

As they departed, Hayden's partner and mentor advised him to go and see several movies a day, studying the actors intently. In short order, O'Toole departed, heading back to Boston and T Wharf. Hayden checked into a cheap, seedy room on West Fifty-Second Street and awaited calls from his agent. A month went by without any calls from Harry Goufrain. It seemed like Hayden was once again back to square one, but his luck, and his life, were about to change drastically. Once again, it was Tom Horgan who would prove to be the catalyst.

• • •

Edward H. Griffith was a fifty-one year-old Hollywood stalwart who had started his professional life as a newspaper reporter and magazine writer.

He had migrated over to the film industry, and by the late 1930s, he had achieved success as a screenwriter, producer, and director. Several of his recent successful films had starred the reigning Hollywood leading lady, the elegant Madeleine Carroll. His newest film project had the working title of *The Southerner*, and its stars would be Carroll and Fred MacMurray. The plot revolved around a southern belle, played by Carroll, who returns home to her Virginia roots after the Civil War with the intention of selling her family property. She has a change of heart and is romantically pursued by a good-hearted local Virginian played by MacMurray. Her love life would be complicated by the arrival from up north of another handsome suitor, a role that hadn't been cast. It was at this point in late winter that Harry Goufrain met with Griffith and showed him the letter written by Tom Horgan. Griffith decided to meet with the handsome sailor.

Sterling Hayden was getting ready to leave New York since he couldn't pay his rent. Suddenly he received a message, resplendent with spelling errors, from his landlord. "Mr. Hagen," it read, "Call Mr. Griffis at Paramount Pictures or Hampshire House."[6] The director from Paramount wanted to interview him. Nervously, Hayden took five walks in front of the building on Central Park South as the time of his appointment with Griffith approached. Entering the Hampshire House at the appointed time, Hayden was treated like expected royalty and was escorted up to the Paramount Suite. He was politely introducing himself to one of Griffith's assistants, whom he had mistaken for Griffith, when the director came bounding into the room. He immediately started peppering Hayden with questions about his background. He then ordered him to walk to the window and stare down at Central Park. Doing as he was instructed, the director asked, "Mr. Hayden, do you always stand with your hands in your pockets that way?"

"No, sir, only when I'm scared," he replied, rapidly pulling his hands out.

"You are nervous now?"

"You're doggone right I am," he blurted out, surprised that he hadn't used profanity.[7]

Next, Griffith had him go through an acting scene and observed him as he read from the supplied script. He noted that the young man had a broken tooth and a scar on his left cheek. Hayden started to explain how he had acquired these during his many voyages when the director raised his hand and cut him off. "Very well now. I think, Mr. Hayden, that we will make a screen test." His assistant concurred with his plan.

The incredulous Hayden could only ask: "Are you serious?" The director assured him that he was and scheduled the screen test for the following Wednesday.

The screen test took place on March 15 in one of Paramount's New York studios. Hayden was ushered in and immediately sent to makeup. As the makeup artist was working on him, Larry O'Toole came bounding into the room. After Hayden wired him about the screen test, O'Toole immediately hopped on a bus to New York, arriving at that precise moment to provide support to his friend.

They headed for wardrobe and on the way O'Toole slipped him a flask, encouraging him to take a swig of bourbon to steady his nerves. After the wardrobe session, it was time for the screen test. They entered the studio and the director greeted him and the crew staged him by a table. This was the silent part of his test, during which Griffith wanted to shoot several poses of the prospective actor. Then the director barked out several scenarios for Hayden to react to: he was on a high floor of a hotel and looking down, observing a woman being hit by a car; he was a skipper of a boat trying to navigate his boat through a deadly storm; he was in Grand Central Station all alone when he finally spots the love of his life and runs to her.

After an hour, the director called for a break. Hayden and O'Toole immediately departed to get a drink. When the duo returned, the spoken part of the screen test was ready to take place. A short time later, Edward Griffith was joined by Russell Holman, head of Paramount East Productions, to watch the recently shot screen test. Hayden frequently blew his lines, but they were fed to him by one of the film assistants. He felt that it had been a dismal failure and before the end, he convinced O'Toole to leave with him. He was already planning on returning to sea.

O'Toole felt just the opposite. He thought the screen test had gone extremely well, based on what they observed. "You're in, I tell ya—You're *in!*" he insisted. Call Griffith, he demanded, and you'll see. Complying with his buddy's directive, he called up to Griffith, who sounded jubilant as he informed Hayden that the test was a success and instructed him to return immediately. He and Holman had a contract for him to sign.[8]

And so began Sterling Hayden's movie career.

• • •

In May 1940, not long after signing his forty-two-page contract with Paramount Pictures, Hayden moved to a Spanish-style house in Laurel Canyon, near Paramount's Hollywood studios. The dutiful son brought his mother Frances to the West Coast to share the house with him. To his amazement, he was now being paid $600 a month—three times as much as he had ever earned at sea.[9] Every morning, he would go to the studio where he had his own dressing room as well as a personal trainer named Jim.

For six days a week, his daily routine remained the same. In the mornings he would have weight training and exercises supervised by Jim. Next came acting lessons, supervised by acting coach Bill Russell, and visits to the publicity department. Hayden quickly learned that the name of the game was to get individually noticed and singled out from the myriad of other aspiring actors vying for their big break. He differed from these others in that he was indifferent; he really didn't care. It was hard for him to take the whole thing too seriously. Many of his fellow aspiring actors had been plugging away for years waiting for their moment in the sun. In Hayden's case, however, the moment came after he had been in Hollywood for only three weeks,

One morning while pumping iron, Jim entered the room with an important message—Edward Griffith's secretary had called and wanted Hayden to come to the office immediately. The young star-in-training quickly appeared in front of Griffith's desk and the director asked him how things were going. Hayden candidly told him he was thinking of giving up the acting effort and going back to sea. Griffith interrupted him, saying "You're about to receive the greatest surprise of your life."[10]

"Sterling," he continued, "I am going to do something that has never been done before in Hollywood. The front office thinks I'm insane. I'm going to star you in my next picture, *Virginia*. You will play the second male lead, next to Fred MacMurray. You will be playing opposite Madeleine Carroll." Hayden claimed to feign surprise as Griffith continued, explaining that he would need to learn how to ride and jump a horse in preparation for his role as a country gentleman from the North. Jubilantly Griffith predicted that when the publicity department learned of this plan, they would go wild.[11]

As Griffith expounded on his plans for the young star, he mentioned one potential problem. "There is one possible hitch . . . Miss Carroll is the star. Miss Carroll has cast approval. It is not an easy thing for a girl in her position to play opposite someone as—as inexperienced as you. She might object."

Leaving Griffith's office after being informed he would be co-starring in a major Hollywood production, despite having no acting experience,

Hayden would claim in his 1963 autobiography: "The strange thing is, I knew all along this would happen."[12]

That summer, the cast and crew of *Virginia* traveled by railroad to Charlottesville, Virginia, where the film was being shot. Upon arrival, the stars, including Hayden, were taken to their lodging at the Farmington Hunt Club. That night, Griffith prepped Hayden for his dinner date with Madeleine Carroll. They arrived at her suite with a gaggle of Paramount crew in attendance. Finally, she arrived and welcomed him. He was immediately struck by her natural beauty. Although she was not wearing makeup and her hair was tied back, Hayden noted: "I knew she was lovely, but nothing like this."[13]

At thirty-four years of age, Madeleine Carroll was one of filmdom's top box-office draws. Her myriad of hits included *Lloyds of London*, *The General Died at Dawn*, *The Prisoner of Zenda*, and Alfred Hitchcock's *The 39 Steps*. A sophisticated Englishwoman, she received a bachelor's degree from the University of Birmingham, and it was during her senior year there that she had landed her first leading role in a school play. Abandoning her plans to obtain a master's degree, she focused on an acting career that soon took off. She and Capt. Phillip Astley of the Kings Guards were married in 1931 before divorcing in 1939. And now, the following year, she was having dinner with her new potential co-star, an actor who had never acted. He was, as she noted, extremely handsome. She invited him to dine with her that evening at the resort's main restaurant.

The unlikely couple hit it off at dinner, very much enjoying each other's company. Hayden was delighted to learn that, like him, she considered acting a means to an end, and her real interest in the profession was in earning enough money to help war orphans in France. In 1938, she had purchased Chateau de Saudreville, just south of Paris, and earlier in 1940, had converted it over to an orphanage. At the orphanage, she supported a number of war orphans, an effort she would continue throughout the war.[14] In response, Hayden shared his dream of buying a schooner in which to travel the world.

By the end of the evening and after several bottles of wine, they parted. There was an instant attraction between the handsome couple. Madeleine Carroll that night let Edward Griffith know that she wholeheartedly approved of his choice for the second male for *Virginia*.

The filming of *Virginia* took place over a six-week period in and around Charlottesville. Hayden was listed in the credits as "Stirling Hayden," and he played the second male lead, a character named Norman Williams.

During the shoot, Hayden often felt foolish and amateurish. In later years, he would fondly recollect how inexperienced he was in the ways of acting; when the director called for him to turn upstage, he had no idea what that meant and turned the wrong way. The one thing he felt strongly about was his physical attraction to the beautiful star of the film. The feeling was mutual and she and Hayden began an affair during the filming.

When the location filming was finished, work on the film continued at the studios in Hollywood. The lovers returned to the West Coast, resuming their affair. One day, they drove up the coast to a secluded house where he had arranged for two friends to be present so they could meet his paramour. They entered and were greeted by Larry O'Toole and Capt. Malcom MacDonald, a Boston Harbor pilot and among the group of his T Wharf drinking buddies. The two had driven out from Massachusetts to meet their young protégé and his glamourous new girlfriend. As was the case when most men met her, they were in awe of her beauty. As usual, O'Toole was his usual charming self.

When alone together that night, Hayden surprised O'Toole by telling him he was not enjoying his acting experience at all. "It's not a life for a man," he explained. "Not for me, it isn't. I'll tell you something, Larry. As soon as this picture is finished, I'm clearing out, fast."[15] As O'Toole pointed out the obvious, that he didn't have enough money to buy his beloved schooner as planned, Hayden shifted his thoughts and for the first time mentioned the war in Europe. "What I want to do is get into the war somehow . . . What I think I'll do is buy me a typewriter and a good camera and be a war correspondent." O'Toole accused him of reading too much Hemingway.

O'Toole pointed out the obvious to his young friend—that he was under contract to Paramount and couldn't just walk out. "They can't force a guy to work when he doesn't want to work," replied Hayden. True, his friend noted, but they could sue him for breach of contract. The bottom line, countered Hayden, was: "They respect you if you don't give a shit about money, if you tell them to take their dough and get lost." Exasperated, O'Toole could only advise him to wait at least a year and raise the money he'd need to buy a schooner before abandoning the film industry.[16]

When the production wrapped on October 2 and the film went into post-production, it was time to build publicity for the film's release, which was expected to take place late that coming winter. Madeleine Carroll had headed back east, while Fred MacMurray refused to go on a publicity tour. The job was left to Paramount's newest discovery, a new actor that they described as "The Most Beautiful Man in the Movies," and "The Beautiful Blond Viking God." He was soon riding in the Christmas Day parade on Hollywood Boulevard along with Roy Rogers and Dale Evans. After New Year's Day 1941, Griffith decided to send Hayden on a publicity tour to accompany the opening of the film on the East Coast. The highlight of the tour was an invitation to the White House where he accompanied fellow stars including Danny Kaye, Lana Turner, and Gene Kelly. As he filed past the president, he said: "Sir, Captain Ben Pine asked me to give you his regards and—" A delighted Roosevelt shot back: "Well, give my best to him. Tell him *Thebaud* should have won those last two races."[17]

The publicity tour lasted five weeks, with the Paramount entourage visiting Richmond, Charlottesville, Norfolk, Baltimore, Philadelphia, Washington, New York, and Boston. The film was scheduled for general release in late February.

Virginia had its New York premiere on January 22, 1941, and *New York Times* film critic Bosley Crowther gave the film a tepid review, reserving most of his criticism for Edward Griffith's direction and screenwriter Virginia Van Upp. Crowther addressed the actors thusly: "Fred MacMurray, as the noble Virginian, is somewhat smug, and Stirling Hayden, a newcomer to the screen, is just handsome and self-conscious as 'the modern carpetbagger (as he facetiously calls himself).'"[18] Griffith was satisfied enough with the onscreen chemistry between Carroll and Hayden that he was prepared to have the two of them in his next film, this time with Hayden as the male lead.

Griffith's new film project was titled *Bahama Passage* and was filmed in various locations in the Bahamas. Production began on May 19, 1941. Playing island business owner Adrian Ainsworth, Hayden was again billed as "Stirling Hayden." His love interest, Carol Delbridge, was played by Carroll. Sterling Hayden, in just his second Hollywood film, was the lead male star, playing opposite an established, beautiful Hollywood star. He had it made.

Or so it seemed.

PART TWO

THE FIRST WAR

"Protect the goddamn boat, and you're gonna protect your own ass."

STERLING HAYDEN, AKA 2ND LT. JOHN HAMILTON, USMCR

CHAPTER SIX

Walking Out on Hollywood

TO THE CASUAL OBSERVER, IT WOULD SEEM THAT STERLING HAYDEN had it made. Only twenty-five years old and having no prior acting experience, he was now making his second Hollywood film and was in a starring role. Once again, his leading lady was the elegant and beautiful Madeleine Carroll. However, the doubts that he had already felt while filming *Virginia* only deepened. Once again, he realized that he didn't enjoy the process of acting and felt foolish performing. In his mind and in his heart, he belonged at sea. And now, during the filming of *Bahama Passage* in August of 1941, another complication arose to add to the anxiety and confusion that he was already feeling. The physical attraction that he felt towards Madeleine Carroll was turning into love.

It seemed an unlikely pairing. He was a self-educated man without a high school diploma who had spent the past ten years as a seaman. The elegant British actress, who was already an established movie star, was ten years older than Hayden and a college graduate, fluent in four languages. As one director recalled, "You could not have found a more mismatched couple. Madeleine was beautiful, gay, witty. Sterling was humorless. All he wanted to talk about was boats."[1] Yet the physical chemistry between these two beautiful people was palpable. As he had learned when he had an affair with Carroll during the filming of *Virginia*, she seemed to detest Hollywood as much as he did. Career-wise, both Hayden and Carroll similarly "marched to the beat of a different drum," as their future career decisions would soon indicate.

When he arrived on Stage 31 at the Paramount lot that August day for shooting, he saw Madeleine sitting there with her new boyfriend. Hayden described him as "lean and tall and he looked like a man should look. He had been ferrying bombers across the North Atlantic."[2] They shot their scene together, but Hayden acknowledged that whatever they had between them personally was, by then, over. Yet he also realized that "suddenly and for the first time, I knew what jealousy meant."[3] When the shooting wrapped for the day, he had to escape, to try and clear his head. He got into his car and drove to the coastal highway and headed south. He didn't stop until he reached Capistrano, over fifty miles away.

After the end of this pointless drive, he turned around and headed north back towards Los Angeles. At that moment, all he could think about was his first love—ships and the sea. His mind shifted to a ship that he had spotted before, so he headed north and drove to Los Angeles harbor. Climbing over the barrier fence, he went down the dock until he arrived at the prize he now sought—the two-masted schooner *Oretha F. Spinney.* The ship had been purchased by MGM in Gloucester for the purpose of filming background shots for the movie *Captains Courageous,* starring Spencer Tracy. After being brought out to the West Coast for the filming, the ship was retired to the dock in Los Angeles harbor. This ship, lying in disrepair, had become Hayden's obsession. After inspecting it that evening, he inquired as to the price. It was for sale for $18,000—money that Sterling Hayden didn't have. He proceeded to fall asleep in the starboard bunk and when he awakened, he had already decided what he was going to do.

Driving back to his home as the sun was starting to rise, he imagined the interaction he would have later that day with Y. Frank Freeman, the head of Paramount Pictures. In his mind, he tried to visualize the confrontation. He would acknowledge how generous and accommodating Paramount had been to him personally. "I also know you have a great deal of faith in my future," he imagined telling Freeman. "But, sir, there are things busting loose inside of me that I simply cannot explain. You know, I want to buy a schooner and you've told me to be patient. Well—I'm sorry, sir, but I just have to have that vessel. Right now!"[4] Noting that two weeks of shooting were left on *Bahama Passage*, Hayden would make a serious threat to the studio head. "It so happens that I appear in almost every scene. This means you cannot finish the picture without me. Unless Paramount buys *Oretha F. Spinney* from MGM and hands her over to me, I shall refuse to report for work." If the studio did buy it for him, he would agree to be the most cooperative actor in the studio and arrange a repayment schedule. If he was unable to make the payments, he would work for free. "I mean that, sir," he would reassure Freeman. "I never meant anything so much in all my fucked-up life."[5]

That morning, the shooting went well on the set. From Hayden's demeanor, Madeleine sensed that something was brewing in her co-star.

Without revealing the purpose, he told her he had scheduled a meeting with Frank Freeman that noon. Gathering up his courage, Hayden reported to Freeman's office at the appointed time. The two growling boxers in the office did little to reassure the young actor. Neither did Freeman's somewhat curt and distant manner. Hayden re-created the conversation in *Wanderer*: "Well, Sterling, what's on your mind today?" Freeman brusquely inquired.

"Mr. Freeman, I just wanted to have a few words with you about this schooner we were talking about last month."

"My God, Sterling, do we have to go through this again? You'll have your precious boat when the time comes. Nobody's going to run off with it. Metro has no use for it, I have no use for it, so just control yourself and concentrate on your acting."

When Hayden countered that he'd have nothing to do when the shooting finished in two weeks, Freeman left the room for a minute and returned to his leather chair. He stunned the young actor with his next statement. "All right now, Sterling, I'll tell you what. I'll try and buy that schooner today. While you're still here if I can. When you finish your work on *Bahama Passage*, you will get a fifty percent interest in the boat as a—as a sort of bonus. You have some peculiar ideas but you'll outgrow them. As a matter of fact, if I was your father I'd be right proud of you."[6]

The surprised Hayden could not even begin to articulate his appreciation, but the studio head told him to forget it. If the actor would complete one additional picture for Paramount, the boat would be entirely his. A beaming Hayden watched as Freeman picked up the phone and called Eddie Mannix, the head of MGM. "You've got a boat somewhere down at the harbor called *Oretha F. Spinney*," he inquired of his rival studio head. "That's right. How much do you want for her? Eighteen five? I'll buy her."[7]

Hayden now had the boat that he had obsessed over. But he was far from content. His inner turmoil would soon cause him to commit to what was tantamount to career suicide.

• • •

The shooting wrapped up on *Bahama Passage* in late August. The next day, Hayden saw Madeleine off at the Pasadena Station, where she was beginning her journey back east to be with her "bomber man" once again. After saying their goodbyes, a downhearted Hayden left for the harbor to do a thorough inspection of the *Spinney*. The dilapidated condition of the ship depressed him even more and he laid back on a stained mattress, staring at the overhead while jealously thinking of Madeleine. In a few minutes he was sound asleep. It was 9:30 p.m. by the time he awaked. Looking around at his cluttered, filthy ship in need of multiple repairs, he decided he couldn't deal with it at the moment. He spontaneously decided that he would visit an old acquaintance from Gloucester who had since relocated to the San Francisco area—Sausalito, to be exact. This would be the first of two visits to an old friend that would come back to haunt Hayden in the years after the war.

Sterling Hayden had last seen Warwick Tompkins in June of 1936 before Tompkins and his wife and two small children set sail from Gloucester and traveled to San Francisco by way of Tangier, Rio, Cape Horn, and Talcahuano in Chile.[8] He published his best-selling book *Fifty South to Fifty South* describing the heroic voyage in 1938. Since relocating to Sausalito, Tompkins had sailed his schooner *Wander Bird* to Hawaii twice and Tahiti once. Tompkins was a master sailor, as well as a published author with an engaging and persuasive manner about him. Hayden admired the man although he readily admitted that he was somewhat intimidated by his intellect. As Hayden described Tompkins: "The only thing wrong was a rumor that he was becoming a radical, but all the same, I envied him his belligerence, his brusqueness, his ability as a writer, and his way of making a go of things even when he was broke. He also had a knack of flouting minor conventions."[9] When Hayden testified before the House Committee on Un-American Activities (HUAC) in 1951, he would describe that visit to Tompkins thusly: "I felt kind of lost in Hollywood, not really being an actor by inclination, and one time when I was feeling particularly low I decided to pay him a visit. I went to San Francisco and saw him. He was at that time, or previously, had become, I believe, an open and avowed Communist. He made no bones about it. He talked about very little else, and he started to deluge me with propaganda."[10]

Hayden was delighted to be in Sausalito, which he regarded as a true "sailorman's town." Tompkins and his wife Gwen appeared to be the same genuine couple he had seen several years before, and they graciously invited Hayden to stay aboard the *Wander Bird* with them. He gladly accepted the invitation. Being aboard a sailing vessel worked its magic on Hollywood's newest star. "Without a struggle, I surrendered myself to the sea: to the wind sounds and the smells of tar and salt, to the feel of splicing tools and marline, to the quiet hours of painting under the lee of the bulwarks and to lying on the deck in the sun, watching the birds perched on pilings pinned to the sky."[11] However, the serenity that Sterling Hayden felt being back in a maritime environment was muddled by his dinner discussions with Tompkins on his first night aboard, which added to the disequilibrium that was already tormenting him.

Hayden had just complimented Tompkins and his wife Gwen on how they appeared unchanged since their last encounter and how the *Wander Bird*, too, appeared to be unchanged. Tompkins startled his young guest by replying, "Oh yes, the old *Bird* is fine no doubt, but one of these days, my boy, you are going to find you can turn your back on the sea with scarcely a backward glance." Hayden suddenly realized that the rumors about the radicalization of Tompkins were very likely true—he appeared to have swallowed the communist line and now he was "as Red as they come these days."[12] His initial instinct was to feel sorry for his older colleague, but Hayden described the epiphany he subsequently experienced in his autobiography *Wanderer*. "But a strange thing happened; I found myself in the grip of a new excitement, anxious to discover just what this power was that had taken my friend and dammed the river of his mind in such a way that it no longer ran to the sea.

"I sensed I was about to stumble upon the key to what was wrong in my life, for the older I grew the more convinced I became that I was flawed in some way beyond my understanding."[13] Hayden continued to describe this newfound conflict that had been awakened by Warwick Tompkins. "I want both worlds at once, the world of ships and the world of social struggle. I was late, too, and I knew it—twenty-five years old, and for all my fighting and searching and voyaging I had yet to come to grips with life . . . Was I too scared to face reality? Too stupid perhaps? Well, then, the best thing I could do was listen to Tompkins with an open mind, and to hell with conventional thinking."[14]

Years later, Hayden would only be able to recall the name of one of the many people that Tompkins had introduced him to during his stay. At a luncheon one day, Tompkins told Hayden that there was a man he wanted to introduce him to, describing the man as "an old warrior in the class struggle."[15] He introduced the man as "Pop" Folkoff. Hayden didn't know anything about the man at the time. Born in Latvia in 1881 and having emigrated to San Francisco in 1904, Isaac Folkoff and had gone as a delegate to the founding congress of the Communist International in Moscow in 1919, and was a founding member of the California Communist Party.[16]

During his visit, Warwick Tompkins took Hayden to Oakland to participate in a labor protest at the waterfront. The International Longshoremen's Union was picketing a ship that was loading scrap iron bound for Japan. Tompkins knew some of the longshoremen, who were invited to have coffee with them. Initially, Hayden was simultaneously intimidated and impressed, thinking, "I felt ignorant and soft, a tourist for the first time in my life. These longshoremen belonged, and I was a phony on the outside looking in."[17] As the meeting progressed, Tompkins dominated the conversation and at times tried to pull Hayden into the discussions. The young actor felt very much out of his league and too uninformed to be a part of the dialogue, and for the moment he very much resented what he perceived to be Tompkins's arrogance and uncompromising opinions.

That evening, Tompkins invited about a dozen guests to the *Wander Bird* for further political discussions. Once again, Hayden felt out of his league as the discussions seemed far beyond his scope of knowledge and awareness. For the first time, he heard about International Brigades that had fought in the Spanish Civil War. A whole new vocabulary was revealed to him, as well as a new group of people. "They kept using words I didn't know—working class, Fascism, solidarity, imperialist, monopolist. It occurred to me that I was in the midst of some very dangerous people, yet they didn't seem dangerous. They seemed different, that's all—more intelligent than the rest, and above all, more concerned."[18]

Hayden, who felt humiliated by his ignorance of these issues, dared not speak. The time passed with agonizing slowness for him as the lively conversations continued all around him and he just listened and observed. Later in the evening, Tompkins turned to him and invited him to talk to the group about his past experiences. After all, reasoned Tompkins, none of the other guests were seamen and they would likely appreciate Hayden's descriptions of his hardworking life at sea. Obliging his host, the young man began to talk and his spoken recollections not only clearly intrigued the other guests, but suddenly they seemed more important to him; they seemed to have taken on a new perspective. They were not merely anecdotes, but real working-class stories that seemed to bring into focus several of the concepts that the rest of the guests had been talking about all evening. The more he spoke, the more relaxed he felt.

The guests seemed truly moved by his recollections, and some were angered by the struggles of the young man who had gone to sea at the age of sixteen. "I shared a part of my life;" he would recall, "and felt a new kinship with them. If I could only feel this way in front of the cameras, I'd turn into one hell of an actor. Perhaps I could revolt and still belong."[19] He came to the realization that he was right about the shallowness of Hollywood, that it wasn't wrong to have dreams and ideals and to want more out of life than an office, a house, and all the other possessions that many aspired to. And in his own antiestablishment way of thinking, he reasoned, "what could be more unusual than the sometime schoonerman who of his own volition tells conventional Hollywood to go to hell and goes back into the world to contribute something to life."[20]

When he left Sausalito, he had made up his mind to pursue a course that would seem to many self-destructive, and certainly it appeared that he was at the very least committing career suicide. But Sterling Hayden never looked at things in a conventional manner. Money and prestige never mattered to him that much. Coupled with his tendencies toward self-hatred and feelings of unworthiness, he decided to embark on a path to redeem his self-respect and to "contribute" to the world in a manner that was revealed to him by Warwick Tompkins and his friends.

He was also determined to win the love of Madeleine Carroll.

• • •

Sterling Hayden would recall the exact date when he performed two life-changing actions.[21] The morning of September 15, 1941, he wired Madeleine who was staying in Stamford, Connecticut. He announced his intentions with a wire that announced: "HAVE ABANDONED THE SHIP DRIVING EAST AT ONCE WILL PHONE FROM BOSTON MUST SEE YOU DO NOTHING RASH STOP LOVE."[22] Later that day, he found himself back in the waiting room of Frank Freeman's office at Paramount. His agent, Bert Allenberg, emerged to speak with him first. He informed Hayden with the expected news that both Freedman and Henry Ginsberg, the head of production at Paramount, wanted to meet with him individually. Before Hayden went to Ginsburg's office, Allenberg hinted at some of the sweeteners that Paramount was considering to offer if Hayden remained with the studio.

"Let me slip you this one thought," offered Allenberg. "I'm not supposed to let on, but just between the two of us, if you stay Paramount is prepared to give you the lead in *For Whom the Bell Tolls*." Hayden admitted to Allenberg that he had not read the Hemingway novel. Undaunted, Allenberg continued: "And, sweetheart, they'll tear up your contract and write you a new one, three pictures a year, thirty thousand dollars a picture. I can't believe it myself, but I happen to know it's true."[23] Hayden didn't say anything when his agent finished and got up to head over to Ginsburg's office as instructed.

Hayden knew Ginsburg by reputation, describing him as the "hatchetman" of the Paramount executives. When Hayden entered his office,

Ginsburg did not rise from his chair or offer his hand. As the young actor sat down, Ginsburg immediately began to live up to his reputation as a tough taskmaster. "Hayden," he began, "I am supposed to convince you not to quit. I'm not going to bother. I haven't the slightest sympathy with you. You are not an actor. You never have been. I doubt you ever could be an actor. You are what we call a Personality.

"We have brought you along until you are what is known as a hot property. You might go a long way in this business. If you would like my opinion, I would say that the odds are against it. You have to care in this business, and you don't give a damn. If you walk out on us, you will never work in pictures again."[24] Ginsberg went on to assure Hayden that he would in all likelihood be hit with a breach of contract suit. Then, after laying out the gloomy picture, he asked the young star if he would consider changing his mind. Hayden replied no, and he was then dismissed from Ginsburg's office and told to report to Frank Freeman's office.

He found Freeman sitting at his desk, puffing away on a large cigar. Freeman immediately pointed out the awkward position in which Hayden had put him. He quickly reminded his young star how well he had been treated by Paramount and by Freeman personally. "When this thing with the boat came up a few weeks back, I acted on my own initiative because I wanted you to calm down and be happy out here on the coast. I may be boss of this studio, but the Board of Directors and the stockholders don't take it lightly when we present newly discovered actors with eighteen-thousand-dollar boats."[25] Hayden readily acknowledged how well the studio had treated him.

Freeman offered to take his young star to lunch to continue the discussion, but Hayden told him that it wouldn't be necessary. Freeman decided to cut to the heart of the matter. Urging the young man to be direct and reminding him that he was his friend, Freeman told him to stop beating around the bush and to get to the matter that was driving his decision to walk out on the studio. Initially, Hayden replied that he didn't feel right as an actor and just wasn't cut out to be one. He also mentioned that with the war raging in Europe, he felt that he had to get out now. Freeman wasn't buying his explanations. He quickly pointed out: "You wanted the boat so we gave you a boat. We jumped your salary. We starred you in two of our biggest pictures. What more do you want? This war thing is nonsense. Our country isn't in the war yet—if it was, then I'd be the first to understand."

"Goddamn it, sir," Hayden replied, "but I can't act and keep my self-respect. It's the only thing I have and I guess I'd better hang on to it."[26]

Again, Freeman wasn't buying the explanation. He continued to puff on his cigar and complimented Hayden for his lofty thoughts, but he could sense that there was a deeper reason behind the young actor's motives. And, Freeman mused, he could understand the lure of a woman like Madeleine Carroll. As an older, more experienced man, he recommended that Hayden step back a bit, assuring him that his fixation for Madeleine would pass with time. Don't act out of passion without calming down and reasoning it through, he advised.

"I don't have to think about it. Madeleine is a big part of my decision, I admit," the young actor confessed. "But I would rather gamble on the thousand to one shot that I'll walk out this door and do whatever it is I have to do," he said as he wiped his eyes. Freeman looked back at him and asked him if he should even bother to make any further offers in an attempt to get his young star to reconsider leaving. Hayden told him not to bother—his mind was made up.

Walking Sterling Hayden to the door, Frank Freeman turned to his now former-star and said, "Good luck. We'll take care of the schooner, and if there's anything I can do, let me know."[27] It was just about noon when Hayden left Freeman's office. He made a beeline to his car and in moments he was off, heading east.

Heading to Madeleine Carroll.

• • •

Hayden journeyed east, stopping only to sleep an hour or so at a time in the back of his car. After several days, he had made it to his destination: Boston, Massachusetts. Shortly after he arrived at T Wharf and the home of his mentor and drinking buddy Larry O'Toole, he was surrounded by reporters who began to deluge him with questions. The word had gotten out that he had walked out on Hollywood. The reporters asked him if the rumor that he was going to be offered the lead in *For Whom the Bell Tolls* was true. They also grilled him on the rumors that his pursuit of Madeleine Carroll may have had something to do with his seemingly rash decision to walk out on his screen career.

"Put yourself in my position," he replied. "You come off the deck of a vessel and they sign you up to a contract and they powder you down and doll you up and Christ—I mean, end up nothing more than a dummy. I couldn't take it, that's all. It's as simple as that." Asked what his plans were, Hayden told them he was going to run down to New York for a few days and after that, "I'm a sonovabitch if I know."[28]

But Hayden did in fact have some immediate plans for the future. First, he would win back Madeleine from her lover from "Bomber Command," as he referred to him. Then he would make what he would regard as a token visit to the war zone. He described his intentions in *Wanderer*, referring to himself in the third person: "Having led an irregular life, he would wage an irregular war—vague imitations of danger, but just this side of bloodshed. Excitement, but no hardship. Good publicity for a cause that was not yet our concern."[29]

He did indeed win the heart of Madeleine Carroll, snatching her from her pilot. They were driving just outside Stamford, Connecticut, when he pulled over. The couple got out to walk in a field not far from Long Island Sound. It was late in the morning of October 3, 1941, and Hayden revealed his plans to Madeleine. Earlier that morning, he had called the father of his old friend David Donovan, who had sailed around the world with him aboard the *Yankee*, then-Col. William J. Donovan, who in July had been named by President Roosevelt as Coordinator of Information. In that capacity, he would develop and head up the United States' first foreign intelligence agency.

"This morning I spoke on the phone with Colonel Donovan," he told Madeleine. "He is sending me to England for three months of Commando and parachute training."

"And then?" asked Madeleine.

"Then I'll come back to help train more civilians until we get involved in the war. And then, we might get married. Maybe we could even keep it a secret for a little while."

"We might," she quietly replied.[30]

• • •

In mid-November, Hayden departed for Europe as a passenger in a convoy of forty-seven ships, escorted by five World War I vintage destroyers. Their destination was Glasgow, Scotland, and from there Hayden would proceed to London. He would be traveling with Col. Robert Solborg, who would be acting as his supervisor and mentor. Solborg had been appointed by Donovan as his first chief of Special Operations.

After studying the British MI6 model of organization, Donovan had decided to create a similar, two-pronged intelligence organization and created the Special Intelligence Branch, or SI, which would be charged with espionage—the secret collection of intelligence information—and the Special Operations Branch, or SO—tasked with sabotage and liaison with underground movements.[31] Donovan would write to FDR on December 22, 1941, to expound on his ideas on the covert warfare that the SO would undertake. First, he explained that in order to harass the occupying Axis troops, two types of guerilla warfare were necessary for different purposes: to set up small bands of fighters under definite leaders, and second, to establish these forces in a military framework in order to satisfactorily carry out their missions. "The principle laid down is that the whole art of guerilla warfare lies in striking the enemy where he least expects it and yet where he is most vulnerable," he explained. Donovan further suggested "that there be organized now, in the United States, a guerilla corps independent and separate from the Army and Navy, and imbued with a maximum of the offensive and imaginative spirit. This force should, of course, be created along disciplined military lines, analogous to the British Commando principle, a statement of which I recently sent you."[32]

OSS (as the COI would soon be renamed) training camps in the United States were not established until 1942. Hence, Hayden was sent to Scotland for his training with British SOE counterparts. Midway across the Atlantic Ocean, he recalled taking part in an antiaircraft drill. Assigned to man and operate a .50 caliber machine gun, he glibly recalled his short Hollywood career as he thought, "If they could see me now, Fred and Bing, and Bob, glued to a fifty-caliber antiaircraft gun, bound for Glasgow, on a secret mission."[33] They arrived in Glasgow on December 7, and while awaiting their train to London, Hayden noticed residents scurrying about and talking in hushed tones about the latest tragic war news. The news had something to do with the United States naval base in Pearl Harbor, Hawaii. After inquiring with one of the passing people, Hayden first learned of the Japanese attack on American soil. He didn't believe it at first, thinking the British were as susceptible to gossip and rumor-mongering as Americans. His reaction was: "The Japs bomb Pearl Harbor? Preposterous."[34] He quickly learned that the rumors were true.

The team arrived in London the following day and reported to the American embassy where, to their surprise and annoyance, they learned that no one was expecting Hayden—nor did they know what to do with him. "What the hell is going on?" recollected Hayden in his autobiography. Describing himself in a third-person narrative, he recalled, "He had sacrificed his career, security, and the company of his tentative fiancée to assist in the war, and nobody gave a damn."[35] Solborg decided to take the matter into his own hands. For about three days, he took Hayden around to different British officers who conducted interviews and briefed Hayden as to the type of work he would be doing. None of the officers were introduced by name, with the whole organization operating in great secrecy.[36]

Hayden had a couple of days to kill before he reported to his first training assignment in Scotland. During that time, he became introspective as he realized that his plan, in essence, to go through the motions of involvement in war and to skirt real danger had rapidly changed with America's declaration of war on Japan and the simultaneous declaration of war on America by the other Axis powers. Inwardly, he felt he was a coward. Recalling his reaction in the third-person, he admitted, "He knew, too, that his burlesque days were numbered, for now that his country found itself in the war there was bound to come, sooner or later, an end to the leeway he needed to operate in. (What I'll have to find is some pretext to detach from the COI. Then I'll simply fade for the duration. I have no business being here, to begin with.)" He angrily reflected that it was the influence of Warwick Tompkins and his "dialectical and historical materialism, and all that crap about the brotherhood of man," that had largely been the major influence on him to pursue the course on which he now found himself.[37] He was a "windjammer man" and would be until the day he died. Adding to his turmoil was the thought that he really couldn't picture the glamorous movie star Madeleine Carroll being married to the captain of a South Seas schooner. With all of these thoughts tearing at him, he left London to begin a three month's training course taught by the SOE. Two weeks of parachute school would follow.

• • •

The Lochaber district was a sparsely populated region of the County of Inverness on the coast of the West Scottish Highlands. With its remote location and limited access, it was an ideal place to set up the Special Operations Executive training schools; the entire Lochaber region was requisitioned by the British government for exclusive use by the SOE. Two miles from the village of Arisaig stood an isolated stone mansion built in 1864 and known as Arisaig House. Arisaig House became the SOE Special Training School, designated STS21. On December 15, 1941, an overcast day, Sterling Hayden arrived at Arisaig House.

The school was staffed by combat veterans of the Argyll and Sutherland Highlanders, an infantry regiment of the British Army. Sterling Hayden reported in to the impressive-looking, thirty-six-year-old commanding officer, Col. Edward G. Young. Young expressed his delight at seeing an American at the school—up to this time, they had not trained any Americans, nor would Hayden train with any other fellow countrymen at the SOE schools. Young quickly got to the heart of the matter by stating: "You have no military background, I am told."

"No, sir."

"Are you by any chance trained as an engineer?" Young inquired.

"No, sir," was again Hayden's reply.

"Just what, Mr. Hayden, is your background?" asked Young, likely wondering what he was supposed to do with this strapping young man with no apparent useful military skills. It was not obvious to him at all why Hayden had been sent there.

"Well, sir, I grew up in small sailing vessels in New England and I went around the world two or three times under sail and then three years ago I took command of a small brig and delivered her from Boston to Tahiti and—"

"But what have you been doing recently?" interrupted the increasingly confused commanding officer. In response, Hayden provided a startling explanation, one that undoubtedly Young had never heard anything remotely similar to from any prior students at the school.

"Well, sir, this is going to sound kind of strange, but a few years ago Colonel Donovan suggested I go out to the West Coast and become an actor."

"Go on," invited Young.

"I guess it had something to do with my being able to use the acting thing as a cover in case we got in the war."[38] With that incredible explanation, Young formally welcomed Hayden to the school.

As he began his training, Hayden noticed that he was training with men of various European nationalities, virtually all of whom had served in combat. As per SOE Training School protocol, men of each nationality were housed in separate schools for security reasons for the duration of the curriculum.[39] The training at Arisaig House lasted for three weeks. In addition to intense physical training, topics taught included silent killing, weapons handling, demolition, map reading, compass work, field craft, elementary Morse code, and raid tactics. The training would commence with a hard run over the unwelcoming terrain of the Invernesshire, a most difficult trek that both men and women trainees would have to complete.[40]

The training was physically demanding, but Hayden was up to the challenge. As part of his regimen while under contract with Paramount, he had a regular program of weightlifting. The success of that program was evident in the bare-chested photographs of Hayden that the studio released. His physical strength no doubt held him in good stead for the demanding hand-to-hand combat training taught at the school. The weapons training and unarmed combat training was designed for close combat only. For this, the students were instructed in the art of "silent killing" by the true masters of the trade: the legendary William Fairbairn and Eric Anthony Sykes.[41] Fairbairn had developed a system of close-in combat while a police officer in Shanghai in the 1920s that came to be known as the "Fairbairn Fighting System." He and Sykes had created the combat knife that would become standard issue for commandos throughout the war. Fairbairn would soon be commissioned by Wild Bill Donovan to set up the hand-to-hand commando combat training in the United States for the Office of Strategic Services in 1942.

Hayden and his fellow students were trained in the use of the Colt .45 and .38, as well as the Sten gun. Their handgun instruction was tailored for close-in killing, based on the Double Tap system of firing two shots at their target while tucking their firing arm into their hip instead of the standard arms extended double hand grip.

The nearby West Highland Line was used to train the students in railway sabotage. The railroad had supplied the school with a train that the students used as they learned to plant dummy explosives and jam communications, and then stealthily slip away undetected.[42]

Hayden trained hard. "So they told him to train and he trained," he would recall, "a pale figure in British battle dress, minus insignia, wearing American hunting boots and no hat—all wrapped up in a Hollywood trench coat. He trained with Dutchmen and Poles and Belgians and French and Danes and Norsemen, all of whom," he noted with admiration, "had been in combat." Despite the growing camaraderie he felt for his fellow European trainees, he became increasingly wracked with self-doubt, feeling that he was going through heroic motions, but knowing that he was not cut from the same cloth as his classmates. He missed the relatively carefree life he had experienced in California with Madeleine and began to feel he had become "hostage to an image of heroism."[43]

Hayden decided that he wanted to remain a civilian and avoid the military when he returned to the United States. He felt he had at least earned some bragging rights that he could use back home. In his autobiography, he reflected on the canned speech that he could give to admirers back home. "Well, the fact is, folks, I've been over in Scotland training with some Commandos from the Argyll and Sutherland Highlanders.

That's right. What? No, I was the only American there at the time; and then they sent me to Ringway Field near Manchester, where I made a dozen or so parachute jumps. What's that? Oh, it's quite a sensation all right. No, you don't get used to it."[44]

At the end of three weeks, Hayden completed the initial training. In a November 1944 narrative that would become part of his personnel file, he reported that he had enjoyed not only the challenges that the commando training presented but also the camaraderie amongst all the students. He described his relations with the instructors who had driven them for the past weeks as "extremely good. They were very, very cooperative and helpful in every way."[45] Once his training at Arisaig was completed, he traveled to his next SOE training school for more advanced training in commando techniques.

For the last phase of his SOE training, Hayden was sent to Ringway Field near Manchester, England, for parachute training and qualification. Ringway had been designated as the top parachute-training school in the Royal Air Force shortly after the war began. All European allied paratroopers received their training there, as did SOE operatives. At Ringway, the students continued with their rigorous conditioning program. As one paratrooper recalled, "At Ringway we lived hard. Before breakfast each morning we went for a three mile run, followed by thirty minutes PT. After breakfast we normally had a 12 to 15 mile 'parachute march.' This meant covering at least 11 miles every two hours and it took some doing while carrying full equipment."[46]

Hayden reported to the jump school on January 4, 1942. His first jump was completed from a balloon at an altitude of five hundred feet. Poor weather prevented him from jumping from an airplane until his fourth jump. On his fifth jump, from a Stirling bomber on January 11, he landed on a frozen cart track, injuring his left ankle, the base of his spine, and his left knee. He was admitted to the Davyhulme Military Hospital and discharged later that day. His discharge diagnosis was "sprained ligament left knee."[47] Due to his injury, his jump school curriculum was cut short and he was assigned further training on the pistol range.

Hayden clearly impressed his British instructors. His evaluation from parachute school stated that he was "a keen and intelligent student." Praising his courage and enthusiasm, it was noted that he jumped without hesitation, but was "inclined to open his legs on landing."[48] The school's commandant further commented that "Sterling Hayden acquired a full knowledge of all the instruction given at this school." Despite his injury and an abbreviated curriculum that was marred by bad weather, he further said, "He was, however, satisfied himself and satisfied us that he had a good practical knowledge of parachuting."[49] From Ringway, he was sent back to the COI office in London, where he filed a report on his experiences and training in Scotland. In London, he received more medical treatment and was issued crutches (that were "much too short") to help him get around.

His parachute school instructors were not the only SOE instructors to be impressed with Hayden. On February 18, 1942, Pulitzer Prize-winning playwright Robert E. Sherwood, who had joined the COI to head up the propaganda division known as the Foreign Information Service, wrote to Col. Solborg to pass along some of the excellent feedback on Hayden that the COI had received from Great Britain.[50] "We have received from London, the following report on Mr. Stirling [*sic*] Hayden, which we should be glad if you would pass on to Mr. Solborg. London has also heard personally from the Commandant of the School how well Mr. Hayden is doing." Another comment read: "This gentleman is showing the greatest enthusiasm in all branches of our work at this School. He has personality and is very popular. He is sparing no pains to learn everything which is likely to be of use to him, and, with further experience, should develop into a first class instructor."

On January 15, 1942, Fisher Howe, the executive officer of the London mission of the COI, cabled both Col. Solborg as well as William Whitney, director of the London mission, that Hayden would be departing via sea transport for the United States on January 17. Interestingly, he included William Donovan on the message's distribution.[51] Shortly thereafter, the COI sent Hayden to Liverpool where he boarded a freighter bound for New York City.

On January 26, 1942, Howe followed up with a message to Thomas G. Early, head of administration for the COI office in Washington, announcing that Hayden's ship would arrive at St. John, New Brunswick, on about January 27, adding that he would be reporting immediately to Washington, DC[52] Once again, Donovan was included on the distribution list, indicating his high level of interest in his son's friend.

On his voyage back to the States, Hayden was once again faced with the reality that perhaps he wouldn't be able to conveniently "hide" from the war effort as he thought he might. The skipper of the freighter, although only thirty-two years old, had survived a torpedoing on a run to Murmansk while he was carrying a load of high-octane fuel. His hair had turned white overnight as a result of that trauma.[53] While midway across the Atlantic, sirens went off indicating that a submarine had spotted them and was preparing to attack. The skipper darted from the wardroom table for the bridge to direct the evasive zigzagging maneuvers. Watching the skipper act so authoritatively and observing the calmness of the mess stewards as the ship started its evasive actions, Hayden was also struck with another self-realization that he was grappling with. He was scared. He, the trained commando, felt his blood "congeal." "A stroke of terror stunned him. And all at once he knew that the thing he feared the most was true. He was yellow."[54]

...

Arriving back in the Unites States, Hayden returned to Washington and reported in to the COI headquarters at Twenty-Fifth and E streets on Navy Hill where he was offered a commission in the United States Army. He refused the offer, explaining that he did not wish a direct commission.[55] At this point, his involvement with the COI was effectively over and he returned to civilian life. The COI calculated his government service to be from November 7, 1941 (when he was sworn into government service to attend SOE training) though January 29, 1942. For this he was paid a per diem of six dollars per day and was issued a check for $504 on February 21, 1942.[56] During his training, he had formulated his plan to avoid military service and perhaps just train future special operations recruits at home in the States. However, the rest of his future plans remained murky. He was in the same situation he was in when he walked out on Hollywood. He only seemed to be able to focus on the here and now, and not on the future. There was only one immediate goal that he wanted to pursue and for this he headed immediately for New England.

Madeleine Carroll was indeed waiting for him and they drove up to a vacation lodge on a frozen lake near Peterborough, New Hampshire, where they were married on February 14, 1942. The newlyweds quickly set up housekeeping in South Norwalk, Connecticut. With his injured leg propped up and facing a roaring fire in their fireplace, Hayden had found some of the contentment he sought. Having gotten through some of the most demanding training on earth, achieving status as a trainer of warriors, and having married a glamorous Hollywood star, it would appear to any observer that young Sterling Hayden was a lucky man. However, once again, large doses of self-doubt and self-hatred would eat away at him. The contentment he felt was only temporary.

He was extraordinarily brutal with himself. As he relaxed at his Connecticut home, his self-analysis once again began to torment him. "Now, where do I go from here?" he asked himself. "I'm flawed inside and I know it. But why did it have to be me? Why, why, why, why, why? Roosevelt was right: we have nothing to fear but fear. Could it be perhaps that this is a trick of fate to compensate for my being tall and strong and good-looking enough to intrigue every girl I meet? Is this a malignancy grafted into my spine to offset the fact that I'm equally at home in a drawing room or a fo'c'sle? If so—what a hell of a price to pay." He asked himself, "Isn't it true that I've been living a lie for years? . . . When is an unemployed victim of the depression not a victim at all? Perhaps when his life is a charade. When is an actor not an actor? When the bulk of his acting is offstage."[57]

He soon found some solace from the haven he had always turned to—the sea. Hayden traveled to Bayonne, New Jersey, and began to work for the Elco Boat Works. Elco, a successful shipbuilding company, had built its Bayonne facility after being acquired as a subsidiary of the Electric Boat Company. At the outset of World War II, the company contracted with the United States Navy to build hundreds of small boats that would achieve legendary status during the war—the Patrol Torpedo boat, better known as the PT boat.

The potential of the PT boat was already capturing not only the attention of the Navy, but the American public as well. Enamored with the exploits of a brash young PT boat commander, Lt. John D. Bulkeley, against the Japanese Navy, the PT boat's successes provided some of the few bright spots in otherwise gloomy news coming from the Pacific theater in early 1942. Among the feats that Motor Torpedo Boat Squadron 3, commanded by Bulkeley, had achieved was the rescue of Gen. Douglas MacArthur from Corregidor and his delivery through five hundred miles of Japanese-controlled waters to safety.

For several weeks, Hayden worked with the test crews at Elco, where they "rammed PT boats up and down New York harbor." Hayden enjoyed the work. After all, he was back on the water and in an environment where he felt genuine and could excel. After several weeks, he realized that maybe this was the way he could contribute to the war effort and perhaps not be the outside viewer that he had already planned he would be. He decided to apply for a commission in the United States Navy. He wanted to go to sea in command of a PT boat. He would be disappointed by the Navy's response.

Sterling Hayden was offered a commission by the Navy, but it was for the rank of ensign, the lowest rank of a commissioned officer. He was somewhat insulted by the offer. Given his vast experience at sea and the fact that he had been master of ships, he felt that he should have been offered a commission as a lieutenant. The Navy didn't agree. In addition, Hayden conceded, "lieutenancies weren't given to men whose education had stopped halfway through tenth grade."[58] In the end, he turned down the Navy's offer, but would take some solace in the admiration from his friends for, in essence, telling the Navy to go to hell. That night, he and Madeleine dined in a little café where he proposed a toast to his wife after she announced that she was going to lend him the money to buy out Paramount's share in the *Oretha F. Spinney*. As his self-doubt continued, he mused over the type of husband that she could have married. She could have married anyone, but she had chosen him, and he was beginning to wonder why. Nonetheless, he was formulating a plan for the immediate future and it involved going back to sea.

• • •

Now that Madeleine had provided him the funding, Hayden headed out to California to pay off Paramount Pictures for their half-interest in the schooner. *Orthea F. Spinney* was now completely his, and he had a lucrative plan not only to make money but to serve the war effort as well. Having obtained an unlimited draft deferment, "on the logical grounds that a man might do more good packing cargo under the auspices of the War Shipping Administration than packing a rifle,"[59] he planned to obtain shipping contracts hauling needed wartime materials, including munitions and explosives. Whatever potential danger that might be posed by German submarines, such work would certainly be counterbalanced by very generous remuneration. If all went smoothly, Hayden figured he could gross between $8,000 and $11,000 per voyage.[60]

He put the schooner in dry dock in Los Angeles and flew on to New York City to negotiate contracts. Given the relative shortage of adequate shipping assets available at the beginning of the war, he was able to quickly secure a contract to carry ninety-five tons of explosives from Port Everglades in Florida to San Juan, Puerto Rico. He next flew on to Nassau and signed up a ten-man Bahamian crew.[61] After the repairs in the dry dock, the new crew left Los Angeles and three and a half weeks later they were transiting the Panama Canal. One of the canal pilots had some sobering advice for Hayden as they arranged the transit. "If I were in your shoes, Hayden, I'd go the rest of the way under sail. If you don't turn that goddamn diesel on, the U-boats may not know you're around. I hope you're well insured anyway."[62] When Hayden replied that the cost of insurance was prohibitive and hence he didn't have any, the canal pilot just shook his head.

Heeding the sage advice he had been given, Hayden captained the schooner out of the canal and made the rest of the journey under sail. Fortunately, they encountered no enemy submarines and after ten days, they arrived in Miami. Having dodged the potential bullet of encountering Nazi submarines, they now had to struggle with the United States Navy. Naval officers boarded the *Spinney* soon after she docked, informing Hayden that because of wartime necessity, they were requisitioning his boat. He argued fiercely with the officers, pointing out that the schooner (serving in its current capacity) was an essential and integral part of the war effort. The Navy wasn't buying the young skipper's arguments and announced that in several days, the ship would be taken by the Navy.

That evening, Hayden assembled his crew and revealed his plan—they would not be going up to Port Everglades, but instead they were leaving that night. Stealthily, they departed from Miami before the Navy realized they had left. The *Spinney* set course for Nassau, arriving shortly at the Paradise Island marina in Hurricane Hole. Madeleine flew down to be with her husband, apparently the first time they acknowledged their marriage in public. Hayden set out to salvage his business venture. Within two days, he had sold all of the schooner's mechanical equipment for $10,000 in cash. He also hired a new crew after the original crew quit upon arriving in Paradise Island.

Three weeks later, the *Spinney* departed for Port Everglades to pick up the cargo of explosives that Hayden had contracted for. Madeleine departed when they reached port and Hayden and his crew commenced loading the explosives onto the schooner. This time, it was the United States Coast Guard that stepped in. Before they could carry aboard the first load, an officer informed Hayden that he was required to have two watertight steel bulkheads and a specially constructed steel case on the deck for stowage of the explosives and the detonators. Hayden was, of course, running his operation on barebones expenses and could not afford to comply. However, he saw great opportunity in this new dilemma. "This was all the excuse I need to default on the explosives contract," he would humorously recall. "I had long held the Coast Guard in high esteem, but never as highly as now. My sailing-ship luck still held."[63]

There were still numerous materials that needed to be transported. Hayden had contracted to transport 112 tons of general cargo for Curacao. In addition to the cargo stowed below, the deck was covered with an additional fifteen tons of rivets and bolts.[64] They were sailing rapidly down the Windward Passage when disaster nearly stuck the schooner in the form of a white squall near Haiti. For the next nineteen days the ship was tossed about and the crew nearly mutinied out of fear of capsizing. Finally, after thirty-two days at sea, they approached their destination—Curacao's capital city, Willemstad. The city's Queen Emma Bridge, the famous pontoon bridge, swung open as the *Oretha F. Spinney* was towed in to a berth. On the left side of the harbor, Hayden could see the large Shell Oil refinery overlooking the harbor. He had no way of knowing it, but the refinery was about to dramatically change his life.

• • •

After the *Spinney* pulled into its berth in Willemstad, Hayden hastily proceeded to unload his cargo. Because of the terrible sea conditions encountered during the transit from Florida, his cargo was pretty much soaked. He had to engage in "endless consultations with brokers, agents, insurance adjusters, and customs inspectors."[65] Business practices and financial matters were things that he had little interest in and even less talent for handling. Nonetheless, he finally managed to sell off his cargo and complete his business in Curacao. Shortly after concluding his negotiations, he met six off-duty United States Marines who were part of Force 1291, the US military unit in Willemstad assigned to protect the Royal Dutch Shell oil refinery. Describing them as broke, bored, and tough, Hayden immediately hit it off with the Marines and he invited them back to the schooner.

Aboard the *Spinney*, the seven men congregated in the aftercabin, and Hayden broke out a case of Haig and Haig Pinch scotch and handed each of his new friends a bottle. He was getting along famously with the Marines and quickly developed a deep sense of admiration for these men dedicated to the Corps. The hard-drinking skipper was in his element with his new buddies, and after finishing their bottles, they decided that the night was still young and they headed ashore to continue. Ending up at the bar in the Hotel Americano, they became rowdier as they became even more drunk. Finally, by 3 a.m., the hotel manager intervened and tried to evict them. He recognized Hayden as a movie star and was willing to cut him some slack and tried to get him to get his drunken Marines friends to leave. The Marines, however, were in no mood to acquiesce to the request so the manager called the police. At this point, Hayden grabbed the manager and threw him out to into the street just as the police arrived. For his noble action in diverting the attention away from his new found friends, Hayden was thrown in jail.

By the following morning, Hayden had sobered up. After calling the agents that he had dealt with in selling his cargo, they arrived at the jail with the money to bail him out. Once again, Sterling Hayden had come up with an impulsive career move. After quick negotiations, he sold the *Oretha F. Spinney* to his Curacao agent for $14,000. He called his new Marine friends to bid them goodbye. Apparently the admiration was mutual, as all six Marines escorted Hayden to the airport to bid him farewell. He was off for New York City.[66]

It was the middle of the night when he landed in New York. He arrived at the Beekman Towers Hotel in Manhattan in the early morning hours of October 26, 1942, where Madeleine was waiting for him. They had champagne with their breakfast as they watched the sunrise from their terrace overlooking the East River. The impulsiveness of his next move indicated the important effect that his newly found Marine friends had on him. "At nine sharp I picked up the phone directory, got the address of the Marine Corps recruiting station, and within the hour I had enlisted for boot training at Parris Island in South Carolina." His self-pride in this action was expressed thusly: "My image shone brighter than ever."[67]

• • •

Interestingly, at the same time her husband was changing his life's direction, Madeleine Carroll had recently made an important career decision of her own that was to change her life. Although one of Hollywood's top leading ladies ever since Alfred Hitchcock's 1935 film *The 39 Steps*, she had always preferred to work on the stage, and she was not enamored with Hollywood in general. In the fall of 1940, a personal tragedy struck Madeleine's family that inspired her new journey, one from which her film career would never recover. In a Luftwaffe bombing raid over London on October 7, 1940, Madeleine's younger sister Marguerite, or "Guiguite" as she was called, was killed.

Madeleine would never truly recover from the death of her sister. In a letter to her parents, she promised she would do everything possible to avenge her sister's death.[68] While visiting British Columbia in November of 1940, she gave an interview to the press where she declared, "I have a personal debt to pay Hitler. I can't be a soldier, but there are ways to pay the Germans back and I shall do just that in all possible ways."[69] She began formulating a plan to leave Hollywood and pursue her personal interests. Ironically, her plan would come to fruition immediately after once of her greatest film triumphs.

Paramount had cast her opposite Bob Hope in the comedy *My Favorite Blonde* that began shooting in the fall of 1941. At the time, Madeleine was the highest paid actress in Hollywood, earning about $250,000 per picture. The filming wrapped in January 1942, at which point she stunned the Paramount executives, much as her future husband had done the previous September, by requesting that they release her from her contract. She wanted to more vigorously support the war effort, convinced that the conflict was the greatest challenge her generation would ever have to face. She wanted to do more than participate in the usual bond-selling tours to aid the war effort.[70] In 1940, she had already donated the chateau that she owned outside of Paris for use as an orphanage. She still wanted to do more. After initial reluctance, the studio heads relented and released her from her contract. Less than a month later, she flew to the East Coast and traveled to New Hampshire, where she and Sterling Hayden were married in February, 1942.

My Favorite Blonde was released in April of 1942 to strongly positive reviews. Madeleine received high praise for her performance, and the film became one of her biggest box-office successes. But she was not interested in making films in the immediate future. She joined the USO and toured the country to raise money for the war effort on bond tours. It became a goal of hers to return to Europe as soon as it was feasible. Meanwhile, she also became a spokesperson on behalf of merchant seamen, no doubt being influenced by her husband's background. At a charity function held in New York City to raise money on behalf of the Seaman's Service in early 1943, Madeleine was the featured speaker. Among her exhortations to the crowd were: "We have the ships, let's not beach them this time." To a reporter who asked her if she was angry over the relatively little credit and attention given to merchant seamen, she replied, "Of course I get angry, we do not give enough to these courageous men."[71]

In November 1943, just as she had obtained American citizenship, Madeleine was finally able to return to Europe. After a brief reunion with her family, she embarked on a mission to support the war effort in Europe that was most unusual for a Hollywood star—as unusual as her husband's activities.

CHAPTER SEVEN

Joining the OSS

AFTER ENLISTING IN THE MARINE CORPS IN LATE OCTOBER 1942, STERling Hayden arrived by bus at boot camp at Parris Island, South Carolina. He was with about seventy other recruits from the New York area. Immediately upon arrival, he received a taste of what life was going to be like for a boot camp trainee, especially one who was immediately recognized as a Hollywood movie star. As they lined up as instructed, their drill sergeant bellowed out: "You! You big guy there in the middle. Take three steps forward!" After Hayden complied, the sergeant proceeded to walk around him twice. Then, striking his own thigh with his swagger stick, he exploded, "So this is the big-shot actor from Hollywood. Well, Hayden, let me tell you if you think just because you're married to Madeleine Carroll you're going to get special treatment down here, you got another think coming."

"Yes, sir," Hayden dutifully replied.

"Because, Buster, let me tell you, and this goes for the rest of you slobs, beginning now I want you to know the shit's on good!"[1]

Hayden was wondering if he had made a big mistake by enlisting. Here he was in boot camp for only a few minutes and he was already being singled out. He quickly came to the conclusion that he needed to seek a commission. As an officer, he figured he surely would not have to deal with such nonsense. He learned that two men were always selected from each recruit platoon and sent to Officer Candidate School in Quantico, Virginia. This was the incentive he needed to stay focused. The rugged, physically fit Hayden performed in an exemplary manner during the seven-week boot camp curriculum. His drill instructor, Private George S. Featherstone, described him as a "hell of a good Marine. . . . Life as a DI would be a pleasure if all were as good recruits."[2] In the end, he was one of the two graduates selected for OCS. He was assigned as a drill instructor for several weeks before being ordered to report to Quantico to begin the Twenty-Third Officer Candidates Class.

Hayden was one of 270 OCS students, virtually all of them recent college graduates. His life at Quantico was somewhat more palatable than his experiences at Parris Island, but he nonetheless found the regimented discipline distasteful and too confining for his individualist ways. He sarcastically observed that "it seemed incredible that any man in his right mind could spend his life in the Service."[3]

After completing his officer training, he was commissioned as a 2nd lieutenant in the United States Marine Corps Reserve on April 30, 1943. He was very disappointed to learn that he was being assigned to the Training Section at Quantico for the next two years.[4] This was not the type of work he had in mind. Now that he was a Marine, he saw himself in a more unorthodox role, one where his background as a sailor and a world traveler could be put to good use. He also detested the fact that he was recognizable to most of his fellow Marines and that his name was well-known. He was looking for a certain type of role, one that could be performed in relative anonymity. He had not sacrificed his Hollywood career to become 2nd Lt. Sterling Hayden, USMCR, a training officer at Quantico, Virginia. But he had two ideas that just might solve his problem. Both ideas reflected the constant out-of-the-box-thinking that he demonstrated his entire life.

The first idea concerned both Hayden and his wife. They were determined to pursue their goals in anonymity and were willing to take legal action to further their plans. That summer, acting on both of their behalves, Madeleine had gone to court and legally had their names changed. By late June, Sterling Hayden had legally changed his name to John Hamilton, a name he would use for official purposes for the rest of the war. Madeleine was henceforth officially Madeleine Hamilton.[5] The second idea involved the Office of the Coordinator of Information (OCI), which on June 13, 1942, had been renamed as the Office of Strategic Services, or the OSS. Hayden had decided that the best way to serve his country as a Marine, while maintaining some of the idiosyncratic individuality that he had always expressed, was to join the OSS. On Saturday, May 1, 1943, Sterling Hayden telephoned Gen. William Donovan and expressed his desire to transfer to the OSS. Donovan told him that he would see what he could do.[6]

• • •

William Donovan, or "Wild Bill" as he was called, was a polished infighter in Washington in charge of the Office of Coordinator of Information, or COI. Franklin D. Roosevelt envisioned a centralized intelligence agency under Donovan's direction but there was stiff opposition to this from FBI director J. Edgar Hoover and Gen. George V. Strong, head of the War Department's Military Intelligence.[7] Both men coveted the position of director of all US intelligence activities for themselves.[8] In June 1942, Donovan met with British intelligence officials to discuss an alliance between their two intelligence agencies. Each had much to offer the other—the British had the experience, training, contacts, and equipment, while the Americans had manpower, wealth, and political reputation.[9] The meeting resulted in the creation of the London Agreements, dividing the world into spheres of control of intelligence activities. Donovan's COI controlled Asia, Australia, Finland, and the Atlantic Islands. The British SOE was responsible for India, East Africa, the Middle East, and the Balkans.[10]

With support from and alliance with the British intelligence officials, Donovan was able to persuade Roosevelt to transfer the COI from presidential authority to the authority of the Joint Chiefs of Staff. The COI would evolve into the Office of Strategic Services, or OSS. But opposition from Gen. Strong continued until Donovan was able to convince Gen. George Marshall to take over the OSS himself. Marshall directed Gen. Joseph McNarney, Adm. Frederick Horne, and Gen. H. H. "Hap" Arnold to create a charter for the OSS. In December, 1942, JCS Directive 155/4/D established the OSS and made it coequal to other military intelligence agencies.

One portion of JCS Directive 155/4/D created Operational Groups, or OGs, which were responsible for "organization and conduct of guerilla warfare" and execution of "independent organizations against enemy targets."[11] These men with commando training would parachute into enemy-held territory to sabotage and harass the enemy and support local resistance movements.

The OGs were looking for men in good physical condition with language ability who were willing to do hazardous duty, had specific guerilla and army training, good judgment and stability, and had political sympathies compatible with the area in which they operated.[12] The OSS was open for business and Sterling Hayden wanted to be part of it.

• • •

To Donovan, Hayden must have seemed like a gift from Heaven. Given his background, he was to all appearances a natural for the OSS, as well as a qualified candidate for the newly formed Operational Groups. Hayden's qualifications were impressive. He had already completed commando training in Scotland with the SOE and was a qualified parachutist. He was a commissioned Marine Corps officer and would complete his OCS training shortly. He had a working knowledge of the French language, was extremely fit, and was eager for the challenge. According to Hayden, the only problem was that he was not scheduled to finish his training at Quantico for another six weeks. He was hoping that Donovan could pull some strings with the Marine Corps to expedite his transfer to the OSS.

The strings that Donovan did pull on Hayden's behalf reveal the high regard that the OSS director had for the young Marine. The very next morning, Sunday, May 2, 1943, Hayden reported to OSS Headquarters for his interviews. Hayden was interviewed by Lt. Cdr. R. Davis Halliwell, the head of the Special Operations branch at OSS Headquarters, and Col. Ellery Huntington.[13] Huntington was the commanding officer of Operational Groups and would soon head the OSS mission to Tito's Partisans in Yugoslavia. Under the section of OG qualifications for special skills, Halliwell commented on Hayden's extensive small boat experience and its potential in commando operations.

Despite having passed the interviews, the OSS Officers Board for selection consideration did not approve Hayden's transfer. In response, Huntington wrote a memo to one of the dissenting board members on May 22, 1943. He ended his memo with a question: "These officers were specifically requested by General Donovan. Does the Board know this?"[14]

The subtle message from Huntington was understood by the OSS Selection Board. On May 24, 1943, they approved the selection of Sterling Hayden for transfer to the OSS. Charles S. Cheston, the assistant director of the OSS, requested that Hayden be transferred immediately from Marine Corps officer training to the OSS, explaining that Hayden was to be assigned as Area Commander for Operational Groups in France.[15] Cheston also wrote to the Selection Board with a none-too-subtle reminder: "Colonel Huntington has interviewed Lt. Hayden, and General Donovan is specially [*sic*] interested in his transfer." Out of Hayden's Marine Corps OCS class, only three men received transfer orders to the OSS.

The Marine Corps was opposed to the premature transfer of Hayden before the end of his officer training at Quantico. In a June 3, 1943, memo to Cheston, Huntington explained that the early transfer would enable Hayden to be part of the French Operational Groups that were being recruited and would be of great benefit to the OSS.[16] However, the OSS did not push the issue, and Hayden eventually completed his final four weeks of training before transferring to the OSS.

Hayden reported to Q Building at OSS Headquarters in Washington on July 15, 1943, to begin his in-processing. On his OSS personnel forms, he listed Emory Land and Irving Johnson as two of his character references, and Lincoln Colcord and Capt. Ben Pine among people he had known for five years. Notably, he did not list Warwick Tompkins on either list. On the section regarding language skills, he listed "yes" for French as far as speaking and writing, and "fair" as far as reading. Under special trainings and proficiency, he listed his qualification as a parachutist and mentioned attending "Special Schools" in Scotland and England in the winter of 1941–42 while employed by COI.[17]

At first glance, it would seem that Hayden was out of place with the other officers at the OSS. Most were college graduates and many had Ivy League pedigrees, in contrast to his tenth-grade education. He sarcastically noted that Brooks Brothers was the official costume-maker for the OSS, and Abercrombie and Fitch functioned as their Quartermaster Corps. It was at the OSS where "businessmen overnight became majors and colonels" and were mixed in with a small number of enlisted men and junior officers who were able and willing to fight.[18] But, like Hayden, many who joined the OSS were unique individualists, men with distinctive talents and a desire for adventure that they perhaps felt wasn't available to them in the conventional armed forces. There was another trait that many of the OSS volunteers shared with Hayden: they were idealists.

The majority of OSS operatives who, like Sterling Hayden, volunteered for action behind enemy lines were under thirty years old. Some of the psychological screening that these applicants underwent was designed to identify officers who possessed an "ability to get along with other people" and a "freedom from disturbing prejudices."[19] Social idealism, the belief in the ability of the common man to improve the world through a common effort, was a shared ideal of many of these men who volunteered. In this regard, Sterling Hayden was right at home with his fellow recruits.

Donovan hired the best candidates, regardless of their politics, who were eager to join the fight against fascism. He was just as likely to hire an anti-Franco communist as he was to hire a Wall Street broker—if that person could help him win the war. After the war, the FBI and the National Security Agency would identify at least twenty-two people who were Soviet sources inside the OSS. Between fifty and one hundred OSS employees actually belonged to the Communist Party of the United States.[20]

In July and August 1943, recruitment for French OGs was in progress and the first group consisted of thirteen officers and eighty-three enlisted men.[21] Correspondence indicates that Hayden was originally scheduled to be one of those officers. However, shortly after his in-processing, Hayden's assignment was changed. On July 21, 1943, G. R. Holden, Assistant Operations Officer, Middle East Special Operations, contacted both OSS Headquarters and Hayden directly, requesting a transfer of Lt. John Hamilton's orders to their theater of operations.[22] They had an immediate position for Hayden in Greece as a liaison officer to the Greek resistance, and Ellery Huntington approved the transfer.

The exact reason why Hayden/Hamilton was selected for the assignment is not clear. He was unable to speak, read, or write the Greek language. Perhaps it had to do with his sailing skills, which would play a crucial part in the upcoming job. Regardless of the reason, it appeared that he was being groomed to be an officer of a liaison team in Special Operations.

After a delay of several weeks, Hayden contacted Capt. Carl Hoffman, the head of the OSS Special Operations. Hoffman promptly cut orders for Hayden and on October 10, 1943, Sterling Hayden, now officially Lt. John Hamilton, embarked on a US Army troopship headed to North Africa. Three weeks later, he arrived at Arzew, near Oran. Billeted at the Navy's bachelor officer's quarters, he was informed that transportation out of Arzew was sketchy at best and could not be predicted. He immediately began to raise hell to get on to Cairo. "I contacted the OSS representative, Mr. Lovering Hill, who took less than no interest in our situation."[23] He finally succeeded in getting on a Navy transport plane to Cairo. He would soon be entering a theater where there was not only a war raging between the Allies and the Axis powers, but one where the Allies, specifically Great Britain and the United States, were waging a turf war over control of covert operations. The British SOE and Donovan's OSS were already clashing over control in the Balkans by the time Hayden, who, for the rest of the war, would officially be known as John Hamilton, arrived there.

• • •

As promulgated in the London Agreements the previous year, intelligence and espionage operations in the Balkans fell under the British sphere of influence. For the SOE, the Balkans fell under the authority of the Middle East headquarters in Cairo. The headquarters had always been dysfunctional and rife with mutual suspicion and intrigue amongst its members. Already the SOE had been through three directors in as many years. Upon arrival at the headquarters in 1943, the OSS personnel assigned to work alongside the SOE quickly noticed the factionalism and bitter rivalry of support for the competing Balkans resistance movements.[24]

Hayden would see the dysfunctionality firsthand when he arrived in Cairo. He couldn't help but notice the opulent lifestyle in which the OSS director lived, observing that his Cairo villa looked like a "bastard version of the Taj Mahal."[25] He reported in to Lt. Col. Paul West, Chief of SO Cairo, whose first words were, "Sit down and tell me what they told you you were going to do here, because it is always interesting to see how different the situation really is."[26] West went on to explain that he was not expecting Hayden's arrival and had no definite assignment for him in Greece or anywhere else for the time being. Staring at the tall, handsome Marine sitting opposite him, West asked, "Haven't I seen you somewhere before?"

"I don't know, sir," replied Hayden.

"Your face is familiar; did you play football in college?"

"No, sir, I never went to college."

"Oh," replied the puzzled officer. Reaching into his desk, West pulled out a sheaf of papers and handed it to Hayden. "I suggest, Lieutenant, that that you study these intelligence reports. Familiarize yourself with the situation in Greece. But I warn you, you will find it a most complex situation."[27]

For the next ten days, Hayden reported in to headquarters and read the daily intelligence briefs for Greece. During this time and for the next few weeks, West was in Washington for high-level conferences. When he finally returned, Hayden tried to pin him down for a definite assignment and he brought up the situation in Greece that he had been studying since his arrival in Cairo. That was now a British function, West informed him. As fate would have it, Hayden was rooming with OSS Maj. Louis Huot, who had just returned from setting up a shipping line in Italy to run supplies though the Nazi-controlled waters of the Adriatic Sea to the Partisans in Yugoslavia. Huot had suggested that Hayden go out to Italy and put his superior sailing skills to use in support of the operation.

Mentioning this to West, he replied, "Well, Hamilton, a report has just come in that there is this man named Tito up in Yugoslavia. They say he's a Communist, but apparently he's in control of a large guerilla organization, so why don't you hop out to Bari, Italy . . . and see whether you can be of service."[28] Orders were promptly cut for Hayden's transfer.

Three days later, Hayden reported to Alexandria to board a British liberty ship where he and a fellow OSS officer were placed in charge of several OSS vehicles on board. After a week, they left Alexandria and reached Taranto, Italy, about two weeks later. After supervising the unloading of the vehicles, Hayden reported in to the OSS's Special Bari Section (SBS), Bari, Italy. He was about to embark on a phase of his military career that would change his life forever.

CHAPTER EIGHT

Yugoslavia

ON APRIL 6, 1941, THE AXIS POWERS INVADED YUGOSLAVIA. BY APRIL 17, it was all over when the Royal Yugoslav Army signed an unconditional surrender. The Germans proceeded to dismember the country, occupying Serbia proper and granting recognition to Ante Pavelic, leader of the Ustasha, a pro-Nazi terrorist militia, as head of the Independent State of Croatia, the western portion of which was occupied by Italy. Italy also occupied Montenegro. Other portions of Yugoslavia were occupied by Bulgaria, Hungary, and Albania.[1]

Soon propaganda began appearing in the western presses about a Yugoslavian hero who, although an officer in the Yugoslav Army, had refused to surrender. Instead, he took to the hills to form a guerilla army. His name was Col. Draza Mihailovich. The bearded, bespeckled Mihailovich and his followers called themselves Chetniks, adopting the name of an anti-Bulgarian guerilla group from the First World War.[2] The Chetniks swore loyalty to King Peter who had fled to London to lead the government-in-exile.

Soon after the British established radio contact with the Yugoslav guerillas in September, 1941, King Peter endorsed his official recognition of the Chetniks. Shortly after, the king anointed Mihailovich as the leader of the Yugoslav resistance movement, appointing him as a general and war minister to the government-in-exile. The British media promptly began to sing the praises of the Chetniks as the first organized underground resistance movement in occupied Europe. The American and Soviet presses quickly followed suit.

The Chetniks, whose roots were in Serbia, were largely a confederation of guerilla bands organized on a territorial basis. It was Mihailovich's intention to consolidate his power to marshal all resources against the Axis invaders. He proved very hesitant to engage German troops out of fear of destroying his manpower and resources prematurely. He also feared German reprisals against the Serbian civilian population should he attempt military actions against the German occupiers. There were political considerations that also drove Mihailovich's strategy. He was a strong supporter of the monarchy and also of Serbia's dominant position in Yugoslavia. He saw little point in risking the slaughter of Serbia's population and the fostering of Croatian dominance as a result. He was determined to take actions against the Germans only when the results could justify the inevitable reprisals that would follow.[3]

At first William Donovan was also enamored with the Chetniks, and in early 1942, he had one of his aides fly to Cairo to negotiate a supply arrangement. Although this came to naught, later that year King Peter visited President Roosevelt in Washington, DC, and also met with Donovan. The OSS leader was impressed with the young king. Promising that aid would be forthcoming, Donovan stated that the Chetniks were "a prime force of resistance in Europe and that Americans would be honored to give it all aid."[4]

Despite the rave reviews of the Chetniks and Mihailovich in the western media, a clearer picture was starting to emerge in London as a result of secret reports originating in Yugoslavia. William Hudson was the first SOE officer to be sent to act as liaison to Chetnik forces in September 1941. His reports started to sing the praises of another Yugoslav resistance group, a largely communist-dominated group called the Partisans. The Partisans were led by a handsome and charismatic man, Josip Broz, whose nom de guerre was Tito. Tito, a Croat, was active in the Yugoslav Communist Party before the war, soon ascending to the leadership of Partisan forces. He initiated active resistance against the Axis occupying forces after the Germans launched Operation Barbarossa—the invasion of the Soviet Union, in June of 1941.

Hudson could readily see the differences in the resistance strategies of the two groups. The Partisans were proactive in attacking the Germans whenever they could. Their aggression stood in stark contrast to the cautious and, at times, timid appearing actions of the Chetniks. Tito appeared to be committed to all-out resistance, whereas Mihailovich seemed more apt to husband resources and wait for opportune moments to strike the Germans. In addition, Hudson's dispatches described open warfare between the Chetniks and the Partisans.[5] In an effort to reconcile their differences, the two resistance leaders met in Struganik on September 19, 1941, and again in Brajici on October 27, 1941. They were unable to reach a consensus. Complicating their efforts was the underlying ethnic rivalry between the Serbs and the Croats, which in London's view, lay at the root of the Partisan-Chetnik conflict.[6]

The Nazis sensed the internal power struggle in Yugoslavia and were happy to throw fuel on to the fire. They installed a collaborationist general to be the puppet ruler of Serbia, and as previously mentioned, appointed Ante Pavelic as the ruler of "Independent Croatia." Pavelic showed his appreciation by having his pro-Nazi militia, the Ustasha, massacre the Serb minority in Croatia. Tito began to charge that the Chetniks were supporters of the murderous acts of the dreaded Ustasha, while Mihailovic countered with accusations of Partisan collaboration with the Nazi and Italian occupiers of Yugoslavia.[7]

By June of 1942, the public perception had already started to change in both the Great Britain and the United States. A massive propaganda campaign against Mihailovich was unleashed, a campaign that had its genesis in the reporting of Hudson. Not only was Mihailovich's inactivity against the Germans being criticized, but reports of collaboration with the Germans had begun to circulate. In December of 1942, Hudson was replaced by Col. S. W. Bailey, whose observations mirrored those of Hudson. He, too, favored more pressure on Mihailovich to be more proactive against the German occupiers. The situation in the Balkans had changed enough so that more aggressive action by the Yugoslav resistance had become mandatory. After the British victory in El Alamein following the Allied landings in North Africa, the Mediterranean had become a major theater of operations. The British realized that supply lines for the Axis powers going through Yugoslavia and Greece needed to be eliminated to weaken Axis resistance in North Africa. As reports of inactivity and possible collaboration with the Germans by the Chetniks continued to surface, Britain's policy began to shift to one of equal support to both the Chetniks and the Partisans. This policy was formally approved by Winston Churchill in January 1943.[8]

Donovan was eager to have the OSS enter into action in the Balkans. As a result of the London Agreements that Donovan negotiated with Great Britain in June of 1942, the Balkans came under British authority, and the United States was required to have all of its actions approved by the British. In July 1943, Donovan negotiated another agreement, whereby he agreed to have OSS operations in the Balkans come under the authority of SOE-Cairo. The arrangement also provided for OSS officers to be assigned to the British missions at both Chetnik and Partisan headquarters. On August 18, 1943, OSS operative Lt. William Mansfield, USMC, parachuted into enemy occupied Serbia to join the SOE mission assigned to Mihailovich's headquarters. Four days later, Capt. Melvin Benson parachuted into Bosnia as the OSS's first representative to the SOE mission assigned to Tito's headquarters.

In an effort to obtain a clearer picture of the two resistance groups and determine which group was more deserving of American aid, the OSS sent another agent to each resistance headquarters. Maj. Linn Farish was selected to join the SOE mission of the Partisans while Lt. Col. Albert Seitz joined Milhailovich's SOE mission. The two men would have dramatically different impressions of their respective host organizations. Seitz would cite difficulties in dealing with his British hosts and document a disturbing discord between the British and the Chetniks. The British were quick to promise Mihailovich supplies, but wouldn't come through and deliver as promised. After a successful raid in which 350 Germans and Ustasha were killed, supplies still weren't arriving as promised. To add insult to injury, the BBC attributed the heroic Chetnik combat actions to the Partisans. After that engagement, Mihailovich lapsed back into a policy of passive resistance.[9]

Farish, on the other hand, had a much more positive experience at Partisan headquarters. This relationship with his British hosts was much more cordial. The British mission was headed up by Brig. Fitzroy Maclean, who had served as a diplomatic attaché in Moscow before the war and was personally selected by Prime Minister Churchill for the Yugoslav assignment.[10] He was very distrustful of Moscow and the communists in general, and was well aware that the Partisan movement was communist-controlled. However, he was instructed by Churchill that the major task for the SOE in Yugoslavia would be to "help find out who was killing the most Germans and suggest means by which we could help them kill more. Politics must be a secondary consideration."[11] Soon both Maclean and Farish would be praising the military actions and commitment of the Partisans. The reports generated by Maclean would have a major influence in changing British policy in Yugoslavia.[12]

Shortly after the invasion of Italy, the OSS established an advance base for its Balkan operations at the coastal city of Bari, designated Special Bari Section, or SBS. One of the officers assigned there was also highly impressed with the Partisans and felt that they were more than worthy of support by the allied powers. He had a can-do, "rules-don't-apply-to-me" attitude and was determined to provide needed supplies to the Partisans. His name was Maj. Louis Huot.

• • •

The personal importance to Hayden of his OSS service in support of the Partisans in Yugoslavia cannot be overstated. It is best described using Hayden's own words in his autobiography *Wanderer*. Again writing in the third person, he explained it thusly: "I remember the man quite well. He was born one afternoon, at the age of twenty-seven, on the east coast of Italy, where the harbor of Bari was scoured by the raw November norther that whined in from the wastes of the Adriatic. Three years later he died in a stucco motel-apartment next to a liquor store at the base of Laurel Canyon, near Schwab's drugstore in West Hollywood.

"Brief as this life span was, it transported him to such heights of exultation as perhaps few men know, because he had, before this, been dead for a long time. So great, in fact, was the shock of his awakening that certain seeds were planted which would lead to his undoing, to his eventual self-betrayal. And he was aware of this at the time."[13]

Hayden somberly went on to write: "I shall tell you what this man went through in the first—or twenty-eighth—year of his life. After that our paths diverged, slowly, so that I never saw him again."

•••

Shortly after arriving at Bari on December 6, Hayden met with Maj. Robert Koch, who would soon assume command of SO-SBS. In addition, he met with Maj. Richard Weil, and in a harbinger of things to come, Hayden reported the meeting with these two officers as "unsatisfactory." Within three hours of his arrival, he was working on the docks with Maj. Hans Tofte and Lt. Robert Thompson. He would later describe his work with these two men, plus Lt. Ward Ellen, as being the first time since joining the OSS that he was associated with men who were really doing a job. They worked an average of sixteen hours a day on the docks supervising the Partisans as they loaded supplies bound for Yugoslavia and offloaded returning wounded fighters.[14]

During his first day on the docks at Bari, Hayden had an epiphany—he described it as a baptism—when a German air raid on the docks suddenly commenced. German Heinkel fighters swooped in as Italian stevedores ran out wildly from three Allied freighters tied up at the pier and began firing back at the aircraft. With bullets and shrapnel flying all about, the Partisans went on with their loading of the ships in spite of the deadly chaos all around them. Hayden wanted to flee and started to run, but realized that he best start on the right foot, so he stopped and lit a cigarette. Seeing him standing there, one of the Partisan leaders called out to him—"Hamil-tone! Please give to me one nice cigarette if you will." As he lit his new colleague's cigarette, he noticed that his hands were perfectly steady. "Good Christ!—he thought—I'm not a coward at that!" Continuing to describe himself in the third person, Hayden wrote: "Hamilton was stunned to discover that almost overnight he had become an integral part of the human race. Never before had he belonged to anything more than a ship. And here he was, still working with schooners . . . but now he was working with men whose spirit made anything he'd seen before sophomoric."[15]

The effort to provide the Partisans with supplies shipped from Bari was actually the idea of Tofte and Thompson. The concept became feasible after the Allies invaded Italy as Tito's Partisan forces were fighting to gain control of the Dalmatian Coast of western Yugoslavia and several offshore islands at the same time. In early September, the two young OSS officers met with Gen. Donovan in Algiers, where they pointed out that once the port of Bari was in Allied hands, they believed that they would find many small Adriatic coastal ships there. They proposed that the OSS should take possession of the shipping and use it to both supply the Yugoslav guerillas and to infiltrate OSS personnel into Yugoslavia. Donovan, who had become increasingly frustrated with continual British attempts to control the OSS in the Balkans, felt that this was an excellent way to exert independence so the OSS could operate freely, and strongly endorsed the plan that became known as Operation AUDREY.[16]

Tofte and Thompson were typical examples of the type of men who gravitated to the OSS. Tofte, a native of Copenhagen, escaped from Nazi-occupied Denmark in 1941. He joined the underground resistance in Europe and migrated to Asia to undergo counterespionage training. He served behind the Japanese lines in Burma. Before joining the OSS in 1943, he acquired coastal shipping experience working for the East Asia Company in China. Thompson, who was born to missionary parents in Jerusalem, was a newspaper reporter in Philadelphia before joining the OSS. Both men were free spirits, imaginative risk-takers, and somewhat averse to authority. Upon meeting them, Hayden quickly sensed that they were kindred spirits, and the three formed an effective working relationship as well as a strong personal bond.

Donovan had the two men accompany him on a flight from Algiers to Cairo, where Donovan's enthusiasm for the plan increased as they began to refine its broad outlines. Arriving in Cairo, the three met with Maj. Louis Huot, acting chief of Special Operations at Cairo on September 12. Donovan instructed Huot to operationalize the plan as described by Tofte and Thompson. Huot needed no further prompting. Another freewheeling spirit, Huot had come to Europe during the 1930s to observe firsthand the rise of fascism in Europe. Serving as a reporter for the Paris edition of the *Chicago Tribune* and later as European manager of an American press service, Huot developed a well-deserved reputation as a daring liberal journalist.[17] Throwing his heart and soul into Operation AUDREY, Huot rapidly began bending the rules and exceeding his authority, and as a result, getting himself into hot water.

Receiving the endorsement of Maj. Carlton Coon, SO branch chief at Cairo, Huot worked at a breakneck pace to bring Operation AUDREY to life. Although Huot and Thompson claimed to have the authority to establish the base and to make necessary reconnaissance to ensure the supplies were being delivered to where the Partisans needed them, the British, who were the senior partner in the theater and greatly resented OSS meddling, would soon complain that Huot had exceeded all authority acting as he did. It became impossible to determine exactly who authorized what, but Huot traveled much faster than staff officers normally traveled, and Donovan appeared to have given his implied endorsement to the operation.[18]

A whirlwind of unbridled energy, Huot, accompanied by Thompson and two Partisans, hitchhiked to Taranto and fast-talked his way in to see Adm. Sir Arthur Power. Huot claimed Power gave him verbal permission to take charge of all coastal shipping in the name of Gen. Eisenhower. Going on to Bari, Huot was able to secure the use of berth two from the British naval officer in charge of the port. Completing his masterstroke, Huot then went to see the British civilian who represented the North African Shipping Board, who, on the strength of Huot's report of his conversation with Power, endorsed the handing over to Huot of all the Yugoslav ships in the port, some thirty or forty vessels, some with crews and ranging from 50 to about 1,200 tons.[19]

On October 9, 1943, shortly after the Allies secured the port of Bari, the OSS had secured the use of berth two for its shipping operation to run supplies to the Partisans.[20] Two days later, Huot was formally able to commence Operation AUDREY. Shipping the supplies to Yugoslavia that he had disingenuously obtained, he often gave the impression to his British allies that he was working under the direct authority of Gen. Eisenhower. As Anthony Cave Brown described the situation: "With a minimum of paper, fuss, and words, Huot and Thompson had crossed two theaters of war, and had obtained authority to act from one field marshal, one supreme commander, at least three generals and one admiral, and several colonels and majors and lesser officers. They had been promised 400 tons of war stores from one officer, 250 from another. They had acquired seventeen ships with crews, berths, and the necessary fuel to operate them, and were in the process of acquiring a further twenty-three. In short, they had acquired control of all the coastwise shipping of a major Italian port through a combination of blandishment and judicious name-dropping. Tofte was to remember: 'Huot was forever making statements such as General Eisenhower directs . . . Admiral Powers orders . . . and General Bedell Smith requests . . ."[21]

In spite of his unorthodox and questionable methods, the fact remains that it was Huot who brought Operation AUDREY, the first major OSS guerilla supply operation, to life. However, Huot's freewheeling ways, accentuated by his outsized ego, were soon to bring about his downfall. Although he started a program that produced impressive results, his behavior was rash and crossed the line into insubordination. A SOE survey party, led by Lt. Col. Samuel Lohan, arrived at Bari to establish a base for Yugoslavian supply operations and were stunned to find that the OSS had already established one. Lohan reminded Huot that Bari was under British control and that Great Britain had overall authority in the Balkans. He ordered Huot to cease and desist and turn all of his operations over to the British. Huot refused to cooperate.

Huot proceeded on to the Yugoslavian islands off the Dalmatian Coast without authorization from the head of the Allied Military Mission in Yugoslavia, Brig. Fitzroy Maclean. He then began negotiations with Tito's representatives, promising an unrealistic inventory of large supplies such as tanks and trucks. These actions would not only infuriate Maclean but give the Partisans the impression that the Americans and the British were in competition with each other and feuding. The British protested loudly to Washington. Huot's actions also served to embarrass both the State Department, whose official policy at that time was to recognize the authority of Chetnik leader Draza Mihailovich, and President Roosevelt, who supported the reestablishment of the monarchy in Yugoslavia once the country was liberated from the Nazis.[22] The British brought in a friend of Donovan's, Lt. Col. the Lord Harcourt, as the senior SOE officer in theater. When he met with Huot he informed him that all shipping operations could continue—but only under SOE command. In a stunning act of disrespect, Tofte reported that Huot told Harcout to "go and fuck himself."[23]

Huot proceeded to take an unauthorized journey into Yugoslavia to personally meet with Tito. The American liaison to the Partisans, Capt. Melvin Benson was stunned to see an American officer arrive in Jajce, the site of Tito's headquarters, knowing that the visitor had no authorization from Cairo or from Brig. Maclean. After spending eighteen hours at Partisan headquarters, Huot compiled a seven-page paper describing, among other things, the Partisan's training methods, a detailed list of supplies, and Tito's ideas on postwar Yugoslavia.[24] He then ordered two OSS officers from the liaison mission to accompany him back. Once again, he lacked the authority to do this. The trip to Tito's headquarters was the straw that broke the camel's back.

Huot had made too many enemies and had behaved too arrogantly to remain in charge of Operation AUDREY. His trip to Jajce provided the final nail in Huot's coffin. Huot's actions had provoked the wrath of the British who protested vigorously to Washington, further embarrassing Huot, who was relieved. Hans Tofte was placed in charge of Operation AUDREY. Huot was ordered to report to the acting director of OSS Middle East in Cairo, Col. John Toulmin. After his meeting with Huot, Toulmin wrote to Donovan, describing the positive results achieved thus far with Operation AUDREY, noting that "this is to Huot's credit." Continuing on, he stated, "He is almost impossible to control and one of these bright days I may have to send him back to Washington."[25] While awaiting transport out of theater, Huot was billeted to share a room with a young OSS member who had just reported to Cairo: Marine 2nd Lt. John Hamilton.

• • •

The team running Operation AUDREY that John Hamilton/Hayden joined the day of the German strafing attack was a team that he was honored to be a part of. Hayden's notes express the highest admiration for team leader, Capt. Hans Tofte, then thirty-three years old. Tofte, who had just taken over for Louis Huot (Hayden consistently misspelled his name as "Hoot" in all of his notes), had established a "magnificent liaison" with the Yugoslavian Partisans, who had implicit faith in his judgment.[26] Rounding out the team was Hayden's colleague LTJG Ward Ellen, who took over responsibility for the ship's maintenance. By the time Hayden joined Operation AUDREY, the team was handling forty-five Partisan steamers. Unfortunately, the operation was also being hampered by the bad blood that Huot had engendered in his relationship with the British.

Hayden reported that Tofte was handicapped in an "uphill battle with the Royal Navy and with various British officers in Bari who were jealous of the American position at the time."[27] He also took note of the fact that the SBS was lending little support to the operation, observing that "in fact, Major Koch, Commander McBane [*sic*] (Commander Turner McBaine, commanding officer of SO-SBS) and Major Weil did everything in their power to hinder the operation."[28] In an effort to mollify the British, when Tofte took over control of Operation AUDREY, the OSS concluded an agreement giving overall control of the operation to the SOE-Bari (Force 133) while the actual movement of supplies to and from Italy to Tito's forces in Yugoslavia would remain the responsibility of the OSS at SO-SBS.[29] For the fiercely independent Tofte, the arrangement was unsatisfactory as he received the unspoken message that the British wanted his operation out of Bari.

The fortunes of war would, in a sense, solve Tofte's dilemma. On December 2, 1943, more than one hundred German bombers attacked Bari and its harbor, causing hundreds of casualties and destroying or damaging twenty-seven Allied cargo ships and transports.[30] One of the ships sunk in the attack at Bari harbor was the SS *John Harvey*, an American liberty ship carrying mustard gas to be used in the event that Hitler resorted to the use of chemical weapons in the Mediterranean. As a result of the release of the gas, the harbor was rendered unusable for several days.[31] Tofte promptly developed alternative plans for his operations.

On December 6, Tofte made a reconnaissance trip about thirty-five miles down the coast to the port of Monopoli. Inspecting the port, he decided that it would be a much better place to conduct shipping operations from, away from the oversight of the British, and also away from his own commanding officer, Maj. Koch, for whom he had a growing dislike. The following day, Tofte notified Lt. Hamilton that he would be in charge of establishing a new base at Monopoli. Loading seventy-five hand-picked Partisans, including stevedores, shipwrights, machinists, and office personnel aboard the 350-ton Partisan steamer *STON*, Hayden took his team down to Monopoli. They began their operations in earnest the following day when five Partisan steamers arrived in Monopoli to be loaded.

The British influence was felt in Monopoli as Hayden immediately clashed with a Royal Navy lieutenant who proved to be an obstructionist. Despite this, Hayden noted with pride that "we managed to load the schooner *ORION* in twenty-three hours, including all night work by lantern light. The *ORION* was dispatched for the Yugoslav island of Vis with 400 tons of hand grenades, rifles, ammunition, clothing, flour and high octane gas."[32] Over the next two weeks, the entire Bari shipping organization in support of the Yugoslavian Partisans was transferred down to Monopoli. Hayden used his authority to requisition whatever housing, warehouses, automobiles, and supplies were necessary. On December 18, Lt. Thompson and the enlisted crew joined Hayden in Monopoli. Tofte remained in Bari "to fight the Royal Navy and try to reduce the damage being done to the Partisan cause by Major Koch, Lt. Comdr. McBane [*sic*] and Major Weil."[33]

When the Monopoli operations were fully ramped up, Hayden commanded quite an armada. He had a fleet of fourteen schooners, six ketches, and two brigantines. Four hundred Yugoslavs—fifty of whom were women—worked for him. The mission for all of the ships and personnel was straightforward and full of danger: they would run the German blockage across the Adriatic Sea to the Partisan island of Vis off the German-held coast of Dalmatia. The ships average cruising speed was seven knots and the nearest point of the Italian coast to Vis was a distance of eighty miles. As a matter of routine operations, the ships would leave Monopoli and navigate through Allied minefields with the hope of reaching the coast of Vis by dawn where they would be hidden on the coast. The next night they would be unloaded and camouflaged again. When the weather permitted, the ships would make the return trip to Italy. An even more hazardous journey was made by smaller fishing boats, manned by very brave sailors.[34]

Working day in and day out with the Yugoslavians, Hayden developed a strong admiration for them. Writing in the third person, he stated: "As the partisan saga unfolded day by day Hamilton found himself committed in a way he had never known before. Night after night he pounded out long letters to people back in the States, to Tompkins in particular, while out on the docks sweating partisan stevedores sang wild Serbian songs. He had never known such men. There was a ferocity about them, not just in the way they looked but in the way they worked, straining and sweating for hours on end, refusing to pause or accept relief until ordered to do so."[35]

Hayden's armada made seventy sailings altogether across the Adriatic and lost only four vessels, despite the German blockade. The tonnage of supplies delivered to Tito's Partisans, although estimated by one report as high as 11,637 tons, was recorded by Tofte as a still-impressive 6,500 tons.[36] Hayden's Silver Star recommendation lists the amount as 7,000 tons.[37] In addition, Hayden and his fellow officers made more than a dozen armed reconnaissance missions into Yugoslavia to determine optimal supply routes and collect vital intelligence.[38] Hayden himself made three reconnaissance missions during this timeframe.[39]

• • •

The men who served under Hayden provided consistent and vivid descriptions of their leader. They painted a picture of a fearless, hard-drinking man with a mercurial temper who inspired loyalty from the men who served under his command. One of these men was D. Perry Moran who was interviewed by journalist Dennis Brown shortly after Hayden died in 1986.[40] On first seeing Hayden in Monopoli, he was quite impressed. "He was built like a tree," he recalled. "He had these broad shoulders and thick arms. Then his torso tapered down to a thin waist. He had a passion for privacy. He was highly selective about who he chose to speak to and who he chose to drink with—till he got drunk. Then he'd drink with anyone." Although he was casual about things like uniform regulations, when it came to boats, he went strictly by the book. Moran recalled that Hayden always ended his mission briefings by saying, "Protect the goddamn boat, and you're gonna protect your own ass."[41]

Upon arrival at Monopoli, Moran was also warned about a touchy subject regarding their commanding officer. "It turns out that after the war started, in an effort to get as far from Hollywood as possible, Hayden changed his name to John Hamilton. These guys warned me not to make the mistake of calling him by the wrong name. When we were with him, he was addressed as Capt. Hamilton. But behind his back, when we talked about him, he was Sterling Hayden."[42]

Like all of his fellow crewmembers, Moran was in awe of Hayden's seamanship and navigation skills. He would go hours without saying a word, always holding his binoculars up to his eyes. He had an uncanny ability to locate secluded coves on the Yugoslav coastline. He was also able to tell time by maneuvering the boat around and looking over the gunnels at shadows cast on the water. The crew had implicit faith in Hayden's leadership.

Some of the anecdotes that Moran shared with Brown also serve to paint a vivid portrait of Sterling Hayden. What emerges is a picture of a mission-driven, no-nonsense leader with little tolerance for anything less than top performance of their nautical missions, despite his tendency to drink his men under the table while in port. One story of a rescue mission nearly gone awry serves well to describe Hayden under fire. It occurred on one of the many missions to Yugoslavia, where they would be delivering gold to the Partisans for bribe money and returning with American airmen who had been shot down in the Balkans for evacuation back to Bari.

On this particular mission, they picked up four airmen for evacuation. Two were seriously wounded and a third was slightly wounded. On the return voyage, they were spotted by two German E-boats. The speedy patrol boats pursued them and fired on them. Their boat was pretty badly shot up, and the slightly wounded airman was hit by German gunfire and now had suffered a serious wound before being able to escape the German pursuers. When they finally approached the Italian coast, they launched two flares, indicating that they had wounded aboard and that an ambulance should be standing by for transport. "As we approached the dock," recalled Moran, "the ambulance was there, but it was further away than it should have been. In its place was a Red Cross wagon. That didn't make any sense. We'd never seen Red Cross wagons in our area before. Anything the OSS did was with tremendous security."[43]

Hayden started shouting to get the Red Cross wagon the "blanket-blank" out of there. As they were tying up, Moran noticed a woman standing there in full Red Cross garb. Standing next to her was the Fifteenth Air Force public relations officer. She was extraordinarily beautiful and he realized, as the crew began running over to him, "Christ, that's Madeleine Carroll. Don't let the boss see her." She had come to Italy and was now with the Red Cross. According to Moran's recollection, she was living in the general's villa and there were rumors circulating that she had been unfaithful to her husband.

"Captain Hayden was in a wretched mood due to this pick-up run which had gone so badly," recalled Moran. "When he saw his wife, he started screaming, wanting to know who had sent this cheap wharf-rat whore down to meet his boat. Then he opened up with profanity the likes of which I have never heard again since that day. Being in the army, I thought I had heard it all, but not the language he used against her."

The public affairs officer, a major, tried to intervene. Hayden initially ignored him, first ensuring that the wounded men were transferred to the ambulances. Next he inspected the boat to assess the extent of the damage inflicted by the Germans and to make sure it was still seaworthy. When he finished this, Hayden astounded all of the onlookers by walking over to the major, an officer more senior than he, grabbing him by the shirt and tossing him into the harbor. He turned to his wife who was stricken with fear and began running from the dock.

"We pulled the major out of the water," recounted Moran. "He started ranting and raving something awful. We told security, 'You better get him out of here before Captain Hayden kills him.'"[44] They all later learned that the visit by Madeleine Carroll was a publicity stunt to highlight her involvement with the Red Cross. Needless to say, the visit was never reported on in the press.

Moran's last mission with Hayden served to exemplify the disdain that he (Hayden) had for the British, who were the senior partners in their theater of operations. They were caught by two German patrol boats and had to fight their way out of the area. Their boat was so heavily damaged during the fracas and their situation was so tenuous that they called the British headquarters for help using open voice transmissions. The British reply was: "Negative, negative, Can't help you, old chap." Hayden was livid; his disdain for the British quickly reached new heights. They managed to fight their way out of the trap and returned to Monopoli where Hayden had decided to let his British colleagues know what he thought of them.

As they approached a British motor torpedo boat, the enraged Hayden ordered his men to fire on the boat. His gunners were nearly paralyzed with fear. Were they going to oppose their captain who would then likely throw them overboard, or fire on the British ship? They decided to fire over the ship, but a few rounds did accidentally hit the torpedo boat's windshield. No one was injured. Very soon after, a British destroyer escort appeared on the scene, flagged them down, and escorted them into the base. The loudspeaker from the destroyer announced to Hayden's crew that they were all under arrest. Hayden was having none of this.

He ordered some of his men to sneak off the boat and get the American military police. Shortly after, the destroyer was surrounded by a group of American soldiers armed with machine guns. After the crew disembarked, the British brought up Hayden on various charges. Moran recalled, "We were all interrogated, and we all denied having received any orders from Captain Hayden to fire on any kind of a British MTB. We denied everything, because he was our captain. We weren't going to allow him to get into trouble any more than he would have allowed us to get into trouble. Eventually the entire matter was dropped."[45]

CAPTER NINE

Bravery, Chaos, and a Rescue Mission

ON DECEMBER 22, 1943, TWO SIGNIFICANT EVENTS OCCURRED THAT were to have a major impact on Sterling Hayden. The first involved Capt. Melvin Benson, the OSS liaison to Tito's Partisan forces in Yugoslavia. Stationed on the island of Vis, Benson was under the direct authority of Brig. Fitzroy Maclean of the SOE. Like many OSS members in the Balkans, Benson was growing weary of what he felt was both the treatment of the OSS by the British as stepchildren to the SOE, as well as the seemingly ineffective relationship that the British had with Partisan forces. The fact that he was the only American liaison officer assigned to cover the islands of Hvar, Brac, Korcula, and Vis grated on him, as he noted that Maclean had fourteen officers and forty-five other personnel to cover the same territory. His frustration boiled over in a message he sent that specifically noted that the British were intercepting communications directed to him from Cairo and using the information so that they could get credit for the American supplies that were delivered to the Partisans.[1]

Commenting on the supply issue in a report on Operation AUDREY, Benson sent a message to Cairo that read in part, "The British are meeting the German threat to these islands with more liaison officers and barmen."[2] Unfortunately for Benson, the message received a general release and one of the recipients was Brig. Maclean, who protested to Lt. Col. Paul West, chief of Special Operations, OSS-Cairo. Benson was ordered to report to Cairo to explain the situation before departing on December 22. The OSS hierarchy anticipated that the matter could likely be resolved with an apology to Maclean from Benson, and SO-SBS believed that Benson could possibly be returned to his duties with the Partisans in about a week.[3] Hence, with Benson's departure, there would be no American liaison officer to the Partisans for a short while. This proved problematic for several OSS members.

Capt. Hans Tofte felt that the absence of an American liaison officer, even for a short period of time, would be an "unthinkable" situation. He felt that his assistant, 2nd Lt. John Hamilton, possessed the ideal qualifications to take Benson's place. Accordingly, utilizing Lt. Cdr. McBaine's authority, he arranged for orders for Hamilton to depart for Vis on December 24. Hamilton would be accompanied by a radio operator to facilitate direct communications with SO-SBS. To maintain the efficiency of the shipping operations, he also sent three officers and three enlisted Navy personnel to accompany Hamilton.[4] Adding to the urgency of Hamilton's assignment was the fact that the Germans had launched Operation Herbstgewitter II, an offensive on the island of Korcula on the very day he was to report in for his new assignment. In his new role as the OSS liaison to the Partisans on the Dalmatian Islands, Hamilton's mission had an added dimension: to assess the state of the German offensive on Korcula and determine whether the island had been overrun and, if so, to set up alternative shipping routes to supply the Partisans. His primary mission was to make contact with staff officers of Tito's headquarters in charge of the coastal area of Dalmatia, situated on the island of Hvar.[5]

Hamilton departed on December 24 via surface craft, but due to extremely foul weather, the boat foundered and sank off the Italian coast. Along with his men, he was able to get back to Monopoli, making the extremely rough crossing the following evening and arriving at the island of Korcula the night of December 25. He arrived just as the mismatched foes were engaging. He noted that approximately 3,500 German and Ustasha troops, well-equipped and with four tanks and air cover, were in the process of driving some 1,500 ill-equipped Partisans off of the island. There was constant bombing by Stukas and ME-109s. During that time, Hamilton noted that he did not see any Allied aircraft.[6]

It quickly became apparent to Hamilton that Korcula was lost, and with his team and the remnants of the Partisan army, he escaped the approaching enemy forces the night of December 26 to the island of Hvar after a treacherous sea journey through enemy-infested waters. They left behind approximately three hundred Partisans to act as spies and spotters. They arrived in Hvar just in time for two days of heavy dive-bombing raids by the Germans in preparation for an apparent invasion of the island. During that time, Hamilton was nearly killed on two occasions. While on Hvar, Hamilton met the Partisan leaders at their headquarters and had a six-hour conference with the Partisan staff officers. Their meeting took place in the open on the headquarters' back porch. During this meeting, he gathered precise information on the military situation on the Dalmatian Islands as well as on the coast.[7] While standing on that back porch, four Stukas descended and bombed the building, killing five civilians. The following day, while driving to inspect the Partisan line of defense, a German aircraft strafed their Fiat, killing the driver.[8] Hamilton and the other surviving passengers unleashed a hail of machine-gun fire at the attacking aircraft, chasing it away. On both occasions, Hamilton survived without a scratch.

Shortly after, Hamilton crossed over from Hvar to Vis on a seventy-foot Partisan schooner. Also aboard were over four hundred women and children refugees. Hamilton found the conditions on Vis simultaneously encouraging and appalling. He noted that Vis was virtually a "young Gibraltar," home to five thousand battle-hardened crack Partisan troops who were veterans of combat in Bosnia.[9] Counterbalancing this positive situation was the humanitarian crisis that was developing on the island. Hamilton found over six thousand refugees living in a town that normally had a population of 1,200. "They had no clothing, blankets, or shoes, and the food allowance was ¼ lb. of bread per day per family."[10] Meeting with the commandant and commissar, he found that they had a lot of faith in American aid that they believed was forthcoming. Reflecting on the fact that all major policy decisions rested with the British, and, to Hamilton's mind, they certainly had no intention of evacuating these civilians back to Italy, he determined that he would return to Italy and attempt to arrange for an evacuation of the refugees.

Before leaving Vis, Hamilton and his team scouted out prospective supply routes on Vis to get the supplies to the other side of the island and subsequently to the mainland of Yugoslavia. He departed Vis, arriving back in Bari on December 31, feeling that, after safely evacuating the refugees out of harm's way, the Partisans and the British had conveyed to him that there was nothing left for him to do.[11] He was also acting in compliance with Tofte's orders to return by midnight on December 31. He didn't realize it, but he was stepping into a hornet's nest, one that also arose as a result of another incident that occurred on December 22.

• • •

On November 8, 1943, a C-53 Dakota aircraft belonging to the 807th Medical Air Evacuation Squadron (MAES) took off from Catania, Sicily, bound for Bari, Italy. Aboard the converted C-47 aircraft were twenty-six American medical personnel, including twelve female nurses. The seemingly routine flight to deliver the nurses and medics to the hospital at Bari to attend to wounded Allied soldiers soon turned out to be a disaster. Encountering treacherous weather over the Mediterranean and Ionian seas, the aircraft soon got lost and was blown farther east over the seas, and finally crash-landed in central Albania, near the village of Elbasan. Fortunately, no one was killed in the crash and they were promptly met by Allied-friendly Albanian Partisans.

The situation was dire for the downed Americans. They were many miles from the Albanian coast on the other side of mountain ridges that separated them from any rescue ports. The harsh Albanian winter weather was the least of their hazards. They were behind German lines, and although their initial rescuers, the Partisans, were friendly, they would have to potentially contend with pro-German Albanian guerillas along any potential evacuation routes. The rescue of the medical team became of the utmost importance to both the American and British governments. The SOE and the OSS were assigned the tasks of locating the nurses and medics and bringing them out of Albania.

The Partisans were soon able to deliver the Americans to members of the British SOE, and the OSS sent Capt. Lloyd Smith to Albania to coordinate the rendezvous and rescue of the medical personnel from Albanian soil. Given all of these factors, it was slow-going. Senior officials grew frustrated over the seeming lack of progress with the rescue mission. This included President Franklin D. Roosevelt, who was closely monitoring the situation and wanted to see concrete results. Returning from Europe aboard the battleship USS *Iowa*, on December 12, 1943, Roosevelt called the SOE headquarters in Cairo directly. A stunned British duty officer answered the phone to hear the voice of the American president who proceeded to express his concerns and demands in a display of rarely used presidential profanity. "This is Franklin Roosevelt," he announced. "Why the fuck is it taking you so long to get those nurses out?"

Before the startled duty officer could even respond, Roosevelt threatened, "Captain, if any of those girls is so much as *touched*, there'll be serious consequences!" After a slight pause, Roosevelt ended his one-way conversation by saying, "They are the flower of American womanhood. They must be saved at all cost!"[12]

Back at Bari, Hayden was put on alert on December 8 and ordered to be ready to depart on a moment's notice to pick up Capt. Smith and the rescued Americans once they reached the coast. To accomplish the evacuation, Hayden had a stripped-down converted ex-Royal Yugoslav Navy PT boat ready to depart from the port of Otranto, located on the "heel" of the Italian boot 125 miles up the coast from Bari. It would be a direct shot across the Strait of Otranto to the Albanian coast to facilitate the pickup. In an act of nostalgia for past accomplishments, Hayden named his boat *Yankee*.

By the third week of December, Lloyd Smith was not able to link up with the downed Americans, whose location could not be accurately determined. The pressure on the OSS and the SOE from the highest levels of the American and British governments was becoming intense. It was then that the SBS decided to insert itself into the situation and attempt its own rescue mission.

On December 22, 1943, Lt. Cdr. Turner McBaine, officer in charge of SO-SBS, contacted Capt. Hans Tofte and instructed him to report to his office. Upon arrival, Tofte saw that four other officers were present for the meeting convened by McBaine. Tofte noticed that Maj. Richard Weil Jr. was among those in attendance. McBaine got directly to the point. He reviewed the entire story of the crash-landing in Albania the previous month on November 8, and the unsuccessful efforts thus far to rescue the medical team. The passengers and crew were believed to have been initially rescued by Albania Partisans. SO-SBS, McBaine announced, would be mounting a rescue mission whereby the five officers present would parachute into Albania to accomplish the mission.[13] The mission was to be headed up by Maj. Weil.

Weil was an unusual breed of warrior, the kind that gravitated to the OSS. Prior to the war, the thirty-seven-year-old was a New York lawyer. A descendent of a wealthy Jewish family in New York that owned the Macy's department store, he was an intellect who loved to quote Aristotle and write poetry. Only grudgingly did he give up a career in literature to enter the family business.[14] Weil had never been in a combat situation prior to leading the rescue mission.

Looking around the room, Tofte had an uneasy feeling as he studied the other members of the newly formed team. That night, he went to see McBaine to express his dissatisfaction with the team's composition. His recommendation was straightforward—one of the five team members should be dropped from the mission; instead, 2nd Lt. John Hamilton should be assigned to the team.[15] During the several weeks that they worked together in Bari and Monopoli, the rugged Marine had impressed Tofte with his work ethic and can-do spirit. He felt it vital that Hamilton be made a part of the rescue mission. McBaine informed Tofte that it was Weil's mission and he would have to take it up with him. In addition, McBaine pointed out that Hamilton had just left for Vis and wouldn't be available to participate. McBaine told Tofte that he was very hesitant to remove the other officer from the mission if he had already been informed of the assignment. Lastly, he informed Tofte that he was leaving OSS-SBS in the morning and the new officer in charge was going to be Maj. Robert Koch.[16]

At 5 a.m. the following morning, a very angry Maj. Weil appeared at McBaine's room and informed him of the conversation that he had the prior evening with Hans Tofte, who apparently, along with Robert Thompson, went straight from his meeting with McBaine to see him. After Weil refused Tofte's request that Hamilton be added to the team, Tofte somewhat arrogantly informed Weil that as he, Tofte, was the only member of the rescue team who had actually experienced combat, he felt duty-bound to go over Weil's head and take his demand that Hamilton be added to the team to the commanding officer of the overall rescue sortie.[17] Weil ordered him not to and stated, in no uncertain terms, that if Tofte went outside the OSS chain of command and sought to go over his head, he would bring him up on disciplinary charges. Tofte ignored Weil's threat and proceeded to argue his case to the rescue sortie's overall commanding officer, who sent an "equivocal" note to Weil. Weil simply ignored the note.[18]

On December 28, 1943, McBaine wrote a memo to Lt. Col. John Toulmin, director of OSS-ME in Cairo. The subject of the memo was "Capt. Hans Tofte, Lt. Robert Thompson, Lt. John Hamilton." After reviewing the details of the proposed rescue mission and Tofte's insubordination towards Weil, McBaine charged Tofte with disobedience of orders, and accused him of bringing discredit on the organization, to the prejudice of the successful completion of the proposed mission. He made three recommendations to Toulmin: 1) that letters of censure be written for Tofte, Thompson, and Hamilton, and that the letters be entered into their official personnel records, 2) that any recommendation for promotion concerning any of the three men be canceled and that the men be notified of this action, and 3) that Tofte be recalled from Bari and given another assignment in the OSS.[19]

On December 30, 1943, Lt. Col Toulmin responded back to Koch.[20] He acknowledged that Lt. Cdr. McBaine had updated him on the situation in Bari. Toulmin, having recently been forced to recall Louis Huot to Cairo after relieving him from command of Operation AUDREY, no doubt was also tiring of the drama coming from Bari. McBaine had brought several weekly reports with him to Cairo and, as usual, there was the ever-increasing demand for more supplies to ship to the Partisans. Toulmin noted with annoyance that every arriving Partisan was claiming a new urgent priority need and it was the job of OSS-ME to provide for the entire theater. It was therefore impossible to provide every request submitted by Tito's men. Testily, Toulmin told Koch: "I wish you would explain this to Tofte."

Tofte had previously written to Toulmin and requested permission that either he or Thompson be allowed to travel to Washington, DC, to directly brief Joseph Scribner, assistant chief of the Special Operations branch, on Operation AUDREY. Toulmin's reaction to the request was unequivocal: "The answer is definitely 'No' and you may so inform him." Tofte had also written to Toulmin requesting the promotion of Lt. Thompson. Toulmin coldly informed Koch that Thompson's promotion couldn't be considered at that time "for obvious reasons."

Toulmin then turned to the personnel situation in Bari. He acknowledged that he had received and read McBaine's memo of December 28 and told Koch: "You will handle this case as you see fit but, if you wish any men recalled you will then advise me." He closed his memo with one last item: "While it is agreed that the moving picture project might be sound, I believe it is premature at the moment." He was referring to a proposal submitted by one of the officers in Bari to make a movie about the Partisans in Yugoslavia and their valiant struggle against the Nazi invaders. The target audience would be viewers in the United States and Great Britain. The officer who submitted the proposal was in fact a genuine Hollywood movie star, 2nd Lt. John Hamilton, USMCR, formerly known as Sterling Hayden.

The already tense situation in Bari was soon to worsen considerably. On December 23, 1943, Maj. Robert Koch replaced Lt. Cdr. McBaine as the director of SO-SBS. Bad blood was already present between Tofte, Thompson, and Hamilton on one hand and Koch on the other. Hayden was highly critical of Koch in his November 2, 1944, narrative. The command structure had already labeled the three officers as loose cannons, despite the results they had achieved thus far with Operation AUDREY. When it was reported to Koch that Lt. Hamilton was seen on the docks at Bari on the evening of December 31, 1944, he was livid and immediately demanded that Hamilton report to his office to explain his absence from Vis. At the time, Hamilton was likely unaware of the feud between Weil and Tofte over the proposed rescue mission. Tofte was barely on speaking terms with Koch and Weil. Koch and Weil were also unaware that Tofte had issued orders to Lt. Hamilton that directed him to return to Bari "no later than 2400 hours, New Year's Eve."[21]

Hamilton reported to Koch as instructed. His explanation for his absence from Vis was, as noted, that the Partisans and the British had told him that there was nothing for him to do so he decided to come back. He did confirm that he had received the communications brought by his radiomen, and Koch pointed out that he was sure that instructions for Hamilton to remain on Vis "were certainly contained in the message brought by the radio men." Hamilton explained that he had left orders for his detachment remaining on Vis and that he was going to return to the island the following day on a British LCI.[22] Koch proceeded to again brief Hamilton on his duties, which included overseeing the shipping of supplies and transport of refugees, the preparation to receive over one hundred Operational Group personnel, and the critical liaison duties with the British. Hamilton again expressed his desire not to return as "there was nothing to do there," but said he would, of course, follow his orders. The meeting ended satisfactorily from Koch's standpoint, and Hamilton was told to return back to Koch's office the following morning, January 1, 1944, at 8:30 a.m., to prepare for his return to Vis.

The following morning, Hamilton failed to report as he had been ordered. Koch was livid, so he drove down to Monopoli with Weil and Maj. Linn Farish. They quickly found both Hamilton and Tofte. Tofte offered the explanation that as a result of a storm, the sea state was too rough to transport Hamilton back to Vis. Hamilton appeared to be hung over, and when questioned about it, he indicated that it was a result of "too much New Years' Eve."[23] Koch noted that there was evidence of a "considerable party" and Koch requested that Hamilton return after lunch while he conferred with Tofte.

The subsequent meeting between Koch and Tofte was in essence an acrimonious continuation of their prior meeting of December 22. Once again, Tofte requested that Hamilton not be returned to Vis, deeming it a waste of his talents and also opining that Vis was bound to fall to the Germans and therefore a waste of a valuable man to send any OSS members there. Koch reminded Tofte that the importance of maintaining a liaison with the British was paramount regardless of Tofte's opinions; the assignment was crucial and the liaison with the British would go on. The matter was settled. Next on the agenda was the subject of finances. Koch indicated his frustration with Tofte's methods in his report to Toulmin on January 3, 1944. "The meeting then turned to finance in which certain principles about the expenditure of money were repeated for the fourth time and a statement was made that money was available for any expenditure but that there would have to be an adequate accounting."[24] Koch then departed the meeting while Farish continued to talk with Tofte and Thompson.

After lunch, Tofte requested that Koch and Farish meet him in his cabin. When the two arrived, Tofte was there, as were Lt. Thompson, Lt. Ellen, and Lt. Hamilton. The meeting began with Tofte dropping a bombshell: he announced "that the five of them conferred and decided that the organization of O.S.S. did not suit them, that they were no longer in sympathy with the organization and that they wanted to be transferred out. The implication was that they were dissatisfied with the present set-up in Cairo and Bari."[25] Trying to remain calm and dispassionate, Koch informed Tofte that there was a word for this conduct in the American Army. He would not discuss the issue with the "committee of five," but would meet with them individually over the next several days. He dismissed the group, but as Hamilton rose to leave, he ordered the young Marine to meet with him immediately.

During the subsequent meeting, Hamilton once again stated his preference not to return to Vis but told Koch that he would dutifully follow his orders. Upon questioning him in an attempt to ascertain if Hamilton concurred with Tofte, Hamilton informed Koch that Tofte had spoken for him without consulting him. He again apologized for missing his meeting that morning, explaining that he had partied too hard the night before. Koch seemed to accept the Marine's word and he dismissed him, ordering him to report for duty in the front office while he and Weil decided what to do about situation with Operation AUDREY.

Near the end of his memo to Col. Toulmin, Koch vented his disgust with Tofte and Thompson. He offered grudging praise for their overall mission accomplishment while simultaneously demeaning their work. "It seems to me that the time has come to end this sort of erratic neuroticism and the alleged 'martyrdom' of the Thompson-Tofte pair. We have all admitted that a good over-all job has been done," he wrote. Questioning whether the two were truly critical to the mission's success, he suggested that anyone spending the time and money that they did on the Partisans would be equally popular. Giving the Partisans credit for the back-breaking work of loading and unloading the ships and then sailing them through enemy-infested water, Koch belittled Tofte and Thompson's contribution by stating: "Our pair have been liason [*sic*] with a bottomless expense account."[26]

With obvious frustration, Koch stated that the situation had gone far enough. Because he found it too confining, Tofte would simply not acknowledge the authority of the OSS. He wanted no oversight or restrictions hampering his efforts. "It is frankly believed that Capt. Tofte does not want to accept any authority except that which is so vague or so far removed as to constitute no regulatory function at all." In Koch's mind, the situation was beyond salvation.

Koch's recommendations were direct, to the point, and harsh. He recommended that Tofte be removed from Bari "or that permission be given to bring charges against him in a *Courts Martial* in Bari." He recommended against transferring him to any other organization. Repeating McBaine's charges from his December 28, 1943, memo to Toulmin, he accused Tofte, Thompson, and Hamilton of disobedience of orders, bringing discredit on the OSS, and jeopardizing the success of Weil's mission. In addition, he singled out Tofte for another serious charge: that of actions tantamount to mutiny. "These charges are repeated and in Tofte's case is added violation of Articles of War 64, 66 & 67—Willfully Disobeying Superior Officer, Attempt to Create Sedition, Failure to Suppress Sedition."[27] He recommended that Thompson, Hamilton, and Ellen, all be removed from Bari.

It was the beginning of the end for Operation AUDREY.

The very same day, January 3, 1944, Lt. Col. Toulmin wrote to Koch in response to both his letter written on Christmas Day, and also the verbal reports given to him by Lt. Cdr. McBaine. Although he had not yet received Koch's letter written on that same day, he was already well informed on the problems with the men running Operation AUDREY. He had already had his fill dealing with Louis Huot. He was in no mood to deal with the situation much longer. "So far as Tofte and Thompson are concerned," he wrote, "I have little, if any, sympathy for their recent doings. I am sure you can handle this matter but, as I stated when I wrote before, I will recall either or both whenever you say the word."[28] Koch now had the green light to proceed with his plans.

On January 8, 1944, Koch officially relieved Tofte, Thompson, and Hamilton from their duties concerning Operation AUDREY. Hayden was disgusted by the way their relief was handled. The Partisans, who greatly trusted and admired the Tofte-Thompson-Hamilton-Ellen team, were not told about their relief until after the fact and, according to Hayden, were "very much distressed" by it.[29] Koch had taken a liking to Hayden and told him he wanted him to learn the front-office end of the operation at the headquarters in Bari pending a new assignment. Feeling that Hayden "had been led astray" by Tofte and Thompson, Koch instructed the young Marine that he was to have nothing to do with them whatsoever.[30]

Disgusted with the whole situation, Hayden requested a transfer to another theater of operations, but suspected that the request never went through the proper channels. Tofte was replaced by Capt. Stephen T. Jacobs, who, according to Hayden, "knew nothing whatsoever of the situation, the business, or the Partisans, and what's more, who cared less!"[31]

Ultimately, Hayden and Thompson would remain at Bari, while Tofte was sent to Cairo for reassignment. Lt. Ward Ellen was the only one of the four who would remain with Operation AUDREY, continuing to supervise the maintenance of the ships.

Over the next two months, the shipping operation was transitioned away from the OSS. The procuring and loading of supplies for the Partisans became the responsibility of the SOE's Force 266, while the sailing of the ships was taken over by the Royal Navy. The OSS-SBS continued to finance the operation through the month of April, but in March 1944, withdrew all of its personnel.[32]

The final official report for Operation AUDREY reflected that the results achieved by the dismissed team of Huot, Tofte, Thompson, Ellen, and Hamilton were due much credit, despite their ignominious removal from the operation. They delivered 155 cargo shipments with a total tonnage of 11,637 tons. Operating forty-four ships, they evacuated twenty thousand Partisan refugees and seven hundred Partisan wounded. The total cost of the operation was $136,103.38.[33] It is perhaps most accurate to state that those responsible for the planning and execution of Operation AUDREY may have demonstrated initiative and resourcefulness more than prudence, but that should not detract unduly from their accomplishment.[34]

Despite his dissatisfaction at being stuck in an office routine, Sterling Hayden was actually quite fortunate that he wasn't brought down by the actions of Tofte. It was not long before he was back in the thick of the action again. In fact, on January 8, the day he officially was relieved, Hayden left on a new assignment—he was heading to Albania to take part in the rescue of the downed American nurses and medics. These were the very same people that Maj. Weil had proposed to go into Albania to rescue, a mission that he would never undertake. Getting underway at midday on January 8, Hayden piloted the *Yankee* to the rendezvous point the SOE camp in a cove designated as Seaview. He arrived shortly after midnight.

It took several trips by rowboat to transport the nurses and medics from the beach to the *Yankee*. No doubt several of the nurses recognized the tall, handsome boat captain who helped them get aboard. Things got underway shortly after loading all of the passengers. Rum was distributed to the grateful rescued nurses and medics as they began to loop south to avoid a naval skirmish that had broken out between Allied and German boats. Most of the passengers became seasick due to the rough seas.[35] At 1:30 p.m. on January 9, the *Yankee* pulled into Bari Harbor amidst much fanfare. A large crowd, led by the commanding officer of the 807th Medical Air Evacuation Squadron, was on hand to greet the nurses and medics and welcome them back after their fifty-eight-day ordeal. Within a couple of weeks, Sterling Hayden would be heading back to Albania on multiple missions.

• • •

During his tour of duty in the Balkans, Hayden developed an unbridled respect and admiration for the Partisans, so much so that other OSS personnel began to suspect he was a communist. He would reflect back on the literature that Warwick Tompkins had encouraged him to read, realizing that it was Tito and his Partisans who were doing the heavy fighting, despite having limited weapons, supplies, and food, while "the legitimate Royal Yugoslav Government was settled down in a command post in Claridge's Hotel in far-off London, issuing communiques as to the efficacy of their man in the field, Colonel Draja Mikhailovitch [*sic*], and his 'Glorious Fighting Chetniks.'"[36] He would later recall: "We established a tremendously close personal feeling with these people. We had enormous, I would say unlimited, respect for the way they were fighting."[37] Seeing the commitment of Tito's communist forces was an eye-opener for Hayden, leading him to deduce that perhaps Tompkins had been right all along in his ideology.

In his barracks, Hayden would receive many books and pamphlets from Tompkins. During Operation AUDREY, he began to write letters back to the United States nightly, especially to Warwick Tompkins. Enthusiastic praise of the Partisan cause and Tito were the main themes throughout the letters. In between missions, Hayden spent a good deal of his time in theater reading communist literature and propaganda and passing it on to his fellow officers, encouraging them to read it as well.[38] After the war, when he testified before the HUAC in 1951, Hayden would state that Tompkins "bombarded" him with communist literature such as *People's World*, *Daily Worker*, and *New Masses*.[39] All of this served to pique Hayden's interest and curiosity in learning more about this theoretical world of Warwick Tompkins that seemed to have been translated into reality by the Partisans.

During this time, he was also frequently corresponding with his other mentor, Lincoln Colcord. One day he received a special gift from Colcord: a copy of Henry David Thoreau's book *Walden*. The book struck a chord with Hayden. Nightly he would read the words of Thoreau and scribble notes in the margins. It was the first book he ever read that confirmed in him his own sense that it was possible to carve out one's own niche in life apart from the common concerns of most men.[40] Thoreau spoke to him, appealing to the individualist that he had always been and always would be.

While at Bari in December of 1943, Hayden conceived of an idea that would showcase both the will and commitment of Tito's Partisans as well as the crucial role of the OSS in helping them achieve their goals. It would take the form of a motion picture.

CHAPTER TEN

Missions to Albania and an Effort in Filmmaking

ALBANIA, NESTLED IN THE BALKAN PENINSULA BETWEEN THE YUGOSLAVIAN provinces and Greece, had emerged from World War I as an independent country. As a fledgling democracy, a monarchy was established when a 1928 coup was staged by Amhed Zog, who proclaimed himself king and proceeded to rule over the poorest country in Europe. His rule ended in April 1939, when the country was overrun by Mussolini's Italian military.[1] After Mussolini's forces attempted to invade Greece from their launching sites in Albania, they were bloodied by the Greek army and driven back where they were set upon by the Albanian resistance forces. In April 1941, Germany invaded both Yugoslavia and Greece, reliving some of the pressure on Mussolini. After the overthrow of Mussolini's regime, German forces invaded and occupied Albania in September of 1943.[2]

The resistance forces in Albania were largely divided among two major groups, paralleling the political situation in Yugoslavia. The communist forces of the National Liberation Front, also called the Partisans, were led by the enigmatic Enver Hoxha. An unabashed admirer of Joseph Stalin, Hoxha was quick to demand aid and supplies from the Allies, although aid was mysteriously not provided by his Russian dictator idol. He did not care for Americans and he openly detested the British. The main competition to the Partisans for control of the resistance movement and ultimately for control of Albania was the Balli Kombetar (National Front), an anti-communist, anti-monarchist movement that often collaborated with the Nazis in their civil war against the Partisans. Also competing with the Partisans was the Legaliteti (Legality Party), a coalition of northern Albania tribes that sought to restore the monarchy under King Amhed Zog. Another similarity to the Yugoslavian situation was the fact that the communist Partisans were willing to openly engage the Nazis whereas the other two groups appeared to prefer not to engage them so as to preserve their resources for their internal struggle against the Partisans.

The British SOE had been involved in Albania first against the Italians and then against the Germans. Their actions were not merely that of supplying and training of resistance fighters, which increasingly meant Partisan forces (as they were the only group willing to engage the Germans), but also active fighting.[3] The Americans initially sent a civilian to Albania as a liaison officer to the British, under whose authority Albanian operations fell, and the OSS then transferred the headquarters of its Albanian Section from Cairo to Bari in late 1943. The Albanian Section of the OSS at Bari was under the leadership of a civilian, Harry T. Fultz, who was a World War I veteran and was very knowledgeable about Albania. The mission of the OSS in Albania was to be the liaison with the British for intelligence gathering, and for the supplying of the Partisans. In addition, they would facilitate the transfer back to Bari of rescued American airmen who had gone down in enemy territory. Lastly, they would also be arranging for the transfer back to Italy of Italian prisoners of war. Unlike the British, they would not be engaging the Germans in combat. The first OSS member to enter Albania was Gy Sgt. Nick Kukich, USMC, who had arrived in theater in October 1943 aboard the same US Army transport ship that brought Sterling Hayden to the theater. Departing Bari aboard the fishing schooner *Sea Maid*, Kukich, along with a British SOE major whom he would be working with, arrived on the Albanian coast on December 31, 1943.

As was the case in Yugoslavia, supply to resistance forces by air drop was unfeasible, so supply by sea from Bari became the logical alternative. The British had established a base of operations in Albania called Seaview to facilitate their supply efforts. It was located in one of the water-level caves along the Adriatic coast that dotted the Karaburun Peninsula, also known as Cape Linguetta. It was a barren location that was both difficult to find and difficult to get to.[4] It was at Seaview that the OSS had set up its liaison base alongside the British. Seaview was the destination where Gy Sgt. Kukich and the British major landed.

Seaview quickly proved to be a distasteful place as the two new arrivals saw it. The cave and the surrounding caves were filthy, lice-ridden, and very ill-equipped, and the place had a terrible stench. In addition, the caves were surrounded by dozens of "scarecrows"—hungry Italian soldiers who were now prisoners and were begging for transport on one of the supply vessels back to Italy.[5]

The major and Kukich soon found a good secondary base for their operations further south down the coast from Seaview. Located one hour's travel time by boat was a much more suitable bay hidden by two mountains, where the water close to the beach was deep enough to allow supply boats to come closer in. The major described the bay as "perfect," noting that it was well-protected and that the entrance to the bay was three times wider than the one at Seaview. The base was named for its location—Grama Bay. Once the base was functional, the OSS and the SOE alternated their operations between Grama Bay and Seaview, depending on German military activity. Most of the men preferred Grama Bay because of its more hospitable conditions. Very quickly, supply operations originating from across the Adriatic at Bari began to ramp up.

• • •

On January 20, 1944, Maj. Koch called Hayden into his office and gave him a new operational assignment. He was to procure an Italian fishing vessel, ensure its operational seaworthiness, and establish a supply operation to the bases on Cape Linguetta on the Albanian coast. In addition to running supplies to Albania under the cover of darkness, his mission would be to retrieve rescued American airmen and to bring back Italian prisoners. Once again, Hayden would bristle at what he considered the interference of the British as he attempted to acquire a vessel. With annoyance, he observed that there were ten ex-Royal Yugoslav Navy motor torpedo boats "doing nothing," tied up to the docks at Brindisi. They had been seized by the Italians when Italy overran Yugoslavia and brought to Brindisi. Because of politics, the British never released them to the Partisans who truly needed them.[6]

Hayden spent a lot of time wrangling and cajoling British officials before they allowed him to acquire a fifty-foot Italian fishing boat, capable of a top speed of eight knots. He put together a crew of Partisans and within two weeks was ready to commence operations out of the port of Otranto. The initial trips to the Albania coast were accomplished despite the fact that their boat was unarmed; the SBS supply department claimed it was unable to acquire machine guns prior to their first two missions. All told, between February 15, 1944, and April 1, 1944, Hayden made ten transits across the Adriatic Sea to both Seaview and Grama Bay. He noted with disgust that after the third voyage the British informed him that it was against their policy for what they termed a "private navy" to operate in British waters.[7] Their mission put them in harm's way in many different ways. The weather in the Adriatic was often treacherous. They had to avoid Allied minefields upon departure and return to base. They had to avoid German sea patrols off the Yugoslavian coast. Had they been discovered, it was likely that the German patrol boats would have great firepower and would certainly decimate them in combat. Lastly, transferring supplies and men between the trawler and the shore by rowboat was fraught with difficulty, and if discovered during the process, the crew would be annihilated. The overly constricting British policies towards their alleged allies only served to greatly increase the stress levels to an already difficult assignment.

In his 1963 autobiography, Hayden only devoted a single sentence to his Albania mission. "In August," he wrote in the third person, incorrectly recalling the month, "they ordered him to pick out a suitable Italian fishing craft, convert her to a minor-league blockade runner, and begin running to the environs of Cape Linguetta, on the Albanian coast, with agents and supplies."[8] In his narrative of November 2, 1944, he described an incident that occurred on one of his Albanian trips. He did not specify whether it was to Seaview or to Grama Bay; he simply described the coast as "treacherous."

After offloading seven tons of rifles and ammunition and one OSS team of agents, he was informed by the British SOE major (who was Gy Sgt. Nick Kukich's superior officer) that he was to take back to Italy sixty Italian soldiers and two officers who had escaped from Greece. The "scarecrows" were jeopardizing the security of Seaview.[9] Hayden had to dodge two German patrol boats on his approach to the drop point. His boat was in an exposed position in the bay with a full moon to rise within the hour. Hayden informed the British major that they would load the men, or at least as many as they could before 2 a.m. By that time they would have to leave in order to reach the minefields off the Italian coast by daylight.[10] At that point, he traveled back to the trawler with nine of the Italians, and assumed that the British would oversee the embarkation of the rest of the men from the beach.

After about forty-five minutes, the sea state was making their departure necessary. They made repeated attempts to signal the men on the shore, but their signals went unanswered. Hayden decided that he and his assistant, Sgt. John Harnicker, USMC, had to go ashore and find out what was causing the delay. On the run in to the beach, the surf was so rough that their boat was swamped. Fortunately, it wasn't damaged, and once they righted it, it continued onto the beach.

When they arrived on the beach, they found six dead bodies beside a cave with the rest of the Italians gathered around their two officers. The six had drowned in the surf while attempting to swim out to the trawler. Hayden and Harnicker were told that the dozen men from the British mission had gone back to their camp, leaving no one to supervise the evacuation. Hayden sent a message to the British major, who in turn sent Gy Sgt. Kukich back with his reply: he was too busy to come down to the beach. The window of opportunity for escape was rapidly closing and Hayden informed the senior Italian officer that they were leaving now and he only had room in the rowboat for him and five other Italians.

It took four attempts through the rough surf to finally reach the trawler and make their getaway. It was then that Hayden learned that both the Italian officers had deserted their men on the beach in an attempt to get back to Italy. Hearing this, the Partisan first mate, who spoke fluent Italian, ordered the two officers to return to their men, but they refused. "Therefore," reported Hayden, "the mate beat them both up with a piece of wood that was handy."[11]

After their uneventful return trip to Italy, the disgusted Hayden approached the Albanian desk at Bari and lodged a formal complaint. He informed them that unless they were to have the full cooperation of the British on the reception end, it was foolish to risk property and good manpower on such an operation.[12] Hayden's complaint only served to further fuel the bad blood between the British and the Americans. While the SOE and OSS attempted to work out a compromise, Hayden made three more voyages across the Adriatic, delivering supplies and agents to several of the Greek islands north of Corfu. It was during this time that the SOE decided that it would take over control of Operation AUDREY and all shipping functions in the Balkans. "This would have not been necessary," opined Hayden, "had the SBS really fought for its rightful participation in what was called 'Allied effort.'"[13]

When he wrote his narrative in November of 1944, it is highly likely that Sterling Hayden had no idea who the British SOE major was that he dealt with in Albania. In an ironic twist of fate, the major was also an actor—Anthony Quayle, who was a major star of the British stage, having been the actor who replaced Laurence Olivier in the Old Vic tour of *Henry V* in London just prior to joining the British Army.[14] After the war, he would go on to a distinguished film career and would be knighted by Queen Elizabeth II in 1985. When he and Nick Kukich reported to Seaview, he became the ranking officer on the scene.

Kukich found it difficult to get along with Quayle, whom he considered aloof and snobbish, an English aristocrat who looked down on Kukich's coal miner roots.[15] Although they worked closely together, it was a tense relationship. Kukich resented being ordered around by Quayle and being excluded from important meetings. He felt that Quayle only wanted minimal interaction with him because he was an enlisted man.

Kukich found a way to retaliate against what he regarded as unfair and demeaning treatment by Quayle. He began withholding intelligence reports from his British superior officer while continuing to send them back to OSS headquarters in Bari. When Quayle learned what Kukich was doing, he was furious and confronted the young Marine. Kukich responded authoritatively, saying, "When you stop treating me badly, I'll share intelligence. I am a representative of the OSS and the American government and I expect to be treated as such. I expect to be treated equally." Following that blowup, Kukich reported, "After that, we got along like Eisenhower and Montgomery."[16] The new, somewhat more cordial relationship between the two men would soon be severely strained over an incident involving the OSS agent known as Lt. John Hamilton.

Anthony Quayle was always very hesitant to talk about his World War II experiences. His autobiography, *A Time to Speak*, was published in 1990, the year after he died. In the book, he paints a very unflattering picture of Sterling Hayden as a result of the incident involving the Italian prisoners that Hayden described in his 1944 narrative. Quayle described the incident as having taken place at the mouth of Grama Bay during a supply mission.[17] In his account of the event, Quayle rowed out to the trawler and urged the crew to bring the trawler closer to the shore to make it easier to transfer the supplies to the shore. His request was met with drunken laughter by the Serbian Partisan crew who proceeded to drop the supplies down to Quayle's rowboat, the first one hitting him in the head, and continuing until the rowboat was nearly sunk.

After Quayle and his men made several exhausting trips between the trawler and the beach, he wrote a "furious note to whoever might be in command of the ship. 'For God's sake, come ashore and speak to me. It is safe to bring your boat in. There is plenty of water.'"[18] Soon after, he saw a small boat leaving the trawler heading to the beach. Once on the beach, Quayle described an "enormous man, a man built on the scale of the Trojan War" get off the boat and walk up to him. He subsequently described his encounter as follows: "An American voice called out, 'Well—what's all the trouble?'" Quayle explained that it was safe to bring the trawler closer to the shore, which would make the transfer process much easier. The response from the American skipper was blunt: "I am the captain of this ship and I do not think it is safe. Therefore, I shall remain outside. What's more, in another twenty minutes I shall up-anchor and sail."[19]

The trawler's captain promptly returned to the ship and shortly after, the men on the beach heard the boat's engines come alive and could hear the anchor chain being hoisted. According to Quayle, "most of the Italians collapsed on the beach in despair; some tried to swim out to the ship. Three were drowned."[20] Adding to his dislike of the American trawler captain, Quayle also described an incident that occurred later at Seaview when he had to leave behind sixty Italian prisoners after a German patrol suddenly appeared. All of the Italians were taken prisoner by the Germans, including some of the ones that the trawler skipper refused to take aboard that night in Grama Bay.[21]

Several weeks later, after recovering from a bout of malaria, Quayle returned to Bari. On his first day there, he walked into the headquarters mess hall and saw, "lunching there, a man I was unlikely ever to forget—a tall, handsome man with the head of an ancient hero. It was the American captain who would not bring his trawler into Grama Bay.

"I turned to the mess sergeant. 'That big man over there, at the long table. Who is he?"

"The sergeant was surprised by my ignorance. 'Don't you know, sir? That's Sterling Hayden, the movie star.'

"I turned and left the room. I had no desire for further acquaintance with Mr. Hayden."[22]

...

In his 1963 autobiography, Hayden was home on leave in the United States when he related an anecdote concerning a mission to Albania to his friend Lincoln Colcord. In this version of the events, Hayden was sent to Albania to pick up thirty Italian soldiers hidden in one of the caves, likely either Seaview or Grama Bay. They had been on the run for over a year, trying to get from Greece to the Albanian coast and then back to Italy. After successfully evading a German patrol boat, Hayden sent his pilot, a Partisan named Ivosevitch, ashore in a rubber boat to arrange the pickup of the Italians. Hayden noticed that Isovevitch had taken a Thompson submachine gun with him, which he assumed was for self-defense, should they encounter any Germans. Hayden described what happened next: "He took a Thompson gun ashore with the rubber boat, and then I heard the firing. He came back on board alone. 'We go!' he had cried. All the Italians were dead. I didn't know what to say to this man whose wife had been raped to death."[23]

It is difficult for the historian to determine what exactly transpired in the incident that Sterling Hayden and Anthony Quayle described so differently. In the last version that was described in *Wanderer*, Hayden might have been taking some poetic license, and his version seems like a creation or an amalgamation of many of his experiences in the Balkans. This was confirmed by Nick Kukich in interviews that he gave to author Peter Lucas for his book *The OSS in World War II Albania*, published in 2007. He described Hayden's story of the murder of the thirty Italians as either a figment of his imagination, or perhaps a totally different incident that could have taken place in Yugoslavia. "It did not happen where we were," explained Kukich. "It could not have happened. We would have known. There were no bodies."[24]

Kukich believed that Quayle actually took two separate incidents—his confrontation with Hayden, where three Italian soldiers did drown, and the capture of the sixty Italians—and combined them into one incident in his book. Kukich was not present at Grama Bay when Quayle supposedly had his confrontation with Hayden; he had heard about it later. The incident involving the sixty Italians took place at Grama Bay, not Seaview, as Quayle had described. Embellishing on the incident at Grama Bay, Kukich explained that the Italians were on the beach, ready for transfer, when they spotted a vessel at the entrance to the bay. Certain it was one of the Partisan trawlers, Kukich prepared to signal their position when Quayle ordered him not to. Quayle was certain it was a German destroyer. "No way is that a German destroyer," insisted Kukich. "It's an Italian ship. I knew because I studied the charts. I knew it was an Italian ship used by us [the OSS]. I went to signal. Quayle ordered me to stop. 'If you signal I'll have you court-martialed,' he said. I argued with him but it was no use."[25]

After being chased from Grama Bay by the Germans, Quayle and Kukich stayed at a house in Dukat. The following morning, looking out the window, Kukich saw a column of the sixty Italians being marched along the road, directed by their German captors. "I told Quayle," he related. "He looked out the window and then he looked at me. He felt guilty. It never should have happened, but it did."[26]

Hayden's Albania adventures ended with his return to Bari on March 20, 1944.

• • •

By mid-spring, Hayden had completed his Albanian mission. He would soon be hampered by medical issues. Upon his return to Bari he was feeling fatigued, had lost weight, and his skin had yellowed. For the next three weeks, he remained in the hospital with what he simply described as jaundice. Most likely he was suffering from a case of acute hepatitis. While in the hospital, he continued corresponding with friends back home and continued to read the leftist/communist literature sent to him by Warwick Tompkins. After his recovery, he reported back to the headquarters at SBS, ready to resume his mundane routine of office work. He quickly became enthusiastically involved in a new project proposed by one of his colleagues.

Together with Lt. Robert Thompson, Hayden conceived of an audacious plan involving a series of sabotage operations in northern Yugoslavia that was tentatively called Operation DRAVO. It would entail a coordinated attack on the German lines of communications in the northern part of Yugoslavia through which practically all German materiel and personnel would eventually have to retreat.[27] The plan called for the OSS to play a major role. After detailed planning and a three-week reconnaissance mission behind enemy lines in Yugoslavia to facilitate the plan, Hayden angrily learned that the British were planning a similar operation. They launched Operation RATWEEK on September 1, 1944, and it was successful in destroying German railway lines of retreat as well as their communication network.[28] As Hayden was to testily recall in his 1944 narrative, the OSS had no apparent role in the operation.

• • •

During the time that Hayden was busy with the proposed Operation DRAVO, he was also involved in a unique project that he apparently conceived of soon after he began working with the Partisans in December of 1943. Impressed with their fighting spirit and also enamored with their communist ideology, Hayden's movie background came to the forefront with a proposal he pitched to headquarters at SBS. The previously mentioned memo sent by Lt. Col. Toulmin on December 30, 1943, acknowledged that while a proposed movie project that Toulmin reviewed was sound, the timing was not right at that particular time. After his disappointment with the result of his efforts for Operation DRAVO, Hayden requested a transfer to a different theater of operations and he was scheduled to go to Caserta, Italy. While awaiting his transfer orders, in May 1944, he resumed his lobbying efforts to create a movie about the

Partisans. It is interesting to note that he did not mention the movie project in either his November 1944 narrative or his 1963 autobiography.

In early May, Hayden wrote to Lt. Cdr. Edward Green, commanding officer of SBS, to formally request permission to shoot his film.[29] He began his proposal for a "Project for Photographic Unit" by noting that SBS now had its own photographic unit consisting of Specialist 1st Class J. B. Allin and Specialist 1st Class Nelson McEdward. The two men has been transferred to Bari the previous December as a result of an agreement between Maj. Walter M. Ross, commanding officer of their parent command, Company B of the 2677th Regiment OSS (Provisional), and Capt. George Vujnovich, operations officer at Bari.[30] Having completed their last assignment, the two cameramen were eager for a new one.

Hayden proposed that he and the two cameramen leave as soon as feasible for Vis, where they would set up their base in the quarters still currently occupied by Special Operations. The facilities on the base had adequate billeting, messing, and also had the capabilities to create a dark room if needed for film development. The mission of the unit would be twofold: "First; To make a photographic record of the Partisan movement as it exists in the Dalmatian Island and Coastal Area," and "Second; To make a film of the activities of the Operational Groups now stationed on, and operating from, Vis. Upon arrival, this officer will outline his ideas to the commanding officer."[31] Hayden added that he had attached his completed script, as well as a schedule of the work that would need to be done for the project.

To assist them with equipment, scripting, and various anticipated tasks, Hayden stated that the unit must be "increased by three non-commissioned officers of the highest possible caliber." Lastly, he requested that the orders from the CO of SBS for the mission clearly state the unit's two clear-cut objectives, and point out that all of the work of the team would be "the responsibility of this officer, who will be directly responsible to the C.O., SBS in his efforts to carry out the twofold mission." In closing, he added one last request to provide himself maximum flexibility to carry out the mission as he saw fit, and to hopefully avoid British interference, by requesting "that full permission be obtained from the director, Force 266 for the Unit to operate freely in the Dalmatian Coastal Area as this officer believes necessary."

On May 19, Lt. Cdr. Green met with Hayden to discuss the proposed film project. That afternoon, he wrote to Hayden with his endorsement. Arranging a temporary transfer of Allin and McEdward to Special

Operations, so they would come under Hayden's personal supervision, he somewhat cautiously ended his endorsement by stating that Hayden must "prepare a written script which shall be approved in advance before any definite steps are launched."[32]

Hayden's proposed film project now had the blessing of his parent command and now Lt. Cdr. Green passed it up his chain of command for their endorsements. On May 30, 1944, Green wrote to the "CO, OSS/Italy" to outline the proposed film.[33] He began by pointing out that the two cameramen had been at Bari for several months with little to do and that their photographic skills were of "relatively little value." Therefore, to better utilize their talents, they were assigned to Lt. John Hamilton "because of his contacts with British, Partisan and American officers and his wide experience along the Dalmatian coast, where the best photographic subjects are located." All of this was accurate, but it is also interesting to note that he did not mention that Lt. Hamilton was actually Sterling Hayden the movie star. It is possible that Green and others at Bari didn't know his real identity, but given his striking good looks and impressive height and physique, this seems highly improbable. Nonetheless, Lt. Hamilton's film background was not brought up in the memo.

Green also pointed out Hamilton's two objectives for the filming: to showcase the activities of the largest resistance and best organized movement in Europe, and to film the activities of the Operational Group personnel currently stationed on Vis. Hinting none-too-subtly about Hayden's sympathetic views towards the communists, Green sought to assure the CO. "While it is recognized that the shooting script which has been prepared by Lieut. Hamilton might be questionable if it were to be used for immediate release, it should be borne in mind that the ultimate results of photographic activity will come under the control of the person who edits the film after it had been developed. If, in his enthusiasm to portray the Partisan spirit, anything should be incorporated which might be of questionable nature, this can be deleted by the consorts before the film is released."[34]

Green recommended that the OSS/Italy approve Hamilton's attached script and "authority be granted to obtain approval for this activity from the British." Once the proper authority was granted, he recommended that Hamilton and his crew depart immediately for Vis. Reminding the authorities that Hamilton was scheduled to report soon to the headquarters in Caserta and emphasizing how vital he was to the mission's success, Green requested that Hamilton be retained at SBS until the mission was completed.

On June 8, 1944, Col. Edward Glavin, commanding officer of the 2677th Regiment (Provisional), provided an endorsement for the mission.[35] He wanted the "Field Photographic Mission" to be coordinated with the Special Intelligence and Special Operations branches prior to undertaking it. With the approval of both parties and several other stipulations, the mission could commence under the control of SO. As an interesting flourish, Glavin wrote across the top of Green's original memo "get name for this mission" and underlined it.

• • •

Hayden's script was entitled "The People Fight."[36] It was eleven pages long and contained 151 scenes. Reading it, one can tell it was written by someone who was very familiar with screenplays and movie staging. Viewing it with contemporary eyes, it seems contrived and overdramatic, even within the context of World War II films that were often instruments of propaganda. What is most striking to the reader is that contrary to one of his two explicit mission objectives, there is no mention of the OSS Operational Group activities on Vis at all. All of the activity on Vis appears to be conducted by the Partisans. On the top of the second page, Hayden wrote, "Today Vis is garrisoned by several thousand Partisans, many of them equipped by the Allies." That is the only mention of any Allied contribution to the resistance effort in Yugoslavia.

Hayden's praise of the Partisans knew no bounds. The stage is set in the opening scene as the dedication solemnly states: "Dedicated to the Yugoslav National Army of Liberation. Which for three bitter years has resisted every attempt made by the Germans and Fascists to annihilate it and by so doing conquer Yugoslavia. These Partisans, under the leadership of Marshal Tito, have given the world an unequalled example of self-sacrifice and an unconquerable will to smash the common enemy.

"As this is filmed over three hundred thousand Partisans are fighting and dieing [*sic*] to free their country. They fight, work and live with one motto—Smrt Fasizmu-Sloboda Narodu DEATH TO FASCISM—LIBERTY TO THE PEOPLE.

"Between battle and burials they sing."[37] At this point, one of the Partisan marching songs arises in the background. Hayden used the image and the sounds of the Partisans singing as they march to battle in several spots in the script.

The script documents the typical Partisan routine from Vis. Boats are loaded and run over to the German-controlled Dalmatian coast under the cover of darkness and are hidden in coves. The boats are hidden during the day as German planes fly over the coast. The following night, under the cover of darkness, the boats go to different unloading points along the coast. He points out the transport of the supplies to inland Yugoslavia over the Velebut mountain range to "the blood-soaked plains of Yugoslavia, the home and the heart of the Peoples War of National Liberation."[38]

In one melodramatic scene showing a boat approaching from the sea and being signaled by lights on the shore, the script solemnly announces: "This is nineteen hundred and forty-four. In 1776 and 1812 it was not much different."[39] This is the only reference to the United States in the script. Describing the Partisan leaders as young, tough, and consumed with the desire to fight, Hayden emphasizes that attacking the enemy is their one objective. At this point, the script calls for five hundred feet of combat scenes to be inserted and notes that it would be obtained later by the unit and inserted into the film at that time.

The script's final scene shows the Partisan brigade marching away into the distance as the sound of the Partisan Hymn begins to swell. As the volume of the music rises, on the screen, just before the fade-out appear the words: "Death to Fascism—Liberty to the People."

• • •

Also that month, Hayden learned that his wife Madeleine Carroll was working at the 61st Station Hospital, a US Army hospital in Foggia, Italy. She had volunteered to become a nurse's aide for the American Red Cross and had dedicated her life to caring for injured servicemen. Foggia was only sixty miles away from Bari, and Hayden's team was still waiting for final approval for their photographic mission. Hayden decided to spend a weekend with his wife, whom he hadn't seen for well over a year. He made no mention of this side trip in his 1944 narrative and mentioned it only in passing in *Wanderer*. Once again writing in the third person, he noted that he found out "his wife had been transferred to the 61st Station Hospital in Foggia, a bombed-out town ninety miles north of Bari. He rested a week, spent one weekend with her."[40]

• • •

Due to the confusing chain of command that had evolved during the course of the war, it became unclear where to next forward the film project proposal to. More significantly, the planning for the upcoming Yugoslav campaign that would become Operation RATWEEK had taken top priority. Accordingly, permission to begin the film project was not obtained.

Sterling Hayden's film tribute to the Partisans and Marshal Tito would never be made.

CHAPTER ELEVEN

Air Crew Rescue Unit and a Loss of Faith

BY THE SUMMER OF 1944, RECOVERY OF AMERICAN AIRCREWS SHOT down over the Balkans became a major concern. Complicating the situation was the shift of Allied support to Tito's Partisans and the virtual abandonment of Mihailovich's Chetniks. This was driven largely by the evolving British policy to support Tito but it was not wholeheartedly embraced by the United States. From Donovan's perspective, there was valuable intelligence to be gained from the Mihailovich and the Chetniks. Capt. George Musulin of the OSS was subsequently assigned as a liaison officer to the Chetnik headquarters effective October 19, 1943. Mihailovich had told Musulin that the Chetniks were holding many rescued American airmen, and the OSS at Bari became aware of this as early as February 1944.[1] Musulin requested to take part in the rescue of the Americans, but under pressure from the British to abandon Mihailovich, he was withdrawn back to Bari in May.

In January 1944, two OSS officers, Maj. Linn Farish and Lt. Eli Popovich, parachuted into Partisan headquarters in Drvar to arrange assistance in rescuing American airmen who had been shot down over Partisan territory. They met with Tito on January 23, 1944, and shortly after their meeting Tito issued orders that the Partisans were to exercise maximal efforts to assist in the locating of downed Americans and bringing them back to where they could safely be evacuated.[2] In addition, Popovich oversaw the construction of an airstrip near Drvar to be used for the rescue missions.

Back in Bari, the outspoken Musulin continued to push for the same consideration for Americans shot down over Chetnik territory. He ran into strong resistance from the British who were then determined to have nothing to do with Mihailovich. He met with Maj. Farish and Lt. Popovich, and also invited Lt. Deranian to discuss the situation. They came to the consensus that maximum efforts to rescue all American airmen, regardless of which territory they were shot down over, should be made, and British politics be damned. Shortly after their meeting, they arranged a meeting with Maj. Gen. Nathan Twining, commander of the Fifteenth Air Force to ask for his support.

They had come to the right man. Twining considered the rescue of Allied airmen downed in enemy territory a top priority. He took great pride in the fact that his air force had made every effort to recover its own people as well as other Allied personnel. His well-known concern in this matter served to endear Twining to his own airmen.[3] The combined efforts of the OSS men, coupled with the enthusiastic support of Gen. Twining, paid off. On July 24, 1944, Gen. Ira Eaker, commander of the Mediterranean Allied Air Force (MAAF), signed the order that created the Air Crew Rescue Unit (ACRU). This new unit would be under the command of Col. George Kraigher and, although officially attached to the Fifteenth Air Force, it would be a totally independent unit. Its sole mission was to locate and rescue Allied airmen downed in the Balkans.

Kraigher initially had two B-25s made available to him, but was told he could draw off of MAAF and BAF resources if needed. He immediately formed two sections for the new rescue command; one would work with Tito and his Partisans, and the other with Mihailovich and his Chetniks. The logical choice to head up the team going to the Chetniks was George Musulin, who was eager for the assignment. The first ACRU mission, named by the OSS as the HALYARD mission, was initially marred by inadequate signals coordination as well as British attempts to undermine the mission. But it succeeded on its fourth attempt to parachute drop Musulin and two enlisted men near Mihailovich's headquarters at Pranjane on the night of August 2. Musulin, an outstanding tackle for the University of Pittsburgh football team in the 1930s, was a giant of a man. He might have been the heaviest American soldier to make a successful parachute jump during the war.[4]

Upon arrival at Mihailovich's headquarters, Musulin learned that about 250 airmen were awaiting evacuation. Fearing the Germans would soon learn of the rescue mission, and recognizing that the runway at Pranjane was too short to accommodate the C-47 aircraft that would be taking the airmen back to Bari, Musulin immediately ordered that the runway be lengthened by 1,800 feet and widened by 150 feet. Three hundred Chetnik workers using sixty ox carts managed to complete the job. The resulting runway was marginal for C-47 operations, but they had no choice. Because of its relatively short length, aircraft would be limited to twelve evacuees per flight.[5]

On August 8, four C-47s landed on the modified airstrip. That night, during the initiation of the HALYARD mission, forty-eight airmen were evacuated back to Bari. The following day, under increased security provided by the Chetniks, 177 American airmen and a number of other Allied personnel were evacuated to Bari. Back at SBS, Lt. Cdr. Green radioed a message to Musulin that "good old Col Kraigher is still floating around in the air four feet above the ground."[6] The success of the first ACRU mission guaranteed that there would be more. In fact, by August another mission was being planned, this time to rescue airmen downed in Partisan territory. This mission would be assigned to an officer who had worked extensively with the Partisans and was, at the moment, waiting for permission that would never be given to embark on a film project—Lt. John Hamilton.

• • •

In early August, Hayden was called in to Special Operations headquarters at Bari and was informed that the film project had been canceled. Events had overtaken the project and a new focus had arisen as a result of the success of the HALYARD mission. On August 5, Hayden filled out personnel paperwork for the new proposed ACRU mission, tentatively designated DEMAGOGUE.[7] In the "Military Record" section of the form he wrote one word: "Unblemished." He listed an interesting, even amusing answer where the form asked for "Marital Status." He wrote: "Yes By God."

On August 17, Lt. John Hamilton was officially designated as the commander of the newly designated HACIENDA mission. This new ACRU mission had a similar goal to its predecessor: to locate and rescue downed American airmen and Allied personnel in Yugoslavia. For this mission, they would be searching in Croatia, in the Partisan area of operations. Also on the HACIENDA team were Hayden's Marine Corps colleague Sgt. John Harnicker and Radioman 3rd Class Joseph Rajacic.

Their mission orders called for them to land in central Croatia and to proceed in an easterly direction toward Slavonia and then swing north, paralleling the Hungarian border. Their mission was to pick up airmen who had been shot down while returning from bombing missions.[8] There are two detailed descriptions of the HACIENDA mission that have survived, both written by Hayden thirty-seven days apart (September 28, 1944, and November 4, 1944). The mission details are basically similar, but his impressions of the Partisans are strikingly different in the two reports. Both reports remained classified for decades but they shed light on what might be the first feelings of doubt that Sterling Hayden experienced concerning the Partisans and the communists in general.

On August 20, Hayden parachuted into Yugoslavia and arrived at the Croatia headquarters of the Partisan 4th Corps. There he met with OSS liaison Capt. George Selig, "who was the senior Allied officer in this mission and who was doing a very fine job."[9] Hayden and Selig conferred with the Partisan Corps command and it was decided that the HACIENDA mission would proceed overland to the 6th Partisan Corps in Slavonia. At this point, the two reports generated by Hayden began to differ, despite the fact they were written less than five weeks apart. In the September 28, 1944, official after-action report, Hayden stated that he landed in Yugoslavia on August 20 and was by himself, adding that the other two team members joined him on August 28. In the November 4, 1944, narrative, he reported that the entire team flew together into Yugoslavia on August 22.[10] This initial discrepancy would be a harbinger of greater and even more profound differences between the two reports.

The journey to Partisan headquarters in Slavonia was accomplished in five days. Crossing German-controlled lines several times, they were accompanied by a Partisan battalion as far as the Sava River. During river crossings, the Partisans would detach addition battalions to cover their flanks. Hayden noted in his narrative that the troops were ill-equipped but their "spirit was magnificent and they showed remarkable training and discipline."[11] The only way that the OSS men could repay the Partisan troops for their assistance was with cigarettes, of which they had brought seventy cartons. They made it to the Slavonia headquarters uneventfully.

After arriving at the 6th Partisan headquarters, the OSS team took over billeting quarters that were vacated by another OSS team that was out on operations with a Partisan division. Hayden's team had to wait eight days to obtain permission to proceed on to Croatian 10th Corps. Upon arrival in Slavonia, Hayden noted with disdain the appearance of the fellow OSS officers who greeted them. "Upon reaching this point we were greeted by ten OSS men, complete with paratroop boots, insignia, and enough equipment for at least a Partisan Battalion." Their plan had been to get into Hungary but they couldn't penetrate the heavily fortified border. "Therefore, after living off the Partisans for upwards of three weeks they flew back to Bari." With disgust, Hayden pointed out, "It is this kind of operation which makes an American really look foolish. The Partisans are unable to understand how or even why we operate."[12]

Finally able to obtain the requisite permission to proceed from the Partisan headquarters, they departed on September 12, heading northeast towards the 10th Corps area of operations. It took them three days to make the journey, which placed them about forty-five miles from Zagreb. They successfully avoided a potential enemy during their journey, one that headquarters in Bari was unaware of. The area was currently being patrolled by the infamous Cossack division, which had over nine thousand men. The Cossacks, whom Hayden noted were beautifully equipped and 100 percent mounted, "enjoyed the reputation of being the most fanatical opposition the Partisans met in all of Yugoslavia."[13] Fortunately, the Partisans knowledge of the area and of their enemy's tactics were sufficient to allow the mission to avoid contact with them. During this time, they found no sign of Allied airmen.

Upon arrival at the Croatian 10th Corps headquarters, they were greeted by Maj. Gordon Allen, commander of the British mission to the Croatian 10th Corps. Hayden was very impressed with the British officer, describing him as "exceptionally able and cooperative. There are few of his caliber in Yugoslavia."[14] Maj. Allen promptly arranged quarters for the three OSS agents. It very quickly became apparent to Hayden that Maj. Allen's men had the entire 10th Corps region well covered and there would be no benefit having the HACIENDA team remain there. Accordingly, he requested permission for a Partisan escort to accompany them as they planned to proceed about seventy miles north into Slovenia. Permission was granted, so the team prepared to leave on September 14. The Partisans had made all of the travel arrangements, including providing pack and riding horses and Hayden notified Bari of the change in their itinerary.

Once again, events in the combat theater of Yugoslavia transpired to interfere with Hayden's mission. Bulgaria and Rumania both had surrendered; as a result, a large number of German troops were now in that border region. The Germans were also beginning to evacuate Zagreb as the Russians were beginning to flood into Serbia. Also, on September 22, strong Ustasha, Cossack, and German motorized elements were reported on all sides of the 10th Corps headquarters. "Partisan Chief of Staff informed this officer that he could not move for at least three weeks," reported Hayden. "Accordingly, Hacienda Mission had itself evacuated to Italy by B-25 on 24 September, arriving at Bari at 1630 hours."[15]

The two reports written by Hayden differ in a key detail. The November 4 narrative stated that they had collected nine airmen who had been shot down and had them returned to Bari. The September 28 after-action report stated that no airmen were rescued. His summary of his experiences in Yugoslavia that end his Narrative report of November 4, 1944, expressed his sense of frustration and disappointment with any OSS accomplishments. "We came here promising big things, and in the long run did almost nothing," he noted. This, he claimed, was in spite of the fine efforts of men such as Linn Farish, Eli Popovich, and Hans Tofte. "The net result has been that our position in the Balkans has deteriorated immeasurably." The other issue he addressed was the deteriorating morale of the junior officers and enlisted men of the OSS in Italy. Virtually all of the men were frustrated by "months of idleness or futile, proposed operations . . . the morale situation was one best described as tragic." Possibly reflecting back on his experiences at Bari and venting his dislike of Maj. Koch and Maj. Weil, he railed against unresponsive commanding officers who, in Hayden's opinion, seemed to be promoted in spite of their incompetence. He summed up his frustration with communist-sounding rhetoric: "I feel that the sooner we realize that this war is one of National Liberation for the heretofor [*sic*] fascist governed peoples of the world, the sooner our war effort will reach its maximum effectiveness. OSS in particular is in a position to foster these Peoples Movements in their fight for freedom."[16]

The most striking difference in the two reports is the opposite feelings that Hayden expressed towards the Partisans in the reports. The narrative descriptions of the Partisans are consistent with the constant admiration that Sterling Hayden had expressed for them since his arrival in the Balkans. In his September 28 after-action report, the views that he expressed concerning the Partisans provide an astounding contrast to his thoughts in the narrative, reflecting a dramatic and largely negative change in his feelings towards them. He began by acknowledging that he had worked with the Partisans for nine months prior to the HACIENDA mission and, consequently, he had an "exceedingly favorable" impression of them. However, as a result of the just-completed mission, his impressions were largely reversed. He went on to elaborate his reasons for his changed opinion.

He stated definitively that the Partisan movement was not an expression of the people's will. All the Partisan units were led by young men who were good fighters but were "completely unable to exercise the judgment and mature responsibility required of men in their position. This is particularly true of the Commissars. These men are politically fanatic and in almost every instance it is they, rather than the Commandants, who hold the final say-so in all matters."[17] The Partisans in general were "high-handed" and arrogant and their abuse of the common people, the peasants, galled Hayden.

It was the farmers and the peasants, according to Hayden, who were truly paying the price of the war. They were forced to billet the Partisan troops, feed them, and supply them with livestock for food, as well as transportation. In return, whenever enemy troops drove through the country, the Partisans fled to the hills and abandoned the very people that took care of them. "The expression 'liberated territory' is pure bunkum in all the territory covered by this mission," declared Hayden.[18] "Partisan territory is 'free' simply because the enemy does not care to use it at the time." The cycle was continuous: the enemy approached, the Partisans would flee, and the farmers were left "holding the bag." The result was the looting of the farms and raping of the women. Hayden had observed the contempt that the common farmers had for the Partisan troops.

The savagery of the internal conflicts that he observed among the Yugoslavs appalled Hayden. He saw hatred among people who differed in religion, race, and position. "Atrocities have been committed on a wholesale scale by the Ustashi [*sic*] and Cossacks that surpass an American's credulity." Having witnessed the evolving civil war between the Partisans and the Chetniks for nearly a year, he closed with a very prescient comment. "One thing is certain—a formal end to the European war will mean nothing in Yugoslavia. The bloodshed there will be endless."[19]

Hayden's report on the HACIENDA mission was forwarded up the chain for endorsement by Lt. B. Nelson Deranian, head of Special Operations-Bari, as an attachment to his October 2, 1944, memo to the Commanding Officer, SO-Washington, via the Commanding Officer, Company B, 2677th Regiment OSS (Provisional).[20] In his memo, Deranian summarized Lt. Hamilton's prior accomplishments since arriving in the Balkans and it is obvious that he thought highly of the young Marine. "After Lt. Hamilton's return," he wrote, "we discussed the situation in Jugoslavia [*sic*] at length; and I was amazed to learn that his attitude towards the Partisan organization had changed completely during his most recent experience with them. However, he retained his sympathy for the people as a whole." Prior to the mission, Hamilton had been a staunch Partisan supporter, "irrevocably and completely convinced of the efficacy of the Partisan movement—its organization and high purpose." After their discussion, Deranian felt that Hamilton had good reasons for his change of heart and for the gloomy conclusions he had come to. Accordingly, he asked Hamilton to write his September 28 after-action report.[21]

Deranian noted that when the Reports Officer read the report, he "expressed amazement at Lt. Hamilton's change of heart," but was a little disappointed that Hamilton didn't include more facts and examples upon which he based his conclusions. Deranian himself felt that Hamilton's remarks expressed a feeling which was supported by his natural tendency to sympathize with the "downtrodden," a common feeling among many of the OSS officers at Bari who had spent some time in Yugoslavia "without an axe to grind" and who had observed things objectively.

Deranian closed by offering further praise for Lt. Hamilton. He described the report as being the conscientious feeling of a man who had given the matter considerable thought and come to the conclusion regarding the Partisans that "I was wrong." "Coming from an officer of Lt. Hamilton's caliber, qualifications, and ability to observe and see things, it deserves attention."[22]

On October 2, 1944, Lt. Cdr. Green signed the first endorsement, offering the noncommittal "Forwarded" as the sole comment in the endorsement narrative, and sent the package to the Chief of Special Operations at OSS headquarters in Washington.

...

How is one to reconcile the two diametrically opposed opinions of the Partisans that Hayden expressed in reports that he wrote only five weeks apart? The opinions expressed in the September 28 after-action report appear to represent an abrupt about-face, a change so markedly different from any of his previous comments that consistently sang the praises of the Partisans that it is hard to believe they were written by the same person. A clearer understanding of how this change came about as well as its meaning can be achieved when one considers Hayden's overall experiences in the Balkans as well as the context of the after-action report, written immediately after his return to Bari.

The September 28 report was an official military/OSS after-action report to his superiors. It would be read immediately and would be endorsed up the chain of command with either a positive, negative, or a neutral endorsement, such as the one Lt. Cdr. Green provided. After reaching Washington, DC, the report was immediately classified and remained so for decades. The November 4 narrative differs in several respects. It was written at the end of his tour in the Balkans, and as its name implied, it was a personal statement of his actions and observations in the Balkans theater of operations. It served as a summary of his experiences along with opinions about the success of the missions, his feelings about superior officers, and so on. It is uncertain who, if anyone, in the chain of command actually read it. It was placed in his OSS personnel file and remained classified for years.

Hayden's sympathies with the Partisans and their communist ideology had been "prepped" by the teachings and the literature provided by Warwick Tompkins. But Hayden was not alone in his admiration for Tito's forces. As previously noted, Donovan's open-minded approach to recruit the best men to defeat the Axis powers often did attract those with a "strong social-democratic orientation." As the British fostered the strong shift toward support for Tito over Mihailovich and the Americans followed suit, SBS had many people whose political views were similar to Hayden's. This was noted by Eli Popovich when he arrived in Bari. He found the communist presence and influence so pervasive that the OSS headquarters there had become known as the "Little Kremlin."[23] The overall pro-Partisan inclination at Bari was palpable to all who visited. While Hayden may have expressed some of the strongest opinions on the subject, he certainly was not alone in his views.

Hayden had come under the influence of Tompkins long before he joined the Marine Corps and the OSS. His initial meeting of the Partisans on the docks at Bari and Monopoli in December of 1943 had a significant influence on him. For the first time, he had found something to believe in, something that he said made him feel he had become an integral part of the human race.[24] At that moment, the theoretical literature that Tompkins had sent him, as well as his previous discussions with him, suddenly seemed to coalesce and make sense. It was those people, the Partisans working with him in Operation AUDREY, that had solidified in his mind the righteousness of their cause. These men sailed with him, worked with him on the Dalmatian coast setting up supply drops, and fought any Germans they would encounter. None of these Partisans were part of a large organized Partisan unit. He would continue to sing their praises, to devour the communist literature that Tompkins would send him and encourage his fellow OSS members to read, and to believe the communist propaganda—until the HACIENDA mission.

During the HACIENDA mission, for the first time Hayden was exposed to organized Partisan combat units, not guerilla fighters. He was stunned by the difference in these people. As he described in his September 28 report, the combat units were modeled on Soviet military units, with political commissars actually having more say on operations than unit commanders. The commissars, often young men barely out of their teens, were fanatical ideologues. They were cruel, compassionless people who, in Hayden's opinion, abused the very peasantry that they claimed they were fighting to free. He greatly resented the abandonment of the peasants and the farmers who were taking care of the Partisan forces whenever an enemy unit approached. He also began to suspect that the military exploits of the Partisan armies were exaggerated and some reports were outright lies.

No doubt, Sterling Hayden was highly conflicted upon returning from his ACRU mission. He would later testify to the HUAC in 1951 about his early experiences in Yugoslavia. Coupled with the literature provided by Warwick Tompkins, he stated, "I was all steamed up. We all were."[25] He would also describe the final effect on him: "At the time . . . there was a sort of a thing churning inside of me that I didn't know how to handle."[26] His experiences in the HACIENDA mission working with the Partisan units must have provided a jolt of reality that began to shatter the idealized image in his mind of the noble Partisans and provided to him a glimpse of the true face of communist totalitarianism. For official purposes, in his after-action report he expressed his honest opinion of Tito's forces, an opinion that stunned his superiors when they read it. Writing his narrative five weeks later, he omitted his harsh criticism of the Partisans, but instead concluded his report with a very gloomy assessment of what the OSS had really achieved for all their efforts in Yugoslavia. Perhaps that gloomy assessment was a metaphor that Hayden used to describe his newfound disenchantment with the Partisans. Perhaps the best explanation of the differences in the two reports was unknowingly given by Nelson Deranian when he described Hayden's newfound contempt for the Partisan organization's hierarchy as it was detailed in the September 28 after-action report, and yet noted that Hayden had retained his sympathy for the people as a whole, as reflected in his November 4 narrative. We will never know, but back in 1944, Hayden may well have suspected that after the reports were filed, they would never again see the light of day during his lifetime.

Although he could not possibly know it, Hayden's newfound gloomy and divergent observations on the nature of the Yugoslavian people versus their political leaders had already been eloquently expressed in an official report forwarded on to Washington only two months prior. After his return from Yugoslavia in June, Maj. Linn Farish was asked by Lt. Cdr. Green to prepare an official report on conditions in Yugoslavia. Farish, who had spent nearly a year in the country, much of it as American OSS liaison to the British headquarters delegation to Tito's headquarters, was a highly respected authority on actual conditions on the ground in the country. He arranged a meeting with two other key officers who were also expert authorities: Lt. Eli Popovich who, as his assistant, had served with him most of his time in the country, and Lt. George Musulin. Musulin had spent months as the OSS liaison officer to the British delegation at Mihailovich's headquarters. There were no more knowledgeable experts about actual conditions in Yugoslavia than these three men. Their combined thoughts provided a devastating critique of the resistance movement, similar to the conclusions that Sterling Hayden would arrive at only two months later. In addition, they harshly criticized the Allied efforts in Yugoslavia and what they perceived to be its failure to accomplish a secure future for the Yugoslavian people. Lt. Deranian forwarded Farish's report in a July 4, 1944, memo to the chief of OSS-Special operations in Washington.[27]

In his prologue, Deranian indicated that "the discussions of these three men helped me to put together the political jig-saw puzzle of Yugoslavia." He also stressed that there was no conflict of opinion between Lt. Musulin, who had served with the Chetniks and held them in high regard, and the other two officers who had served with the Partisans. Deranian and others had attended the discussions and were able to get a clear picture of what was actually happening in Yugoslavia. So clear and persuasive were the points made by the three officers that rather than write his own report of the conference, Deranian had elected to forward Farish's actual report of their consensus meeting, stating, "Such a report would be almost a repetition of Major Farish's observations on the subject."

The situation in Yugoslavia was extremely confusing, according to Farish, almost beyond the comprehension of an impartial outside observer. Both sides were at fault for the present situation. "In the case of Marshal Tito and General Milhailovich, both sides tell exactly the same story of incidents which occurred at certain places on the same dates, the only difference being that each side places the blame on the other . . . Both sides proclaim as their aim, a Free, United and Democratic Jugoslavia [*sic*] with a form of government determined by the free electorate of the people after the country has been freed of the occupier." Yet the Chetniks insisted that the Partisans wanted to superimpose a communist tyranny on the country, while the Partisans claimed that the Chetniks goal was to restore the monarchy that was "corrupt, fascist, and dictatorial." The crux of the problem, noted Farish, was that "Both sides believe that their first enemy is the other, with the Germans and Bulgarians second . . . They are their own worst enemies."[28]

As Hayden was to note in his September 28 report, Farish described the vast majority of the people in Yugoslavia as simple, peasant types, regardless of which province he encountered them, who were to a large degree apolitical. They were strong-willed people with tremendous endurance and personal courage, although he interestingly added that they "love intrigue and gossip, and are the most profound liars I have ever met." He sensed no great urge for revolution among them. They simply loved their countryside, their homes, and their flocks. "They want something better, but, measured by our standards, what most of them ask is not a great deal; a good government, their King and their church, schools, more roads, shoes, clothing, and a few modern conveniences, better farming equipment, and some new livestock."[29] The people's desires were relatively simple—it was the political leaders, primarily Tito and Milhailovich, who had fostered a civil war among the people for their own ends in their quest for power. Their efforts were geared more towards the situation in Yugoslavia after the Axis powers were defeated, rather than the immediate task of defeating the Axis powers.

The Allies had not done well in Yugoslavia, opined Farish. They had never presented a united front to the Yugoslavs, but instead engaged in power politics themselves. While implying criticism of the diminished status of the United States bestowed by Great Britain and the minor role played by the Soviet Union, he bemoaned the fact that they had not established "one Military mission composed of duly constituted high-ranking officers of at least Great Britain, the Soviet Union, and the United States, who could have called all the conflicting parties together and taken such steps as were necessary in the form of a provisional government and military command to the end that the civil war was stopped and the maximum effort directed against the enemy."[30] Having stated his feelings on the subject, Farish went on to state that it did no good pining for what should have been done.

Was it too late to draw all the factions together into one group that would direct its efforts against the Axis enemy instead of each other? Farish was more hopeful in this regard, stating: "As far as the great mass of the people are concerned, it can be done because they are weary of fighting each other, but eager to fight the enemy." Only a few people from each side, the ideologues and the self-serving power-hungry, would prevent such a union from happening. Only a few, compared to the millions who had suffered as a result of their misguidance by their supposedly concerned leaders.

Farish's final major point was that there was one great power that might have prevented or at least stopped the disintegration of Yugoslavia into a civil war, but it was never used. "The United States if America is mentioned in the same breath with God in Yugoslavia. We were the one nation on earth to whom the people believed they could turn for unbiased, unpolitical aid, and advice without having to pay something in return."[31] Significantly, he went on to clarify this comment: "I am speaking now of the common man, not of Marshal Tito, General Milhailovich, or any one of the members of the government or leaders in the various factions." Citing the care and compassion with which all the common people of Yugoslavia, regardless of political persuasion, treated downed American airmen, Farish again lamented the squandered opportunity to unite the people of Yugoslavia.

Already hinting at the role of British incompetence in over-controlling OSS efforts in theater, he also criticized the Russians for their meager participation in providing the Yugoslavians with urgently needed supplies while trying to take claim for American supply drops. "Nothing here should be construed as anti-British, anti-Russian, or anti-anything. They are merely statements of facts intended to point out that we do have a very direct interest in what is taking place in Yugoslavia."[32]

Farish concluded his analysis by stating that it was inconceivable that the combined efforts of Great Britain, the United States, and the Soviet Union couldn't bring an abrupt end to the civil wars in Yugoslavia and assure the people a guarantee of free elections after the war. This portended poorly for the future because, as a result, "the Yugoslavians with their wild, turbulent, strong-willed nature, have abandoned reason and resorted to force." He asked: Was this the shape of things to come? His gloomy assessment would be mirrored in a similar assessment made by Sterling Hayden two months later. "It appears to me," Farish concluded, "that indications in the past few months are that there has been less emphasis placed on the fight against the enemy and more preparations for the political struggle to follow the ending of the war."[33]

Sterling Hayden's belief system, one that he had so recently embraced with enthusiasm, was now very much tainted as a result of his time spent with the Partisan military leaders. He now had seen the sharp dichotomy between the common people that he admired so much and the ruthless Partisan leadership that simply used the people to achieve power and their political aims. For the first time, he began to question the cause to which he had devoted himself, after seeing what Maj. Linn Farish had so eloquently described. These were realities that armchair American upper-class socialist intellectuals, such as Warwick Tompkins, could not imagine. Hayden needed a new sense of reassurance and reinforcement. As fate would have it, he would get that reinforcement fairly soon when he went back on leave to the United States. Although that reinforcement would help restore his beliefs to a degree, they were irreparably altered and would never be the same again.

• • •

Upon his return to Bari, Hayden received orders to return to Washington, DC, for reassignment. In addition, upon arrival in the United States, he would be granted thirty days leave. On October 30, 1944, he received a detaching fitness report, signed by Lt. Cdr. Green.[34] The report indicated "Superior" grades for motivation, ability to work with others, and physical ability. He received "Excellent" grades for practical intelligence and stability. Under the remarks section, it stated: "He is essentially a seaman and has demonstrated great skill in handling small vessels on clandestine missions along the Dalmatian Coast. He has great courage and has shown an almost reckless disregard of his own life where duty is involved." Under the section "Complete Reasons for Return to U.S.," it cited that his mission was complete and that the progress of the war limited his further usefulness in the Balkans, concluding: "He is a valuable man and should be made available for other Theaters without delay." Under "Recommendations," where it asked if his further use in the OSS was recommended, it stated, "YES, definitely."

Upon detaching from SBS he traveled to Naples where he boarded a troop ship bound for the United States. When he arrived in New York City, he went to Grand Central Station and boarded a commuter train headed for Darien, Connecticut. He was going to where his "duty lay" and spend some time with his mother. Having contacted her in advance, Frances Hayden had driven to the Darien train station and was waiting for him as the train pulled in. It was a joyous reunion and as they hugged, his mother greeted him using her nickname for her only child, "*Well*, Buzz, how good to see you, my dear."[35]

Driving through the Connecticut countryside, Hayden was struck by the sense of calm, peace, and most of all, safety. He was grateful that there was no snow on the ground; after months of dealing with the Balkan winters, he had his fill of snow. After a short while, they arrived at the home he shared with Madeleine at Wilson Point in South Norwalk, where Frances had been living ever since both Sterling and Madeleine had left on their World War II endeavors. After arriving, Hayden went to his bedroom to unpack, pulled out a bottle of liquor and poured himself a drink.

Mother and son commenced their somewhat awkward reunion in front of the fireplace which was handsomely decorated with flowers and ivy curtains. "Now, Buzz, stand still and let me look at you," she ordered as the two stared at each other for a few seconds. The sight of her tall, handsome son in the uniform of a (newly promoted) first lieutenant in the United States Marine Corps, impressed her greatly and filled her with pride. Handing her son a plate full of molasses cake cubes, he took one and then downed the rest of his drink. They walked over to the sofa for some catching-up time. "Now, sit down and tell me all about it," she requested.

"All about what, Mother?"

"About what you did in the war."

"Mother, didn't you get my letters?" he asked somewhat surprised.

"Hah, I certainly did *not*," she shot back. She watched her son get off the sofa after refusing more of her molasses cakes and head over to make himself another drink. Hayden had been a diligent letter-writer while overseas and was no doubt angered by his mother's revelation. "Oh Buzz, I'm so sorry to see you're still drinking," she ruefully said. The words struck a sore spot within him. He was well on his way to becoming an alcoholic, albeit a highly functioning one. "I've got to pull myself together," he thought to himself, noting his mother's anguish. He would try to focus on reading and relaxing, but it was no use—he was only kidding himself. A few minutes later, he gave in. "Defeated, he flung himself erect and went for another drink."[36]

...

As the DC-3 began its descent into Bangor, Maine, a hungover Marine was awakened by the flight attendant. Startled, the Marine asked the attendant where they were. "We're approaching Bangor, Maine, Lt. Hamilton," replied the attendant. "Bangor," thought Hayden to himself. "I must have called Lincoln Colcord." In no time, he was at the home of his friend in Searsport, Maine. It was a wonderful respite for him to be back on the New England seacoast that he loved so much. Adding to his sense of rest and contentment, he was again with his old friend and mentor. As expected, the conversation centered on Hayden's first love—the sea. And, inevitably, the alcohol flowed freely. The two friends downed much buttered rum as the talking and reminiscing progressed. After a while, it was Colcord who abruptly changed the subject.

"I don't mind telling you, Sterling," he began, "you had me worried there for a time with your letters full of this socialistic nonsense."

"There was more to it than that," his young friend replied.

"Of course there was. But I know you pretty well. I know you're inclined to be headstrong, inclined to jump in with both feet without thinking things through."[37]

When describing this conversation in *Wanderer*, Hayden recalled the inner turmoil that was pulling him in two directions. Colcord now represented the grounded, real-world mentor whose love of the sea and all things nautical coincided with Hayden's attainment of success in that field, but was, like his movie career, not truly fulfilling. The conversation had not gone the way he had expected. While speaking with Colcord, he was also thinking of Tompkins, thinking that perhaps this was the way of the world, that romance really went with dreams. "Maybe it was the rum," he reasoned. "Maybe so long as I kept on getting loaded I'd never have a chance, because the rum unleashed a flood of non-sea thoughts, of desires to join in the common cause and do something about changing the world a little."[38]

As their conversation continued, Hayden grew irritated with Colcord. Colcord appeared to have no interest in the Partisans, despite the heroic tales that Hayden had just recounted which he felt had conveyed a nice blend of maritime adventure and social comment. As the hour grew late, his mentor again offered his opinion. "Well, Sterling, it bothers me that you're still a radical. And I know what you're thinking, too. You're thinking I'm an old fogy who doesn't know what's going on." Hayden quickly concurred. "Well, let me tell you something," Colcord countered. "I went through my socialistic period in my late twenties, and it lasted a damn sight longer than it will with you. This whole thing is nonsense. You wouldn't last ten days in a totalitarian state."[39] He counseled the young man to go to the West Indies once the war ended, get a schooner, and start a charter business.

"I'm not sure I'd last there either, not anymore," responded Hayden. His reason was this: "Because all my life I've escaped. Now I'd like to take a hand in things."

"Oh balls!" retorted Colcord. "What we have in this country is *freedom*. What would happen in your Communist world if two men talked like this?" He answered his own question by drawing his finger slowly across his throat.[40]

As the hour approached midnight, Colcord went off to bed and Hayden sat there, thinking of their conversation and continuing to drink rum. It was as if his friendships with Lincoln Colcord and Warwick Tompkins were a metaphor for his newly ambivalent feelings for the Partisans that resulted from his experiences in the HACIENDA mission. Tompkins had fueled his idealistic and somewhat glorified view of the Partisans as exemplified by the Yugoslavs he worked with in Bari and along the Dalmatian coast. As a result of his interaction with these people, as Colcord noted, the headstrong Hayden had jumped in as an impassioned advocate for their cause without thinking it through. It was Colcord who represented a blast of reality concerning the Partisans. In his younger days, he too, had embraced socialist ideology but the reality of rigid socialism and communism, and their lack of individual freedom, had soured him; hence, his warnings to his young friend. For once, Sterling Hayden had embraced something that he had believed in, something bigger than himself and his accomplishments at sea or as an actor. His disappointment that resulted from his work with the Partisan military leaders had been a blow to his beliefs, a reality that Lincoln Colcord was quick to point out. That night, all Hayden could do was to continue to drown his ambivalence in alcohol.

He needed to restore his damaged faith in the Partisans and in communism. He decided to wait until Colcord was asleep and then make a call to the West Coast, a call to Warwick Tompkins. He needed the ideological reinforcement that only Tompkins could provide. As he expressed it: "When I got home on leave in December 1944, one of the first things I wanted to do, purely on an emotional basis, was go back and see Tompkins and talk to him about this thing, which I did."[41] It was a trip that would come back to haunt him several years later.

• • •

Hayden flew to the West Coast and stayed with Warwick Tompkins as a guest aboard *Wander Bird*, which was moored at Sausalito. He stayed with Tompkins for about a week and attended nonstop meetings arranged by his friend. As he described the week: "I flew out to the coast and basked in the reflected glory of the Partisan movement. Tompkins sort of showed me off as an exhibit."[42] In preparation for what he knew was going to be an exhibition of Tompkins's protégé—the movie star turned Marine hero—Hayden had decided to quit drinking and smoking.

Nightly, the Tompkins would host many of their friends who requested that Hayden regale them with his experiences working with the

Partisans in Yugoslavia. When the topic would veer off of his personal experiences in the Balkans, his insecurities about his "sweeping ignorance" would surface, forcing him to stick to the subject of his adventures in Yugoslavia.[43]

Several times the gatherings would take place at the home of Tompkins's brother-in-law, Dr. Ellwood Lyman. The fascinated guests would pepper Hayden with questions about his future. Hayden didn't know what his next OSS assignment would be, but he was hoping he would be sent as an OSS liaison to other guerilla groups fighting in Europe, particularly in Spain. The guests seemed more focused on his future after the war had ended. Someone recommended that he return to Hollywood and resume his film career. "There's nothing so wrong with being a picture star," the guest advised. "You could go around the country in between films. You could talk to kids in school, not about socialism because you don't know much about it, but about the questions that have been troubling you."

Another guest chimed in, observing how people were drawn to him. Hayden, he claimed, could fit in with all kinds of people, from seamen, to laborers, to the wealthy set who lived on Nob Hill. "Also," added Tompkins "you can write and you can talk—once you loosen up . . . you can reach the big audience, too."[44] Hayden took all the well-meaning advice of Tompkins's friends under consideration, but he really wasn't thinking that far in advance.

Part of Warwick Tompkins's plans for his young friend was to introduce him to influential fellow travelers. During his second night in Sausalito, Tompkins took Hayden to dinner where he got reacquainted with Isaac Folkoff, who Tompkins called "Pop." As previously noted, Folkoff was one of the founders of the California Communist Party.

On another occasion, Tompkins took him to the offices of the *Daily People's World*, the Communist Party's daily newspaper on the West Coast. There, Hayden was introduced to William Schneiderman and Harrison George, both senior Communist Party officials. The four of them departed for the San Francisco waterfront after their meeting to have drinks aboard a Russian ship.

At a subsequent group get-together at Dr. Lyman's home, Hayden was introduced to another special friend of Tompkins, a man who was an "outstanding figure." Prior to arrival, Tompkins informed his young friend that "Steve Nelson will be there. He is quite a guy." There were about fifteen guests in attendance, and once again, the guests asked Hayden to relate his Yugoslavian adventures and also his impressions of the Partisans. Steve Nelson had a special interest in the young Marine's impressions as he had served as political commissar of the Abraham Lincoln Battalion during the Spanish Civil War. He was a senior official of the Communist Party of the United States at the time of his meeting with Sterling Hayden.

At the end of his week with Warwick Tompkins, Hayden flew back to the East Coast armed with more of the communist literature that Tompkins always seemed to have in limitless supplies. In spite of the career advice of all of the people he had just met during his stay, he still didn't have a definite plan for himself once the war would end. He wasn't sure he wanted to return to Hollywood, despite the relatively easy and lucrative life that it would provide him. But the time with his leftist friend had provided the counterbalance to the influence of his other significant friend, Lincoln Colcord. Once again, their diametrically opposed thoughts on social structure served as the metaphor for Hayden's newly acquired ambivalence towards the Partisans. His time with Tompkins and his friends helped relieve the doubts he had experienced since the completion of the HACIENDA mission and filled him with a new resolve. "I think the main thing was," he recalled, "it planted a seed in me that said if I could do something about the conditions of the world I could probably justify my position as an actor with a good salary and good working conditions. This wasn't concrete, but it was something boiling inside of me."[45]

Arriving back in New York City while awaiting further OSS assignment, he was determined to see if there were other guerilla movements similar to the situation in Yugoslavia that he could possibly be of some use to. He wired back to Tompkins, asking if he had any contacts in that regard who could advise him. Tompkins promptly wired back a name for Hayden to contact: V. J. Jerome. Victor Jeremy Jerome was a Communist Party spokesman and at the time was the editor of *The Communist*. Hayden did contact Jerome but their meeting went nowhere. A meeting with a colleague arranged by Jerome also proved to be unhelpful to Hayden. A final meeting was arranged by Tompkins for Hayden to meet Allan Case. Case had run for Congress in the 1936 elections as a Communist Party candidate from New York. Although he was very interested in Spain and arranged for Hayden to meet friends who were knowledgeable about the underground situation in Spain, it didn't prove useful to Hayden.

It was time for Hayden to return to OSS headquarters in Washington for a new assignment.

CHAPTER TWELVE

European Theater

SHORTLY AFTER NEW YEAR'S DAY 1945, STERLING HAYDEN REPORTED to OSS headquarters in Washington for reassignment. On January 12, 1945, Hayden received his new assignment as the head of an OSS intelligence unit attached to the Intelligence section of the United States First Army. In preparation for his new job, he was formally transferred from Special Intelligence-Middle East theater of operations to Special Intelligence-European theater of operations, the following day. In addition, on January 16, he was enrolled in Station W, a one-day course held in Washington that assessed candidates who would be assigned to headquarters and rear bases overseas rather than to operations in the field. He was deemed qualified for his new assignment after completing Station W's Class W-196.[1] Orders were cut for Hayden to fly to Paris to report to the G-2 (Intelligence) Officer of the First Army and subsequently forwarded to the Navy Air Transportation on January 19 to arrange transit.

Perhaps the most interesting facet of his stay in Washington was a dinner invitation to the White House that he received. Hayden had a private dinner with Eleanor Roosevelt and Creekmore Fath, a Washington power lawyer who was currently on active duty with the US Army and serving in the White House in the Office of War Mobilization and the Department of Interior. Once the dinner ended, Hayden was asked to tell of his exploits. Although he admitted to feeling "acutely uncomfortable," he discussed all aspects of his Balkan experiences and expressed his desire to someday join future guerilla movements. Mrs. Roosevelt offered no suggestions.[2]

...

On February 2, 1945, Sterling Hayden left the United States bound for Paris to ultimately report to the G-2 (Intelligence section) of the US First

Army, which was then in Germany. Later that month, he achieved another milestone in his military career. On February 14, he was promoted to the rank of captain in the Marine Corps. In addition, recognition was being accorded to all members of ACRU missions who had participated in the efforts in the Balkans. A Letter of Commendation for members of the HACIENDA mission had worked its way through the chain of command during this timeframe. It was finally signed off on April 25, 1945, by Lt. Gen. John K. Cannon, commanding general of Mediterranean Allied Air Forces and sent to Col. Edward Glavin. It cited each member of the team for "their superior performance of duty while assisting in the establishment and operation of Air Crew Rescue Unit teams in enemy-occupied territories." In an embarrassing typographical error reflecting a lack of attention to detail, it listed Hayden as "1st Sgt. John Hamilton."[3]

After arriving in Paris, Hayden's orders were endorsed and while he was awaiting transportation to the First Army headquarters, he spontaneously decided to call his wife Madeleine, who was living at 44 Rue Foch. In an anecdote that he only revealed shortly before he died, he described the phone call. "We were headed for divorce and hadn't seen each other for a couple of years but I thought it would be fun to take her out. I called her one evening at her hotel apartment and a man answered. 'I'd like to speak to Miss Carroll, please.' The man said, 'May I ask your name?' I answered, 'What's yours?' The man answered, 'General Dwight Eisenhower,'" Sterling chuckled. "I hung up."[4]

Madeleine was very active in the American Red Cross and her efforts were greatly appreciated by the Allied command, Eisenhower in particular. They had become friends and on occasion did dine together.[5] As implausible as the story might seem, Eisenhower was, in fact, in Paris during February. For her efforts on behalf of the American Red Cross, Madeleine Carroll would be awarded the French Legion of Honor[6] as well as the US Medal of Freedom.

After arriving in Paris, Hayden's orders were endorsed and he was transported by jeep towards the First Amy headquarters near the Belgium border, where the First Army was occupying the Ardennes Forest. The Battle of the Bulge had just ended, signaling the last German offensive of the war. As the jeep was approaching the Belgian town of Spa, the young driver asked Hayden a question he had heard numerous times during the war. "Captain, haven't I seen you somewhere before?"

"Not that I recall," Hayden gruffly replied.

"Captain," continued the inquisitive driver, "if you don't object to the question, is that there a German soldier suit you have on?"

"I'm a Marine."

"A United States Marine?" responded the surprised driver. "Man, you must be lost or something!"[7]

Arriving at Spa, Hayden was quickly billeted and then reported to the senior US First Army intelligence officer, Col. Benjamin A. Dickson, designated as G-2 Officer. Dickson had proven his superior intelligence abilities by predicting the German counterattack that would be known as the Battle of the Bulge in his G-2 Estimate No. 37 of December 10, 1944. The report had been suppressed by his superior officers who wanted to propagate the impression of a defeated German army on the run.[8] Hayden met with Dickson and his staff the following night. As they all took part in devouring a bottle of cognac, Hayden presented his orders. Dickson expressed surprise that a United States Marine had been sent to his headquarters. Before he could respond, Dickson surmised, "Don't tell me. You're OSS—ten thousand dollars says you're one of Donovan's beagles. Right?" After Hayden confirmed the guess, Dickson informed him, "Well, if you're looking for Hitler, he's not here."[9]

As the liquor continued to flow, everyone seemed to enjoy meeting the "new guy." Dickson went on to explain to the others all about the OSS, calling it "the most fantastic damn organization" in all of our armed forces. "Its people do incredible things," he explained. "They seduce German spies; they parachute into Sicily one day and two days later they're dancing on the St. Regis roof." He continued to describe the OSS in this fashion, much to the amusement of all at the meeting. Dickson concluded his analysis by declaring "ninety percent of this has not a goddamn thing to do with the war."[10]

Hayden seemed to enjoy meeting the hierarchy of the G-2 department. It proved to be a different story when he met the head of the OSS detachment to whom he would be directly reporting to. Stuyvesant Wainwright II was about as different from Sterling Hayden as could possibly be imagined. A descendent of Peter Stuyvesant, the last Dutch governor of New York City, he was also related to financier Jay Gould and Gen. Jonathan Wainwright. A graduate of Yale University Law School, he had joined the US Army as a private when the war broke out and was soon commissioned as an officer. He was promptly transferred to the OSS. His patrician, blueblood background was in direct contrast to Hayden's working-class background. He was also five years younger than Hayden. A conservative Republican who would ultimately become a Wall Street lawyer and a member of Congress, his views were diametrically opposed to Hayden's communist sympathies, and he frequently derided Hayden's political views. Hayden enjoyed showing his disdain for his boss by frequently rendering the communist clench-fist salute to Wainwright. Hayden's disrespect ultimately enraged Wainwright, resulting in his recommendation that Hayden be sent to a court-martial.[11] That particular recommendation was never endorsed or acted on.

Hayden took a suggestion from Col. Dickson and had himself attached to the Political Intelligence branch of the G-2 headquarters, thereby escaping Wainwright's clutches. He began working for Maj. Shepard Stone, and life in general was much improved for Hayden. His work was not nearly as exciting as it had been in the Balkans. Stone assigned six sergeants who were fluent in German to Hayden. Their job was to search for genuine anti-Nazis among the German population that they were encountering as the Nazi war machine collapsed.

Traveling the nearly one hundred miles from Cologne to Marburg, Hayden's unit encountered a phenomenon that many Allied soldiers would also experience—it seemed that everyone in Germany had opposed the Nazis. Virtually every German that the unit encountered would claim they were anti-Nazi. Their hypocrisy disgusted Hayden. "It was tough," Hayden was told by these people, as they waved their handkerchiefs and proceeded to wring their hands with joy, "to have lived under Hitler. But, only the night before, they had heated the water that would quickly yield this democratic douche."

"The real anti-Nazis were dead, or in exile, or in Belsen, Auschwitz, Buchenwald," he bitterly noted. "Names, we thought at the time, that would teach us all a lesson we'd never forget."[12] There must have been some genuine anti-Nazis he reflected with disgust. But they couldn't find them, other than scattered pockets of communists in the bigger cities like Dusseldorf and Essen. By May of 1945, Hayden's mission for SI attached to the US First Army was largely concluded and he was about to go on to another less than glamorous assignment.

On May 5, Hayden received verbal orders from his commanding officer relieving him from duty with the Headquarters OSS Detachment and he was ultimately transferred to the Field Photographic Branch. His orders, dated May 24, assigned him as "field officer in charge of intelligence photographic documentation project team."[13] The orders requested expedited clearances "be immediately cut pending transfer procedure to send Capt. Hamilton to the Bremen-Hamburg areas to carry out an urgent operational assignment." He found himself assigned once again to the unit that had worked with him on his ill-fated motion picture project.

Germany had unconditionally surrendered to the Allies on May 7, but the OSS ordered Hayden and his team to proceed to fifty-three different ports throughout Germany, Denmark, and Norway. Their mission was to compile a photographic survey of bomb damage and overall port conditions. After being briefed on his mission, Hayden sarcastically asked his superior officer, "Why? Are we getting ready for the third world war?"[14] He noticed the colonel's apparent lack of amusement at his question. The team proceeded to scour Germany, inspecting the designated ports and then quickly completed its survey of the other two countries. By the end of the summer, their mission was completed. Japan surrendered on August 15, and the war was officially over after the signing of the surrender documents by Japan aboard the USS *Missouri* on September 2, 1945. Like all American servicemen, Sterling Hayden was eager to go home to the United States.

...

In September, Hayden was briefly reunited with his wife Madeleine in Paris. After her work in Europe, she was not eager to return to America. They both sensed that their marriage was over. They realized how little they really had in common and the ten-year age difference had always been a problem for her. The reality was that they had lived together only for a total of four months in their entire three-and-a-half-year marriage.[15] During their short visit, they agreed that Hayden would obtain the divorce in Reno, Nevada, when he returned to the United States.

Hayden felt no sorrow over their impending divorce. "Oddly enough, I didn't feel sad. When you can't love properly, you can't be properly sad."[16] He had gone to her apartment to drop off several boxes of rations and intended to leave after their discussion of divorce. Before he departed, Madeleine asked, "Would you have just one glass of sherry?" He agreed. The awkward conversation was interrupted by a knock on the door. It was an old colleague from his Yugoslavian days. "This," noted Hayden, "was the excuse I needed, the crutch that would take me away.

"My wife," he explained, "is busy. I was just leaving. We will dine together, non?" With that, the befuddled friend politely kissed Madeleine's hand goodbye. Hayden did the same and they left.[17]

It would be three decades before they would see each other again.

...

In mid-November 1945, Sterling Hayden left Europe and arrived back in the United States on November 22. Administratively, all OSS personnel from the Navy Department came under the authority of the Naval Command branch at OSS headquarters. On November 26, Hayden reported in to the Naval Command to begin the separation process. He had served thirty-seven months in the military, twenty-three of them overseas. His decorations included the World War II Victory Medal, the European-African-Middle East Campaign Medal with two Bronze Stars and a bronze arrowhead, a Letter of Commendation, and the Yugoslav Government Order of Merit.[18] During his exit interview, he expressed no desire to remain in the military. His interview form indicates that he had accrued eighty-one separation points, enough to qualify for discharge after the surrender of Japan ended World War II.[19] The interviewer promptly forwarded the interview containing the requisite information up the chain of command.

That same day, a message was released by the commanding officer of the Naval Command naming four officers to be "transferred out of Strategic Services Unit, or discharged, whichever is applicable."[20] One of the four officers was Capt. John Hamilton, USMCR. Hayden was formally discharged from the United States Marine Corps on December 24, 1945.

On February 28, 1946, Hans Tofte submitted a three-page recommendation on behalf of Hayden to have him awarded a Silver Star. The recommendation documented in detail Hayden's heroic actions during Operation AUDREY. The recommendation received positive endorsements as it worked its way up the chop chain. On July 31, 1946, Capt. John Hamilton, USMCR, was awarded a Silver Star for gallantry in the performance of his military duties by the commanding general of the Mediterranean Theater of Operations, United States Army.[21] The citation succinctly read: "For gallantry in action in the Mediterranean Theater of Operations from 24 December 1943 to 2 January 1944. Capt. Hamilton displayed great courage in making hazardous sea voyages in enemy infested waters, and reconnaissances through enemy held areas. His conduct reflected great credit upon himself and upon the United States Armed Forces."

PART THREE

THE SECOND WAR

"I don't mean to attach any importance to myself as an individual who is out of balance, but I have had the feeling that my appearance before the committee could serve a very useful purpose."

STERLING HAYDEN, HUAC TESTIMONY, APRIL 10, 1951

CHAPTER THIRTEEN

Joining the Communist Party in Hollywood

AFTER HIS DISCHARGE FROM THE MARINE CORPS, STERLING HAYDEN wrestled with the dilemma of what to do with his life. His initial thoughts had nothing to do with resuming his film career. He struggled internally with two forces that seemed to pull him in different directions—to return to his first love, the sea, or to pursue what he described as "the political thing." He would later claim that in spite of his political interest, it never occurred to him to join the Communist Party during that time.[1]

Immediately after his discharge on Christmas Eve, Hayden traveled to New York City. Shortly after his arrival, he was contacted by Russell Holman, a local New York agent for Paramount Pictures. They wanted the budding movie star, who was now a war hero, back in the fold and were prepared to pay him well to return to the studio. Although this wasn't in his initial plans, the pragmatist in him realized that he needed the money, and what Paramount was offering him, he couldn't logically refuse. He signed a sweetheart deal with the studio: they would pay him $1,500 a week for the first year and $2,000 a week the second year, while guaranteeing him four months off each year, from June through September. Hayden initially envisioned using those off months to perhaps go on the lecture circuit, talking about the evils of and the fight against fascism.[2] After signing the contract, he also made a personal commitment to himself—he gave up smoking and drinking.

From New York, he next drove across the country to Reno, Nevada, as his next order of business was to obtain a divorce from Madeleine Carroll. He checked into a rooming house next to the local library. The manager of the rooming house looked on as he unloaded his pile of books from his car, mainly leftist literature by authors such as Karl Marx, Vladimir Lenin, and Eugene Debs. He was prepared to hunker down in

Reno for six weeks, the minimum time required to establish residency so he could obtain the divorce. He would describe his stay in Reno as a "prison sentence."[3]

He vowed that he would spend his days mirroring the hours that the Partisans kept in Yugoslavia. From sundown to sunrise, he would work; from sunrise until noon, he would rest; and from noon until sundown, he would walk in the fields and nearby mountains.[4] He had good intentions, but he was soon battling with his two obsessions: women and alcohol. The tall, handsome movie star had no problem finding women to sleep with, and soon he was drinking heavily, consuming his beloved aquavit, and smoking heavily. However, with his senses dulled by alcohol, he started to think about his life, and soon his self-doubts, as well as large doses of self-hatred, began to emerge. Sitting alone on the back porch and looking up at the stars, he was already berating himself for returning to Hollywood and for what he considered his numerous personal failures. "Everything was going or gone: marriage, war, my militant future going. A big boy full of busted resolves and shattered resolutions."[5]

He labeled himself a quitter, a man who was awarded a Silver Star and didn't know why he was so honored. Perhaps, he sarcastically reasoned, it was award for "'quitting with valor': quitting the COI; quitting a naval commission; quitting the *Spinney*; quitting the ranks of enlisted men; quitting the Marine Corps and switching to the OSS, then switching from OSS-Bari to OSS First Army . . . Quitting the sea and the films and the ranks of men who fought for principles; then walking from Madeleine's arms into the cold embrace of Paramount."[6]

It is highly likely that his marked disappointment with the reality of what he learned about the true face of the communist Partisans was also grating at him as he struggled to retain the idealism that he initially felt for the fight against all forms of fascism. Maybe, he reasoned, the totalitarian, top-down dictatorship of communism that he has witnessed wasn't much better than the fascist dictatorships that he opposed. Added to this conundrum were the doubts he experienced when he was drunk about his own commitment to "the cause." "What did I care for labor? For racial discrimination? For civil liberties and the war between the classes? Oh, I cared in my own fashion. I cared just enough to embrace these things as props, flailing away night after night at semi-drunken parties."[7]

The painfully long six weeks finally ended in March. He had established his Nevada state residency and could now file the divorce papers.

His divorce from Madeleine Carroll would be formally granted on May 8, 1946. Meanwhile, he needed some spiritual rejuvenation. He left Reno and headed for the West Coast to see Warwick Tompkins.

• • •

Sterling Hayden arrived in Sausalito in late March and joined his friend Warwick Tompkins aboard his schooner *Wander Bird*. He would recount to the HUAC that this visit also lasted about six weeks. The only thing of significance he would recall about his stay was that Tompkins proposed that he write a book about his young friend. Tompkins, in addition to being a skilled sailor, was a published author. He proposed to Hayden that he write his biography. The angle that he would be using was along the line of "the development of a typical nonpolitical American youth into a militant participant in the class struggle."[8] Somewhat amused by it all, Hayden initially agreed to the project.

Throughout the war, Hayden had also kept up a regular correspondence with his other mentor, Lincoln Colcord. Colcord, the former radical, was upset with the choices that Hayden was making. Specifically, he warned Hayden that he was probably being used by the Communist Party, especially in regard to the proposed biography. Using Tompkins own words—that the proposed biography would demonstrate how a former "escapist sailor," actor, and war hero had emerged as a "leading figure in the anti-fascist struggle at home"—Colcord demanded, "Just what is the anti-fascist struggle at home?" He warned Hayden that if he agreed to have his past written up for Stalinist purposes, he would regret it for the rest of his life.[9]

A few weeks later, Tompkins came down to the Los Angeles area and met with Hayden over a period of about three weeks. He took copious notes on Hayden's life and experiences, eventually writing about seventy-five thousand words. The project started to grate on Hayden's nerves and no doubt the warning from Lincoln Colcord was also weighing on his mind. He began to have real doubts about the project. Finally, after several more weeks, he had had enough of the proposed biography. He contacted Tompkins and told him that he was calling the whole thing off.

• • •

Perhaps it was the idea of being the subject of a book that solidified his desire to become a writer. The fact that he had no background in writing was not a deterrent. After all, with absolutely no acting training of experience, he had already starred in two major Hollywood movies. Nonetheless, it was at this point that he began to seriously consider trying his hand as a writer. Shortly after returning to Hollywood, Hayden rented an apartment where his furnishings included a desk and a typewriter. He believed he was ready to begin this latest endeavor.

He quickly found that he couldn't initiate any writing projects. He was perplexed by his inability to jump in and accomplish something that he felt was very important to him. He could become a master seaman, become a Hollywood matinee idol, join the United States Marine Corps and the OSS, and serve with distinction in World War II, yet he couldn't face the challenge of sitting on front of a typewriter. Years later, in 1982, he would recall the situation in an interview. "But I couldn't write," he recalled. "Even then I was fighting something I'm still fighting, something called a depression, stress, alcoholism. Obviously I'm an alcoholic. At the time I didn't know it, but I couldn't figure out why I couldn't harness myself and function. I seemed to have functioned well in ships. Why couldn't one write?"[10]

• • •

One morning in early June, Hayden awakened in the home of yet another woman he had slept with but whose name he couldn't remember. Indicative of a familiar pattern, he was hung over, struggling to get himself together for a meeting with his agent, Bert Allenberg. He would ruefully recall that at the time, his home was a dressing room at Paramount Pictures, and that he "had $13,000 in the Melrose branch of the Bank of America. I call myself a 'progressive.' I am one of Paramount's stars."[11] Driving away from his latest paramour's apartment, he instinctively headed towards Newport Beach.

It had occurred to him that his home should be a boat and he was determined to find one that morning. Prowling the bay for a while, he came upon a schooner that brought back many memories. It was a boat that he knew well—his first Schooner, *Puritan*. Scanning all of the boats moored at the docks, an abandoned, worn boat caught his eye. It needed a lot of work, but it would not be a challenge for Hayden to get it seaworthy again. Immediately meeting with the yacht broker on the premises, he initially offered $13,500 cash for the *Wetona*. Two hours later, he bought the boat for $14,000 cash.

By three o'clock, he was at Bert Allenberg's office. Despite not having any film offers, he wanted to see what his agent's plans were for him and

Sterling Hayden at sea as a teenager, undated. Courtesy of Catherine Hayden.

Captain Sterling Hayden as King Neptune (seated, center) during the "crossing the line" ceremony aboard the *Florence C. Robinson*, January 1939. From the Sterling Hayden Collection, Howard Gotlieb Archival Research Center at Boston University.

Hayden aboard the *Aldebaran*, December 1939. Courtesy of Catherine Hayden.

Sterling Hayden publicity photo from Paramount Pictures, 1940. Note his first name was spelled "Stirling" in his first two films. From the Sterling Hayden Collection, Howard Gotlieb Archival Research Center at Boston University.

Still photo from Hayden's first film *Virginia*, 1941. L to R: Fred MacMurray, Madeleine Carroll, Sterling Hayden. From the Sterling Hayden Collection, Howard Gotlieb Archival Research Center at Boston University.

Sterling Hayden in Boston, 1941. From the Sterling Hayden Collection, Howard Gotlieb Archival Research Center at Boston University.

Madeleine Carroll, the Duchess of Windsor, Sterling Hayden on the set of *Bahama Passage*, 1941. From the Sterling Hayden Collection, Howard Gotlieb Archival Research Center at Boston University.

Sterling Hayden (on right) as a second lieutenant in the United States Marine Corps assigned to the OSS, Monopoli, Italy, 1943. For the duration of the war, he had legally changed his name to John Hamilton. Courtesy of the OSS Society.

Sterling Hayden at Parris Island, 1942. Courtesy of Catherine Hayden.

Hayden as Dix Handley in *The Asphalt Jungle*, 1950.

The Hayden children—Matthew, Gretchen, Christian, and Dana—peer over the stern of the *Wanderer*, 1959. From the Sterling Hayden Collection, Howard Gotlieb Archival Research Center at Boston University.

Hayden aboard the *Wanderer*, off of Sausalito, 1959. Courtesy of Catherine Hayden.

Hayden aboard the *Wanderer*, undated. From the Sterling Hayden Collection, Howard Gotlieb Archival Research Center at Boston University.

Sterling Hayden, Nantucket Island, 1961. Courtesy of Catherine Hayden.

Hayden's barge *Who Knows*, docked in front of the Hotel Bellevue, Dordrecht, the Netherlands, 1968. Courtesy of Catherine Hayden.

Hayden aboard *Who Knows*, flanked by sons David and Andrew, 1970. Courtesy of Catherine Hayden.

Sterling and Kitty Hayden at a film premiere in New York City, 1979. From the Sterling Hayden Collection, Howard Gotlieb Archival Research Center at Boston University.

Hayden aboard *Who Knows*, 1979. In the background is the famous Pont des Arts that spans the River Seine. Courtesy of Catherine Hayden.

Sterling and Kitty Hayden in front of their home in Wilton, Connecticut, 1982. Courtesy of Catherine Hayden.

Sterling and Kitty Hayden, September 1985. By this time he was gravely ill with cancer. Courtesy of Catherine Hayden.

The Hayden family scatters Sterling's ashes to the sea, May 1986. Courtesy of Catherine Hayden.

if there were any prospects on the horizon. Earlier, Allenberg had informed him: "Nothing doing yet. Relax, Baby, they're paying the money, aren't they?"[12] The receptionist immediately offered apologies as Allenberg had been delayed at Fox and was going to be late for their meeting. Not a problem, replied Hayden, as he settled down to think of a name for his new boat. Considering several possibilities, he finally settled on *Quest*. As he continued to peruse boating magazines, an attractive woman entered the room. "No longer a girl, but graced with a certain look. She is clinched up tight beneath a beige wool suit, a trench coat slung over her arm. We know each other well."[13]

The girl was a secretary in Bert Allenberg's office named Bea Winters. She was already one of Hayden's many friends but she had been specifically pointed out to him by Warwick Tompkins. She and her husband were active in leftist politics, and Hayden admired them for their intellect and their ability to talk on virtually any subject affecting the world, while "all I can do is to drink three to their one and try to look intelligent."[14] After discussing commitment to "the cause," she finally asked him, "Well, when are you going to stop talking and do something?"

"Such as?" he asked.

"Join the Party."

Reaching into her purse, she pulled out several forms and Hayden impulsively signed them, indicating his willingness to join the Communist Party. Almost immediately, he began to feel awkward about joining. Once again, he asked himself, was he running, quitting, searching? He would testify to the HUAC that his initial impression after signing the form was: "This is ridiculous."[15] Perhaps his ambivalence towards his action that day was best summed up when he lay in the bunk of his newly purchased schooner that night and he wondered if there had ever been a man who bought a schooner and joined the Communist Party both on the same day.[16]

...

Shortly after signing his membership papers, Sterling Hayden attended the first meeting of his party branch or "cell," as they were referred to. The membership of the cell consisted of people from Universal, RKO, Columbia, and Paramount studios. To "protect" Hayden, he was assigned to a cell that consisted of what he called "back workers"—carpenters, electricians, etc. There were no other movie stars in his cell. A typical meeting would consist of "from 10 to 22 or 23 people. I think they were happy if they had more than 8."[17] The meetings that he attended over the next six months were conducted exactly the same way. Only first names were used. They were held several times a month at the homes of different members. At the end of each meeting, members would be given the address of the next meeting. No drinking was allowed, although nearly everyone smoked throughout the meetings. The very first meeting was at the home of a man Hayden could only identify as Hjalmar, who was the recording secretary of the cell.

The meetings started promptly at 8 p.m. and lasted three hours. The first hour was devoted to the local Hollywood scene. Issues such as wages and labor-management relationships were discussed in detail. Hayden would recall that he rarely contributed to these discussions. The next hour was "devoted to intensive study of Marxist-Leninist principles." The words were strange to Hayden—writing in the third person, he recalled, "'surplus value,' 'proletariat,' 'bourgeoisie,' and 'deviationism.' Why, hell, the only deviation he is familiar with has to do with a compass. His lack of knowledge appalls him. This is not what he had in mind, and not what he came to hear."[18] He began to tune out the discussion almost immediately.

During the last hour, the world situation would be discussed. He enjoyed this session at his first meeting. He felt that this was at least relevant, departing from the theoretical babbling that served only to bore him. From the situation in China to the accusations that several famous industrialists were already laying the groundwork for the next world war, Hayden felt that at least he was learning something, although he was hesitant to participate in the discussions. "Still he remains aloof;" he wrote in *Wanderer*, "perhaps he is the only at home these days with nonpolitical people, who know as little as he does."[19] At the end of that first meeting, he learned that Bea Winters, a member of his cell, had arranged for him to meet a man named "John," an important person in the Communist Party hierarchy. They would meet privately later that night.

Hayden arrived at a Sunset Boulevard restaurant for the scheduled meeting. Soon after he arrived, "John" walked in. Hayden would later recognize from him subsequent newspaper reports. "John" was John Stapp, a full-time Communist Party organizer for Southern California and chairman of the Hollywood section of the state of California's Communist Party. He was not affiliated in any way with the film industry. Stapp sat down, cigarette dangling from his lips and ordered black coffee while Hayden ordered a scotch. Hayden's initial impression was that

Stapp seemed to be the real thing, the "genuine article, not a hothouse revolutionary." He also immediately sensed that Stapp saw right though him, "as I see through myself sometimes."[20] Stapp promptly asked him why he had joined the Party.

Hayden replied by citing his Yugoslavia experiences and the inspiration he felt fighting with the Partisans. He described the Yugoslav situation before the war as similar to what was currently occurring in the United States, with "plenty of ruthless bastards up on the top of the heap, and there were a number of intellectuals in the middle; but when the going got rough and it was time to be counted, it was the Communists who stood up and fought."[21] Probing further, Stapp solicited Hayden's thoughts on what they thought they were fighting for.

Stapp wanted to know if Hayden had any trade union background experiences. Hayden replied that he hadn't really—he only belonged to the Screen Actors Guild. Stapp smirked derisively, replying, "Some union." He challenged Hayden on why he hadn't belonged to any unions such as the Atlantic Fisherman's Union in all the years he had gone to sea. Hayden patiently explained that Gloucester vessels were non-union. Continuing on as he dragged on his cigarette, Stapp inquired if Hayden had ever been a scab, which Hayden denied. What if the studios found out that he had joined the Communist Party and fired him in spite of his contract? asked Stapp. "To hell with it," replied Hayden. "I'd go back to sea." And if he was called in front of a congressional committee and forced to testify if he had ever been a member of the Communist Party? Hayden had no immediate answer, finally saying that he'd have to think about it.

After the interrogation, Stapp looked at his watch and finally cut to the heart of the matter. "Why do you suppose I wanted to talk with you this way?"

"I have no idea," replied Hayden.

"Well, don't worry about it," shot back the Party organizer as he put his hat back on and rose from his seat. He suggested that they leave separately since he was often followed. As he departed the restaurant, Hayden ordered a double scotch. He would recall that the meeting reminded him of his previous meeting with V. J. Jerome and gave him the impression that Stapp was deciding if Hayden would measure up. "He didn't say anything to me at all. I think that he said he doubted that I'd make a good Communist, but I am not sure."[22] While there is no actual record of Stapp's impression of Sterling Hayden that resulted from the meeting, Hayden's description leads one to agree with his assessment.

He likely appeared to Stapp as more of an uninformed amateur dilettante than a committed revolutionary. It is reasonable to assume that in Stapp's mind, Sterling Hayden could function as another celebrity "useful idiot" in service to their cause.

Future events would prove Stapp wrong.

...

By the mid-1930s, the labor force in Hollywood was ripe for organization and collective bargaining through unionization. Two opposing forces would descend on Los Angeles and vie for control of the unions representing the workers who worked behind the scenes in every movie production. First was the International Alliance of Theatrical Stage Employees (IATSE), founded in New York City in 1893. By the 1930s, IATSE was dominated by the mob and used strong-arm tactics to keep its membership in line. A second, more militant force emerged to challenge the IATSE for control of the Hollywood unions in the mid-1940s, when the Conference of Studio Unions (CSU), led by Herbert Sorrell, was formed.

In September of 1946, the CSU went on strike for the second time in a year. About that time, Sterling Hayden was attending another cell meeting. While the location of the meetings tended to vary, by the summer they were mainly held in the home of Abe Polonsky, an acclaimed screenwriter who had written the screenplays for influential films such as *Body and Soul*. Polonsky had joined the Communist Party in the 1930s and served in the OSS in Europe during the war. Although Polonsky initially didn't attend the meetings held in his home, he later became a regular at the meetings. Hayden had the impression that he was, in fact, the leader of their cell. At that meeting, Hayden was given an assignment by the cell leadership.

As previously noted, Hayden was the only actor and certainly the only recognizable celebrity in the group. He was also a member of the Screen Actors Guild (SAG) and for that reason he was uniquely qualified for the assignment. At the time, the Communist Party was sympathetic to the cause of the CSU and its cells were encouraged to foster support for Sorrell's union. "I was told that it would be very helpful and important," recalled Hayden, "if the Screen Actors Guild could be swung into line in support of this strike."[23] His first action in this regard was to attend a large cocktail party attended by "60 or 70 people," all actors and actresses interested in the strike.

While there is no doubt some members of the SAG were sympathetic to the CSU cause, whether Hayden may have had any success in his efforts to steer the SAG actors to supporting the CSU strike is questionable. The SAG did have a turn towards progressivism under the presidency of James Cagney, who served as the SAG leader from 1942–44. However, by mid-October of 1946, the strike had turned violent, with five homes of IATSE members being bombed. This happened in spite of SAG efforts to mediate the dispute. The accusations were immediately directed at Sorrell's CSU and at Sorrell, whose consistently bellicose and uncompromising behavior was losing him supporters. Many opponents of the CSU felt that their strike was part of a long range Communist strategy to control the motion picture industry.[24]

In a further effort to resolve the strike, a delegation led by SAG president Ronald Reagan traveled to the American Federation of Labor meeting in Chicago in September. His efforts were unsuccessful. He came away from the negotiations believing that the CSU did not want to settle the strike unless the IATSE was completely destroyed.[25] The SAG membership began to shift its support to the IATSE. It was the beginning of the end of the CSU. In early 1947 the strike ended and the CSU was destroyed. In July of 1947, the United States Congress, overriding President Harry S. Truman's veto, passed the Taft-Hartley Act. An amendment to the National Labor Relations Act of 1935, the Taft-Hartley Act, among other things, put limits on what Congress considered unfair labor practices by unions, also requiring union leaders to assert that they were not Communist Party members or acting on behalf of the Communist Party.

More importantly, the stage had been set for Washington to begin its investigation into Communist infiltration and influence in the film industry.

• • •

By the fall of 1946, Sterling Hayden was already becoming disillusioned with the Communist Party. He was increasingly disturbed at the mind-control efforts that seemed to be at the root of his cell's philosophy. Just as he had become disgusted with the Communist style of "democracy" as he observed how the Communist leadership dealt with the common people during Operation HACIENDA, he quickly became disgusted with the direction in which his cell of the Communist Party was moving. It is also possible that the Hollywood conflicts between the studios and the labor force didn't, in his mind, quite equal the exhilaration he felt when fighting for a people's freedom from Nazi fascism in Yugoslavia. The issues, which were becoming murky towards the end of his tour in the Balkans, had become even murkier in his current environment. Hayden had always been too much of his own man to fit into any rigid organization. Reflecting on his reasons why he left the Party the following year, he stated: "Because I'd rather be wrong on my own terms than be right on somebody else's say-so. Also I was scared, just a little."[26] In an interview given in 1984 he explained it more colorfully. "I decided right away it wasn't for me. My first thought was 'Fuck the revolution, what about my date with Charlene?' I wasn't committed. Also, I couldn't read dialectic and historical materialism, though I tried."[27] In another interview, given in 1977 to talk show host Tom Snyder, Hayden stated, "I got out, I must say quite candidly, primarily because I'm not a man who can take discipline."[28] In any event, Hayden—the only film star in his Communist cell—resigned from the Party in December of 1946, only six months after he had joined.

• • •

The next year, 1947, would prove to be a pivotal year in Sterling Hayden's life. A series of events were converging that would entangle him in both personal and professional crises. Once again, these events centered around women and politics. Both would nearly destroy him.

Shortly after his divorce from Madeleine Carroll, Hayden met Betty Anne De Noon, a beautiful blonde divorcee and they soon became smitten with each other. Like Hayden, the twenty-three-year-old De Noon shared a passion for sailing. They were soon inseparable and married in May of 1947. Hayden would describe the first ten months of their relationship as truly wonderful, giving him "the peace I've never known before."[29] Beginning in January 1947, they lived aboard Hayden's boat moored in Santa Barbara's harbor.

At first they each became the entire world for each other as they appeared to turn their backs on the rest of the world. "No parties no politics no meetings, just work on the ship all day and read and dream all night. The feel and smell of the sea, and the cries of the birds. What more could any man want?"[30] With his new sense of contentment, Hayden also curbed his drinking. But even this new sense of fulfillment with a beautiful, strong-willed wife seemed to bring him only temporary relief from his constant search for something in which to believe. By the time they left on their honeymoon in June, the marriage was already starting to come undone.

They drove across the country from Nevada to Gloucester, Massachusetts, where they planned to spend time with his old colleague Larry O'Toole and his wife. They spent the entire journey fighting with each other. By the time they checked into the Yankee Clipper Inn on the Gloucester waterfront, the Haydens were barely speaking to each other. As they silently checked into their room, Betty finally spoke, insisting that they cancel their plans for the evening's get-together with the O'Tooles. She did not want to watch the movies that Hayden and O'Toole had taken of a hula dancer in Tahiti, chiding her husband that he was so insecure that he had to "show old movies to his friends of a dame dancing the hula—some broad he laid in Tahiti."[31] Hayden promised there would be no movies that night.

The night evolved just as Betty had feared it would. Despite the efforts of the extremely extroverted O'Toole and his wife Ida to engage their friend's new wife, Hayden realized that she showed no warmth at all to the O'Tooles. No doubt the movie projector that O'Toole had set up had fueled her anger from the moment they arrived. Hayden had brought a bottle of his favorite aquavit and, as Betty knew they would, Hayden and O'Toole proceeded to get drunk. Finally, it was Hayden who called for the light to be extinguished so they could begin the movie. Making matters worse, a very drunk O'Toole walked over to Betty as the film flickered on the screen and planted a kiss on her forehead, exclaiming, "Hiyah, Mommy, having a good time?"[32]

As the image of the sailors and the boat approaching Tahiti appeared, Betty's anger grew. By the time the topless hula dancer appeared, she had had enough. As Hayden and O'Toole leered at the dancer, Betty got up and left to go back to the Yankee Clipper Inn. Hayden remained to finish the entire film with his friend. When the confused O'Toole asked what happened to his friend's wife, Hayden covered for her, saying she was tired from the drive.

Driving back to his hotel, Hayden contemplated why he had done exactly what his wife had insisted he not do. He had no real answers, but the thoughts he expressed that night spoke volumes about the true love of his life. "Nothing too bad can happen," he reasoned, "as long as the ships last and the sea doesn't disappear." If his marriage failed, he could always sell the *Quest*, go to Europe and buy a large vessel and return to sea.[33] He arrived back at their hotel room to find Betty was awake.

"Sterling, I want you to drive me to Boston in the morning, I'm flying back to the coast."

"Very well," he replied.

"And mark my words," she ominously threatened, "I'll get even with you if it's the last thing I do."

"Have it your way," was his only response.[34]

Their honeymoon in Gloucester lasted exactly one day. It would serve as a harbinger of what was to come in their turbulent marriage.

However, in 1947 even more trouble was coming to Sterling Hayden, this time on a professional level that would potentially ruin his film career. The House Committee on Un-American Activities was coming to Hollywood. Its target: Communist infiltration into the film industry.

CHAPTER FOURTEEN

Searching for Subversives in Hollywood

THE COMMUNIST PARTY'S INVOLVEMENT IN HOLLYWOOD AND THE ORIgin of what would become its archenemy, the House Un-American Activities Committee or HUAC, both came into existence within two years of each other. In 1936, the Communist Party (CP) had decided to become active in the movie industry and sent out two people to organize "fellow travelers" in Hollywood. Dispatched to the movie capital to set up a Hollywood branch of the CP were V. J. Jerome, a cultural commissar, and Stanley Lawrence, a CP organizer. The appointed head of the Hollywood branch was screenwriter John Howard Lawson.[1]

The House Un-American Activities Committee had its origins back in 1938. Founded as the temporary Special Committee on Un-American Activities by Congressman Martin Dies (D-Texas) and Congressman Samuel Dickstein (D-New York), it was chaired by Dies and was informally known as the Dies Committee. Its mandate was to investigate disloyalty of private citizens towards the United States as well as to investigate subversive activities on the part of American citizens. Spurred on through the efforts of Congressman John Rankin (D-Mississippi), it was renamed the House Un-American Activities Committee and became a permanent committee of the House of Representatives in 1945.

Just prior to the beginning of World War II, in an effort to counter growing fears of Soviet espionage and subversive activities in the United States, Attorney General Francis Biddle drew up a list of organizations that were designated as Soviet-controlled front organizations. The list, known as the Biddle List, contained eleven organizations, including American League Against War and Fascism, the American Youth Congress, the League of American Writers, and the National Negro Congress. Throughout the war years, the threat of Communist infiltration of American life, or "the Red Menace," was never far from the thoughts of government officials, especially FBI director J. Edgar Hoover.

In 1947, with the Cold War heating up around the world, President Harry S. Truman could not allow his critics and political enemies to believe that he was soft on the communist menace. In March he promulgated what became known as the Truman Doctrine, pledging increased aid to Greece and Turkey to combat Soviet communist expansionism in Europe. He could scarcely afford to be any less tough on communism at home. On March 22, 1947, he signed Executive Order 9835. Known as the Loyalty Order, it established for the first time a loyalty program intended to stamp out communist influence in the United States government. The Federal Employee Loyalty Program authorized the FBI to do extensive background checks on all federal employees. As a direct result of the signing of Executive Order 9835 into law on April 3, 1947, an updated version of the Biddle List was issued. Now called the Attorney General's List of Subversive Organizations, the greatly expanded list included many organizations believed to be Communist front organizations. With this background, HUAC turned it sights in earnest on Hollywood.

Congressman J. Parnell Thomas (R-NJ), chairman of HUAC, called for hearings to commence in the fall of 1947 to examine Communist infiltration and subversion of Hollywood. The film industry's initial response was that of disgust and frustration. "Hollywood is weary of being the national whipping boy for congressional committees," complained the Association of Motion Picture Producers (AMPP). "We are tired of irresponsible charges made again and again and again and not sustained. If we have committed a crime we want to know it. If not, we should not be badgered by congressional committees."[2] In spite of these objections, in September HUAC issued subpoenas to forty-one members of the Hollywood community, with an emphasis on screenwriters.

Of the forty-one persons subpoenaed to appear before the committee in Washington, nineteen of them announced their intentions not to cooperate with HUAC. The hearings began on October 20, 1947. During the first week of the hearings the initial members called proved to be friendly witnesses. Studio head Jack Warner provided the committee with a list of persons he felt were communists. Novelist Ayn Rand found communist propaganda in the smiling faces of Russian children in *Song of Russia*.[3] Actor Robert Taylor expressed his contempt for communists and their sympathizers in Hollywood and expressed the opinion that if it were up to him, they would all be shipped back to Russia. It was during the second week of the hearings that the "unfriendly" witnesses were called to testify.

Eleven of the nineteen subpoenaed witnesses who announced their intention not to cooperate were called in front of the committee. Playwright Bertolt Brecht, after denying that he ever applied to become a member of the Communist Party, promptly fled the country. The other ten were all prominent screenwriters and directors. Many of Hollywood's biggest stars and prominent directors protested what they felt was a threat to freedom of speech as guaranteed by the United States Constitution. To counter what was perceived as the unfair inquisition that the HUAC was conducting against free speech in the film industry, the Committee for the First Amendment (CFA) was formed in Hollywood.

The Committee for the First Amendment was organized in Hollywood largely through the efforts of directors John Huston and William Wyler and screenwriter Phillip Dunne. The committee's core basic tenet—that "any investigation into the political beliefs of the individual is contrary to the basic principles of our democracy. Any attempt to curb freedom of expression and to set arbitrary standards of Americanism is in itself disloyal to both the spirit and the letter of the Constitution"—was strongly endorsed by many of the Hollywood establishment. This included Katharine Hepburn, Gregory Peck, Henry Fonda, and Ava Gardner.[4] One of the active members of the new committee was actor Alexander Knox, most widely known for his portrayal of President Woodrow Wilson in the 1944 film *Wilson*. That September, Sterling Hayden received a phone call from Knox, telling him about the new committee they were forming and asking him to join. Hayden replied that he would think it over. Soon thereafter, Hayden attended a gathering in support of the newly formed group at the home of Ira Gershwin, where several hundred Hollywood celebrities were also in attendance. The spokesmen for the group were Huston and Dunne. Impressed with the group's membership and leadership, as well as the message they conveyed, Hayden decided to join. The committee, as reported in *Daily Variety*, "plans a backfire against the House Un-American Activities Committee via a drive to battle the top headlines out of Washington each day," while carefully noting that the membership "declared themselves to be anti-Communist."[5]

The CFA issued a formal statement alleging several abuses by the HUAC, the most serious of which was that HUAC was running, in essence, a criminal trial, but that none of the accused was given the privilege of self-defense statements or the right to cross-examine their accusers. The formal statement was signed by twenty-eight prominent members of the Hollywood community. Among the signatories were Sterling Hayden and his wife Betty.[6]

The committee decided to send a delegation to Washington to attend the hearings when the unfriendly witnesses were to testify to see if the hearings were conducted fairly. Hayden was one of the members of the delegation that attended. Also attending were Humphrey Bogart and Lauren Bacall, as well as Danny Kaye, Frank Sinatra, and Groucho Marx. The fifty-person delegation made multiple stops along the way to Washington to drum up support. Arriving in the nation's capital, they presented their formal statement to the clerk of the House of Representatives just before the hearings were to resume. Heads turned as Hayden and his fellow movie stars seated themselves in the gallery at the start of the week when the questioning of the unfriendly witnesses began on October 27.

The ten unfriendly witnesses, who would become known in history as the Hollywood Ten, were comprised of eight prominent screenwriters and two prominent directors. It may or may not have been known to many of their Hollywood celebrity advocates in the audience that day that most of the unfriendly witnesses had been or still were members of the Communist Party. The screenwriters were Alvah Bessie, Lester Cole, Ring Lardner Jr., John Howard Lawson, Albert Maltz, Sam Ornitz, Robert Adrian Scott, and Dalton Trumbo. The directors were Herbert Biberman, and Edward Dmytryk.

The Hollywood delegation's plan was to arrive for the hearings on October 27 just when Eric Johnston, president of the Motion Picture Association of America, was set to testify. They felt that the presence of the Hollywood delegation would bolster Johnston's testimony. Prior to their departure for Washington, William Wyler had briefed the group about the importance of timing and perception for their mission. He told them to stay away from unfriendly witnesses. He knew the news media would say they were there defending communists when their purpose in going to Washington was "to attack the House Un-American Activities Committee and not to defend any Communists."[7] Their well-meaning strategy was soon shattered by HUAC chairman J. Parnell Thomas.

Thomas masterfully manipulated the situation to put the Hollywood delegation in a bad light. As the delegation seated itself, Thomas changed the order of witnesses and instead of calling Eric Johnston, he called as the first witness John Howard Lawson. Lawson, head of the Hollywood branch of the Communist Party, proved to be an extremely combative and belligerent witness. However sympathetic to Lawson any member of the delegation of members of the CFA might have been, his shouting, insolent performance put him and the other Hollywood Ten in an extremely bad light from the beginning. This all played directly into Thomas's hands when later that afternoon at a news conference, reporters suggested that the Hollywood delegation's presence at the hearings would be interpreted all over the country as support for Lawson. The demoralized committee members lasted one more day of testimony and left Washington feeling foolish and defeated. "We've been had!" they told each other.[8] The well-intentioned Committee for the First Amendment had accomplished nothing, and their situation continued to spiral downhill after the end of the HUAC hearings.

Each member of the Hollywood Ten refused to answer the questions posed to them by the HUAC, the most important of which was, "Are you now, or have you ever been a member of the Communist Party?" Towards the end of the week, Eric Johnston testified that he would never "employ any proven or admitted Communist because they are just a disruptive force and I don't want them around."[9] On November 24, the House of Representatives voted 346–17 to hold the Hollywood Ten in contempt of Congress. If the CFA thought that they would find sympathy with their cause from the studio executives, they were badly mistaken.

On the same day that the HUAC was voting to find the Hollywood Ten in contempt of Congress, fifty Hollywood executives were meeting in New York City at the Waldorf-Astoria Hotel, representing the Motion Picture Association of America, the Association of Motion Picture Producers, and the Society of Independent Motion Picture Producers. The studio heads that participated in the meeting included Louis B. Mayer of Metro-Goldwyn-Mayer, Dore Schary of RKO Pictures, Harry Cohn of Columbia Pictures, and Samuel Goldwyn of the Samuel Goldwyn Company. After two days of deliberations, the group issued a policy statement that came to be known as the Waldorf Statement. The statement was nothing less than a wholesale endorsement of the HUAC's actions. Eric Johnston, as president of the Motion Picture Association of America, read the statement to the press. The opening paragraph set the tone: "Members of the Association of Motion Picture Producers deplore the action of the ten Hollywood men who have been cited for contempt of the House of Representatives. We do not desire to pre-judge their legal rights, but their actions have been a disservice to their employers and have impaired their usefulness to the industry."[10]

Other key elements of the Waldorf Statement left no doubt what the policies of the studios would be. "We will forthwith discharge or suspend without compensation those in our employ and we will not re-employ any of the ten until such time as he is acquitted or has purged himself of contempt and declares under oath that he is not a Communist." Studios would never employ a communist or anyone who advocated the overthrow of the United States government. Acknowledging that there was a risk that innocent people could be hurt in the process, the group vowed to be vigilant against such a possibility. Thus, on November 25, 1947, the Hollywood blacklist was born.

Almost immediately, the Committee for the First Amendment began to implode. One Washington newspaper issued a report that one of the CFA members who had traveled to Washington—Sterling Hayden—was actually a communist. William Wyler was incensed by the accusation and called the committee members together. He requested that they all raise funds to be used so that Hayden could sue for libel. Hayden, of course, knew that the accusation was true. The idea to raise funds was dropped and the particular issue died down.[11] Hayden had dodged a bullet—at least for the time being.

The Committee for the First Amendment continued in its death spiral. It had failed in its mission, instead appearing to represent communist sympathizers. The studio executives—the very people who had provided the actors with comfortable and, in many cases, lavish lifestyles—had made their position on the matter very obvious. The stars, understanding the studio heads' support of the HUAC, began backtracking. In December, Humphrey Bogart and his wife Lauren Bacall held a press conference during which Bogart described the Hollywood delegation's trip to Washington as "ill advised, even foolish."[12] Bogart went even further, writing an article that appeared in the March 1948 issue of *Photoplay* entitled "I'm No Communist!" that proved to be the final nail in the coffin of the Committee for the First Amendment.

In the following years, the Committee for the First Amendment was branded as a Communist front organization. Members of the committee would hotly deny the accusation. Years later, William Wyler, one of the group's founders and leaders, would state: "Of course the Attorney General said it was a Communist front, and apparently a front organization is what the Attorney General decides. But it was *not* a Communist-front organization. There may have been some communists in the group, but then there are probably Communists in any organization. The point is, they did not run the Committee, and a Communist-front organization is one that is run by Communists. *We* ran the Committee and we were not Communists."[13] Hayden's views on the Committee mirrored those of Wyler. "I thought it over very carefully, and I assured myself that—I may be wrong, but my conclusion was that this was in no way a Communist front at the time," he recalled in 1951.[14]

The members of the Hollywood Ten, having been found in contempt of Congress, were put on trial, and in April 1948, each was found guilty. Each was sentenced to a year in jail and fined $1,000. The Ten appealed the ruling and the case made its way up to the Supreme Court. The court refused to hear the appeals, and the Hollywood Ten all served their sentences starting in 1950. The Hollywood hearings conducted by the HUAC were suspended while the appeals of the Ten worked their way through the judicial system. With the Hollywood Ten finally being jailed, the hearings would resume in 1951. That year, Sterling Hayden's past flirtations with communism would finally catch up with him.

• • •

The years 1947 through 1949 were difficult for Sterling Hayden. His relationship with his wife Betty evolved into one of continual conflict, probably inevitable considering the strong-willed, independent nature they each possessed. Throughout this time, the Haydens lived together on various boats moored not far from the San Pedro hills. Initially, their devotion to each other excluded the rest of the world. "We ate each other up," he would recall.[15]

He was desperately unhappy during this time. His recollections in *Wanderer* would often reflect this combination of depression and self-doubt, coupled with a measure of self-hatred. "I lived in a downward spiraling, diminishing, darkening world. I lived on a ship that was no ship, with a wife who was no wife (no fault of hers) . . . But I had been the golden boy, capturing the imagination of the crowd, born to the sea. I had been the man who didn't care, who thumbed his nose at all the proper things beloved of proper people . . . But now the past was dying. I had raked its coals till all that remained was ash. My stories were all told out. No new friends came, and only sleep was pleasing."[16]

The stresses of his home life were intensified by two major factors: his heavy drinking and his professional inactivity, despite his enviable salary. He had evolved into a highly functional alcoholic, one who was able to infuse a bizarre bit of self-discipline in his destructive habits. "I drank a great deal," he would recall, "but drew the line at real benders. Apparently the same force that prevented me from giving myself to life also blunted the self-destructive process. I could drink till I passed out. But, always, four hours later I would roll out, plunge or shower, then bundle up and read till dawn, when I ran or walked or cycled or rowed for hours. Then I'd settle back and drift though the daylight hours like a ghost, with never a drink till dusk."[17] Greatly exacerbating his self-destructive behavior was his lack of work in Hollywood.

He had no regrets about his decision to leave the Communist Party. In the summer of 1947, he was contacted by actress Karen Morley, a member of the Party cell to which he had once belonged. She arranged a meeting at Hayden's home and came quickly to the point of her visit. She asked Hayden to consider coming back into the Party. With all the personal demons tormenting him at this point in his life, coupled with his disenchantment with the Party and communism in general, it was the last thing he would consider doing. He flatly refused but Morley countered by asking him to contribute money if he wasn't willing to rejoin the Party. This, too, Hayden refused. As he was escorting her to the front door, she turned to him and said, "I hope you realize that having made that decision, it will be extremely hard for you to ever get back in." He tersely replied: "Nothing will please me more."[18]

In late 1946, he co-starred in a film for Paramount Pictures entitled *Blaze of Noon*. This adaption of an Ernest K. Gann novel was a story about the early days of aviation and was notable for the return to the screen of both Hayden and another young World War II veteran, William Holden. Released in early 1947, the picture generated little box-office enthusiasm. Hayden would not work at all in 1947, despite collecting a salary of $70,000 from Paramount. In 1948, he made two more films: *El Paso* and *Manhandled*. Both were released in mid-1949 and were box-office flops. "Both were abortions," described Hayden, "conceived and dead in less than three weeks."[19] His infrequent work schedule was killing him, fueling his drinking. "From June 1946 to June 1949 I worked 75 days—out of 1,095. The rest of the time I did nothing."[20]

In the summer of 1948, Hayden read that famed explorer and adventurer Thor Heyerdahl was coming to the Los Angeles area for a series of lectures. The previous year, Heyerdahl had sailed five thousand miles across the Pacific Ocean from South America to the Tuamotu Islands in a hand-built raft, attempting to test his theory that cross-ocean travel by ancient peoples could prove a link between Polynesia and South America. He would recount his exploits in the best-selling book *Kon-Tiki*. Fellow sailor Hayden had been very impressed with Heyerdahl's voyage and he invited the explorer to stay with him and Betty aboard their schooner. Heyerdahl accepted Hayden's gracious offer and for two days, shared his vast and fascinating experiences with his host.

The second day of the visit, Hayden invited his mother to come over and meet the famous explorer. It would turn out to be a visit with profound personal consequences for Hayden. In front of their distinguished guest, Frances Hayden asked her son why he hadn't attempted something along the lines of Heyerdahl's voyage. Her annoyed son mumbled something to the effect that he hadn't believed that the voyage in the flimsy raft was even possible. "Well," responded his mother, "I must say, Buzzie [*sic*], it would be a good deal better than sitting here the way you have been doing."[21] The criticism of her son in front of their distinguished guest struck a chord with Hayden. He had been sensitive to his mother's opinions all of his life. Now that he was emotionally at rock bottom, drinking heavily and still struggling to establish his real identity, the comments in front of Heyerdahl served as a wake-up call to him. Interestingly, he came to the immediate conclusion that his mother needed psychiatric help, and he promptly determined to get her that help. It would prove to be one of the key decisions of his life, but the result of his decision would have nothing to do with his mother.

• • •

Sterling Hayden frequently described his visits with his psychiatrist in the last third of *Wanderer*. He never mentioned the psychiatrist by name, nor did he explain how he came to be seen by this particular doctor. He did confirm that he initially brought his mother to see him and they talked about her for over an hour. Hayden's request was simple: he wished the doctor could make her understand that "she has to get off my back."[22] The doctor countered by suggesting to Hayden that, as a result of what he had learned by speaking to his mother that morning, perhaps he (Hayden) would benefit from some intensive psychiatric help. At first, Hayden seemed surprised by the doctor's suggestion, sitting there in silence while smoking. He then unexpectedly had a fresh insight into himself and his life. "Nothing else has worked: not the running, searching, drinking, screwing; not the battling, and the dreaming; not the escapism or the Communism or the nihilistic thinking. I nod my head: 'Yes, I know that. Maybe I've known it for a long time.'"

"Think it over, why don't you?" recommended the doctor.

"I don't have to think it over," he resolutely replied.[23]

Ten years later, he would refer to the decision to enter psychoanalysis as a turning point in his life. He would always consider his dealings with psychiatry to be a positive thing that helped him in the crises he was soon to encounter. He had an ambivalent feeling towards his psychiatrist, both praising the good he felt resulted from the man's efforts and damning his style, which was basically to let Hayden vent while he listened, rarely speaking himself. "To your dismay," he noted, again writing in the third person, "the analyst seems maliciously detached. You thought he would give you a hand when things got rough. Some laugh. The joke is on you—at twenty-five bucks an hour. Five hundred bucks a month you pay for the honor of lying flat and talking to a blank screen. Fuck you, Doc."[24]

As it turned out, the man Hayden called "Doc" was not a medical doctor, nor was he a PhD. He had three years of post-graduate training in psychology, but no doctoral degree. His name was Ernest Philip Cohen and he had a thriving Hollywood practice that included many of Hollywood's elite. Cohen, who joined the Communist Party in 1939, could claim luminaries such as Lloyd Bridges and John Garfield as his patients. Many of them were either members, former members, or were somehow affiliated with the Communist Party. Like Sterling Hayden, many of them were ultimately called before HUAC to testify when the Hollywood hearings resumed in 1951.

Cohen occupied a unique position given the Communist Party's hostility towards psychoanalysis and its general rule against its membership undergoing treatment with psychiatric practitioners. The Party considered psychoanalysis as inconsistent with Marxist principles: you were subjecting yourself to the propaganda of the enemy. Psychoanalysis was considered to be a tool of the class enemy to justify the inequities of society by attributing them to flaws in personality rather than the system. Another issue underlying the Communists' disdain for psychoanalysis was that, as a result of the doctor-patient relationship, the patient would reveal to the doctor everything about themselves. There was a great fear that the Party's security as a secret organization would be compromised.[25] Seeing a psychiatric practitioner was grounds for expulsion from the Party. Screenwriter Bernard Gordon, a Party member, commented on this dilemma in his memoirs. "Party or therapist? This was a choice most of us were reluctant to make. A solution was found. The Party came up with a 'safe' therapist who had been a party functionary in Seattle and who had a dialectical-materialist attitude, rather than a strict Freudian one, towards social and personal problems. Enter Ernest Philip Cohen."[26] Hence, Cohen was one of the few psychiatric practitioners acceptable for active and former party members. Exactly who recommended him to Hayden is not known.

Many of Cohen's patients had interactions with him similar to Hayden's and noted his unorthodox manners. Treating members of the same family was not a problem with him and he had no set fees—patients paid what they could afford. It was not unusual for Cohen to socialize with his patients. They all called him Phil during their treatments. Like Hayden, they all became very dependent on him. "This all led to what was called a transference, in which the patient becomes extremely dependent on and close to the therapist," recalled Gordon, "who, in effect, becomes the surrogate father, mother, lover, or whatever the patient needed. In this state, the patient opened up completely and related his innermost thoughts and feelings so that they could be examined by both parties."[27]

Like Hayden, Gordon became dependent on his sessions with Cohen and was totally open with him. When Gordon learned that many of Cohen's patients, including Sterling Hayden, were testifying as friendly witnesses when the HUAC resumed its hearings in 1951, he was stunned and felt betrayed by his psychologist. It would later be revealed that Cohen had a strong working relationship with attorney Martin Gang, who also had a clientele of the Hollywood elite that was virtually identical to Cohen's. Included among Gang's clients was Sterling Hayden. Yet Gordon offered this assessment: "I feel obliged to say that, along with many of my friends who were patients of his, I believe that I benefitted from therapy with him . . . Perhaps the blend of Freud and Marx that Phil Cohen practiced was useful, even if the practitioner himself turned out to be a Hannibal Lechter."[28]

• • •

In a session with Cohen in mid-to-late 1949, Hayden revealed to him an issue that gives insights into both Hayden's desire to be taken seriously as an actor and his insecurities. He realized that his career was stagnating and that, at best, he was developing into a "beefcake" B-movie star who would never be taken seriously. A few days earlier, his agent contacted him and told him he was about to get the break that would make his career. Taking him over to MGM Studios, he had made an appointment for Hayden to meet with director John Huston concerning Huston's next film project, a crime caper titled *The Asphalt Jungle*. Hayden, of course, already knew Huston from their membership in the Committee for the First Amendment and their journey as members of the Hollywood delegation to the 1947 hearings.

Upon entering Huston's office, Hayden was immediately greeted with Huston's magnetic charm and made to feel like he was the most important man in the world to the director. Instructing his secretary to hold all of his calls, he got right to the point with Hayden. "May I tell you something?" he asked. "I've admired you for a long time. They don't know what to make of a guy like you in this business. Maybe we'll change all that.

"Now, Sterling," he continued, "I want you to do this part. The studio does not. They want a top name star. They say you mean nothing when it comes to box-office draw—I told them there aren't five names in this town that mean a damn thing at the box office. Fortunately, they're not making the picture. I am. Now let me tell you about Dix Handley."[29] After describing Dix Handley, the character Huston wanted Hayden to play, he pointed out one problem. The studio did insist that Hayden do a screen test for the role. Huston was confident that it would go well. Although promising to do his best, Hayden wasn't so sure.

Lying on Cohen's couch the next day, Hayden shared his anxiety. The session started out similar to all the prior ones, with Cohen instructing his patient to speak whatever came to his mind. Hayden remained silent for a few minutes, contemplating how he and his wife were fighting more than ever despite the psychoanalysis that Hayden had assumed would help the situation. After a few minutes, Cohen instructed him to verbalize what he was thinking. It was at that point that Hayden exploded.

"All right," he exclaimed. "You want what comes into my mind, I'll give you what comes into my mind: I'm in plenty of trouble, Doc; haven't worked in a hell of a long time. So far as this town's concerned, I might as well be dead. Paramount fired me. Everyone knows that. I'm spending fifteen hundred bucks a month just to keep on living. Nothing coming in, and there's five thousand left in the bank. These aren't the right thoughts, are they? I ought to be talking about crawling between the babysitter's legs, but I can't because yesterday something exciting happened."[30]

After recapping his meeting with Huston, he laid it out for his therapist. "Goddammit, I've got to land this part. If I do, I'm all set." Elaborating on his insecurity, he got to the crux of his concern—the screen test. "Tests are rough, the worst thing about the whole racket. I always tense up in front of the camera. I don't want to, but I do. Now for the next few days why can't I just sit up and talk to you man to man and maybe you can explain this fear to me?" Once again, Cohen continued to listen and not speak.

Hayden continued to explain how important the role was to him. This was the first time in his autobiography where he seemed to express a desire to become a competent actor and to be taken seriously. This could be the role that would make his career. But first he had to get over his fear of the upcoming screen test. "Why do I always freeze?" he asked. "Shit! I went through the war. I jumped out of bombers. I played kick-the-can with E-boats when all we had was a lousy forty-foot dragger with six machine guns and a top speed of six knots. Yet whenever I get a close-up in a nice warm studio I curl up and die. Why?" In his typical laconic style, Cohen merely observed that their time was up. "Articulate sonofabitch" was all Hayden could think to himself.[31]

The day of the screen test, Hayden arrived early and realized with some surprise that he didn't seem nervous. All good actors are a little nervous when they audition, he reflected. Maybe he just wasn't a good actor, he ruefully mused. Entering the studio, he watched the screen test of another actor who was auditioning for the part of Dix Handley. Despite his pledge to Phil Cohen that he would give up smoking in preparation for his screen test, he reached into his pocket and pulled out a cigarette. He took a deep drag and watched as the other actor departed and they called out his name. As he walked to the set, John Huston appeared and placed his arm around Hayden as he escorted him to the stage. He introduced him to Jean Hagen, who would be playing Handley's love interest and then gave Hayden his sage advice. "Kid, play it the way it feels best. Lie down, sit up, walk around, do any damn thing you please," instructed Huston. "Wherever you go, we'll follow. Take your time. Let me know when you're ready."

For a minute, Hayden just sat there, and then he looked at Huston, who nodded back at him. "Action!" he yelled. And Hayden froze, just as he feared he would. But only for a moment. Jean Hagen read her lines to him, asking him to tell her about his dream and suddenly, for the first time in his acting career, something happened. "Then slowly my joints unlock, I shiver a little, and for the first time I begin to act." He responded as Dix Handley, sharing Handley's tragic past with his girl, Doll. Hagen, as Doll, responded to him in a way that made the scene believable and took him deeper into character, an experience he had never felt before.

The more Dix spoke about his troubled past, the more difficult it became for Dix to control his emotions. "I want to go on," explained Hayden, "but all I can do is sit on the edge of the bed. I know there's more I have to tell her. I try to speak but the pain won't let me. I rock back and forth, and something inside me feels like it's tipping over. My eyes begin to back up, but this is a sound stage and guys like me don't cry in the middle of the morning." When he looked up at Jean Hagen, she was in character, with an understanding warmth in her eyes. That bond was all he needed, "so I just let go and I feel the goddamn tears rushing down all hot and the next thing I know they cut the arcs and the work lights come up softly."[32]

Thanking everyone on the set, Hayden felt the urge to leave immediately. As he was departing, Huston caught up with him. Still unable to look up after the unexpectedly emotional screen test, Hayden heard Huston tell him what he had wanted to hear for a long time. "The next time somebody says you can't act, tell them to call Huston."[33]

The Asphalt Jungle was released in May of 1950 to wide critical acclaim. Starring Sam Jaffe, Jean Hagen, Louis Calhern, James Whitmore, and Sterling Hayden as Dix Handley, it is considered a crime classic and has been the inspiration for numerous film noir "heist" films. It was also the film that marked the credited film debut of Marilyn Monroe. The film was nominated for four Academy Awards. Hayden's portrayal of Handley drew wide praise from the critics and is today considered possibly his finest screen performance. In 2008, *The Asphalt Jun*gle was selected by the Library of Congress for preservation in the National Film Registry as it met their criteria for being considered culturally, historically, or aesthetically significant.

• • •

It would seem that Hayden had achieved a milestone, with his career turning in the right direction. With the money he made and the assumption that more work would be coming, he and his wife moved their family off the schooner and into a home in a star-studded Hollywood neighborhood. But there were other factors that were intervening that would keep him coming back to Phil Cohen's couch. His drinking had continued, and his relationship with his wife Betty continued to be a combative one. Betty had become extremely jealous of other women with whom her husband worked. By the summer of 1950, their third child was due. Son Christian was born in August of 1948 and son Dana was born in June of 1949. They would be joined by a sister Gretchen, born in September of 1950. The Haydens would have one more child together, Matthew, born in July of 1952.

Despite his lauded performance in *The Asphalt Jungle*, he had no new film offers and he shared this frustration with his therapist. Meanwhile, an event that occurred halfway around the world started Hayden thinking about another possible crisis to confront. He was right to worry. In June of 1950, North Korea crossed the thirty-eighth parallel and invaded South Korea. Hayden, a member of the United States Marine Corps Reserve, was subject to a possible recall to active duty. The thought of coming back to the Marine Corps did not bother him. It was the thought of a background check prior to being reactivated that worried him greatly. His six-month tenure as a member of the Communist Party would surely come back to haunt him. In addition, the Supreme Court had refused to hear the appeal of the Hollywood Ten. He knew that the HUAC hearings would resume in the near future.

He lay on Cohen's couch, venting his fears to his laconic therapist. "I'm in the Marine Corps Reserve. Since the war started, I've felt this thing closing down around me. Suppose they call me up and we come to the loyalty part: 'Are you now or have you ever been a member of the Communist Party?' If I say no, I perjure myself. If I say yes, and the word gets around, then I'm dead." He continued on, bemoaning his lack of additional film offers since making *The Asphalt Jungle*. He then brought up a key issue to share. "I had a talk yesterday afternoon with my lawyer about how to protect myself. He thinks we should write a letter to J. Edgar Hoover asking if there isn't some way I can admit having been a member in the Party without screwing my whole life up."

"That seems reasonable," responded Cohen.

"I'm not so sure. The F.B.I. isn't going to let me off the hook without my implicating people who never did anything wrong—except belong to the Party."

"Didn't your attorney suggest the F.B.I. would probably treat the information confidentially?" asked his therapist.

"Yes, he did: but from what I've heard about the bureau and its ties with the Un-American Activities Committee, I sure as hell doubt it."

"Maybe you should try another attorney."

"I can't afford it," shot back Hayden. "And besides, Martin Gang is a powerhouse in this business; maybe someday I'll need him." Hayden went on to spill his guts out to Cohen, expressing his frustration with the position he was in and the bitterness it left him with. "You know, I don't know why I got out of the Party, any more than I know why I joined." Expressing an opinion that would differ substantially from testimony he would give to HUAC less than a year later, he went on to state: "I could say a lot of things about those people I knew in the Party-and you know something? It would all be good. I never heard anything that was subversive."[34] He shared with Cohen his plan to take out a two-page ad in the Hollywood trade papers, reading him the prospective ad. "You loud-mouthed, self-styled patriots in this business better wake up. I was in the Party for six months. I know a bit about what goes on. You think those people are trying to subvert your precious Hollywood? They're not. They happen to believe in planned social order. They look up to Russia as the leader of the world socialist movement . . . Now, you people allegedly believe in free competition. You want the world to follow in our footsteps, so you invest billions of bucks all over hell and gone trying to influence people. Yet when the socialist world does this you scream 'foul.'" He declared emphatically: "That's what I'd like to say."

"Why not do it?" asked Cohen.

"Because I haven't got the guts, that's why," he shot back. Hayden's response was symbolic of the conflict that was literally driving him to drink, offering a clear window into the confusion and self-hatred he was feeling. Here the man who had heroically, fearlessly, and sometimes recklessly fought the Germans in the war, the man who had spent his entire life searching for an identity and a cause to truly believe in, now realized that he couldn't even believe in himself. As a result, he was, in his mind at least, a coward. "Maybe because I'm a parlor pink. Because I want to remain employable in this town long enough to finish this fucking analysis. Because when it comes time for the divorce I'd like to be able to see my children, and the courts downtown are full of judges who would look askance at a divorced man who was an ex-Communist to boot. That's why! How many reasons do you want, sitting there on your throne?"[35]

The session with Phil Cohen just described comes directly from Sterling Hayden's 1963 autobiography. It is interesting on several levels, not the least of which is that he mentioned his attorney, Martin Gang, by name and yet never mentioned the name of his psychiatrist. In Hayden's exchange with Cohen, one gets the impression that Cohen either doesn't know Gang, or at most is vaguely aware of who he is. Since *Wanderer* was published in 1963, several facts have come to light concerning these two men. It appears highly likely that these two not only were very aware of each other but, in fact, were working in tandem closely with many Hollywood stars in addition to Sterling Hayden.

Since 1931, Gang was a partner in the firm of Gang, Tyre, Ramer, and Brown, providing legal services to many in the Hollywood community. Hayden had engaged Gang earlier to handle his contract negotiation issues. A well-known liberal, he was a member of, and financial contributor to, the Committee for the First Amendment, and he had offered to represent Dalton Trumbo in his breach of contract suit against Loew's, Inc.[36] During the interim period between the end of the first set of HUAC hearings in 1947 and the beginning of the second set of hearings in 1951, Gang changed the focus of his practice to coincide with the direction that the political winds were blowing, encouraging his clients to cooperate with HUAC. He did not view this as hypocritical. Rather, he saw himself as a "frustrated crusader," trying, "to keep a lot of innocent people from being hurt unnecessarily."[37]

After the Hollywood Ten were cited for contempt of Congress, Gang contacted two members of the defense team who were representing the other subpoenaed witnesses. He advised them that, in his opinion, unless some real service could be performed by the eight remaining members following the same procedure that the Ten followed, "they should not sacrifice themselves to no useful end."[38] Gang's proposal was to wage a vigorous public relations campaign when the hearings resumed. A witness should issue statements that they were testifying voluntarily without conceding the right of the committee to ask, but since the issue had been raised and would be decided by the courts, he would be answering the questions under protest. Gang was sure that this tactic would prevent the witness from being blacklisted.[39]

Another technique utilized by Gang included never having his clients invoke the Fifth Amendment if asked if they were ever a member of the Communist Party. He reasoned that "because if that person had been a member of the Communist Party and had gotten out, he had no right to plead the Fifth Amendment because he was not guilty of any crime unless he had lied about not having gotten out."[40] In Gang's philosophy, contrition, not confrontation, was the way to prevent blacklisting.

In his efforts to assist his clients, Gang cultivated a close working relationship with William Wheeler, the HUAC investigator from their Los Angeles field office. Engaging in what Victor Navasky described as "strategic socializing," Gang would often invite Wheeler to have dinner with him and his clients so that Wheeler could get to meet and speak to them informally. It usually worked in Gang's favor since Wheeler would often not pursue subpoenaing Gang's client after meeting with them, being convinced that they were in the clear. "So there again I did my clients a favor and I also did Wheeler a favor. I don't know what it proved about me, but Wheeler was doing a job, and what I tried to do was to present the facts to him in such a way that my clients would not be unnecessarily hurt. And if that's a crime you can convict me."[41]

Gang would get to refine his technique many times over the next few years while dealing with HUAC. He would explain his actions thusly: that a lawyer's obligation is simple—to serve his client's interests. And for his Hollywood clients their best interests were easy to ascertain: to not get blacklisted. "I didn't tell them what to do," he later declared, "I only told them what the choices were."[42]

It is interesting to note that Cohen's patient list contained many of Gang's clients. It is also interesting to note that many of these people became cooperative witnesses in front of HUAC and would name names. This seeming coincidence, coupled with the unusual interaction of Cohen, Gang, and Wheeler, was examined by Victor S. Navasky for his 1980 book *Naming Names*, as he explored the dynamics of the tactics of both men, as well as their professional relationships. In a series of interviews conducted in 1974, Cohen confirmed that he had indeed been the psychologist of choice for the Communist Party and his practice income soared from their referrals. As a result of his patients' becoming cooperative witnesses starting in 1951, he fell out of favor, telling Navasky that his practice suffered greatly.

Cohen told Navasky that he had met William Wheeler at a football game and they discovered that they had mutual friends in law enforcement. Through these friends, Cohen would find out if one of his patients was subpoenaed and then ask the patient for permission to speak to Wheeler. Once he obtained the patient's permission, he would say to Wheeler, "'When so-and-so left [the Party] he really left.' That kind of thing. And I would often, when talking to so-and-so, persuade him he was better off talking to Bill rather than holding back and trying to be a hero against his own conviction."[43]

When asked directly if he helped Cohen, Wheeler provided the following startling response. "He (Cohen) said, 'If you subpoena one of my patients, I'll try to condition him to testify.'"

Condition or convince?

"What's the difference?" responded Cohen. "It was part of the therapy. The whole thing."[44]

Navasky has labeled Wheeler, Gang, and Cohen as the triumvirate of opinion trustees: Wheeler, the Democratic "good guy" investigator for HUAC, who was willing to make it as painless as possible for those who were willing to play the game; Gang, the attorney, who was only looking out for his clients best interests and saw no point in them sabotaging their careers; and Cohen, who could "condition" his clients to become cooperative witnesses. The three of them, who saw themselves as basically humanistic liberals, functioned collectively as a support system for those ripe for cooperating with the investigators.[45]

...

In the summer of 1950, Martin Gang had convinced Sterling Hayden to be proactive and to go directly to the FBI. With Hayden's permission, Gang wrote to FBI director J. Edgar Hoover. The letter was written on July 31, 1950, a little more than a month after North Korea had invaded across the thirty-eighth parallel.[46] Hayden is never identified in the letter. Gang simply began by stating: "This office has a client who has discussed with us a problem which I believe can only be answered through your organization.

"In June of 1946 this young man, in a moment of emotional disturbance, became a bona fide member of the Communist Party in the State of California. In November of 1946 he decided that he had made a mistake and terminated his membership and his association with the Communist Party." Gang stressed that since November 1946 his client had had no connection whatsoever with the Party, although Hayden actually quit the Party in December of 1946.

Gang described his client's military service during the war with the United States Marine Corps, including his Silver Star award for gallantry. He did not indicate the client's occupation, although it would not have been very difficult to deduce that, with Gang acting as his attorney, he was more than likely employed in some aspect of show business. He did confirm that the client was not engaged in any activity where security was involved. "He is concerned with the fact that his brief membership in the Communist Party, as aforesaid, may operate to prevent the use of his services." He described his client as being married with young children.

Gang described the essence of the problem: Conditions might develop "so as to require an answer . . . to the question 'Are you now or have you been a member of the Communist Party?'" His client could honestly answer that he was not currently a member of the Party. "He could not answer the rest of the compound question without (a) either lying or (b) if he told the truth he would probably find himself unable to earn a living.

"While it must be admitted that a mistake was made in 1946, it does appear that justice requires some method by which one mistake does not operate (a) to prevent the United States from making use of the services of our client, (b) to prevent our client from earning a living."

Gang proceeded to assure Hoover that his client was perfectly willing to be interrogated by the FBI so that the organization could be assured of his sincerity and of the truth of all the previous statements.

Gang ended the letter by getting to the crux of the issue. Gang and his client desired the interrogation by the FBI so that if the "compound question" was asked of him, presumably by the HUAC, he would be permitted to respond "'Please inquire of the Federal Bureau of Investigation.' The Federal Bureau of Investigation could then notify the prospective employer that there was no reason for not employing our client." Gang respectfully requested a response from Hoover at his earliest convenience.

Hoover did promptly reply to Gang, writing a brief letter on August 15, 1950.[47] After thanking Gang for making the facts available to him, Hoover expressed his regrets. "I regret to inform you, however, that it had been a long-standing policy of this Bureau not to grant a clearance to any person and I am, therefore, unable to assist you in the manner which you suggest." Shifting gears somewhat, Hoover, noting the FBI's investigative jurisdiction in matters concerning the internal security of the United States, recommended to Gang "that your client furnish our Los Angeles office with details concerning his membership in the Communist Party together with the nature of the party activities during that period." Hoover provided the name of R. B. Hood, special agent in charge of the Los Angeles office, as the contact with whom Gang could arrange his client's interview.

Later that month, Gang arranged the interview with the FBI and accompanied Hayden to the FBI headquarters. In route, Hayden began to get cold feet. Gang reassured his client that he would feel better after he completed the interview.

When they reached their destination, the two proceeded to the FBI field office. There they were greeted by special agent R. B. Hood, who offered an appreciative welcome. "Mr. Gang, of course I have no way of knowing what it is your client wishes to say this morning. But I would like to avail myself of this opportunity to congratulate you both on the decision you have made. If it is of any value to you, Mr. Hayden, I might also say that you are not alone in your predicament." As Gang left to make a phone call, Hayden had a request to ask of Hood. "I do not wish to disclose the names of other persons who might be in some way involved."

"Mr. Hayden," responded the FBI agent, "it is not the function of this Bureau to approve or disapprove. You have indicated a desire to assist the Bureau in its investigative work and I leave it to you what you say or do not say. However, I would suggest that if you are going to co-operate with the Bureau, you do so to the fullest extent of your ability."[48]

With that preamble, Hood called in a gray-haired investigator who was a specialist in Hollywood affairs. Hayden was left in the room with the interrogator and the interview began.

He spoke for more than an hour. When it came to specific names, Hayden tried to be as vague as possible, using expression such as, "No, sir, I never did know their last names," and "No, sir, the actors and actresses I met were never identified as belonging to the party." When he was finished, the agent complimented him, telling him that his contribution that morning was invaluable. Departing the premises, he got into the car with Gang, who subtly tried to reassure his shaken client. "There now, that wasn't too bad, was it?" Hayden would eventually give testimony to the FBI on two more occasions.

Arriving home after the first FBI interview—"the Confession," as he referred to it— Hayden was devastated. Alone in his backyard, he began to attack a bottle of rum to console himself. He recalled the time when Cohen advised him that on occasion alcohol, when properly handled, could bring relief. It wasn't working; he felt no relief that night. Betty called to him, asking when he was coming to bed. "Just as soon as I kill this bottle, that's when I'm coming to bed," he replied.[49]

The next paragraph that he recorded in *Wanderer* spoke volumes about his state of mind that night. "I might as well have said, 'I'm sorry. It's no use. We never had a marriage. The man who is coming to bed once this bottle is killed isn't the man you married. That guy is dead, because today he finally sold out all the way.'"

CHAPTER FIFTEEN

Naming Names

IN APRIL OF 1950, THE APPEALS OF THE HOLLYWOOD TEN REACHED THE United States Supreme Court. The court refused to review the convictions and each member of the Ten was fined $1,000 and received prison sentences of up to a year. The stage was set for the resumption of the HUAC hearings in Hollywood. Armed with another recent Supreme Court decision, the committee was going to insist that subpoenaed witnesses name names.

...

The HUAC resumed its hearings on communist infiltration of Hollywood and the motion picture industry on March 8, 1951. The committee was chaired by Rep. John S. Wood of Georgia, and attorney Frank S. Tavenner Jr. served as counsel and chief interrogator. On that day, only one witness was called to testify and he wasn't actually a member of the Hollywood film community. It was Victor Jeremy Jerome, Communist Party cultural commissioner and editor of *The Communist*. Jerome was represented by attorney Ralph Powe of New York City. Jerome promptly refused to answer most of the committee's questions, citing his right against self-incrimination. While acknowledging that he was a writer and an editor, he refused to provide any additional specific details. Members of the committee grew frustrated with what they interpreted as Jerome's evasions. Congressman Harold H. Velde of Illinois then asked Jerome, "You do agree that this is a legally constituted committee of the Congress, do you not?"

"I do, sir," Jerome replied.

"Do you agree that we are attempting to determine what subversive forces exist in this country?"

"I do, sir,"

"Do you refuse to cooperate by answering questions as to those subversive forces?" asked Velde.

"My position is to cooperate the best I can," responded Jerome. "I believe, however, I am entitled to invoke a constitutional privilege granted me against self-incrimination."[1]

For the remainder of his total of two hours of testimony before the committee, Jerome refused to answer specific questions regarding his past employment and potential involvement in organizations that could be considered subversive. He also refused to answer questions regarding any particular people that were brought up by committee members. In each case, he cited his constitutional privilege against self-incrimination. The committee adjourned its hearing that afternoon and would not resume its hearings for nearly two weeks.

• • •

On March 21, 1951, the HUAC hearings resumed and the first witness called was actor Larry Parks. He was thirty-one years old when he achieved overnight stardom playing the lead in the 1946 biopic *The Jolson Story*. The highly successful film spawned a sequel, *Jolson Sings Again*, in 1949, also starring Parks. The actor had joined the Communist Party in 1941 but had left by 1946. Parks was determined to be a contrite, cooperative witness but he, too, was determined not to name any of the people he may have associated with during his tenure in the Communist Party. The session involving the genial, well-meaning witness and the aggressive, abrupt HUAC committee members proved to be a tortuous inquisition for Parks.

After Parks's request to read an opening statement was denied, the committee members pounced on him, asking him about various groups that he was a member of, if there were any communists in these groups, and, if so, who they were. As was the pattern for the rest of the hearing, when asked to specifically name names, Parks declined to do so. His answers throughout the session as to his memberships and contacts were somewhat vague and seemed deliberately coached to prevent him from perjuring himself. "I don't believe so, I don't recall being affiliated with that at that time,"[2] "I don't recall," and similar phrases appear throughout the transcript of the hearing.

Throughout the morning, Parks begged the committee not to ask him for specific names. In his plea, he actually hit on the crux of the issue that indicated that the hearings were to a great degree more theater than fact-finding: the committee already had the names. "On the question of naming names," responded Parks, "it is my honest opinion that the few people that I could name, these names would not be of service to the committee at all. *I am sure that you know who they are* [emphasis added]. These people I feel honestly are like myself, and I feel that I have done nothing wrong. Question of judgment? Yes, perhaps."[3] Later in his testimony, Parks would repeat his belief that, among the few people he knew who were fellow members of the Communist Party, "you probably know their names."[4]

Parks's contention that he did not want to name names, largely because the committee already had the names and hence was a secondary issue, was actually supported by committee member Congressman Francis E. Walter of Pennsylvania. Walter asked Chairman Wood to direct a question to Tavenner, and Wood approved. Indeed, why was it necessary to have Parks name names when the committee already had them? "How can it be material to the purpose of this inquiry to have the names of people when we already know them?" Wasn't the key issue what the organization did and hoped to accomplish, how it had or attempted to influence the thinking of the American public through the arts? "So why is it so essential that we know the names of all the people when we have a witness who may make a contribution to what we are trying to learn?" he asked.

Tavenner responded by insisting that some of the witnesses they hoped to interrogate had evaded service of process and hence couldn't be brought to the hearing. In addition, he claimed that the committee was entitled to receive proof of information which it had in its files as a result of previous investigations. Walter was not impressed with these arguments. "But isn't it far more important to learn the extent of the activity and what the purpose of the organization actually was than to get a long list of names of bleeding hearts and fools, suckers, hard-boiled Communist politicians? . . . As long as we have a witness willing and anxious to cooperate in carrying out what I conceive to be our purpose, I think the rest is all immaterial."[5]

The actual intent of getting witnesses to cooperate by naming names was later best described by researchers Larry Ceplair and Steven Englund, who wrote: "These unseemly rituals served no legislative or investigation function for the Committee—no amendments or additions to federal law resulted. HUAC needed no further fodder for its grinder; its research had been thorough. The 'name game' substantiated the witness' 'conversion' by demonstrating his or her willingness to betray former comrades. There was no alternative to this deed, virtually no way out for even the 'friendliest' and seemingly most 'sincere' penitent."[6]

Before recessing for the morning, Parks reaffirmed that it was out of a sense of idealism and naivete that he had joined the Communist Party. When asked if he was entirely out of sympathy with the communist philosophy in the years since he left the Party, he replied without hesitation. "I certainly am. I think any power that is trying to, in my opinion, take over the world in this manner, I think is wrong."[7] He affirmed that in the event of armed conflict between the United States and the Soviet Union, he would unquestionably bear arms for the United States. The hearing then recessed, but Parks's ordeal was far from over.

In the afternoon when the hearing reconvened, Parks's attorney Louis Mandel requested that Parks be allowed to read his personal statement. After initially refusing the request, Chairman Wood allowed Parks to proceed. The three-minute statement was a powerful plea. Parks began by stressing the loyalty to the United States of his entire family and ancestors, and then delved into the personal agony he was feeling. "I don't think I would be here today if I wasn't a star," he accurately stated, "because you know as well as I, even better, that I know nothing that I believe would be of great service to this country. I think my career has been ruined because of this, and I would appreciate not having to—don't present me with the choice of either being in contempt of this committee and going to jail or forcing me to really crawl through the mud to be an informer, for what purpose? . . . I don't think this is American. I don't think this is American justice. I think to do something like that is more akin to what happened under Hitler, and what is happening in Russia today."[8]

The remainder of the session was basically a rehash of the morning's questioning. Parks again pleaded not to have to name names, and the session ended without him doing so. It was to be a short-lived reprieve. Later that afternoon, in a closed executive session, Parks was presented with the option that he correctly predicted would occur. The committee informed him that he would either cooperate and name names, or he would likely be charged with contempt. Tearfully, Parks gave in and gave the committee ten names of people he felt were to be members of the Communist Party. Parks's second prediction also came true. The career of this "reluctant" friendly witness was ruined and he was blacklisted, in spite of having cooperated with the demands of the HUAC. On March 24, 1951, two days after cooperating with HUAC, the headlines of the *Los Angeles Examiner* declared: "LARRY PARKS LOSES $75,000 SCREEN

ROLE."[9] His last starring role was in the Stanley Donen production *Love is Better Than Ever*, costarring Elizabeth Taylor. Filming was completed in January of 1951, but as a result of the HUAC hearings and Parks's testimony, the release was delayed until March of 1952. He would star in one more movie filmed in England in 1955 and would finally return to the screen in America in a costarring role in John Huston's 1962 production *Freud*. It would be his final film appearance.

• • •

On the afternoon of March 21, two more witnesses were called in front of the committee. As cooperative and penitent as Larry Parks tried to be, these two witnesses proved to be totally uncooperative and their testimonies were quite brief. The first was actor Howard Da Silva, who was accompanied by two attorneys. Da Silva proved to be not only uncooperative but defiant and belligerent. Immediately after being sworn in and before he identified himself for the record, he demanded to read a statement that he had already released to the press. Wood refused to allow him to read his statement. The initial clash set the tone for the rest of Da Silva's appearance.

Other than providing minimal biographical information, Da Silva adamantly refused to answer any of the committee's questions. His feelings and attitude toward the hearing was best summed up when he stated: "At this point, may I object to being called to testify against myself in this hearing. I object because the first and fifth amendments and all of the Bill of Rights protect me from any inquisitorial procedure, and I may not be compelled to cooperate with this committee in producing evidence designed to incriminate me and to drive me from my profession as an actor."[10] The transcript of the hearing is rife with examples of the mutual contempt that both Da Silva and the committee felt towards each other. In the end, the committee was unable to obtain any names from this most uncooperative witness.

The last witness to testify that day was actress Gale Sondergaard, who was represented by the same two attorneys as Da Silva. She was placed in a very awkward position as a subpoenaed witness, since her husband was screenwriter and director Herbert Biberman, one of the convicted Hollywood Ten. Other than essentially just confirming her identity, she refused to answer virtually all of the committee's questions. Like Da Silva, she was an uncooperative witness, although not belligerent or defiant like her predecessor.

The combined testimonies of Da Silva and Sondergaard took about an hour. The transcript of both of their testimonies occupied thirteen pages of the HUAC hearing transcript, as compared with the thirty-five pages that it took to record Larry Parks's testimony. The committee adjourned after its executive session on March 21, 1951, and would not reconvene for over two weeks. The next witness would be represented by an attorney who was the ultimate Hollywood insider who had well prepared his client. The attorney was Martin Gang, and his client was matinee idol Sterling Hayden.

...

Any relief that Sterling Hayden may have felt after his testimony to the FBI in August of 1950 was short-lived. While Hayden and Gang had hoped that his FBI testimony would exempt him from the possibility of having to testify before the HUAC, Hayden still wasn't that confident. His frustration at not being able to find any film work was stressful enough when coupled with the volatile relationship he had with his wife. He also began to lash out at Phil Cohen, feeling that he, in conjunction with Gang, had subtly forced him to go to the FBI. He seriously considered leaving analysis (he would do this shortly after and seek treatment with another psychiatrist) and began to vent his anger at Cohen. "I'll say this, too," he told Cohen at one of their sessions in late 1950, "that if it hadn't been for you I wouldn't have turned into a stoolie for J. Edgar Hoover. I don't think you have the foggiest notion of the contempt I have had for myself since the day I did that thing . . . Fuck it! And fuck you too."[11] As usual, Cohen just listened and didn't respond.

During this time period, one interesting and potentially lucrative film role was offered to him though he turned it down. His agent had secured an appointment for Hayden at Lesser Production Enterprises. The studio head, Sol Lesser, was very interested in Hayden. Johnny Weissmuller had retired from the Tarzan film series following his last Tarzan film, *Tarzan and the Mermaids*, was released in 1948, considering himself too old to continue in the franchise. The role went to actor Lex Barker, who did two Tarzan films for RKO Studios. Lesser wanted Sterling Hayden to take over the role from Barker. As he indicated in *Wanderer*, Hayden wasn't the least bit interested in the role, although he promised Lesser that he would think about it. When Lesser then asked him to take off his shirt so that he and his associates could see their "Tarzan," Hayden politely refused and left. The words his stepfather once spoke to him came back as he drove away from the meeting: "You are going to grow up to have a forty-six-inch chest and a size-three hat."[12]

In early 1951, Hayden was finally offered a starring role in a film he wanted to act in. He was cast as a minister experiencing a crisis of faith in *Skid Row*. Filming began on March 15, 1951. While having lunch in the studio commissary in late March, a United States marshal approached Hayden and handed him a neatly folded, salmon-colored document. It was the culmination of all of his worst fears: a subpoena to appear in Washington, DC, as a witness in front of the HUAC. Panicking, he found a pay phone and called Martin Gang to tell him that he had been served with a subpoena. As a reflection of how tumultuous Hayden's life was becoming, Gang asked him, "Who by, your wife?"

In a hushed voice, Hayden told him, "No . . . by the House Committee on Un-American Activities."

"Well, is that so? All right, we'll have to move fast. I'll contact Wheeler, their Hollywood investigator. Meet me tonight—my office—eight o'clock sharp . . . And, by the way—better bring your wife—and also you might wear that rosette that goes with the Silver Star."[13]

The meeting was also attended by HUAC general counsel Frank Tavenner. Gang and Tavenner immediately locked horns, with Gang reminding Tavenner that Hayden had already given his statement to the FBI and that should have sufficed for the HUAC.[14] Tavenner retorted that the committee's actions were merely investigative and that it was Hayden's "duty and privilege to tell the whole truth before this duly constituted body."[15]

Soon after, the studio executives at RKO were panicking. They called an emergency meeting that was attended by eight or ten top executives and asked Hayden and Gang to attend in order to brief them. When they arrived, the executives jumped all over the two of them, asking for any updates. "Nothing," responded Gang. "The schedule stands. The testimony will begin at the end of next week, maybe before."

"Hayden, I must be frank with you," shot back one of the studio's New York executives. "This entire venture has been placed in serious jeopardy . . . My colleagues and I placed great faith in you, in spite of your discouraging career in recent years. We gambled. Gambled half a million dollars on you. Now what do we do?"

Gang offered little solace when he informed them that "it just may be that we'll have to testify sooner, before the end of the production. It might be dangerous to wait too long, with public hostility and all." With that, one of the local executives began bemoaning the fact that Hayden was scheduled to be in virtually all of the remaining scenes. Gang had to convince the committee to postpone the hearing, he insisted.

It was the New York executive who had the final say in the matter. After pausing for a few seconds, he calmly announced, "Gentlemen, I have confidence in Hayden. Look for God's sake at his war record. This boy is no Red. He's our boy. He's no radical dedicated to force and violence. Right, Sterlin'? True or false, I ask it?"

"I think it will be all right," mumbled Hayden.

The New York executive adjourned the meeting by declaring: "Sterlin'—one word of advice. Go straight, tell the truth. Ask yourself: 'What will my children think?' Always make them proud of you."[16]

• • •

On April 9, 1951, Hayden flew from Los Angeles to Washington, DC, accompanied by his wife Betty. He was in a somber mood when the plane finally touched down in Washington. A crowd of news reporters crowed around the couple as they entered the terminal and were met by Martin Gang and William Wheeler, the HUAC's Hollywood investigator. Wheeler had been in Washington for several days, arranging details of the upcoming hearing and making arrangements to make sure that the hearing proceeded as he, Gang, and Cohen had planned. In a driving rain, the four of them got into a limousine and headed for their hotel. During the trip, Gang showed Hayden reports provided by the FBI, documenting his December 1944 trip to San Francisco while on leave, as well as letters that he had written during the war to Warwick Tompkins. Recalling this, and other potentially adverse items uncovered by the FBI—including a trip that Hayden had taken to the printing plant of the People's World where he wrote on their bulletin board, "Smrt Facizmu—Sloboda Barodu" (Slavic for "Death to Fascism—Freedom to the People")—Hayden interrupted his attorney. "Martin, why go through all this crap? I don't have to be reminded of what I did. I've told the truth all along and I'll tell the truth today. They're not going to trip me up." Unable to restrain himself from exhibiting the downward spiral of his self-esteem, he added: "I may be yellow, but I'm not a liar too."

"Why do you keep on saying that you're yellow?" protested Wheeler.

"Because I am," he snapped back. "Can you think of a better reason?"[17]

• • •

The night of April 9, Sterling and Betty checked into their hotel and Sterling informed his wife that he was going to have dinner with an old friend. He met his old Gloucester colleague Norm Hatch in the hotel's restaurant, eager to obtain Hatch's counsel in spite of his apparent confidence in front of his attorney. Sterling was well aware that Hatch was wise to the ways of Washington and could help him deal with his upcoming testimony. After a distinguished career in the United States Marine Corps as a combat photographer, Hatch was a senior advisor to the secretary of defense and a White House consultant. If ever there was a man adept at maneuvering through the ways of Washington and dealing with Washington bureaucrats, it was Norman Hatch.

Despite the reassurances of Gang, Sterling remained somewhat uneasy about testifying before the committee. "He wanted to talk with me because he was afraid that he wouldn't know how to talk to the committee," Hatch recalled. "I told him not to be too harsh, not to lose his temper; don't do it that way." He also told his friend that the committee already had the information they were allegedly seeking and would be able to tell if he was being evasive or deceptive. Gauging Sterling's response that night and also reacting to his testimony the following day, Hatch concluded, "I think he did listen to my advice. We respected each other."[18]

• • •

On the morning of April 10, 1951, the House Un-American Activities Committee was called to order at 10 a.m. by Chairman John S. Wood. Over 300 spectators were in attendance to observe the proceedings in Room 226 of the Old House Office Building, leaving standing room only. In addition to Wood and the other committee members, eight committee staff members were present, including counsel Frank Tavenner and investigator William Wheeler.

Sterling Hayden was led into the room and taken to the small table facing the committee members, topped off with a yellow tablecloth and a microphone. He dressed the part of a solid citizen, in his "costume" as he referred to it: a brown tweed suit, a button-down shirt, and a loose-knit tie. In his left lapel was his Silver Star pin. Off to his side he saw a solid wall of television cameras and media photographers. Directly in front of him a CBS-TV cameraman lay on his back, shooting into Hayden's face. Betty Hayden and Martin Gang were out of the camera's range. He was promptly sworn in and agreed to answer all questions truthfully and to the best of his ability. The ordeal he feared was about to begin.

The hearing, and his testimony, in fact would be another performance for the cameras, albeit a critically important one to his future. The entire testimony was scripted in advance. Frank Tavenner had in his hand a forty-page scripted compilation of questions and answers that had been collaboratively worked on by Martin Gang, William Wheeler, and Hayden himself. He knew that his job today would be relatively easy—after all, he had a cooperative witness who would not be taking the Fifth Amendment. Also, as Larry Parks had readily pointed out, the committee already had the names that it sought. What the committee really wanted was a witness to demonstrate appropriate contrition by providing the names that the committee already had. Gang, Wheeler, and Hayden had paved the way by scripting the questions and the answers in advance. Gang, with Wheeler's agreement, had also given guidance to Hayden when it came to the topic of naming names. "Don't guess: unless you saw a card or it was a closed meeting, you can't be sure someone was a member of the Party, so you shouldn't name him."[19]

After providing the obligatory personal identification and data, Tavanner asked him when he first went to sea. At age fifteen, replied Hayden, quickly proceeding to explain that by age twenty-one, he had obtained his master's license and took command of a ship and began making long sea voyages. At that point, Tavenner asked him, "During that period of time, did you become acquainted with Capt. Warwick Tompkins?" "Yes," replied Hayden. "I met him when I was 14, in Boston Mass. He had a schooner and I wanted to go to work on it, but he said I was too young. I never got to know him well personally at that time."[20] Hayden subsequently explained how he got into the acting profession.

After the brief introduction phase, Tavenner began honing in on Warwick Tompkins. Hayden provided direct and open answers, aided by the ten pages of notes in front of him, the result of the collaboration of his legal team. The first nine pages had notes typed out on index cards. The tenth was an index containing dates, names, places, and an itemized list of all donations that he had made over the years that could be in any way considered seditious by the committee.[21] In a sense, it was almost like he was performing on the stage, with a script and cue cards to assist him. His script called for him to come across as a well-meaning and idealistic patriot who made a mistake and was, in essence, asking for forgiveness. It also called for him to name names—the price of forgiveness, according to the HUAC.

Tavenner asked Hayden if Tompkins was on the West Coast when he came to Hollywood. Hayden confirmed that Tompkins had moved his base of operations from Boston to San Francisco by that time. Feeling lost and depressed in Hollywood, Hayden told the committee that he decided to go see Tompkins. "I decided to pay him a visit," he explained. "I went to San Francisco and saw him. He at that time, or previously, had become, I believe, an open and avowed Communist. He made no bones about it. He talked about very little else, and he started to deluge me with propaganda."[22]

"Were you a Communist at that time?" asked Tavenner.

"No. It had never entered my head."

Tavenner asked if he had ever met any other people, as a result of his acquaintance with Tomkins, that he knew then or found out since were Communist Party members. Hayden recalled one person for the committee. When he visited Tompkins on his schooner sometime in 1941, he was introduced to "an old warrior in the class struggle, 'Pop' Folkoff." Hayden thought that he was a retired tailor at that time and professed ignorance as to why Folkoff was so highly regarded by Tompkins. Unbeknownst to Hayden, Folkoff was at that time a senior founding member of the California Communist Party and acted as a liaison between the Communist Party of the USA and Soviet intelligence.

Tavenner then dug deeper into the relationship between Hayden and Tompkins. "What was the way in which Captain Tompkins went about consulting with you regarding communism? Tell us a little more detail about that."

Hayden's response appears to have been perfectly scripted to cast Tompkins in the role of an evil Svengali and himself as an uneducated, unworldly, naïve rube who now expressed remorse for what he had done. It was also a fairly accurate description. "All right, sir. If I may change the word, I wouldn't say he consulted with me. I think he recognized I was at a peculiar stage in my life. I was sort of betwixt and between. The sea had always been my calling. This was now denied me, or I had denied myself it. I was feeling restless and dissatisfied in Hollywood. He used the device of talking and talking and asking why I didn't read more. I had never thought in political terms at all. That was another world, which I am not particularly proud of today."[23]

The questioning shifted to Hayden's brief Hollywood career and his decision to abandon it in 1941 after two movies. The next several pages of testimony were dedicated to the wartime career that Hayden had left Hollywood for. As he explained: "All during the summer of 1941 I was churning inside, thinking about the war. I would like to claim, but I can't claim, I knew the country was in danger, but I knew something was going on, and I wanted to get in it," he recalled.[24] In detail, Hayden explained how he contacted "Wild Bill" Donovan and was accepted for commando training, how he turned down a US Navy commission, how he used a schooner to haul war freight, and how he ultimately enlisted in the United States Marine Corps. After changing his name legally to John Hamilton—"I changed it because I wanted to get away from Hollywood as much as possible. When I was in boot camp there seemed to be a good deal of curiosity about Hollywood. So I changed my name"[25]—he was commissioned as an officer and using his connection to Donovan, was accepted into the OSS.

He provided succinct but accurate descriptions of his wartime experiences in Italy, Yugoslavia, Albania, and would later describe his service with the First Army in Europe. He provided just enough detail about his wartime service for the committee and the viewing public to know that they were hearing the exploits of a genuine American war hero.

In keeping with the strategy of Martin Gang, the committee had agreed not to flat-out ask, "Were you at any time, or are you now a member of the Communist Party?" The background leading to Hayden's decision to join the Party had to be described first, as a prelude to the matter of why he ultimately did decide to join. This began with a key question that was posed to Hayden: how close was his relationship with the members of the Yugoslavian underground, the Partisans? "We established a tremendously close personal feeling with these people," he responded. "We had enormous, I would say unlimited, respect for the way they were fighting. I think that respect was reciprocated. We tried to do the best we could. We got quite steamed up by it, I myself was steamed up considerably by it. I had never experienced anything like that, and it made a tremendous impression on me. We knew they were Communist-led, we knew they had commissars, but there was very little discussion of that. We couldn't discuss those things very much because we didn't know the language."[26]

"And you were fighting a common foe at the time," added Tavenner.

"That we were, and I think we conducted ourselves fairly well."

"You say your relationship with the Partisan movement had a deep effect on you. What do you mean by that?"

"Precisely this: As I have, I believe, mentioned, in 1940, when I was still a young actor, and in 1941, I had had conversations with this man Tompkins. I wish I could describe my first reaction, because I think it would be typical of the experience so many people have had. I was appalled at the idea of what he was telling me about, but I did listen. He would give me literature, propaganda, and I would scan it briefly and burn it up.

"When this Yugoslavia thing came up, I wrote to him. I began writing, 'Maybe you were not so wrong. These people are doing a magnificent job.' I thought I had better figure this thing out.

"He, in turn, reciprocated by, I would say, bombarding me with Communist literature—*People's World, Daily Worker, New Masses,* and others I can't remember. I was impressed by the fact that the reports of that thing printed in the United States in this literature were accurate as regards the Partisans in Yugoslavia. This had an effect on me because it made me conscious of what these people knew that apparently the rest of us didn't know. That was about the size of it at that time.

"I engaged in quite a lot of correspondence with Tompkins at the time. I was all steamed up. We all were . . ."[27] When Tavenner asked if Hayden had engaged with political discussions with the Partisans, he replied, "No. I would honestly say not at all; not at all . . . I remember a couple of times when I would have a story in some of this literature Tompkins sent me, I would show it to them, and they were very pleased. There were no involved or detailed political discussions at all; not at all." In an interesting, and no doubt planned, omission, Hayden was not asked if he engaged in political discussions with his fellow American servicemen. If he had to provide an honest answer to that question, it could have been revealed that he avidly read communist literature while in Bari and passed it on to his OSS colleagues, encouraging them to read it.[28] The revelation that he sought to have the US military make a movie singing the praises of the communist Partisans' war efforts (while barely mentioning the US military) might also have been exposed.

Tavenner asked Hayden to summarize the "net result" of the effect that the correspondence with Tompkins, coupled with his experiences with the Partisans, had on him at that time. The question was surely intended to contrast the political thinking of Sterling Hayden in 1944–45 with his current beliefs. Hayden replied: "At the time—I'm glad you put it that way—there was a sort of churning inside of me that I didn't know how to handle, but it seemed there was something in this world that I ought to find out about. That was the net result of the whole thing.

"When I got home on leave in December 1944, one of the first things I wanted to do, on a purely emotional basis, was go back and see Tompkins and talk to him about this thing, which I did. I flew out to the coast and basked in the reflected glory of the Partisan movement. Tompkins sort of showed me off as an exhibit."[29] Before leaving the part of the testimony concerning his experience in Yugoslavia, Tavenner asked him to confirm that he received an award from the Yugoslavian government for his wartime services. He confirmed that he was awarded the Order of Merit, the second highest award that the Yugoslavian government could present to a combatant. "So you received a Silver Star?" asked Tavenner, referring to the award from the US for combat valor.

"Yes, sir,"

Tavenner had successfully established that Sterling Hayden was a) a patriot who gave up a promising film career to serve his country; b) a man of action who not only received a commission in the United States Marine Corps, but volunteered for and was accepted by the legendary OSS; c) a distinguished combat hero in World War II, which culminated with him being awarded a Silver Star; and d) an idealistic, well-meaning, and somewhat naïve person who was greatly influenced by what he had experienced working with the Partisans in Yugoslavia and Albania. He also confirmed the notion that Hayden had come under the malevolent influence of a Svengali-like mentor who was a committed communist. So Tavenner then switched his line of questioning to expose the extent of the influence that Warwick Tompkins had on the young Marine when he arrived home on leave in December 1944. It is most interesting to note that Hayden's marked change of heart towards the Partisan movement after Operation HACIENDA was not brought out at this time, nor would it be during his entire testimony. It seems strange, since that testimony underscoring his realization of the true evil nature of the Partisan leadership certainly would have worked strongly in his favor. It is likely that he didn't share this with Gang or Wheeler. He never mentioned his change of heart towards the Partisans in his 1944 narrative, nor did he mention it in *Wanderer*. The only record of this is his after-action report from Operation HACIENDA.[30]

Hayden told the committee about his December 1944 leave period back in the United States. Omitting both his visits to his mother and Lincoln Colcord, he went on to describe his visit to Tompkins on the West Coast as "a merry-go-round." He told the committee that he was interested in hooking up with some guerilla organizations for his next assignment and felt that Tompkins could point him towards the right people for this. Tompkins was delighted to have his young protégé back and took him around to meet various people. Hayden proceeded to name these people for the committee, names of known communists such as Isaac Folkoff, William Schneiderman, Harrison George, and Steve Nelson. These names were already well known to the committee. He also gave the name of Tompkins bother-in-law, Dr. Ellwood W. Lyman, as the host of the meeting where he met Steve Nelson. After nearly a week on the West Coast, he said, he went east to Washington.

Asked to describe the effect that his visit with Tompkins had on him, he explained, "Well, I was at the time, I think, trying to look ahead, figure out what I wanted to do after the war. I didn't know if I wanted to go back to Hollywood or not. I felt sort of reluctant to accepting what seemed to be the very lucrative and easy life Hollywood had offered me before and probably would again. I think the main thing was, it planted a seed in me that said if I could do something about the conditions of the world I could probably justify my position as an actor with a good salary and good working conditions. This wasn't concrete, but it was something boiling inside of me."[31]

Learning that the OSS did not have a new assignment for him at the time, Hayden explained that he contacted Tompkins for advice on guerilla movements similar to the Partisans and that Tompkins had put him in touch with V. J. Jerome, whom he contacted at the offices of the *Daily Worker* in New York City. He described for the committee his uneventful and somewhat bizarre meeting with Jerome, as well as his unproductive meeting with Joe North, who was another contact that Tompkins had provided him.

"Did you also go see a person by the name of Allan Chase, who is an avowed Communist, having been a candidate for Congress on the Communist ticket?" asked Tavenner. Hayden confirmed that he had met with Chase, but was unaware that he was a communist. "I didn't know he was a Communist. I thought he possibly was. He was particularly interested in the situation in Spain." Once again, Hayden confirmed that nothing had come of the meeting. He did receive "two or three" letters of introduction to friends of Chase on the off chance that he was able to get to Spain, but he burned them when he arrived in Paris en route to his next assignment. The questioning about Jerome, North, and Chase—following the requested description of the effect of the week with Tompkins in San Francisco—further served to paint a picture of a dedicated Marine on leave, on a personal quest to see how he could make the world a better place. In describing the course of this idealistic journey, he was able to publicly name more names (already known to the committee) while having Tavenner himself declare that they were communists when he asked Hayden the questions. This scripted approach provided a nonconfrontational air to the entire testimony and portrayed Hayden as an honest, candid witness who had nothing to hide.

Hayden was then asked to describe his work in his next assignment with the G-2 Division of the US First Army Headquarters. After he provided details of his assignment, Tavenner asked him if Warwick Tompkins continued to send him communist literature during this time. Hayden confirmed that they continued their correspondence but could only vaguely recall details.[32]

After his discharge from the Marine Corps in late December 1945, Hayden recalled for the committee his quandary over plans for civilian life. "At the time I remember there were two forces working inside of me. One was to go back to sea; the other was this political thing. At the time, I would like to say—and this is accurate to the best of my recollection—it had never occurred to me to join the Communist Party. It never occurred to me. It seemed this whole thing had introduced me to a new world that up to that time I had never known." After failing to raise money for a schooner, he told how Russell Holman of Paramount Pictures had signed him to a contract while he was in New York. "Did Holman know of your past associations and connection with Capt. Warwick Tompkins?" Tavenner asked.

"I doubt he did. He may have. I don't think he did. I don't know . . ."

"At the time of your second employment by the moving-picture industry, did your employer have any knowledge, as far as you know, of your associations with other Communist functions in California, such as William Schneiderman and Isaac Folkoff?"

"No," Hayden responded. "I think that was more or less lost in the shuffle of the war. There was so much going on, and I was fortunate enough to come out of the war better, publicitywise [*sic*] or otherwise, and they felt I had done pretty well in the war and let it go at that. There was no detailed analysis of what happened."[33]

Continuing with his departure from Nevada once he obtained his divorce from Madeleine Carroll, he described his trip to San Francisco to see Tompkins again in March of 1946 and Tompkins's efforts to write Hayden's biography. It was at this point that the hearing shifted into Hayden's membership and involvement in the Communist Party, starting in mid-1946. The questioning would provide ample opportunities for him to name various people who were members of the Party with him. He had done well thus far in his role of the confused idealist looking to make the world a better place after his distinguished military career. It was now time to pay penance for his subsequent actions and to show that he would cooperate as fully with HUAC in public as he had already done in private.

Tavennar asked Hayden to tell the committee how he became a "card-carrying member, or dues paying member, of the Communist Party." Admitting that "I continued to talk, I would say almost incessantly, about this thing built up in me in Yugoslavia and the feeling I wanted to do something for a better world," Hayden then recounted the story of how Bea Winters, after hearing him talk repeatedly along those lines, challenged him to do something about it—namely, to join the Communist Party. He recalled that he felt ridiculous, but signed the papers anyway. Tavenner asked several questions about Bea Winters and Hayden confirmed that it was Tompkins who had told him that she was a member of the Party. Hayden stated for the record that he joined the Party sometime between June 5 and 15, 1946.

Hayden was asked to describe his Party group, or "cell," as it was referred to. He explained why he was the only actor in the group. "I was told that for security reasons I should not be with any prominent people in any phase of endeavor at all in the motion-picture industry, but should be with people known as back-lot workers, carpenters, electricians, and so forth, and so on."[34] He described the meetings in detail and provided several names to the committee, but, as he explained, only first names were used. He only knew the full name of Bea Winters. The committee, as per the game plan, fed full names to Hayden, asking, "Do you know . . . ?" and "Were you acquainted with . . . ?" Hayden confirmed that he knew screenwriter Abe Polonsky and that he had later joined his cell, although he (Hayden) knew little about Polonsky's activities on behalf of the Party. He verified that he knew screenwriter Robert Lees, as he was also a member of the cell.

Tavenner continued, asking the witness what the purpose of the cell was—in other words, why they held the meetings. Hayden explained that they were largely discussion groups about two main topics: what was going on in the movie industry, in regard to such matters as labor conditions, and the world situation—"theoretical diagnoses, and so forth," he said.

"In other words," shot back the counsel, "part of the time was devoted to the study of the principles of the Communist Party?"

"Yes," agreed Hayden.

Tavenner asked him if he had any particular assignment while he was a member of the cell. Hayden promptly mentioned the labor strikes initiated by the Conference of Studio Unions. He recalled that he was told by the cell leadership that it would be very helpful and important if the Screen Actors Guild could be influenced to support the strike, and he described his efforts in that regard. He explained how he had attended several large Hollywood functions where he interacted with several other actors who were sympathetic to the cause of the CSU. He was quick to point out to the committee the following: "I would like to say at this point there were a great, great many people involved here. I don't know what percentage of the actors and actresses involved were a long, long, long way from being Communists in any sense of the word, so far as I know."[35]

Tavenner's next question was carefully worded and was perfectly in harmony with Gang's instructions to all of his clients who would testify as friendly witnesses. Referring to the group of acquaintances in the Screen Actors Guild that he was trying to influence, Tavenner asked: "Are there any of that group whom you can identify as members of the Communist Party, to your knowledge? I am not asking you for names of people generally who were with you in this project, unless they were known to you to be members of the Communist Party."

"I understand. I wouldn't hesitate to say Karen Morley, inasmuch as in 1947, a long time after I had completely severed any and all connections with any form of Communist activities or endeavor, she came to me and asked me to come back, so I certainly think it is safe to assume she was a member. Over and above that, it would have to get into the realm of conjecture, which, frankly, I am somewhat doubtful of."

Describing his interaction with the Screen Actors Guild during that time, Hayden was able to provide more names. While the meetings sometimes took place at Karen Morley's home, they moved from place to place, including the home of actor Morris Carnovsky. "Are you acquainted with a person by the name of Lloyd Gough?" inquired Tavenner. He was, replied Hayden, and he confirmed that Gough was often at the meetings. "Do you have any knowledge on your own part to whether or not he was a member of the Communist Party?" asked the counsel.

"Well, I would say it would probably be safe to assume that he was."

"I don't want you to assume it," shot back Tavenner.

"I have absolutely, categorically, no knowledge that he was." It was not mentioned that Lloyd Gough was Karen Morley's husband. Hayden also confirmed that he knew actor Howard Da Silva and that he attended the same meetings. When asked if he had knowledge that Da Silva was a Communist Party member, Hayden stated: "Only in his behavior before this committee."

After naming fellow members of the Party as well as perceived sympathizers to the committee, Hayden was asked why he broke with the Communist Party. This provided him the opportunity to read a well-scripted statement that allowed him to chastise himself in public for his past actions and to repudiate everything about the Party. He began by thanking the committee for the chance to clear the air. "As I think is abundantly clear—and I don't make any apology—I do not mean to imply that I was dragged into the thing in any way, shape, or manner. I went into the thing voluntarily. Certainly I think it was the stupidest, most ignorant thing I have ever done, and I have done a good many such things, but I did go into it with a very emotional and very unsound approach. I hadn't been in very long—I would say it took me 3 or 4 months to realize the true nature of what I had done.

"I would like to say at this time, without launching into a long dissertation on this thing, that one thing that decided me once and for all against the whole business was the manner in which everything is predetermined. I think that I had become susceptible to and, in a sense, perhaps, a victim of the idea that they had a form of democracy in mind. That was in my mind during the Yugoslav days and the time I joined. I found the belief is that they have the key, by some occult power, to know what is best for people, and that is the way it is going to be. I think any Communist or pseudo-Communist who pretends it is other than this is falsifying the fact.

"When I learned about this and began to think about it and digest it a bit, I decided to get out, and I got out.

"I would like to take this opportunity, if I may, to briefly state for the record a sort of synopsis of my complete association with anything that was Communist or might be construed as Communist front. I would like to lump it and say categorically that is all there is to it, and anybody who insinuates it is not, is mistaken."[36]

In a carefully choreographed move, Tavenner asked Hayden if, since the time he had left the Communist Party, had he become a member of any other organization affiliated with the Communist Party, had Party leanings, or was a Party front. This provided a perfect segue to the Committee for the First Amendment. Recounting how he had left the Party in December 1946, he told the committee about being contacted by Alexander Knox and his request that he (Hayden) join the new organization that would be headed shortly out to Washington to attend the HUAC hearings in October of 1947. "I thought about it very carefully, and I assured myself—I may be wrong—but my conclusion was that this was in no way a Communist front at the time," he stated.

Hayden quickly came to the defense of the Hollywood people who went with him to Washington on behalf of the Committee for the First

Amendment. "I would like to go on with the people who did join. I think you are probably familiar with the membership list of that organization, and if it has since been determined that this thing was spearheaded by Communists, believe me these people didn't know it. The people who lent their names and gave money to this Committee for the First Amendment, to the best of my knowledge certainly had no idea that it was a Communist front, any more than I had."[37] Asked for the names of those who were prominent in the CFA, Hayden recalled that Ira Gershwin had hosted several hundred people at his home. He was vague on names, but did mention Humphrey Bogart and his wife Lauren Bacall, as they had appeared to be the leaders of the trip to the HUAC hearings in Washington. He identified John Huston and screenwriter/director Phil Dunne as the group's spokesmen.

Tavenner probed Hayden's memory as to whether, during his time of membership in the Party, he was acquainted with any communist activity on the part of any high official of the motion picture industry. He related only one instance to the committee—when Bea Winters arranged for him to meet "an important man." Hayden described his somewhat strange meeting with "John," who he later realized was John Stapp, head of the Hollywood section of the California Communist Party. When pressed for any other examples of Hollywood luminaries whose activities indicated membership in the Communist Party, Hayden could not recall any. Seemingly out of the blue, Tavenner asked: "Were you acquainted with Edward G. Robinson?"

"I met Mr. Robinson backstage at a rally for Israel one evening, and chatted with him a couple of minutes before he made a speech."

"Did he attend any Communist Party meetings which you attended?"

"No," responded Hayden.

"Please proceed to sum up what you had in mind saying," instructed Tavenner, moving on.[38] Seemingly in the course of having Hayden testify, the HUAC counsel continued his technique of throwing out names in the form of questions to the witness, thereby assuring that these names were inserted in the record, whether Hayden had "damning" testimony against them or not. Hayden then produced a meticulous accounting of all of the dues and donations that he paid to the Communist Party. He assured the committee that all of the transactions were done prior to his leaving the Party, with the exception of $100 that was donated to the Committee for the First Amendment in 1947.

Hayden was asked to describe his interaction with Karen Morley in the summer of 1947. He recounted her attempt to entice him back into the Communist Party as well as her suggestion that he consider donating money as an alternative.

"In other words," Tavenner asked, "in Hollywood there is such a thing as a passive membership, or a contributing membership, without attending meetings and so forth?"

"That's the way I understood it."[39]

It was at this point in the scripted testimony that Hayden would be asked to amply document the sincerity of his convictions regarding his break with the Communist Party. The HUAC counsel acknowledged Hayden's cooperation with the investigators, and asked him if he had taken any other actions that would indicate good faith on his part. "I believe I have," he replied. "One month after South Korea was invaded, through my attorney a letter was sent to Mr. J. Edgar Hoover, Federal Bureau of Investigation, in which was set forth the fact that for a period of 5 to 6 months I had been a member of the Communist Party, and with the world going the way it was, it seemed entirely probably [*sic*] that a conflagration would develop, and I hope, if that was the case, my services would not be denied, if the Marine Corps could use me, on the basis of this mistake I had made.

"I have a photostatic copy of that letter I would like to produce or read for the record." Tavenner immediately allowed him to produce it, and Martin Gang's letter to Hoover, dated July 31, 1950, was read entirely into the record. When Hayden had finished, Tavenner coyly asked if they had received a reply. When Hayden replied affirmatively, Tavenner asked that he read it also into the record. After he had completed this, Hayden recounted his three visits to the FBI headquarters in Los Angeles to provide documentation of his prior actions.[40]

Frank Tavenner was coming to the end of his questions for Sterling Hayden. He concluded his inquiry by asking Hayden if he had anything else to add. Hayden's obviously scripted response seems almost like a combination of an overly fawning apology to the Committee and a "Dear Abby"-like advice column response to other former Hollywood sympathizers. "I would like to say that I appreciate very much, very, very much, the opportunity to appear here today. I think there is a tremendous service to be rendered, not only to the country at large but to the motion-picture industry and also to those individuals who find themselves in a similar position to mine.

"I have heard that there are many, many thousands—I have heard there are hundreds of thousands—of ex-Communists who don't know what to do about it. I would like, if it is not presumptuous, to suggest in all humility that perhaps some provision could be made by law to permit people who had a similar experience to make their position known and clear, so that they could get this thing off their chest, because, believe me, it is a load to carry around with you."[41] In so many words, Hayden was telling people who were worried about their former communist leanings or affiliations to come to HUAC, testify about the serious mistake in judgment that they had made, give the committee names that they already had (and allow the committee to throw the names out to you in hearings if needed), and to grovel sufficiently. There was a chance that all would be forgiven after such an appearance. Hayden would hate himself for the rest of his life for what he had just done and was advising others to do. As he stated in *Pharos of Chaos*, a documentary film about his life filmed in 1981, "I was a shit. A total goddamn shit."

Tavenner responded by pointing out that Chairman Wood had broadcast a statement not long before that had advised the very actions that Hayden had just suggested, inviting "those who were in this category to make that fact known to this committee, and they would keep it in confidence if that was desired, but to make known their participation so that it would be a matter of record now as to just what their participation had been, . . . and there had been a very fine response to that."[42]

"I didn't realize that," Hayden obediently responded.

• • •

After a brief question by Congressman Frances Walter of Pennsylvania, Congressman Clyde Doyle of California began his questioning of the witness. Doyle seemed to want more precise and specific answers from Hayden. His questioning appeared to have the intent of getting into the crux of Hayden's thinking, as if to serve as a metaphor for all the idealistic naïve people who had made similar choices and now regretted them. He began by honing in on Hayden's previous statement that he was grateful to the committee for the opportunity to get this thing off your chest. "Then you added, 'Believe me, it is a load.' What did you mean by that?" The next five pages of the HUAC testimony record would display the interrogation of Hayden by Doyle over his motives for leaving the Party.

Hayden again reiterated his naivete in joining. "As I have indicated, I went into the thing of my own free will, impulsively, stupidly, but I did get into it. When I realized I was wrong, I got out."

"What happened to cause you to come to the conclusion you had committed error?"

"One of the prime things was taking refuge in certain amendments to the Constitution. At the time I was pretty much of a greenhorn, but as soon as I realized the Communists were taking refuge under the amendments to our Constitution that they under no circumstances would permit others to take—"

"Taking refuge from what?" interrupted Doyle.

"Taking refuge in the Fifth Amendment," replied Hayden, "or the First Amendment and considering that their political connections could not be questioned." As an example, he pointed out that many of the Hollywood communists or suspect communists had taken the Fifth Amendment in the course of HUAC's investigations and hearings.

Doyle didn't quite buy that explanation, pointing out that Hayden had quit the Party four years earlier, in 1946. "What did you discover prior to the time you resigned which caused you, if anything did cause you, to come to the conclusion that you could not consistently continue longer as a member of the Communist Party?"

"One thing was when I became aware of the totalitarian idea of communism, which had been obscured by the fog of the war years." Doyle wanted more specifics and a clearer definition from Hayden. He pressed him again: "When you say you discovered the totalitarian nature of the Communist Party, what do you mean by that? What does 'totalitarian nature of the Communist Party' mean to you that caused you to resign?"

"That a very few people, or a certain group of people, know what is best for the majority, and the will of the majority has no bearing on what is done for the majority, That, I believe, is wrong."

Doyle's next question served to confirm the nefarious intentions of the Party, and it would be Sterling Hayden who would, as the former insider, corroborate what the committee already believed. He solemnly asked, "Did you discover at any time that the Communist Party was encouraging devious ways to upset or overthrow or overcome, by force if necessary, the republican form of government that we have under our Constitution in the United States?"

"I certainly believe that to be the case," responded the witness, paying his penance in public.[43]

• • •

Doyle's next line of questioning was a rehash of Tavenner's inquiry into the composition of Hayden's cell activities, the frequency of meetings, and the two names—Abe Polonsky and Robert Lees—he was able to recollect. Again, Hayden explained his efforts to get the Screen Actors

Guild to support the CSU strike. Doyle returned to Warwick Tompkins, asking Hayden if any of the literature that he provided indicated that the Communist Party was interested in revolution against the American form of government.

"As I recall, it was always couched in other terms, I think a more perceptive person would have seen it. I did not at the time," responded Hayden.

"Do you believe the literature you received from Tompkins did advocate the overthrow of the American form of government?"

"I think that was the ultimate objective; yes." Hayden went on to deny that he had any of the literature still in his possession. In response to Doyle's question as to where such literature could be obtained currently, Hayden identified the Lincoln Book Store in Hollywood, which he had last patronized in 1946.

Doyle continued to press Hayden on his previous testimony. "You stated you came to think there was a great service to do the country and the industry. I suppose you were referring to the moving picture industry. Does the moving picture industry, in your judgment, need any service in connection with who are and who are not Communists and who were Communists previously, and if so, what service?"

In response, Hayden reiterated his thought that if these people "felt they could stand up and be counted on the facts, it would clarify the situation." Hearing that, Doyle asked if the film industry was being active in "cleaning up" the situation. Not satisfied with Hayden's response, he rephrased his question: "I will ask it this way: To your knowledge has the moving picture industry been endeavoring to clean up its own house?"

"I certainly think it has."

"Do you think it is doing a pretty good job of it?"

"I think it is; so far as I know."

Doyle decided to shift gears with the final phase of his questioning. At first, he seemed to be mocking Hayden's naivete with questions that almost asked him how he could be so obtuse. But there was a motive for his questioning that soon became apparent. He went back to Hayden's previous testimony when he said that the feeling was boiling inside of him and that being an actor with high income and pleasant working conditions would allow him to do something about conditions in the world in general. "What were the conditions that you were boiling up inside about, that you wanted to help correct?"

Hayden related his irregular background and unconventional way of earning a living by always being at sea. "I suddenly found myself making a lot of money and not doing a great deal of work for it, and I felt a responsibility I should have had earlier as an American citizen. I never thought politically before. All of this came to focus at one time, and, unfortunately perhaps, the increment that set it off was my experience in Yugoslavia."

In response, Doyle seemed to come to Hayden's rescue and threw him a lifeline when he stated: "At the time you were not interested in any economic conditions facing our country; it only involved your personal boiling up inside?"

"That is very close to being correct."

"Am I correct?" Doyle insisted.

"You are very nearly correct."

"It was a personal matter?"

"Yes," replied the witness, assuring the world that he was not part of an overall evil scheme by the Communist Party to overthrow the government. It was simply the personal feeling of a young, naïve man trying to make the world a better place that caused him to mistakenly do what he had done. It was now time for Doyle to continue on with his "babe-in-the-woods" portrayal of Hayden as a rube who couldn't see he was perhaps being used by the Communist Party. He addressed Bea Winters's signing him up for the Party in June of 1946. "You were told you could not be a member of a cell where all the members were actors, for security reasons, didn't it then occur to you there was something phony or dangerous about the Communist Party, when, for security reasons, you could not belong to a cell where actors belonged?"

"Yes; it did," replied Hayden.

"What occurred to you?"

"As I said before, it was a rash move, an impulsive move, but I was under such a head of steam at the time I simply did not think the thing out very carefully. I went ahead anyway."

"In other words," Doyle helpfully interjected, "you were so enraptured with the Partisans of Yugoslavia, their bravery and heroism, and you had so tied yourself up with Tompkins and others, that you could not immediately withdraw from the Communist Party?"

"I could have withdrawn, but I couldn't see clearly at the time. I think that is accurate."

Doyle asked if Hayden could come up with any of the security reasons as to why he could not be in a cell with other actors. The only thing that Hayden could think of was that he was an employee of Paramount

Pictures and if it came out that he was a member of the Communist Party, he would have likely been fired.

After succeeding in having Hayden perceived as an idealist with a personal agenda as opposed to a malevolent communist agenda, and who didn't question the suspicious placement of him in a non-actors cell out of fear of losing his job, it was then time to turn back to the evil Svengali who was largely the cause of Hayden's troubles. He brought up Warwick Tompkins's proposed biography of Hayden, a project for which he had written 75,000 words before Hayden "came to" and told him to call it off. "What was it that caused you to 'come to' sufficiently to go to this longtime friend of yours, advisor. He had been an advisor, I take it? . . . What gave you the backbone to go to him? What did you discover about the 75,000 words."

"The first draft he had knocked out actually fell by the wayside when I realized what I had done. It was not the book. I never read the book."

"Was the book published?"

"Heaven forbid," responded Hayden. "No." He went on to explain that Tompkins had typewritten a first draft and that his (Hayden's) wife had frequently suggested that he get it back from his former mentor. He did not mention the warning and advice he had received from Lincoln Colcord. "Do you feel if you made a demand on Tompkins for it you would get it back?" asked Doyle.

"I have no idea."

"Did you accept money or anything of value for the script?"

"Nothing whatever. I have heard since that he has been expelled from the party. I don't know anything about that," Hayden concluded. With that, Doyle had finished his questioning of the witness.[44]

• • •

The next inquisitor for the HUAC was Congressman Harold Velde of Illinois. Velde began by complimenting Hayden for his cooperation with the committee, but noted that his recall of "the names of your associates in the Communist Party are, for some reason, a bit obscure, and I can understand why." He was interested in tracing Hayden's communist association from World War II, beginning with the Partisans. Hayden was able to provide the name of three Partisan leaders, but when asked if he had ever met Tito, he admitted that he had not.

Next, Velde wanted to know the names of his fellow OSS members that he served with in the Balkans theater. Hayden replied, "American

OSS officers in Bari, Capt. Haus [*sic*] Tofte; Lt. Bob Thompson; Lt. Ward Ellen; Lieutenant Benson; Sgt. John Harnicker, Marine Corps; Major Koch; Maj. Linn Farish, who was killed in Greece. I guess there are a lot of others. Their names don't come to mind."

Velde inquired of Hayden "if any of those you have listed are known to you to be or have been members of the Communist Party, so state."

"To my knowledge, none of them had any connection whatever. These were simply fellow officers or enlisted men with whom I worked."

Velde continued with the precedent set by Frank Tavenner and began to name names on behalf of the witness. "Was there an OSS officer from Pittsburgh?" he inquired, obviously knowing that there was. Hayden acknowledged that there were a number from the Pittsburgh area but he could recall only three. "Were they members of the Communist Party? Can you identify any of them as members of the Communist Party?" pressed Velde.

"No," replied Hayden, who then served up the name of a fellow OSS officer for the Committee to tarnish. "I have heard subsequently that one of them, George Wuchinich, was in some way connected with the Communist Party. The others were strictly anti-Communist."

"Will you tell the committee how you felt, or know, that George Wuchinich was associated with the Communist Party?"

"I don't know when or how I heard it, but at some time since the war I heard that mentioned," admitted Hayden.

"Scuttlebutt?"

"Let's say scuttlebutt," agreed the witness.

This singling out of George Wuchinich by both Hayden and the committee is significant, as both he and Hayden were considered the most pro-Partisan members of the OSS team in Bari. That in itself was noteworthy because, according to team member Eli Popovich, the communist presence and influence in Bari had become so pervasive that the OSS headquarters there had become known as the "Little Kremlin."[45] Since Wuchinich was of Yugoslavian ancestry, he and George Musulin, a native of Pittsburgh and also of Yugoslavian descent, were the first OSS officers sent to Cairo to be prepared for infiltration into Yugoslavia in May of 1943. In November of 1943, Lt. Wuchinich parachuted into Slovenia to assist the Partisans. After his return to Bari, his outspoken support and admiration for the Partisans led other officers to charge that he was a communist. Similar to Hayden until he had his dramatic change of heart after Operation HACIENDA, Wuchinich was felt to have such a strong affinity for the Partisan movement that his fellow officers considered him more of an advocate for Tito's cause than an impartial observer who was capable of unbiased assessments from the field.[46] Wuchinich was awarded the Distinguished Service Cross for his actions serving in the Balkans.

After the war, Wuchinich returned to Pittsburgh where he hosted a weekly radio show, *Keep America Free,* and was executive secretary of the American Slav Congress, which sought support for left-wing movements in the Balkans. As the Red Scare evolved in the late 1940s, he was labeled as a "dangerous Communist" although he had never actually joined the Communist Party.[47]

Having managed to get George Wuchinich's name into the record, Velde quickly changed the subject, instead asking Hayden to tell again about his trip home on leave in December of 1944. Once more, the topic would switch to Warwick Tompkins. "Have you seen Mr. Tompkins recently?" inquired Velde.

"The last time I saw him was 2 years ago when my wife and I were living on a boat at San Pedro and he and his wife and son, who had worked for me once, strolled by. We discussed nothing."

"You had no conversation with him?"

"No conversation except about boats."

Hayden again described his activities during the December 1944 visit, and repeated the names of Dr. Ellwood Lyman and Steve Nelson after Velde prompted him to do so. Asking Hayden to recount the conversations he had with Nelson aboard Tompkin's schooner, he recalled that they were just general discussions, with Hayden relating his stories of his work with the Partisans. Velde threw out several other names: Leo Baroway and Isaac Folkoff, whom Hayden had also met through the introductions by Tompkins. Once again, Velde directed the conversation back to Tompkins. "Where were you staying at the time?"

"On Tompkins' schooner."

"Was Tompkins the sole owner of the schooner?"

"I think he and his wife."

"Is he a wealthy man?" inquired Velde.

"I would say he is anything but wealthy. I think that—well, that is getting into the realm of conjecture again."

Unwilling to drop the subject, Velde continued: "There are degrees of being wealthy, like everything else."

"He is a man who has led a rather spectacular career in the South Seas, in Europe, in Paris, as an artist and writer, and he attempted to make the schooner pay and the schooner never paid."

"You mean by taking passengers?"

"College boys in the summer; yes."

Hinting at a possible nefarious motive that Tompkins may have had, Velde asked Hayden: "You said he was one of those who influenced you to become a member of the Communist Party?"

"He forged the first link, you might say."

Velde concluded his questioning by throwing out more names and asking Hayden if he had met them or had they been present at any of the meetings aboard Tompkins's schooner: Bernadette Doyle and Louise Bransten. Doyle had been secretary of the Alameda County Communist Party, while Bransten was a wealthy political activist resident of San Francisco and Communist Party member. To the best of his knowledge, Hayden couldn't be certain. With that, Velde yielded to the next committee member.[48]

• • •

Congressmen Bernard W. Kearney of New York and Donald L. Jackson of California were the next committee members to question Hayden. Kearney proceeded to ask a few widely varying questions. Referring to Larry Parks's previous testimony—in which he stated that no writer in Hollywood could color a picture for propaganda purposes—he asked Hayden if he agreed with that assessment. Hayden emphatically supported Parks's view, although he admitted that it would have been more of a possibility in years past. Did Hayden know if any of the convicted Hollywood Ten, whom he mistakenly identified as actors, had again been employed by the film industry? Hayden had no idea. "I understood you to say in the meetings you attended there was discussion, indirectly, of the overthrow of the Government by force and violence?" queried the general.

"There was a discussion of what they called dialectics," recalled Hayden, referring to the dialectical materialism that is the theoretical foundation of Marxism. In response to Kearney's next question, he didn't recall that any well-known leaders of the Communist Party ever attended any cell meetings that he was present at.

Kearney directed his questioning again to Karen Morley and Warwick Tompkins. In response to Kearney's question, Hayden replied that he did not know if Karen Morley was still a member of the Party. At that point, Kearney turned the floor over to his fellow committee member, Donald Jackson.

After inquiring if he knew Tompkins's present whereabouts, to which Hayden pleaded ignorance, he asked if he had had any further contacts with Bea Winters, and Isaac Folkoff. Other than running into Winters in a market and saying hello, his answer was no. Jackson next posed a series of rapid fire questions having to do with Hayden's first two films, *Virginia* and *Bahama Passage*, before proceeding to ask: "Would you say those people in the motion-picture industry who have for some reason or other associated themselves with the Communist Party or with front organizations, either as active members or as fellow travelers, lend their efforts to the party knowing the ultimate goal of the front organizations for which they appear?"

"I think that covers a lot of ground. I certainly think no, that the majority did not," opined the witness.

"The majority did not?"

"No. I think that is particularly true of the Committee for the First Amendment."

Jackson continued with questions concerning the production of *The Asphalt Jungle* before returning to the topic of the bogeyman, Warwick Tompkins. "Was Captain Tompkins personally acquainted with people in the movie colony?"

"Not to my knowledge. He once visited me on the set."

"Did you attend any parties or affairs with Captain Tompkins in Hollywood?"

"No; never did."

Referring to the biography of Hayden that Tompkins had worked on, Jackson attempted to link the project with Hollywood and its potential to subtly influence the public by presenting communism in a positive light. "Was it ever intended that the story he was doing on you was to be made into a script?"

"Not to my knowledge; not to my knowledge. He has had no experience in screen playwriting at all. I think he had one idea in mind, which is the one I outlined. I have read random remarks in trade papers that certain phases of my activity would make a good story."

"But whether he had that in mind, you don't know?" pressed Jackson.

"No, I don't."

Shifting gears again, Jackson asked Hayden if he knew Herbert K. Sorrell. Hayden knew who he was but he had never met him. Was Hayden ever asked to support the strikes? Referring to the meetings he attended with numerous actors and actresses on behalf of his cell, he replied, "The whole focal point of the activity of this group of actors and actresses was to swing the Screen Actors Guild in favor of Sorrell's CSU."

Jackson ended his inquiry by asking: "Do you consider, Mr. Hayden, that in your own mind you have been completely fair and completely frank with the committee, and that you have named for this committee every member of the Communist Party in the moving-picture industry of whom you have personal knowledge."

"I do."

"Mr. Hayden, has any member of your family, either by blood or marriage, at any time been a member of the Communist Party?

"No; they certainly have not."[49] With that response, Chairman Wood turned the questioning over to Congressman Charles E. Potter of Michigan.

Potter began his questioning by addressing the influence that Hayden's OSS service with the Partisans had upon him. "Mr. Hayden, I was interested in the influence that the Partisan movement had on you, and I am wondering what your observation would be of that same influence on other Americans who happened to be in the OSS aiding the Partisan movement in Yugoslavia. Do you believe you were an exception or that other individuals closely identified with the Partisan movement would be susceptible to the Communist ideology through that association?"

"I can only say that to the best of my knowledge I know of no one else affected similarly. We were all deeply moved, but I have no way of knowing that anyone else had a parallel experience."

"Through your contact with other American military personnel, did any of them at that time feel, or did you discuss among yourselves, that communism was a political star which we should tie onto?"

"We never got into any of that."

"You never discussed that?"

"Not that I remember, not at all. All our work and conversation and thoughts seemed to be filled with just what was actually going on."

Hayden's responses to Potter's previous questions concerning the OSS were absurd and dishonest. Reading the transcript, it seems as if Potter's questions were intended to again portray Hayden as the idealist and hapless rube—the sole OSS member to be mesmerized by the Partisans. It seems incredible that no committee member pointed out to him that only a short while earlier he, with the able assistance of Congressman Velde, had ratted out George Wuchinich as a probable Communist Party member. Although much documentation concerning the OSS personnel in Bari would remain classified for years, the strong political influence of support for the Partisans versus support of the Chetniks, affected many of the men. As previously noted, Wuchinich and Hayden were well known for their outspoken support of the Partisans and were suspected of being communists by many of the other OSS men. In addition, Eli Popopvich, who had served with the Partisans as part of the OSS liaison to Tito's headquarters, had documented that OSS Bari was jokingly referred to by some as the "Little Kremlin." He had become so suspicious of the personnel in Bari that he filed the report of his last mission in Yugoslavia with Robert Murphy, American political advisor to the Supreme Allied commander in the Mediterranean theater rather than forwarding it through regular OSS channels.[50]

It is surprising that Hayden did not bring up the conclusions that he reached when he returned from Operation HACIENDA. His apparent about-face and harsh critique of the Partisans could have only served to help him in his dealings with HUAC, although it potentially could have painted him in an unfavorable light for having joined the Communist Party less than two years later. The after-action report would remain classified for many years and, as noted, he never referred to this change in his opinion in *Wanderer*.

In response to Jackson's follow-up question, Hayden denied that he had any knowledge of efforts made during the war to recruit military personnel into the Communist Party. Jackson abruptly turned to Hayden's efforts to influence the Screen Actors Guild to support the CSU strikes. "How successful were you with the other group?" he asked.

"I am sure, as a matter of fact, the move was very unsuccessful. It ran into the board of directors of the Screen Actors Guild, and particularly into Ronald Reagan, who was a one-man battalion against this thing. He was very vocal and clear-thinking on it. I don't think many people realized how complex it was. I know I didn't. There was little headway made."[51]

Potter next returned to the activities of Hayden's cell, asking about discussions, how they could increase their membership, and similar topics. "Would you say it is difficult to be a half-hearted member when you are a member of a cell?" he asked.

"One of the most impressive things about that group was the dedication of the people to it."

"Was that through discipline?"

"I don't know how to answer to that. As far as I know, there was little or no discipline."

After a few more questions concerning financing of the cell and monetary contributions that Hayden had made, Jackson yielded his time to Congressman Morgan M. Moulder of Missouri.[52] Moulder's first question once again attempted to portray Hayden's actions as those of an individualist, not those of one genuinely enamored with the communist philosophy. "Referring to your testimony of the Communist movement having a tremendous effect on you following Yugoslavia, as I understand, that was caused not because of your sympathy with the Communist philosophy, but was stirred by the struggle of a minority group seeking to achieve economic security?"

"No," Hayden said. "The only thing we were struggling against was the Nazi occupation forces. We knew many of those people had been underground for years, but the one struggle we saw was against the Germans."

Continuing on along those lines, Moulder attempted to shift back to the influence of Warwick Tompkins, asking if Hayden's membership in the Communist Party was the result of "continual solicitation of an acquaintance of yours" that had "followed the exciting period that you had encountered while in Yugoslavia?"

"I think that is right."

"During the period of your membership in the party, you decided that the philosophy they were discussing was not in accord with your philosophy of government?"

"Yes," agreed Hayden. "In the first place, if I may say so—and I say it because probably a good many people have been in a similar position—I never understood it. I was constantly told if I would read 40 pages of *Dialectical and Historical Materialism* I would understand communism. I never got beyond page 8, and I tried several times."

Moulder ended his questioning by stating that he understood that the request to have Hayden appear before the committee was not done to impugn his loyalty but to secure information regarding communist activities. Hayden concurred with the assessment. "I believe your courageous services in the Marine Corps and in the OSS deserve commendation, and your testimony in my opinion has been straightforward and honest . . . From the testimony adduced here before this committee, I can reach only one conclusion, so far as I am concerned, and that is that you have joined with us in our efforts to expose the evils of communism; that you are an intensely loyal American citizen and you deserve commendation for the services you have rendered as a Marine Corps soldier and for your testimony before this committee."[53]

Congressman Doyle was again recognized, and he queried Hayden about his previous statement that in 1944, he had built up a tremendous curiosity and he went to see Tompkins about it. What were the reasons behind this decision? "It so happened he came to me," Hayden explained. "I think it is one of the characteristics of our country and of all democracies that as a rule we don't endeavor to impress upon people—I think we don't attempt to do it enough—the things we believe in. Communists are the opposite. They give you no peace. When a Communist like Tompkins finds anyone at all susceptible, the pressure is on unremittingly."

"Did you find anything going on in the world as to activities of the Communist Party in relation to what was going on in America or other freedom-loving nations, and if so, what?"

"Only that this whole totalitarian Communist move [*sic*] is a tremendous force in the world."

"When you refer to this totalitarian movement, what is that movement, in your judgment?" asked Doyle.

"An endeavor to take over the entire world."

"Are you testifying now," Doyle dramatically inquired, "that the intention and purpose of the Communist Party of the United States is to, by force, take control of the United States of America Government?"

"Yes; I do," Hayden solemnly responded.

Doyle asked if he felt the same way when he quit the Party in 1946. Hayden responded that he did. What inducements did the communists, specifically Karen Morley, offer him to rejoin the Party? What arguments did they present? None, responded Hayden. "There was very little argument. One thing I learned was that you cannot argue with a Communist. His mind is made up, and you can talk from now until breakfast and it won't do any good."

"I am now going to ask you a question," Doyle dramatically announced. Stating the obvious—that Hayden was sitting before a duly constituted committee of the House of Representatives, every member of which was elected every two years by the American people—did he, Sterling Hayden, believe that the HUAC was, in his judgment, serving "a useful purpose? Is it serving a necessary purpose? If so, to what extent, and if not, why? Is that a fair question?" Hayden agreed that it was. Doyle continued on. "I am really asking for your honest-to-God truthful opinion." Praising Hayden's frankness and cooperation, Doyle asked him: "If you have any criticism of the manner in which this committee functions, I would like to know what that criticism is. You have now been before us for 3 hours."

Hayden immediately and obediently could think of no criticism. Doyle set up the witness to be the role model and inspiration for all communists and ex-communists in Hollywood when he asked him: "Have you any suggestions to make of ways and means in which we might be more helpful in meeting this problem of the determination of the Communist Party of the United States to overthrow, if necessary by force, our Government?"

Hayden dutifully replied that the recent suggestion made by the committee "that people come up and speak up, is the thing I came here today thinking it was an extremely fine thing, a constructive thing.

"I don't mean to attach any importance to myself as an individual who is out of balance, but I have had the feeling that my appearance before the committee could serve a useful purpose, I hope it does."

Congressman Velde returned to query Hayden, asking him to once again recall his trip to San Francisco while on leave in 1944. He pressed the witness to recall the names of who else attended the gatherings aboard Warwick Tompkins's schooner. Unable to definitely recall names, Velde very helpfully supplied several, asking Hayden if he had met Steve Murin, Dwight Freeman, and Freeman's wife Pearl. Murin was the founder of the Hawaiian Civil Liberties Committee, a group that was formed to defend a couple of school teachers who had been fired for being suspected Communists. Dwight Freeman had been sent after the war from San Francisco to help organize Hawaii's Communist Party, a finding that had been brought out in previous HUAC hearings. Although he was somewhat familiar with the names, Hayden couldn't recall if he had met them.

Velde returned to the time of Hayden's OSS service in the Balkans. "Going back to the Yugoslavia operations as a member of the OSS, what do you feel was the general attitude of the OSS toward the Partisan Movement?"

"The feeling was high and strong. I was only associated with the Partisans. One man, named Gov Muslin [*sic*], I met him on leave, and he was pro-Mihailovitch [*sic*]. There was every shade of opinion," noted Hayden. He was actually referring to the previously mentioned Capt. George Musulin, who along with George Wuchinich, were the first two OSS officers intended to become liaison officers in Yugoslavia. Musulin soon after served as the OSS liaison to Milhailovich's Chetnik forces. Velde asked about the attitude of the OSS toward the Chetniks.

"Until Tito merged [*sic*], I think we were following the British dictate, which was to support Mihailovitch [*sic*] and the Chetniks," Hayden accurately stated.

"Wasn't the attitude of the OSS members at that time to belittle the efforts of the Chetniks?" asked Velde.

"No. There was a certain element of OSS officers who, I believe were pro-Mihailovitch [*sic*] and stayed that way. Others started that way and swung to Tito."

Velde shifted back to the "did you know . . ." technique of throwing out names for Hayden to recall. Among them was Gregory Khiefets, the KGB officer assigned to the San Francisco consulate. When Hayden denied knowing Khiefets, Velde finished by asking: "Then to the best of your recollection you have never met a member of the Soviet diplomatic force in the United States?"

"Not to the best of my recollection," replied the witness.[54]

Once again, Congressman Potter returned to the questioning, asking a question that likely had occurred to other members of the committee and deserved answering by the witness. "How does it happen that Bea Winters was the one who talked you into becoming a member of the party when your good friend, Captain Tompkins, was the one who constantly advocated the Communist cause? Why didn't Captain Tompkins approach you to become a member instead of Bea Winters?"

"I can only imagine he was waiting for a tactical approach. And he was living in another district," was the nondescript reply. After several general questions concerning the cell he belonged to, Potter asked a question that was perhaps a subtle message intended for those who worked in motion pictures. "From the testimony that you have given before this committee, and the forthright manner in which you have given the testimony, do you expect any reprisals from this testimony by the motion-picture industry?"

"I do not," replied Hayden. "I have thought about that. I will be frank, I have thought about it. Whether it is natural wishful thinking or confidence, I don't know, but I feel that when the mistake of 5 months is weighed against other things, I really don't see a justification for it." In what looks like a carefully scripted exchange, Potter expressed his assumption that people in the motion picture industry knew of Hayden's involvement in the Communist Party. Hayden strongly disagreed. "I was subpoenaed to appear before this committee approximately 5 days before I started working in the picture in which I am now engaged. At that time there was considerable consternation on the part of the producers, simply because I had been subpoenaed. They asked that I issue a statement denying past or present affiliation. I issued a statement denying present affiliation."

"So you think it came as a distinct surprise to them?"

"I think today's testimony will come as quite a surprise."

Potter's last question provided an opportunity to differentiate Sterling Hayden from a previous witness, allowing the committee to once again throw that witness, Larry Parks, under the bus. "When Mr. Parks was here recently he said he belonged to a select group of actors. You had no knowledge of that while you were a member of the party?"

"I was under the impression that no such group existed."

"And were you surprised when you heard the testimony of Mr. Parks?"

In a final act of piling on by the committee, ably assisted by Hayden, he replied: "I was. I never had a firm opinion about Larry Parks. I do not know. I know in these meetings of actors occasionally it would be suggested that perhaps Parks would support something, and it was always said, 'No, he would not.' I remember that clearly."

Chairman Wood briefly peppered Hayden with questions about finances of the cell, as well as how often it met and what topics it discussed, all of which were items that had been previously covered. He again expressed amazement that Hayden could only recall two or three names of cell members for the committee. "You leave with this committee the impression you did not get sufficiently curious about your associates to inquire as to who they were?"

"That is right."

"And you cannot tell us a single name of others in that cell?" he once again probed.

"I cannot."

Congressman Velde returned with a question: "Did you attend a Progressive Party rally at Madison Square Garden in 1947?" The main speaker at the rally was former vice president Henry A. Wallace, who would run for president in 1948 on the Progressive Party ticket. Hayden replied that he and his wife Betty attended the rally. Could he identify any communists who attended that rally? Hayden denied that he could. "Can you tell the committee what prompted you to attend that rally?" asked Velde.

"I think I can. As I said, the entire year of 1947 I was not working. I was under contract but I did not work. I stayed on the boat in Santa Barbara. I was married in May of that year and my wife and I went east for 4 months. Then I began to feel a desire to at least participate in something of a constructive nature. We were in New York on our way to the west coast when this rally was being held . . . it was the same feeling that motivated me in joining the Committee for the First Amendment when I was approached. It was a desire to talk about something outside of the weather, which was what we had been talking about all summer in Maine."

With that last potential land mine—Hayden's attendance at a rally endorsing a man perceived to be soft on communism—successfully defused, it was time for the denouement of the day's hearing. Congressman Doyle led off. "The law under which this committee functions, as far as jurisdiction is concerned, provides that we may inquire into the extent, character, and objects of un-American propaganda activities in the United States. Have you any information which you can give this committee which you have not already given on that subject? If you have, will you give it to us, please? Do you understand my question?"

"Yes," the witness solemnly replied. "I believe I have covered just about everything I possibly have access to in my own mind."

"The law also provides that we shall inquire into the distribution and diffusion within the United States of subversive and un-American propaganda that is instigated by and comes from foreign countries. Have you any information on that?" Hayden denied he had any helpful information.

"Did you acquire any information on that while you were a member? . . . Or before or at all?"

Hayden replied no to both.

"You have testified twice, in answer to my questions, that you are satisfied one of the objectives of the Communist Party of the United States is to forcibly overthrow, if necessary, the form of government set out by our American Constitution. Have you anything to add as to the ways and means they would undertake to accomplish that objective?"

"I do not."

It was time for one last humiliation that Hayden would have to endure in order to fully pay his penance. It wasn't enough that he had publicly named names as the first cooperative and willing witness. He had to confess that there were additional names he had provided the committee. Both Tavenner and Chairman Wood asked Hayden one last time about names he could recall of acquaintances that he could definitely state were Communist Party members. Wood asked: "I understand that the list of names you have given the investigators are in addition to those you have named before this committee." After Hayden concurred with this, Wood then inquired: "And do I understand those names have been furnished the investigators by you only upon some conjecture you have that they may have been members of the party?"

"My feeling is that the only ones I know to have been members are those active in the cell and Karen Morley. Any others would have to be conjecture."

"That is not entirely responsive to my question," Wood pointed out. "Do I understand that the list of names you have furnished the investigators, that you have no knowledge as to whether they have ever been members of the Communist Party or not?"

"That is true. I do not know."

"But your purpose in furnishing the list of names to the investigators was that by proper investigation on the part of the investigators of the committee itself, that their connection to the Communist Party might be revealed with reference to some of them?"

"I think if they were asked it would be developed."

"Was that your purpose in furnishing to the staff of this committee that list of names?"

"It was."

"And no other reason?"

"No, sir." [55]

In other words, people named on the list provided by Hayden were guilty until they could prove they were innocent (if indeed they were). That was Hayden's benevolent purpose in assisting the committee in that manner. He had paid his penance to the fullest extent.

Hayden's self-contempt over what he had just done jumps out of the pages of his autobiography. Recalling Congressman Moulder's compliments to him, he sarcastically imagined a response and a conversation with the studio executives who days before had worried about the effect that his testimony would have on the current film production. "Oh, thank you, sir, so much. Hey execs back out on the coast! Your boy came through. It is okay. You will not lose your dollars . . . Do you hear me? Is it okay—for me to come back to work tomorrow?" Continuing on in that vein, he noted: "I think of Larry Parks, who not ten days ago sat in this very chair and by pleading with the Committee—by begging them not to make him crawl through the mud—consigned himself to oblivion. Well, I hadn't made that mistake. Not by a goddamn sight. I was a real daddy longlegs of a worm when it came to crawling."[56]

Congressman Doyle asked one more question about Karen Morley, and then it was over. After three hours and fifteen minutes of testimony, the committee officially adjourned at 1:15 p.m. Sterling Hayden's immediate ordeal was over. The record of his testimony would occupy forty-five transcript pages (in contrast to the thirty-five pages that it took to record Larry Parks's hearing). But did his testimony save his career, or would he find himself an unemployable pariah like Larry Parks? He would soon find out.

• • •

Martin Gang was elated with the way the hearing had gone. As they departed the hearing, he buoyantly reassured Hayden. "Mark my words, boy," he predicted to his handsome protégé, "you are going to emerge from this thing bigger than ever before. I wouldn't be at all surprised if you became a kind of hero overnight. Wait till they hear about your testimony out on the Coast tonight . . . Why, you're going to end up smelling like a rose."[57] Gang's prophecy would prove to be correct. That night, Hayden flew back to the West Coast. While changing flights in Chicago he bought the local newspapers to see if there was any coverage of his testimony. To his shock, he saw a report entitled "HAYDEN PAL DIES." The United Press reported that Lawrence J. "Larry" O'Toole, artist, sailor, and adventurer, had died that morning at the age of forty-two.[58] His best friend had suddenly died at the very moment when Hayden was testifying before the HUAC.

The following morning, he was back on the set of *Skid Row*. It was almost as if nothing had happened the day before. In less than two weeks, filming was completed. The film was retitled *Journey into Light* and was released in September. Less than ten days after he completed the film, he had another major film offer. He would be starring with Bette Davis in *The Star*.

Gang was right. Hayden was hailed as a courageous hero by many in the film industry. Among the laudatory cables he received from members of the film industry was one from good friend William Holden and another from SAG president Ronald Reagan. Even Paramount Pictures president Frank Freeman offered his congratulations via telegram.[59] His career took off, and throughout the early 1950s, he would star in over thirty films, including a few that would become cult classics. Among these were *Johnny Guitar, Suddenly,* and *The Killing*. Throughout this period, however, he lived with the self-disgust that his testimony before the HUAC had generated. "Not often does a man find himself eulogized for having behaved in a manner that he himself despises. I subscribed to a press-clipping service. They sent me two thousand clips from papers east and west, large and small, and from dozens of magazines. Most had nothing but praise for my one-shot stoolie show. Only a handful—led by the *New York Times*—denounced this abrogation of constitutional freedoms whereby the stoolie could gain status in a land of frightened people."[60]

After a dysfunctional childhood that was followed by a solid career as a sailor, Sterling Hayden had quit Hollywood and ended up fighting his first war against the Nazis with distinction. In order to protect his fledgling movie career, he fought a combined war with himself and the HUAC, and compromised himself in order to emerge victorious in achieving his goal, although the cost to his self-esteem rendered it somewhat of a Pyrrhic victory. It seemed in 1951 that the worst was at last behind him, but he was about to embark on another battle. This time, the foe would be his wife.

PART FOUR

LATER BATTLES

"To me, the greatest delight in life is just to say hello to people going by."

STERLING HAYDEN

"He tried."

STERLING HAYDEN, WHEN ASKED WHAT HIS EPITAPH SHOULD BE

"What the hell difference does it make, left or right? There were good men lost on both sides."

QUOTE BY BRENDAN BEHAN, TAPED ON THE WALL OF
STERLING HAYDEN'S SAUSALITO APARTMENT WHEN HE DIED

CHAPTER SIXTEEN

Divorce and Escape

WITH HAYDEN NOW STEADILY WORKING AGAIN, HE RESUMED HIS psychoanalysis, this time with a new psychiatrist. Much to Hayden's relief, his new therapist was much more talkative and interactive, but also "heavy-handed" and "caustic." Still, Hayden felt he wasn't making progress. His therapist quickly discovered the source of his problems. His marriage to Betty was extremely volatile. They had already separated five times, reconciling each time. Why, asked the therapist, did he stay in the shattered marriage? Hayden lamely replied it was for the sake of their four children. If they divorced, he feared Betty would become involved in a new and equally volatile and unstable relationship. "But what chance do they have now?" countered his doctor, "in a home full of hatred."[1] A divorce seemed like the only logical course, given the totally unsatisfactory situation. Once again, Hayden returned to the subject of his children. He was obsessed with his desire to get custody.

"I was wondering," he asked, "just why I'm so damn obsessed with this question of custody. Thousands of men with kids go through what I'm involved in. They make up their minds even though they're sick at the thought of being cut off from their kids."

"I believe if we knew the answer to that question," his therapist astutely observed, "you would need no further treatment."[2] To assist his patient with his dilemma, he pointed out that Betty did not have custody of her daughter from her first marriage. Hayden should look into those circumstances, his doctor advised. It had never occurred to Hayden to investigate that before. He decided to have his lawyer help him to look into his wife's previous divorce.

Hayden was no longer working with Martin Gang, but instead with a younger lawyer in the firm. His almost quixotic quest to obtain custody of his children nearly drove his attorney to drink. He had filed for divorce in December of 1951, and on April 24, 1953, the courts granted the

Haydens an interlocutory divorce. The movie star harangued his lawyer into accompanying him to the country clerk's office where they searched the records. After digging through multiple files, they found what they were after. There was enough dirt on Betty in the file to convince Hayden to pursue his custody battle for their children. He laid out his plan to have private detectives tail Betty and obtain evidence to show that she was an unfit parent. As his exasperated attorney listened to Hayden rage on about catching Betty in the act, he finally interrupted him to point out a legal reality: "The fact that you are saddled with an interlocutory decree of divorce. The property settlement is in effect. All of this works in her favor—gives her plenty of latitude to go on with her life."

"Okay then," countered his client. "I'll reconcile and stick around for a couple of months. That will dismiss the present divorce. Then we'll start over from scratch."

"You are prepared to do a thing like that?"

"You're goddamn right I am."[3]

With that, the lawyer pointed out the precariousness of such a plan. Hayden already owed the law firm a lot of money. Private detectives would add to his financial burden. Hayden brushed those arguments aside, claiming he would continue to grind out "crap pictures" and "crap television" shows to generate the money. Reluctantly, his attorney agreed to support his client's somewhat dubious plan. He ended the session with some stern and prophetic advice. "The most important part of the deal is this. Custody is never settled. Matters of custody aren't like normal litigation. Don't ever forget I said that. We're going ahead because you won't listen to reason." He also felt compelled to add an editorial comment: "You aren't the smartest client I have, but you just might be the most stubborn."[4]

Following his plan, Sterling and Betty reconciled, but not long after, the Haydens once again separated and Hayden again filed for divorce from his wife. This time, he was armed with information obtained by the private detectives that he had hired to follow Betty. They produced evidence that she had had six affairs while she was still married to Hayden. Confronted with this, Betty voluntarily surrendered custody of the children in an agreement signed on June 5, 1955.[5] On August 28, 1955, Hayden was granted a divorce from Betty. During the proceedings, he told the judge that she "forced the breakup of their marriage by trying to run his life so completely that he could no longer stand it."[6] In the media's coverage of the divorce proceedings, they described the reason for the divorce as given to them by Hayden: "henpecking." Legally, it was mental cruelty.[7]

• • •

Hayden now had custody of his four children and he was determined to be a model father to shield himself from any further actions by his ex-wife. "If ever a man was obsessed with the challenge of fatherhood, I was that man," he would recall.[8] He was determined to provide an idyllic life for his children that would erase the memories of the constant fighting that he and Betty had engaged in throughout the years of their marriage.

Renting a spacious home in the Hollywood suburbs, he settled down to the life of an active community participant, all for the sake of providing stability for his children. He joined the PTA, enrolled the boys in the Little League, and put his daughter in ballet school and signed her up for piano lessons. He even joined the local Democratic Club.[9] In his own words, "he was the pillar of the town, and none of the neighbors suspected that a large share of his devotion stemmed from his need to 'create a proper father image' (to use his lawyer's phrase) that could, should the need arise, be presented to the judge in the Domestic Relations Court."[10] Reflecting back to that time in Sterling's life, Norm Hatch praised his friend's efforts with his children. "He really did a job on them," Hatch said.[11]

He was quick to acknowledge that his ability to pull off his role as "father of the year" was in large part due to his friendship with nearby neighbors Turnley and Flora Walker. Turnley Walker was a television writer who had been stricken with polio as a youth. His wife Flora was a "dedicated homemaker and militant community spirit." Being a community activist, it was her "sponsorship" of Hayden in the community that allowed him to be accepted as a model father figure. The Hayden family and the Walker family became fast friends.

• • •

In January of 1958, Hayden went to court to have his named legally changed from John Hamilton back to Sterling Hayden. The reason he gave was that Hayden was his children's name, and he had been using it professionally since returning to the film industry. On January 13, his request was granted by the court.

By early 1958, Hayden was undergoing a personal crisis because of the continuing conflict with Betty, who had initiated another battle for the custody of their children, the mounting bills he was accruing, and his general hatred of acting. He was now forty-two years old. If he was going to make a break, time was running out. He explained his dilemma early in his autobiography: "We are brainwashed by our economic system until we end up in a tomb beneath a pyramid of time payments, mortgages, preposterous gadgetry, playthings that divert our attention from the sheer idiocy of the charade . . . The years thunder by. The dreams of our youth grow dim where they lie caked in dust on the shelves of patience. Before we know it, the tomb is sealed."[12]

His self-denigration continued in earnest. While there was nothing wrong with being an actor, with the exalted status and financial rewards that come with it, he reasoned, simply because one "photographs well," seemed all wrong. Why, then, did he do it? How did he reconcile these feelings with the fact that he was a highly paid actor? He never really could, and he freely admitted that he hated the work. And why get into the dilemma in the first place? "Simple. The same deficiencies of character that led me into Hollywood prevented my escape."[13] Hayden's advisors kept presenting film opportunities to help him ease his financial burden, but they kept forgetting that he was a man who didn't care about making money. By his own admission, he had never invested any money because he didn't believe in accepting unearned income.

After turning down several film opportunities, Hayden decided to act on his instincts. In March of 1958, he began to arrange his break from Hollywood. His first step was to take his schooner *Wanderer*, which he had purchased on Christmas Day 1955, for $20,000, from Los Angeles to San Francisco. After obtaining photographs of his four children that were passport-suitable, he returned them to their mother for the next month while he worked on his breakaway plan. In June, he hired a first mate, Spike Africa, an unconventional free spirit not unlike Hayden. That summer, Hayden pulled *Wanderer* into the Anderson and Cristonani's Shipyard, just south of San Francisco. In order to finance the shipyard work, Hayden obtained a $15,000 mortgage on the ship. Under Africa's watchful eyes, the ship underwent the much-needed overhaul which was completed by the beginning of August. Hayden admitted that other work was needed, but "what we didn't have we could do without."[14]

Hayden had actually been contemplating the journey for two years. He would secure financial backing and then take a largely amateur crew and sail from California to Scandinavia, transiting the Panama Canal. They would film the entire voyage, capturing the flavor of the voyage and then break the film into segments suitable for television. He ran into a brick wall in his attempts to obtain financing for the voyage. He approached over eighty possible investors, but each one turned him down. "Why risk capital in such a venture," he ruefully recalled, "when the sponsor and the network cried for blood and guts and sex?"[15] Undaunted, he proceeded to begin to select a crew for the voyage.

In June of 1958, Hayden had placed an ad in the personal columns of the *New York Times, San Francisco Chronicle, Territorial Enterprise, Saturday Review,* and *Christian Science Monitor.* It read:

> VOYAGE UNDER SAIL
>
> 100-ton ex-Pilot schooner sailing from San Francisco August 15 for Copenhagen Sept. 15, 1959 [*sic*]. Need six active intelligent young men and women. Send details to Sterling Hayden, Box 655—Sausalito, California.[16]

He received two thousand replies within a month of the ad's appearance. In addition, several people just showed up at the pier, gear in hand and ready to go. Some of the applicants were real eccentrics not fit to take to sea with him. Most were just good people who, like Sterling Hayden, searched for adventure, loved the sea, and were genuine free spirits.

One of the respondents to Hayden's ad was a nineteen-year-old college student named Dennis Powers. When he read the ad, Powers had just finished his sophomore year at Occidental College, and he and several of his fraternity brothers wrote to Hayden, requesting that they be considered for the voyage. Powers was an art major and mentioned in his letter that his favorite authors were Herman Melville and Joseph Conrad. Shortly after that, Hayden contacted him and arranged a meeting in Hollywood.

Over half a century later, Powers would recall the first meeting with Sterling Hayden that took place in Hollywood in June of 1958. "I was totally intimidated by him at the meeting. I didn't know much about him."[17] The interview, which lasted twenty minutes, went very well. Towards the end, Powers provided a detail that he thought would be the showstopper: He didn't know anything about sailing. Unfazed, Hayden replied, "Well, you've read about it and for me that's very important."[18] As they parted, Hayden told them he would be in touch. Almost immediately after that, Powers was delighted to receive a card form the actor, inviting him to come up to the San Francisco Bay Area to see the *Wanderer*.

Arriving in San Francisco later that month, Powers remained in awe of his new acquaintance. "I felt like Ishmael. I didn't know anything and here I was meeting with Ahab!"[19] There were already several other applicants working on the schooner, performing all the required nautical tasks such as painting and helping to properly maintain the decks. It soon became obvious that Hayden was using the interview process as a way of obtaining free labor to prepare the schooner for the long voyage. It was also a way for him to evaluate qualifications, as well as the potential of each applicant for teamwork. Over the next few weeks, many prospective crewmembers would rotate through *Wanderer* until Hayden made his final crew selection. Powers was thrilled to be one of the selectees. Having just turned twenty, he was the youngest crewmember selected. Although he had no sea experience, he proved to be an excellent team player, something that was critically important to Hayden. In addition, he loved Hayden's children, as well as first mate Spike Africa's three children, and they all responded well to him. Describing the crew of *Wanderer*, he said: "We became a family."[20]

Hayden had no trouble obtaining an adequate crew. All told, his plan called for a crew of thirteen adults and seven children. Hayden would be taking his four children, and Spike Africa and his wife would be bringing their three children. The crew would also have a doctor as well as a teacher to provide schooling to the children. In addition, to provide photographic documentation of the voyage, Hayden brought along famed photographer Dody Weston Thompson, who would act has a filmmaker's assistant for him.

In preparation for the voyage, Hayden had arranged for ten tons of fresh water, six tons of fuel, a four-month supply of food, and three hundred charts to be brought aboard. In addition, he also brought aboard over five hundred books. There was one item that he did not have and had no intention of obtaining: a radio or even a basic receiving set. This omission would prove to be critical in the legal action that would be forthcoming. One complicating factor that Hayden had not planned on, which suddenly put the whole trip in jeopardy, was his ex-wife Betty. She acted quickly when she learned of her ex-husband's plan to sail to Scandinavia with their children. On August 25, her lawyers filed an injunction against Sterling Hayden, prohibiting him from taking the children with him.

Clearly frustrated, Hayden had to inform the crew that their departure date was going to be pushed back first to September, then to November 1. The trial was again delayed, with the departure date slipping to November 15 and then to December 1. Finally, the court date was set for December 4. All along, Hayden suspected that Betty's lawyers were dragging their feet and drawing out the legal process in the hope that he would call off the voyage in frustration. If that was their intention, they truly misjudged him and underestimated his resolve.

In fact, the delay in departure actually seemed to help Hayden from a monetary standpoint. During the waiting period, he was finally able to get financing for the voyage. It came from Republic Pictures, which agreed to finance the filming of the voyage with two promissory notes totaling $50,000. Hayden later concluded that the deal was definitely not in his favor. He would have to agree to sign away 40 percent of the ownership of the finished film. Yet he was so desperate for the money that he instructed his attorney to draw up the papers to consummate the deal. His lawyer was staunchly opposed it. "Suicide," he said, "you'll regret it as long as you live."

"Draw up the papers," instructed Hayden.

"You'll be in so deep you'll never get out—unless you go for a bankruptcy bath."

But the stubborn client insisted: "Just fix us up with the papers." His attorney was unable to talk Hayden out of the deal. A few weeks later, Hayden signed the contract with Republic Pictures. Even as he signed the papers, he had misgivings. The contract stipulated that if he failed to produce a film, he would have to reimburse Republic Pictures the $50,000 that they had loaned him. The contract bound Hayden to star in four to six pictures for the company, and he would be obligated to pay the film company 50 percent of his gross earnings until the studio made back the money they had fronted him. Despite his own doubts over the wisdom of obligating himself in this fashion, he decided to proceed with the financially reckless path that was so typical of the way he conducted his entire life. Describing the situation in his own words, he stated: "To hell with it. I'd worry about it later. The only thing to do was battle it out for the court's permission—then get to Scandinavia as planned and come through with the film en route."[21]

The financial windfall allowed Hayden to settle the mortgage on the schooner and pay for the provisions for the planned voyage. Much to his relief, none of his recruited crew left despite the prolonged delays. As he waited for his day in court, he assessed his financial status in his mind. The numbers were grim. He had possibly $1,000 in liquid cash, but he owed money everywhere. He was $6,000 in debt, owed his own lawyers over $10,000, plus another $5,000 to Betty's attorneys.[22] It was typical of Sterling Hayden's approach to money.

On December 4, 1958, the hearings finally began. The crux of the argument that Betty Hayden's lawyers utilized was the dangerous nature of the proposed voyage in the *Wanderer*. The schooner, they argued, was old, obsolete, and decrepit. To a master sailor such as Hayden, the arguments were baseless. True, he would acknowledge, the ship didn't have a lot of fancy bells and whistles, but a real sailor had no need for these things. As far as the claim that the ship was obsolete, Hayden sarcastically observed, "I laugh, for the winds and the seas don't change. Has the circular storm grown obsolete? Or the heave of a long ground swell?"[23]

When he was on the witness stand being cross-examined by his ex-wife's lawyers, they attempted to indicate the real danger posed by the fact that *Wanderer* had no radio for communication with the outside world. Hayden's response was indicative of his confidence in his superb seamanship skills as well as his philosophy of the relationship between man and the sea. "Why go to sea under sail at all," he proposed, "if you're so concerned with security? Why not go as a tourist, as a kind of frozen vegetable buying your way across the world surrounded by running hot water, epicurean cuisine, swimming pools, and tiny-tot programs, mommy and daddy programs—designed for your delectation, and designed to quarantine you from the contagion of elemental wonder and awe known only to simple living? For navigation I rely on simple tools: sextant and chronometer, charts and parallel rules, and a precious selection of passage-worn triangles made of celluloid gone yellow over the years."[24] It was an explanation that only a true seaman would understand and appreciate.

When the hearings ended, the waiting began as the judge deliberated the case. Finally, on January 14, 1959, Hayden received a telegram from his attorney Grant Cooper. The judge would be receiving all counsel in his chambers the next day at 2 p.m. to announce his decision. Cooper promised to call Hayden immediately after the session. The next day, Los Angeles Superior Court Judge Emil F. Gumpert was lavish in his praise of Sterling Hayden as a father and was very sympathetic to him in his battle with his ex-wife. "In forty-three years at the bar and at the bench," he stated, "the author of this opinion has never heard a more forthright witness than the plaintiff, nor one who indicated a more zealous desire to be completely honest, truthful, and factual . . . The uncontradicted evidence . . . compels the court to express the wish that all children might be blessed with a love and devotion, a concern and care, equal to that which this father has bestowed on his offspring."[25]

Hayden would retain custody of his children, but the judge added a stipulation: he could not take the children with him on the proposed voyage on the *Wanderer*. The judge had ruled that the schooner was not safe for such a long open-sea journey. Sterling Hayden and *Wanderer* were legally enjoined from sailing with the children aboard. Betty had won that point.

While the legal proceedings were in progress, Hayden sat in his cabin aboard *Wanderer*, staring at both the phone and the clock. At roughly 2:30, the call came through. Cooper called collect from a phone booth in the courthouse to deliver the judge's verdict. After his client accepted the charges, the attorney's initial words were ominous. "Sterling, this is Grant . . . now listen, fellow, I have some bad news—"

"Don't tell me I lost custody of the kids?" interrupted Hayden.

"No, God no, nothing like that. But the voyage is off—did you hear me?—the court rules the voyage is off—"

"Yeah, I heard you—you're not kidding are you?"

"Sterling, I wouldn't kid about this—why, I've never been more stunned or disappointed in my life—" Cooper offered to read his copy of the judge's ruling over the phone, but Hayden was in no mood to hear it and instructed him to mail it to him. "I'll be goddamned that's all I can say just yet," he angrily explained.

"Don't be upset," his lawyer countered. "Let me tell you something'll make you feel better. There's every reason to believe that if we wait nine or ten months, then go back to the court, they'll give us—"

"The hell you say," exploded Hayden. "I've been in that court system fourteen times in the past eight months—that's enough—"

"Look, fellow, don't get carried away. I'm trying to help you. Within a year, I promise you, we'll go back and get permission to take the children out of the country—you can sail the schooner and they can fly from port to port to greet you as you come in—I know that's not what you want but we have to be practical sometimes—"[26]

The conversation quickly trailed off. It seemed that Hayden had lost his battle to voyage around the world with his children aboard the *Wanderer*. But it only appeared that way.

• • •

With the voyage in limbo, Hayden's agent approached him with another financially rewarding proposition. Warner Bros. was preparing the film version of Sloan Wilson's bestseller *A Summer Place* and they wanted Sterling Hayden for one of the starring roles. It would be a six-week shoot in Big Sur and for his co-starring role, he would be paid $40,000. His agent, Joe Grippo, was sure Hayden would grudgingly sign on for the project. His client was broke and needed the money, plus it looked doubtful that the proposed Scandinavian voyage would ever take place. Grippo anticipated that he would have to coerce his complicated client into accepting the role, but to his surprise, Hayden readily agreed to accept the film role. Asking Hayden if he wanted to think it over before committing, Hayden somberly replied, "I know when I'm licked I guess."[27] Filming was scheduled to begin on February 10. It was all a smoke screen. Hayden had no intention of making the film. He was going to be at sea.

. . .

To all observers, it appeared that Hayden had lost his battle. He confirmed to the United Press that he was indeed going to take the role in *A Summer Place*, as he had committed to. His only plan, he stated publicly, was to sail *Wanderer* down to Santa Barbara. His planned departure would take place on January 18. But the issue of finances still dogged him. It was one thing to go to sea completely broke. It was quite another to do it while defying a court injunction.[28] He had never been so deeply in debt. By his own calculations he would need at least $10,000 to realistically embark on his proposed journey. In addition, violating the injunction would make him a fugitive from the law, rendering him unable to pull into any American port without being subject to arrest. His itinerary had called for *Wanderer* to transit the Panama Canal, visit the West Indies, and then make Atlantic coast stops at Charleston, South Carolina, Washington, DC, New York, and a number of New England ports, including Gloucester, Massachusetts.[29] Then they would proceed to navigate across the Atlantic and arrive in Scandinavia. Now, he told his crew that they would be taking one final sail down to Santa Barbara.

Before leaving San Francisco, Hayden looked over his contract with Republic Pictures. He saw a possible means in which to obtain the $10,000 that he would need. The contract stated that of the $50,000 loan, $10,000 of it remained on deposit to be drawn when he had legal permission to sail. He knew he had to act quickly. He placed a call to his contact at Republic Pictures and laid his cards on the table: he needed $10,000 before the close of business that very day. A period of silence followed, and then his friend spoke. "I think I follow you, Hayden; you're planning to sail without the kids, is that it?"

"Yeah, yeah, Jack, sure, that's it," he replied, lying through his teeth.

"Well, in that case, I don't see why . . . All right, I'll start things moving—take a few days, of course."

"I need it today."

"This I can't understand. Why the big rush?"[30]

Hayden began to offer a multiplicity of reasons, until his friend agreed to arrange for the money, contingent upon Hayden signing a document attesting to the fact that he would not be taking his children on the voyage. This Hayden readily agreed to.

While the money was being arranged, Hayden grabbed a cab and headed for the Branch Hydrographic Office to pick up navigation charts. None of the charts had anything to do with a route to Scandinavia. Rather, they were all of Pacific Ocean areas. After spending $200, he left with the charts under his arm. Next, he took a taxi to the French consul. There he obtained visas for Tahiti for all of the crewmembers. One thing he could not obtain were the passports for his four children. They were locked up in a federal building as per court order. His next stop was the Custom House, where he obtained a bill of health and listed his destination as Jakarta, Indonesia. After purchasing fresh meat and vegetables, designating a power of attorney, and canceling the insurance on the schooner, he checked back with the *Wanderer* via telephone. It was lucky for him that he did.

He had received an urgent message to call Roger Davis, a lawyer at the firm of Loeb and Loeb, who handled Republic Picture's legal affairs. Calling collect from a phone booth, Hayden was able to reach the lawyer, who had some bad news. As counsel for the company, he informed Hayden that he couldn't approve of Hayden's request for the money. "It's not as simple as you seem to think," he lectured the actor. "I have a copy of the court's order. It states very clearly, page 6, line 26, and I quote: 'The proposed ocean voyage is enjoined' unquote."[31]

Wanderer was not going anywhere.

He arrived back at the ship while the crew was eating lunch. Gloomily, he entered the cabin and found Spike Africa and his wife Red inside. Eyeing the charts under his arm, Spike assumed they were good to go. Hayden broke the news to them—they didn't have the money to embark on the voyage. Watching the couple, Hayden realized that he would never be so fortunate again to find such a couple (who were also bringing their three children along on the voyage) who seemed so perfectly suited to work with him on their planned adventure. People who, like him, were willing to walk away from the material world and embark on a bold adventure, to turn their back on money and material goods and to really live life.

At 2 p.m., the phone rang. It was his colleague from Republic Pictures. "Sterling?" he began. "Don't ask me any questions, but you're going to get your money. It's on the way, should be in Sausalito by five-thirty. Bank closes at six. That's all. Have a good trip."[32] Hayden hadn't spoken a word. The Africas were not privy to the conversation.

Arriving at the bank five minutes before closing time, Sterling Hayden was able to acquire the funding he needed for his planned journey. He reported back aboard the schooner as the sun was starting to set. Prepare to get underway, he informed his crew. They were going to take their last voyage together—to Santa Barbara. He then placed a call to Norm Hatch in the Washington, DC, area and he revealed his real plan to him. Hatch strongly advised against it, pointing out that if he defied the court order, he could be considered a fugitive from justice. "I can't pay attention to them," Sterling retorted. Hatch appealed one last time to his friend but admitted, "That didn't work."[33]

At 11 p.m. on January 18, 1959, *Wanderer* got underway with the four Hayden children aboard, allegedly for Santa Barbara, 310 miles south. Hayden guided the ship to a point just outside of the twelve-mile limit. There, he assembled the crew and made an announcement. They were not going to Santa Barbara; they were bound for Tahiti. Explaining his reasons and concluding by saying, "This is what I want to do," he then asked the crew for their input. As Dennis Powers recalled, "After all we had done together in preparation, were we going to say no?"[34] As Hayden would recount to *Parade* magazine that summer, "There was a moment of silence, followed by a faint cheer."[35] *Wanderer* set a course west for Tahiti and Sterling Hayden, in violating the court injunction, became a fugitive from United States justice.

CHAPTER SEVENTEEN

Wanderer to Tahiti and Back

ONCE *WANDERER* LEFT SAN FRANCISCO BAY AND ENTERED THE PACIFIC Ocean, the weather took a turn for the worse. For over a week, *Wanderer* was wracked by violent storms, causing every crewmember, with the exception of Hayden and Spike Africa, to become seasick. The stormy ocean made the decks too dangerous for the children, leaving them confined below. Hayden briefly considered going back, but after consulting with his first mate, opted to press on. Once the storms abated, the rest of the five-week journey went smoothly.

Hayden proved to be a no-nonsense taskmaster. He expected his orders to be carried out immediately without question and for all crewmembers to be punctual for the "four hours on, four hours off" duty schedule. He expected the same work ethic out of each of them that he expected of himself. "He was the captain," recalled Dennis Powers. "We believed in him."[1] All navigation was done by their captain using a sextant and charts. Although *Wanderer* had an engine, it was never turned on during the voyage. His seamanship skills intimidated them. One day, while they were in the middle of the Pacific Ocean and Powers had the steering wheel, "Hayden came up me and said, 'You know what—we are farther from any major body of land than any place on earth right now!' I was like—oh my God!"[2]

After three and a half weeks, *Wanderer* anchored off of one of the islands of the Marquesas Archipelago. For most of the amateur crew, it had been a difficult voyage for the first week and once the weather stabilized, Hayden pushed the crew to his standards. The reality was that Hayden was not happy with the performance of several of the crewmembers. He had only pulled the ship into the Marquesas to give his crew a short break that they requested. He informed them that he would have just as soon pushed on to Tahiti. As they anchored, he told his shipmates that the honeymoon was over and things were about to change. Hayden was about to learn that he was pushing them too hard.

It culminated in a confrontation on the second day in the Marquesas. It was precipitated when he berated Spike Africa in front of several crewmembers. Sensing that he had perhaps been too strident, he called a meeting. To the assembled crew he stated, "Okay boys, let's make it simple. In a way I'm sorry I blew up as I did—and in a way I'm not . . . Now I'm not going to mention any names because we know each other pretty well and you know who I mean when I say that there are two or three of you don't give a good god damn about this ship . . . a sailing ship is no democracy either. Ten percent of this crew has done ninety percent of the work; and that's wrong, and it can't go on—and I guess you know that."[3]

Once finished with his piece, Hayden invited each crewmember to speak theirs. One by one, they vented, and their complaints were nearly uniform. They didn't like the authoritarian and sometimes disrespectful manner that Hayden displayed to the crew. The reality was that they were volunteer amateur adventurers and Hayden was a serious, dedicated sailor for whom the sea was a passion. They wanted a chance to see some of the Pacific islands, to enjoy the journey, and not just race to Tahiti. He had a hard time realizing that his passion for ships and sea was not something that was ingrained in his crew. The crew, in turn, couldn't know the extent of Hayden's inner turmoil over his custody battles and his constant self-doubt. In his moments of solitude on the voyage, he had continually castigated himself again over his failure to make an effort at writing, a thought that was eating away at him and becoming an obsession. The crew had total confidence in their captain's abilities and were in awe of his seamanship. But they were intimidated by him, and they finally vented.

The last crewmembers to speak were Spike Africa and his wife Red. "You should—some of you—be ashamed of yourselves," declared Red. "That's what I think. You're spoiled. This trip is the best thing that ever happened to some of you, and you're letting the ship down. You're bored, you say. All right, so you're bored; you're bored because you're lazy."[4] Spike spoke last. The first mate captured the essence of the problem precisely. "You expect everyone to feel like you and I do about this ship. It won't work. It won't work because this is 1959 and people don't know about what these ships mean." He finished by offering his captain a lesson in effective leadership: don't ever chew him out in front of the crewmembers. "I've been chewed out by some experts, believe me.

But never in front of the crew. It's not right. It's bad—bad for a man's self-respect."[5]

Hayden took all of the crew's feedback to heart. He decided to stay a few days in the Marquesas and let them relax and enjoy the island. He, too, kicked back and spent much time with his children. Spending days ashore with them, even they noticed that he seemed more relaxed. It proved to be an effective strategy, both for Hayden personally and for his amateur adventurers. The crew was revitalized when they got underway and as a result, the journey to Tahiti was uneventful and more enjoyable.

• • •

After a five-week voyage across the Pacific, *Wanderer* finally sailed into Papeete, Tahiti, the capital of French Polynesia. *Wanderer* made a grand entrance into Papeete's harbor. There to witness the schooner's arrival was a man from San Francisco who would become a close friend to Hayden, Barnaby Conrad. Like Hayden, Conrad was an American original. A writer and best-selling author, he was also an adventurer who had once been a bullfighter in Spain. In addition to once serving as author Sinclair Lewis's secretary, he ran a bar in San Francisco named El Matador after his best-selling book *Matador*. The bar was a favorite watering hole for many San Franciscans, including Sterling Hayden, with whom Conrad became a good buddy and drinking partner. His 1994 book, *Name Dropping: Tales from My Barbary Coast Saloon*, described his ten years as the club's owner. He had been to Tahiti on a prior visit and he returned for several months in 1959. It was during this visit that he witnessed his friend's triumphant arrival.

In *Wanderer*, Hayden described the arrival in a low-key manner, but Conrad's description is much more vivid and serves to highlight Hayden's superb seamanship skills. "When his huge schooner, all sails up, flew into Papeete harbor, hundreds of people came to watch. Generally, a boat of this size comes in under power and escorted by a pilot boat. Never had anyone seen such a large schooner enter with all sails up, drop anchor, drop all sails but the mainsail, and with no power but the wind, *back* into the slip. A great roar went up from the crowd as they watched."[6]

When he went ashore, Hayden learned that a San Francisco district attorney had issued a warrant for his arrest, charging him with "kidnapping my own children, contributing to their delinquency, and a host of other things that are hardly worthy of mention."[7] In fact, on January 26, Betty's attorneys had filed charges of kidnapping and child neglect, and on January 29, she was able to get the authorities to issue a warrant for her Hayden's arrest. However, Tahiti was beyond American legal jurisdiction and he was free to pursue time with his children there.

• • •

Not long after arriving in Tahiti, Dennis Powers made arrangements to return home to Los Angeles as he was to begin his junior year of college. He would be the first crewmember to return to the United States. He quickly learned that the *Los Angeles Times* was infatuated with the story of Sterling Hayden and the voyage of *Wanderer*, as attested to by the dozens of newspaper articles saved by his family. He was quickly mobbed by reporters on his return to Los Angeles, seeking juicy details for their readers. Powers provided three "take home" points for all media members to digest. First, that Sterling Hayden was a superb sailor with remarkable seamanship skills. Second, that *Wanderer* was an extremely seaworthy ship and safe, despite reports to the contrary. Lastly, that Sterling Hayden was an incredible father. His children were to most important things in the world to him.[8]

• • •

Hayden rented a bungalow near the Conrads, who would see him nearly every day. The Conrads introduced Sterling to a Tahitian-Peruvian girl named Nita Wanamaker; they seemed to hit it off very well. Although he would claim that he was happier than he had ever been in his life, Conrad could sense the inner turmoil that seemed to define Sterling Hayden, the individualist who could never quite belong or find contentment. To Conrad, his friend brought to mind Robert Louis Stevenson, noting that "he seemed to have, as someone once said about Robert Louis Stevenson, 'an incapacity for happiness.'"[9] During this time, Sterling shared the first pages that he had written of what would become his autobiography. Conrad was stunned by his friend's literary talents. After a few months, Sterling grew tired of Nita and began a relationship with fashion model Betsy Pickering, who was visiting Tahiti and decided to stay with him for several months.[10]

That summer, Hayden decided to give a series of interviews, explaining why he had embarked on the seemingly perilous voyage and why he had taken his children along with him in defiance of the law. In July of 1959, *Parade* magazine featured an article written by Hayden titled "Why I Defied the Law." Describing himself as currently a voluntary exile from the United States, he offered some explanations that elucidated his philosophy of life in general, a philosophy he would later repeat in his 1963 autobiography. "The purpose of this voyage," he explained to readers, "is to make films for television, films dealing not just with the sea and faraway places but with certain fundamental questions. One of the questions is: Why does the vast majority of men, as Henry Thoreau said a century ago, lead lives of quiet desperation? One year ago I gave up my home and plowed everything I had in the world into this venture."[11] It was escape that he sought—from the trap of everyday life, from going through the motions of a career he despised. He no longer wanted to live in quiet desperation.

And why had he violated the injunction, thereby subjecting himself to criminal liability and potentially endangering his children's lives? He described the "eleventh-hour" delay tactics utilized by his ex-wife in an attempt to sabotage the journey. He pointed out that "the court ruled that I was to retain full legal and physical custody of the children because their mother was—in the words of the court—not a fit person to control their lives."[12] The court had also ruled that *Wanderer* was unsafe and had enjoined the trip. But there was a third key factor in the court's ruling that motivated Hayden. "It ruled that, while the mother was unfit, she was nevertheless entitled to have the children with her part of the time. This I will not agree to unless forced into it. I don't enjoy clashing with the law that I have always lived by, and clashing with a judge whom I respect . . . I wish to protect my children. If in doing this I must clash headlong with a court of law, then so be it."[13]

The reaction of the Hollywood community was initially supportive of Hayden. As reported in a newspaper story on August 16, 1959, "When the 42-year-old skipper put 3,600 miles between himself and the courts of law, Hollywood applauded . . . at first . . . They later woke up to the fact that he had scuttled a burgeoning movie-TV career and was flouting the law." The article quoted from a letter that Hayden had sent his agent before his departure, in which he claimed that he had "sold out for years" by filming "pathetic trash." He continued: "I am a decent enough man; not too bright, perhaps, but impelled by some ideas as to convention and principle. I was sustained by my determination to break out—and now is the time to go." His agent would very astutely comment on the character of his client. "Sterling was born in the wrong century. Progress robbed the world of his great love, the seagoing sailing vessel . . . In these days when man is surveying outer space, he is seeking a forgotten yesteryear."[14]

• • •

Being in Tahiti for most of 1959 gave Hayden time to think and reflect on his life. He had finally succeeded in "breaking away" from the Hollywood life that he disdained, but what would be his next move? In reality, he didn't have many options open to him. Although Dody Thompson did a photographic record of the voyage of the *Wanderer*, the film for which he had obtained the financial backing of Republic Pictures never came to fruition. Also, by the end of the summer, he was running out of money.

Still, he did a lot of reflecting on his life, and one of the inspirations that came to him was to finally commit himself to writing. It was at this point that the genesis of his autobiography came to him—he would tell the story of his life, intertwined with of the story of the voyage to Tahiti. The title for his book would be the name of his schooner, *Wanderer*. The title fit him like a glove.

Throughout his time in Tahiti, Hayden received telegrams from his agent, informing him of various film and television offers, none of which he was inclined to accept. As the summer closed out, he came to a somber realization. "1959 was fading fast and so was this odyssey of mine that I had begun back in January. One result was a feeling of relief—after running away comes the time to run back home. Another feeling was of sadness, of conclusion. Nothing lasts, save anxiety."[15] It was time for him to perform a self-assessment and try to objectively evaluate what he had actually accomplished. "Nothing tangible, certainly nothing I could show on a statement of profit and loss. And yet I felt something was coming to life inside. Even as the voyage was about to end, I sensed that its momentum might endure."[16]

His plan now became clear in his mind. He would have to sail back to the United States, sell his schooner, and put his children back in school. Then he would battle it out with all of his creditors and, most importantly, he would write his book and fulfill his years-long desire to become a writer. Before heading back across the Pacific, he wanted one last fling. He would take his children and crew and sail to Taurita, a safe beach cove on the northeast shore of Tahiti. It was there that the Hayden family would have their last chance to frolic in the wild. All the time, Hayden knew they would be heading back soon and he cherished the time together with his children. "Here just now, for better or worse, is a family, five people solitary, marking time until they return to a world of chaos."[17] And he worried. He worried about the life his children would face upon return without a mother to watch over them. He worried about himself. "And who will mother the father—a man all adrift in the tropics? You can swagger around with no visible means of support, but how do you make a family into a family without a woman around?"[18]

It was time to begin the journey back home. But first they had to return to Papeete to make preparations for the voyage back across the Pacific Ocean.

...

It began with a very inauspicious start after they arrived back in Papeete. To obtain money to buy provisions for the return journey, Hayden went to the bookkeeping department of Etablissements Donalds, Ltd., a Tahitian trading company with whom he had arranged to hold his money in lieu of any real banking agency. There he was stunned to learn that he had miscalculated and, in fact, owed them over $2,000. Once again, Hayden's indifference to financial matters had come back to haunt him. He had overspent his account and was deeply in debt.

He knew full well he couldn't turn to his bank—there was nothing in his account, and his debts back home were sizable. He was suddenly struck with a degree of panic. "Moments ago I lolled in a tropical clime," he recalled. "Now this zone I inhabit is polar."[19] Once again, his ample supply of self-hatred seemed to get a hold over him. Stranded in Tahiti, with his four young children in tow, was no place to be broke. He now realized that "the hard-boiled bastard who had thumbed his nose at Hollywood," not to mention the law, would have to grovel to the Hollywood power structure to ask for the money for the return trip home.

He immediately sent out a flood of telegrams to Hollywood in an attempt to get assistance in financing the voyage. He first contacted Republic Pictures, where he was forced to admit that he did not get any of the filming done that he had contracted with them to do. If they sent the financing that he needed, he offered to do a film stressing the romance and beauty of the "escapist" lifestyle, a sort of modern Swiss Family Robinson saga.

He also sent telegrams to his attorney Grant Cooper, as well as several other friends, asking them for loans. While awaiting replies, he was getting acquainted with his newly recruited crew. For the return trip, he would have only six crewmembers, a very minimal crew for the five thousand-mile open-sea voyage. Spike Africa and his family had departed earlier from Tahiti, so there would be no adult women on the long trip.

Replies to his cry for help started coming back to Tahiti by telegram, but they were not encouraging. As expected, the film company was in no mood to further expend funds to Hayden after he had breached his contract with them. His attorney Grant Cooper strongly advised against trying to solicit individual loans from friends, as Hayden had requested. Instead, he informed his client that he was mailing him a private proposal for a personal loan to tide him over. There was no amount specified in the telegram.

Cooper quickly followed up with another telegram, this one warning his client of potential legal issues upon returning to the country involving his new crew. He warned Hayden that his crew, five of which were not US citizens, had to have US passports or permanent visas when they arrived in the country. If they didn't possess either of these documents, they would be deported within twenty-nine days of arrival. Failure to comply by that time would result in their arrests and deportations. In addition to the substantial fines that would be imposed, *Wanderer* would be seized until the fines were paid off. As if this wasn't enough bad news to absorb, Cooper advised that Hayden go to the nearest US consul in Fiji or Pago Pago to work on these issues.[20]

At this point, Hayden was becoming frantic as he continued on with what he called his "deficit waltz." After meeting with an American colleague he knew on the island, he was able to come up with an immediate loan of $2,000, allowing him to pay off his debt to Etablissements Donald, Ltd. His friend promised him more money to fund the voyage back to America. He would soon have the money he needed to buy provisions for the *Wanderer*'s voyage back home. At least it seemed that way.[21]

...

The plan called for *Wanderer* to depart Tahiti on October 4. Hayden had wired back to the States that they would be arriving in San Francisco on November 15, 1959. Everything seemed to be falling into place until just before he purchased his supplies. Then a telegram arrived at the schooner delivering the bad news: his benefactor's wife had frozen his funds in a divorce proceeding. He would have to look elsewhere for funding.

He was back to square one, and he was running out of time if he was to make the October 4 departure date a reality. Hayden was once again forced to grovel for the funding, this time with a reclusive exile millionaire who shared his "violent dislike" for Los Angeles. Traveling to the man's isolated plantation, Hayden spent five hours talking to him, explaining his dilemma. When the meeting ended, the reclusive millionaire loaned him $1,000 at 6 percent interest, payable by the end of the year.[22] The trip was back on.

As the provisions were being brought aboard, Hayden's luck continued. They were less than three days from departing when a taxi pulled up to the pier alongside *Wanderer* and three passengers piled out and headed up the gangplank. It was an Italian film crew in Tahiti to film a documentary, but their equipment had not arrived. Their leader recognized Hayden and knew of the *Wanderer*'s proposed voyage. He offered to buy all of Hayden's film equipment for $2,000, an agreement immediately accepted by Hayden.

Wanderer was going to make its October 4 departure date.[23]

...

On the morning of Sunday, October 4, 1959, the crew of *Wanderer* made its final preparations to get underway. They were scheduled to leave Tahiti at noon, and Hayden was making last-minute inspections of his schooner. After fully provisioning the ship, he had $40 remaining in his wallet. Walking alongside the ship, he ran his hands down the planks of the hull, self-critically noting, "If I knew myself as well as I know this vessel, I'd be of some use to the world."[24] Walking back into town one final time, he spotted his friends Carlos and Agnes Palacios, who had come to wish him well and to also give him a departing gift.

Palacios handed Hayden a photograph of Palacios and his wife, and it was the inscription that Carlos had written across the bottom that touched Hayden's soul. "Many men come to Tahiti looking for something that does not exist," he wrote. "You came looking for life, I think. Perhaps you did not find it but you found what must come first—yourself. Affectionately."[25] The friends embraced for the final time and the skipper of the schooner *Wanderer* headed back to the ship, boarded his vessel and ordered the crew to make immediate preparations to get underway. By noon they had pulled away from the pier.

The Hayden family was heading home.

...

On the evening of November 15, 1959, the schooner *Wanderer* was approximately ten miles west of the Golden Gate Bridge. They were arriving home on the date that its master, Sterling Hayden, had promised they would. The crew had sailed for forty-one days, traveling 4,450 miles across the Pacific Ocean, under the direction of Hayden's superb seamanship. They had averaged a speed of 4.47 knots over the course of the voyage.[26]

With the lights of San Francisco clearly visible, *Wanderer* was approached by the San Francisco pilot boat *California* which sent a harbor pilot via one of its small boats to join Hayden on the bridge and guide the schooner into San Francisco Bay. The pilot, a skilled sailor named Koshkin, exchanged greetings with Hayden, complimenting him on the just-completed voyage. "Well, Hayden," he said, "you made it right on the nose. Here, I brought you the morning Chronicle. Herb Caen says in his column you'd be home on the fifteenth—damned if you didn't make it with two hours to spare." Pacing briefly around the ship before they commenced the entry into San Francisco Bay, Koshkin offered another sincere compliment to the skipper of the *Wanderer*. "This is a great old vessel," he said admiringly. "Wish I'd been with you."[27]

Going below for a cup of coffee, Koshkin delivered a bit of good news. He reached into his pocket and then handed Hayden a check from Grant Cooper for $15,000 to use for a mortgage on the ship. Delighted with this development, all Hayden could humorously think was that not all capitalists were bad. The two men talked as Hayden related with pride how well the children had handled the return voyage, not requiring so much as an aspirin. Koshkin informed him that he was going to face immigration problems, a situation that Grant Cooper had warned him about. Accordingly, *Wanderer* was going to have to anchor at a quarantine station and await clearance. When Hayden informed the pilot that he had only enough fuel left to travel another four to five miles, Koshkin assured him that he would have fifty gallons of fuel brought aboard before the schooner got underway.

When the boat bringing the necessary fuel came back to the schooner, the crew had a surprise for the master of the *Wanderer*. They handed him a large box containing fresh bread, fresh milk and butter, two cartons of ice cream, and a small, well-frosted cake. Attached to the box was a note: "This is for those kids." Although it was near midnight at that point, Hayden went below and awakened his four children, announcing "Roust! We're having a celebration: ice cream, cake, the works."[28] Just before midnight on November 15, 1959, Sterling Hayden and his children celebrated their return home as the schooner *Wanderer* entered San Francisco Bay.

• • •

In accordance with the law, *Wanderer* tied up at the quarantine anchorage, and the crew spent the night aboard. At 6 a.m. the following morning, a Coast Guard boat pulled alongside and the official boarding party came aboard, welcoming the Hayden family and the crew. The foreign nationals were to be retained aboard. Shortly after, a cabin cruiser came alongside carrying several of Hayden's colleagues, including Spike Africa and Al Cristofani, who had overseen the refurbishing of *Wanderer* prior to the voyage to Tahiti. They warmly welcomed him back and as they all embarked for the shore, several boatloads of reporters followed close by. As they pulled up to the pier, Hayden could see a multitude of people taking pictures of their arrival, and many people on terraces in the hills overlooking the bay peering at them through telescopes. The only thing that put a slight damper on the moment was when Spike Africa told him that the Walkers were not able to make it out there for his arrival. Anticipating the legal maelstrom that Hayden was walking back into, the Walkers did want to let him know that he could leave his children with them as he attempted to extricate himself from his difficulties with the law.[29]

The legal battles resumed a month later. He first went to court on December 18, 1959, to determine who would have custody of the children over the upcoming Christmas. Sitting in court only a few feet from his ex-wife, he would recall that he never had felt such blinding hatred for anyone. When it was his turn to testify, Hayden tried to explain to the judge that "an unfit parent doesn't become fit simply because it is Christmas time."[30] The judge cautioned him against such rhetoric, informing him that he had the authority to rule that neither parent would have custody of the children over the holiday period if he adjudged that course the appropriate one. Hayden humbly apologized for his characterization.

After Betty had her turn on the witness stand, the judge recessed the court for ten minutes before reconvening to announce his decision. Upon returning, the court was informed that Sterling Hayden was free after the first of the year to move to San Francisco and to "try and write your book or whatever it is."[31] Hayden was instructed to pack up his children's things as the judge ruled that they would be spending the next twelve days with their mother at Betty's sister's house. They would be returned to Hayden on New Year's Day. Hayden impulsively blurted out that he just had to see his children on Christmas Day. That aspect of his ruling hadn't occurred to the judge. Using the logic of King Solomon himself, he quickly ruled that Hayden could see his children for five or six hours on Christmas Day. Court was then adjourned.[32]

On January 7, 1960, it was time for Sterling Hayden to appear in court to face the consequences of his defiance of the court's previous ruling forbidding him from taking his children out of the country aboard

Wanderer. Once again, the case would be adjudicated in the Superior Court of Los Angeles and, much to Hayden's benefit and relief, the presiding judge would again be Emil F. Gumpert. Just prior to Gumpert delivering his ruling, Betty's attorneys attempted to file a motion disqualifying the court. Angrily, he denied their request. Gumpert then launched into a soliloquy, defending Hayden and ruling in his favor. Addressing specifically Hayden's actions defying the court order, Gumpert stated: "The voyage, Hayden has admitted, was a willful defiance of the law that tends to impede the administration of justice . . . Despite this, in a true effort to do justice, every situation much be considered on its merits . . . For years he has labored to shield the children and give them a normal childhood . . . His act was regrettable and foolish, but this court accepts his sworn statement that he meant no disrespect to the court."[33]

At that point, Gumpert came to the denouement of his ruling. "It is the ruling of this court that Hayden be sentenced to a fine of five hundred dollars and serve five days in jail." After pausing for dramatic effect, he added, "The sentence is suspended."[34] Hayden would later recollect: "I later had a drink with that good judge. He told me he didn't want to give me any sentence, not even a suspended one. But he had to do it as a sop to motherhood."[35]

The suspended sentence absolved Hayden of any penalties for his violation of the court order. While his legal troubles with the state of California were now resolved and he retained custody of his children, his business troubles persisted. He was still in breach of contract with Republic Pictures, which was not in a forgiving mood. The studio took Hayden to court, and on August 5, 1961, the issue was ruled on in a San Rafael, California, courtroom. Marin County Superior Judge Harold J. Haley noted that according to the terms of the contract that he had signed with Republic Pictures, to obtain financing for his voyage Hayden had signed two promissory notes with the studio. In return, Hayden had committed to either begin filming a television series in Tahiti and then finding a sponsor, making eight pictures for Republic, or paying the money back. Noting that he failed to do any of the three, Haley ruled that Sterling Hayden owed Republic Pictures a total of $49,518.[36]

Hayden's legal issues ended with him retaining custody of his children, which was his main concern. There would be no criminal consequences as a result of his having taken the children to Tahiti on *Wanderer* in defiance of the court order. And once again he was deep in debt.

Things were returning to normal.

CHAPTER EIGHTEEN

A New Bride and Literary Acclaim

LIVING IN DEBT WAS SOMETHING HAYDEN HAD DONE HIS ENTIRE LIFE and it never seemed to bother him. He always had acting, a profession he despised, as a fallback to pay the bills. After the court suspended his sentence on January 7, 1960, he was free to pursue his desire to write. Ironically, the adventure aboard *Wanderer* and all of the media coverage that it garnered kept Hayden in demand as a performer. Shortly after the court verdict, Hayden was contacted by CBS television. They wanted him to star in their monthly anthology series, *The DuPont Show of the Month*, in a production of the classic Edith Wharton story *Ethan Frome*. After being offered the title role, Hayden immediately accepted. CBS signed Julie Harris to play the female lead in the show. Originally conceived as a taped production, the studio decided to present the show live instead. Accepting this role was a decision that would change his life.

In Tahiti, during his many moments of solitude and reflection, he wondered how his family would be able to get along without a woman in their lives, how he would be able to go on without a woman to love. While in Tahiti, Hayden had affairs with two women. When he returned to the United States, he had been divorced five years and was looking for a more permanent relationship. Arriving in New York City to begin rehearsals for *Ethan Frome*, he contacted Betsy Pickering to ask her out. By this time, she was no longer interested in any potential long-term relationship with the peripatetic actor who had four children and was perpetually broke. She recommended that they get together with a group of friends for dinner.

That night, realizing that she was pushing him away, Hayden asked the women at the table if they could recommend any single girls for him to go out with while he was in New York. The women quickly compiled a list of seven or eight eligible candidates for him to call. The last name on the list was Catherine Devine McConnell, a beautiful socialite known as Kitty, who had been divorced for two years from Neil McConnell, with whom she had a young son, Scott. Hayden contacted most of the women on the list but after going out with each of them, he simply didn't find any of them interesting enough to ask out again. That brought him to the last name on the list and he decided to call Kitty McConnell.

McConnell was living in a midtown New York apartment with her son and their nanny, a British woman named Agnes. When Hayden called, Kitty was not at home and Agnes answered the phone. Hayden explained to her why he was calling. Agnes was impressed with his manners and conveyed the message to Kitty when she got home. Kitty would recall the conversations fifty-five years later in detail.[1] Agnes expressed her approval: "He sounds so nice on the phone. I want you to go out with him," she recommended. Kitty returned the call. Hayden introduced himself and told her that he would like to take her to dinner. She agreed and they made plans to get together.

Kitty had broken up with her boyfriend about a month before although they continued to speak with each other. During a subsequent phone conversation, she mentioned to him that she had a date with Sterling Hayden. "Isn't he an actor?" she inquired. She associated his name with westerns and since she wasn't a fan of the genre, she hadn't seen any of his movies. Her life was also about to be changed forever.

As fate would have it, the night he and Kitty were to go out Sterling received a phone call from Betsy Pickering, asking him to pick her up at her apartment. He assumed that they were getting together for a night out and he promptly called Kitty to cancel their date. When Hayden arrived at the model's apartment, he was surprised to find her wearing a fur hat and dressed like she was leaving town. In fact, she wanted Hayden to give her a ride to the airport as she was leaving on a ski vacation. Disappointed and angry, Hayden agreed to drive her and after arriving at the airport and waiting for her flight to board, he was recognized by a New York newspaperman—who just happened to be Kitty's ex-boyfriend. The newspaperman looked for a pay phone and called Kitty. "Didn't you say that Sterling Hayden had asked you out?" he inquired.

"Yes, he did. He broke our date," she informed him.

"Well, he's here at the airport with another woman," he responded. Calling to Hayden, he put him on the phone with Kitty. The two began talking, and Kitty was amused by his banter. She suggested, "Why don't you come over after the plane takes off and we'll have a nightcap?"

"I'd love to," he replied.

As soon as she hung up, Kitty realized she had invited a man over that she had never previously met and knew little about. In addition, her nanny Agnes was away at the time. She immediately thought of an excellent means of securing an escort for the evening. She called her brother Robert, who lived in the same apartment building, and invited him up to her apartment. He promptly showed up in his pajamas and a bathrobe. Hayden arrived at the apartment about 10:30 p.m. the night of February 5 to find a beautiful woman answering the door and also a man in his pajamas sitting nearby. Kitty introduced the two men to each other, and Hayden was relieved to find out that it was her brother.

Sterling Hayden would later describe his feeling when he first laid eyes on Kitty McConnell thusly: "When I opened the door, I felt like I was hit across the chest with a board . . . She was so beautiful."[2] He felt an immediate attraction to the stunning young woman. As Kitty began serving drinks to the two men, they began arguing with each other over Fidel Castro. Robert hated Castro—he worked for *Reader's Digest* and when Castro came to power he had nationalized *Reader's Digest*'s holdings in Cuba. Sterling, on the other hand, was an admirer of Castro. They argued for several hours while the amused Kitty listened. Finally, it was time to depart.

As he was leaving, Sterling turned to Kitty and asked, "Will you have dinner with me? Tomorrow?"

She thought he was terrific looking.[3] "I'd love to," she replied.

The couple went out for five straight nights for dinner. She recalled him wearing what he described as his only suit and even a derby hat. One night they went dancing, the only time they ever danced. Their attraction grew and both were smitten. The routine continued: rehearsals for *Ethan Frome* for Sterling during the day, and evenings together with Kitty. On their fifth dinner date, Sterling proposed to Kitty. She would recall his unique proposal. "I can see you want to change your life. Throw in with me and I'll take care of you."[4] She immediately accepted, even though they had known each other for only five days. "I was impulsive too," she would recall with a smile.[5]

Ethan Frome was broadcast live on February 18, 1960, with a few interpolated taped segments.[6] The show drew praise from the critics, who declared that *Ethan Frome* was an exciting production. "That it was exciting was due to skillful performances by Julie Harris and Sterling Hayden, playing the unhappy lovers . . . Hayden was convincing as the long-suffering failure of a husband."[7]

On March 2, 1960, Sterling Hayden formally announced that he and Catherine Devine McConnell were engaged to be married and that the wedding would take place a week later in Sausalito, California.[8] The ceremony was held in the late afternoon of March 9 at the waterfront home of Hayden's friend, contractor William Pomeroy. Earlier that day, two private detectives were detained outside of Hayden's Belvedere home. They had been hired by an attorney for Hayden's ex-wife Betty to see if his fiancée had spent the night there with Hayden. She had not. She had spent the night before the wedding in a hotel in Sausalito. Ironically, the two detectives later came back to his door and told Hayden how much they admired him and that they had been hired on behalf of Betty. Hayden invited them in and they all had a drink together.[9]

March 9 was Kitty's twenty-ninth birthday. The wedding was attended by seventeen people, including the bridal couple. Turnley Walker served as Sterling's best man. During the ceremony, Kitty's hands were shaking so much she had to have Sterling place his wedding band on himself. At the reception, he opened a fortune cookie. The message inside read: "Seek happiness for its own sake, and you will find it."[10]

Several years later, Hayden would recall to an interviewer: "Then, providentially, I met a girl and married for the third time. This is the first time I've ever felt really married; the first time I've ever loved anyone; the first time I've had the capacity to love anyone."[11]

During their entire marriage, Hayden would always address Kitty in private with his own term of endearment. One of his favorite poems was Edward Lear's 1871 nonsense poem "The Owl and the Pussycat." Sterling was conversant in French and loved the French translation of the poem, the title of which was "Le Hibou et la Poussiquette." For the next two and a half decades, through triumphant and turbulent times, for Sterling Hayden, Kitty was "Puss" or "PQ," his personal abbreviation of "Poussiquette."[12]

Sterling Hayden would be married to Kitty Hayden for the rest of his life.

• • •

When Sterling returned from Tahiti, he selected a unique home in which to live. He rented an old, broken-down golf course clubhouse that belonged to the Belvedere Country Club in Belvedere, California, on San Francisco Bay. It was to this home that the newly married couple settled in with their five children. Kitty's first impression was that it was a wreck, but she set about making it a home for the new family. In addition to having her beautiful furniture shipped from her New York home, she oversaw several improvements to the house. In short order, she transformed Sterling's ramshackle bachelor house into what she described as a wonderful home for the family.[13] The domestic bliss in Belvedere was not to last.

• • •

Shortly after the family had settled into their Belvedere home, Sterling sought a quiet place in which to work. In nearby Tiburon, the Northwestern Pacific Railroad had recently vacated its facility on the waterfront, and Sterling rented a room on the second floor of the old train depot. There he would concentrate purely on writing. It was an ideal location, only five minutes from their home. Sterling would write all morning, come home for lunch and a nap, and then return to the depot to write for the rest of the afternoon. He would accept no acting offers until he was finished. Looking out over the water, he was able to finally come to grips with what he really wanted to accomplish: to produce a meaningful piece of writing. During the voyage of the *Wanderer*, he had often questioned himself. "Why did you never write? Why, instead, did you grovel along, through endless months and years, as a motion-picture actor?" he had asked.[14] Now he had his chance and he would see it through. He was determined to write not just another celebrity memoir but rather "a book that people won't forget."[15]

Even though he was apparently retired from the motion picture industry, there was ample interest in him as a result of the Tahiti voyage and the attendant publicity. Accordingly, Hayden was able to obtain a $2,000 advance from Doubleday & Company to write his autobiography. At first it seemed like the opportunity he had long sought, but it quickly became apparent to him that the publisher had only expectations of a Hollywood scandal saga, as they would not provide him with editorial assistance. Hayden angrily returned the advance money, despite being broke as always. To pay his accumulating debts, he had been forced to sell his beloved schooner, *Wanderer*.[16] But, as he had always done, Sterling Hayden was determined to do it his own way.

He had always been diligent in keeping journals his entire life. Now, with a stable family and no distractions from the film industry, he was able to concentrate exclusively on his autobiography and a new writing career. He proved to be a prolific writer and he produced a lengthy draft that he became increasingly dissatisfied with. It had become unwieldly and he realized he that he needed help with the editing process. He would have to turn to a professional writer for help.

Sterling asked a friend if she knew of anyone who could assist him in the editing process and who would be willing to work "for peanuts." The friend promptly contacted her colleague, June Osterberg, a writer for the *San Francisco Chronicle*. Osterberg drove out to Sausalito to meet with Hayden at the Tiburon train depot and quickly fell under his spell. "At 45, he was no longer golden-haired, but I was a gibbering schoolgirl in the presence of this famous movie actor. His photo from a movie magazine was taped to the wall of my room when I was in high school," she recalled.[17] During the interview, he made it clear that he planned to remain detached from Hollywood and was determined to become a professional writer. Would she help him pare his story down and turn it into a real and worthy book—for two dollars an hour? She readily agreed.[18]

Beginning early that spring, Hayden and Osterberg worked together closely as they refined the manuscript. She would take his handwritten, barely decipherable notes and transform them into a lucid, typewritten record. In addition to enjoying Hayden's company, she was also greatly impressed by his writing. "He was coherent in his thinking and articulate," she recalled. "He had a head full of sailing lore and held passionate convictions. This was not a frivolous, typical movie actor's biography. My job was not ghostwriting."[19] By June of 1961, they had produced ninety-eight well-written pages, eleven chapters in all. Armed with this material, Hayden traveled to New York City to find a publisher for the book. He quickly succeeded in his quest. The publisher Alfred A. Knopf was impressed with the movie-star-turned-writer's work and offered him a contract with a $6,000 advance on royalties. Hayden was assigned to work with Knopf's chief editor, Angus Cameron.

• • •

With his book contract in hand, Hayden's writing nearly became an obsession for him. As a result, he would display a developing pattern of behavior that he would exhibit for the rest of his life, the pattern that had its origins when he rented the train depot in Tiburon for his writing. Wherever his perceived needs led him, he would pursue it regardless of the effect on others. His self-indulgent behavior would ultimately affect his wife and children, as well as his health. If he needed to be alone to write, then he would be alone. If he became bored and wanted to move the family, they would follow his desires. He wanted no further distractions from his writing at this point in time and he soon thought of a way to free himself from the obligations of family life. It began as a result of an advertisement he read in the book supplement section of the *New York Times*, in March of that year.

An advertisement for the Summerhill School in Suffolk, England, caught his eye, and for months he considered the possibility of enrolling his children there. The school, founded in 1921, was the creation of Scottish writer A. S. Neill. It was a progressive school with an unusual curriculum whereby the students themselves decided what their daily activities would consist of. Nearly half the student body was from America. This free-thinking approach to education appealed to the individualist who was Sterling Hayden. There was another major reason why Hayden was contemplating sending his four older children—then ages thirteen, twelve, eleven, and nine—to boarding school.

On August 27, 1961, Hayden wrote to A. S. Neill inquiring about the possibility of enrolling his children at the school.[20] As background, he explained the trials and tribulations that his children had endured in recent years. "They have been offered up on that sacrificial altar erected throughout this land and known as 'The Custody Fight'; complete with judges, courts, detectives, lawyers, photographers and headlines half a foot high." Hayden explained that he wanted to get the children out of this type of environment, as he was "trying to buy them a final crack at security—through you—So it is."

While Hayden's described motives were indeed pure, there was another factor at play. The fact was that after having custody of the children for six years—in the wake of years of court battles with his ex-wife, years of trying to be the model single father in California, and his single-parent responsibilities on the voyage of the *Wanderer*—he was drained. The role of father never came naturally to him. Now he had additional responsibilities, namely a new wife and earlier that year they had their first child together, a son named Andrew. On top of this, he was now pursuing his dream of writing, and with the new book contract, he was coming close to achieving this goal. He needed to concentrate on the book and didn't want all of the distractions of children and family life. He explained to Neill: "All of which I only mention because the job of writing seems to destroy the capacity I always had for playing with and understanding the kids at least to an extent."

Hayden heard back from the school in a letter dated September 4, 1961.[21] They offered to enroll the Hayden children for the semester beginning September 28, even if they arrived a little late. In addition, they offered Hayden the discount in tuition that he had requested when he explained that he was still heavily in debt as a result of the *Wanderer* voyage. Even with the discount offered by the school, the annual tuition would have cost over $7,000, money that Hayden didn't have. This likely proved too rich for Hayden's blood. His handwritten note on the bottom of the letter from Summerhill, dated September 15, simply stated: "Am not able send [*sic*] children this year. Appreciate offer . . . Impossible charge."

• • •

An alternative plan rapidly developed in Hayden's mind. He was bored with Belvedere after a year and a half, and the wanderer in Sterling Hayden's soul again began to assert itself. He now felt that he could write more effectively if he returned to his roots and went back east. He uprooted the family and they moved to Nantucket Island, Massachusetts, in the fall of 1961. Hayden drove with the boys to Massachusetts in his Volkswagen bus while Kitty flew back to the East Coast with Gretchen and their new son Andrew, who was born in February of 1961.[22] Shortly after the Hayden family arrived on Nantucket Island, they were spotted by a woman who wondered where the large family was going to live. The woman had rented the large home of John Macrae Jr., chairman of the board of E. P. Dutton Publishing Company, for the summer, but she was in the process of vacating the house. She felt that the house would be perfect for the Hayden family's needs, and after seeing it, they agreed to rent the house. The move to Nantucket would be the first of seven family moves during their first eight years of marriage. The burden of the family logistics for all of the moves would fall to Kitty.

Writing to a friend on February 12, 1962, Hayden admitted that the move to Nantucket was a mistake.[23] "All is not well here," he began. "The move was a big mistake. You cannot go home again! New England is so dead it would make you ache. People here have deteriorated past all telling. They do nothing but take care of one another and watch TV and root for Goldwater and worry about the fallout hitting the scallops. None of which gets to me." The Hayden children hated Nantucket and Kitty was unhappy with the schools. "Planning on a speedy return to the SF area come June," he reported. "Don't know who will finance same unless it's my wife."

He already had a plan of action. "What I want to do now is come back—find some sort of house in Sausalito, lease or buy a CABOOSE (for an office), run the bastard on a siding within sight of the Bay and get to work on the next book. That's what I *want* to do. And it follows therefore that I'll probably end up acting in a picture to tide the family along til [*sic*] the book can begin to earn." By mid-1962 the Hayden family was once again on the road, headed back to California.

Arriving in Belvedere, Kitty purchased a beautiful Tudor home that had been built in 1906. Sterling hated it, but it became the Hayden family residence for the next three years. Shortly after the family settled back into the San Francisco Bay Area, Hayden was on the waterfront across the bay in Sausalito and he spied the retired ferryboat *Berkeley*. The boat had been retired from service in 1958 by a wealthy businessman who converted the boat into a gift shop called "Trade Fair." The *Berkeley* was moored directly across Richardson Bay from Belvedere, where Richardson Bay merges with San Francisco Bay. Contacting the owner, he arranged to rent the pilot house for his workplace. There he would continue his writing. Every morning, he would row his whaleboat across the bay to his new pilot house office on the *Berkeley*, and when he was finished with his writing for the day, he would row home to Belvedere.

...

It was appropriate that he used the name of his schooner, *Wanderer*, as the title of his book. He would tell the story of his life and frame the segments around the story of the recently completed voyage. His language was highly descriptive, and he would often shift between first- and third-person narratives in telling his story. For a first-time author, it was a remarkable effort. Before he was satisfied with his final product, he had completed six bound earlier drafts, with over two thousand pages of notes.[24] After nearly two years of work, *Wanderer* was published by Knopf on October 21, 1963. It became a critically acclaimed bestseller. He dedicated the book to his wife Kitty, and in an interesting form of belated apology, he also included Warwick Tompkins in the dedication.

Critics heaped praise on Hayden's writing, hailing him as an authentic writer in the tradition of Joseph Conrad and Herman Melville.[25] *Kirkus Reviews* offered reluctant praise, concluding that "taken as a whole, it is the interesting story of an interesting man . . . Hayden has produced a surprising book that will be read."[26] Robert Kirsch of the *Los Angeles Times* would declare upon the book's rerelease in 1977: "Like Fitzgerald, Hayden is a romantic. His writing about the sea evokes echoes of Conrad and McFee, of London and Gadsworthy . . . Beautifully done."[27] He had done it—not only had he written a book as he had always wanted to do, but he had produced a well-written, honest, extremely self-critical bestseller that received praise from critics all over the country. As he told an interviewer after the book was released, "I think I wrote it because I wanted to leave behind something of value, something of which I could be proud. Perhaps every man wants, essentially, to do this. I've always respected writing more than any other form of activity a man could indulge in . . . I'd like to be remembered as someone who produced a work of literary merit."[28]

Perhaps even more impressive than the excellent reviews that *Wanderer* received from literary critics and professional book reviewers was the response from the general public. Housed at the Sterling Hayden Collection at the Howard Gotlieb Research Center at Boston University are three thick folders containing hundreds of letters written to Hayden from citizens all over the country singing the praises of his book. What is striking about the letters is that many go on for multiple pages and are very emotional, indicating what a chord that *Wanderer* had stuck with them personally. Many readers identified with the individualist exemplified by Hayden, a man who went his own way and candidly told his story, revealing warts and all.

Wanderer, which was rereleased in 1977 and 1998, would endure. It was and is considered a classic example of autobiography.

CHAPTER NINETEEN

Radical Redux

DURING THE WRITING OF *WANDERER* AND THE SUBSEQUENT EDITING process, culminating in the book's release in October 1963, and throughout 1964, Sterling Hayden had a "rebirth" as a radical. His passion for the underdog and social justice had never dimmed, but during this timeframe he would exhibit his progressive beliefs in very public settings. Why he chose to have this short-lived public rebooting of his radical days can possibly be seen in the context of recreating his past in *Wanderer* and the editing process that shaped the final version. It would involve him working with a vanguard of the Old Left, his editor at Alfred A. Knopf, Angus Cameron. Cameron had achieved notoriety in 1947 when, as an editor at Little, Brown and Company, he refused to have his company publish George Orwell's biting satire on communism, *Animal Farm*, as it offended his leftist sensibilities. In addition to being forced out of his job, in 1951 he became an uncooperative witness at the HUAC hearings probing communist influence in the publishing industry.[1]

Hayden's stepson, journalist Scott McConnell, has read the earlier drafts of *Wanderer* that are now housed at Boston University, as well as the correspondence between Hayden and Cameron, which reveal Hayden's great affection for Angus Cameron. In prior drafts, Hayden dedicated his autobiography to leftists and communists—namely, Cameron, Paul Robeson, Vincent Hallinan, and Harry Bridges—and "to their cause and their comrades throughout the world betrayed by me in 1951."[2] McConnell noted that the original draft of *Wanderer* was 30 percent longer than the final product and that Hayden was not happy with the changes that Cameron had made. In particular, he was displeased with the editorial changes involving his characterization of the members of the Communist Party and his distaste for them, issues that ultimately led to his decision to leave the Party. Although he expressed to Cameron an "enormous sense of failure" in seeing that his work required so much "drastic overhauling," he soon thereafter apologized and ultimately approved the final manuscript.[3] It was, as McConnell described, "the political bowdlerization of his own autobiography."[4]

During his testimony to the HUAC in 1951, Hayden gave the following reason for his decision to leave the Communist Party: his belief that their thought processes sought mind control over their members and their dogmatic belief that emphasized that everything is predetermined. The supreme individualist, Hayden had trouble accepting this and left the Party. While the original draft of *Wanderer* was intended to praise the Party and criticize himself, his description of the Party members highlighting their dogmatism, discipline, and single-minded emphasis on a life devoted to political goals was not the philosophy that Angus Cameron wanted depicted, so it was edited out of the published version of *Wanderer*.[5] Instead, in the more toned-down version of his autobiography, Party members come across more as thoughtful idealists, "concerned" to be sure, but really nothing more than woolly headed participants in a "Marxist" debating club.[6] Any sinister intent of the Communist Party, then vying with the West for control of Europe and ultimately for a possible nuclear confrontation with the United States, was not touched upon.

Also removed from the original draft of *Wanderer* was Hayden's discussion of Thoreau's *Walden* and its profound influence on him. Thoreau's concept of rugged individualism, which had strongly appealed to Hayden, meant absolutely nothing to these people to whom the Party itself meant everything and individuality was scorned. The rigid-minded, doctrinaire attitude of his fellow Party members served only to alienate Hayden from them. In the words of McConnell: "As much as he may have wished to, he could not accept discipline in the Party's sense of the word. This was not a difference over politics, about which Sterling thought little, but simply over the spirit in which one lived one's life."[7] Also edited out by Cameron was the postwar influence of Lincoln Colcord.

Despite the editorial softening by Angus Cameron—whom Hayden would refer to in a 1964 interview as "a wonderful man named Angus Cameron"[8]—*Wanderer* remains a compelling, well-written autobiography that is striking for its candor. In 1951, Hayden was forced to pay penance to the HUAC and the Right in order to preserve his career and to assure him custody of his children in his looming divorce. He did so, but he carried feelings of guilt and regret over his testimony for the rest of his life. By going along with the editorial changes made by Cameron in softening the portrayal of the Party and its members, Hayden had now, in a sense, paid penance to the Left for naming names to the HUAC. He had never lost his passion for leftist causes. As he told an interviewer in 1964, "Curiously, I feel more radical in my beliefs today than I did when I was a member of the Party. This poses a question in view of the witch-hunt affair: Is it the Party, or is it the presence of injustice, which presents the real problem?"[9] Now, in this era of *Wanderer*, he would publicly pursue his passions.

• • •

As *Wanderer* was undergoing the editorial process, Hayden came up with an idea to showcase his beliefs. He remained an admirer of Fidel Castro and his regime promising "direct democracy" in Cuba.[10] He proposed a new book project to Angus Cameron: he would write a travelogue that would culminate with him sailing into a harbor in Cuba. Acknowledging that he would likely be arrested, he had discussed the matter with Harry Bridges, former Communist Party member and head of the West Coast Longshoremen's Union. Bridges felt confident that working people in the United States would "vouch" for him and the Cubans would release him, allowing him to tell the real story of the new Cuba.[11]

Cameron was not at all interested in the proposed project. Despite this rejection, Sterling still wanted to pursue it but had a problem that frequently reared its ugly head with him—he was broke and couldn't finance the trip. He turned to his wife Kitty. Ever the pragmatist and certainly the levelheaded one when it came to finances, Kitty knew her husband only too well and had deliberately never intermingled their financial affairs. She thought the project was absurd and would not give him the money.[12] He subsequently turned to friend, fellow author Eugene Burdick, and was able to borrow the money from him.[13] In early October of 1962, Hayden began the planning for his proposed trip.

World events soon overtook his planning. On October 14, 1962, tensions flared between the United States and the Soviet Union over Cuba in a standoff referred to by historians as the Cuban Missile Crisis. The two superpowers stood on the brink of nuclear war. On that day, aerial surveillance photographs taken by the CIA's U-2 spy planes flying over Cuba revealed the presence of medium-range and intermediate-range ballistic nuclear missiles sites under construction on the island. The administration of President John F. Kennedy weighed its options to counter the bold move by the Soviet Union to place nuclear missiles on Cuba, only ninety miles from the United States. Kennedy decided on a blockade of the island, although he used the term "quarantine" as "blockade" would indicate an actual state of war. The United States Navy sailed into the Caribbean to enforce the quarantine with orders to stop any ships, especially Russian ships, from reaching the Cuban shore. The next thirteen days were tense as the world was poised for a possible nuclear confrontation between the two superpowers.

As the possibility of a US invasion of Cuba loomed more likely, on October 27, a large protest against US policy towards Cuba, as well as a counter-protest, took place at Civic Center Plaza in downtown San Francisco.[14] One of the key speakers opposing the quarantine imposed on Cuba by the Kennedy administration was Sterling Hayden. About 1,200 people attending the rally heard him and other speakers rail against the US policy. In a particularly venomous accusation he made during his speech, he compared the administration of John F. Kennedy to the Third Reich.[15] At the other end of the plaza, about 500 people attended a rally in support of US policy. Soon a shoving match ensued, but no overt fighting erupted between the two groups.

The following morning, as a result of secret ongoing negotiations, the Soviet Union announced that it would be dismantling its missile sites in Cuba in exchange for the US pledging not to invade Cuba. Concurrently the United States agreed to dismantle missile sites in Turkey, whose missiles were aimed at the Soviet Union, within a short time interval. The Cuban Missile Crisis, which began with the quarantine on October 16, ended on October 28 as the world stepped back from the brink.

And Sterling Hayden would never make his symbolic voyage to Cuba.

• • •

Hayden was always interested in racial equality and during this period he would exhibit his support in a very public forum. In 1963 and 1964, the civil rights movement was sweeping the country and nationwide protests and demonstrations occurred frequently. Hayden was very vocal in his views on civil rights. "I think the Negro movement is an extraordinarily exciting thing," he explained to an interviewer in 1964, "not because of the horror of it, but because of what it offers. The Negro movement makes me hope that . . . there's some slim chance that this country might get back on the track it was originally intended to ride."[16] He had already spoken in a public forum on race relations when he took part in a program presented at the Grace Cathedral in San Francisco on February 17, 1964. He was part of an invited panel that discussed "The Church and the Racial Crisis."[17]

The San Francisco Bay Area was erupting in racial protests in the early 1960s. The largest occurred at the swank Sheraton Palace Hotel on March 1, 1964. Hundreds of protesters showed up at the hotel to picket, protesting the hiring practices of the hotel. At issue was the fact that blacks could be hired as maids or bellhops but were not hired to staff the front desk or other jobs that would give them more responsibility.[18] The protests spread to other sectors of the city. One of the next industries targeted was the automobile showrooms on Van Ness Avenue. On April 11, 1964, about 300 protestors descended on Automobile Row, where the "Big Three" automakers had showrooms.[19] They were protesting the lack of any black salespeople in any of the dealerships. Among the protestors was "red-bearded actor Sterling Hayden." They singled out the Cadillac showroom specifically, and General Motors acknowledged that they had refused to sign a statement that would require the hiring of a quota of non-white employees. A four-block span of protesters effectively shut down Van Ness Avenue, and shortly after noon, the arrests began. It took three hours to totally clear the street.

In all, 226 protesters, including Hayden, were arrested and charged with disturbing the peace, unlawful assembly, and disobedience. At arraignment, bail was set at $276 each. Sterling appeared in court the next month, but he dreaded the prospect of being locked up in a jail cell. In addition, he likely felt that his presence with the protesters had made the point he wished to achieve. Accordingly, he pleaded *nolo contendere,* thereby avoiding any jail time.

• • •

After his 1964 arrest during the Automobile Row protest, Sterling Hayden did not appear at any other public protest forums. Despite his absence from subsequent public forums, the issues of racial inequality, identification with the underdog in society, and economic disparity always offended his sense of right and wrong and tugged at his conscience. He would remain outspoken on these subjects, but his brief resurgence as a public figure in the protest movement, a highly visible "radical reborn," had effectively ended. The reasons for this were myriad, including his efforts to write his next book, his increasing alcohol abuse and dependence, and his wandering, restless spirit that would eventually lead him to spend several months every year in Europe. Radical causes were never far from his heart. He became almost like a college professor who taught controversial topics in the classroom and encouraged student dissent but declined to participate in campus protests. Growing up in the Hayden household, his children were exposed to discussions of class, capitalism, and revolution among other topics. He became, as Scott McConnell described him, "a revolutionary in the living room."[20]

CHAPTER TWENTY

Return to Film

STERLING HAYDEN HAD NOT MADE A FILM SINCE *TEN DAYS TO TULARA* in 1958. Things were about to change significantly.

Hayden first worked with director Stanley Kubrick in 1956, starring in *The Killing*. This was Kubrick's first full-length feature film shot with a professional cast and crew.[1] Kubrick wanted to have Hayden star in the movie, and Hayden was impressed with the young director. He pulled some strings for Kubrick, helping him to obtain financing for the film project and agreed to take a lesser salary to enable Kubrick to make the film.[2] *The Killing* received good reviews from the critics upon its release and today is considered a film noir classic. Kubrick rose to Hollywood prominence with his next two films, *Paths of Glory* and *Spartacus*. These films cemented his reputation as filmdom's most creative young genius, despite the mediocre performance of his subsequent film, *Lolita*. For his next film project, he envisioned Sterling Hayden appearing in one of the key roles.

Kubrick had read author Peter George's 1958 Cold War thriller *Red Alert* and began work to bring it to the screen. Shortly after beginning work on the screenplay, he got the idea to turn the story into a dark, satirical vision of the Cold War—in essence, a black comedy. After hiring Terry Southern to assist him in writing the screenplay, Kubrick obtained the necessary financing and began the casting process. Peter Sellers was the choice to star in the proposed film, now titled *Dr. Strangelove or: How I Learned to Stop Worrying and Love the Bomb*. Sellers would play three roles in the film: The president of the United States, a Royal Air Force group captain, and the title role of the ex-Nazi scientist, Dr. Strangelove.

The second key role was played by dramatic actor George C. Scott. Portraying Gen. Buck Turgidson, Scott delivered an uncharacteristically hilarious and manic performance that the critics highly praised.

The other key role was that of Gen. Jack D. Ripper, a US Air Force brigadier general and commanding officer of a Strategic Air Command base. Ripper, insanely obsessed with the notion that the Soviet Union was attempting to conquer the West by fluorinating the water supply, orders several B-52 bombers to drop nuclear bombs on the Russians. For this role, Kubrick convinced Hayden to return to the screen for the first time in nearly six years. Filming in England during the latter half of 1963, Hayden delivered a performance that redefined him as a stellar character actor and became the first of several superb post-*Wanderer* performances that he would deliver. Critics applauded him for his cigar-chomping portrayal of the lunatic general.

The scene where he lectures Peter Sellers (as RAF group captain Mandrake) on the communist plot to "sap and impurify all of our precious bodily fluids," and to cause "loss of essence," remains hilarious to watch to this day. It is difficult to believe that Hayden still, at that time, remained very uncomfortable in front of the camera. His many years away from the camera no doubt contributed to his discomfort. It all came to a head during the filming of this particular scene with Sellers.

Although the number of takes would vary somewhat depending on whenever Hayden would relate the story, he had an extremely difficult time with the filming of that specific scene. It required thirty-seven takes to get the scene done properly. "That story has become a constant in my repertoire. But it's also unassailable. Because what turned out to be Jack D. Ripper's performance, particularly in that long scene with Peter Sellers off-camera, was an actor fighting to survive. And I just got worse and worse and worse, which is what inspired Stanley Kubrick to say that beautiful thing to me: 'The terror in your eyes may be the quality that one wants in Ripper.' But I would suggest to you that few things on this earth are as pathetic as an actor out of control, which I was."[3]

Dr. Strangelove was released in January 1964 to largely positive reviews. Prominent *New York Times* film critic Bosley Crowther wrote: "It is all right to show the general who starts this wild foray as a communist-hating madman, convinced that a 'Red conspiracy' is fluorinating our water to pollute our precious body fluids. That is pointed satire, and Sterling Hayden plays the role with just a right blend of wackiness and meanness to give the character significance."[4]

Dr. Strangelove proved to be a sort of renaissance for Hayden, who seemed to have re-created himself as character actor. As he approached the age of fifty, the years of smoking and alcohol abuse had already taken a toll on his matinee idol looks. Still handsome, he now was a more grizzled version of his former self who looked somewhat older that his actual age. During the coming years, he would find a most unusual treatment for both his uneasiness in front of the camera, as well as his alcoholism.

...

In 1965, Sterling and Kitty Hayden were traveling to across the country aboard the Burlington *Zephyr* when the train made its scheduled stop in Chicago. As they waited, a vice president of the Burlington Railroad came aboard, looking for another railroad executive. Unable to find him, he recognized Hayden and shortly thereafter the men were enjoying drinks together. Hayden mentioned that he would like to buy a caboose to restore and use as an office. The VP responded that it would be possible to buy a business car, as the railroad would occasionally sell off some of its properties. Since he was broke at the time, Hayden declined to make an offer.

About three weeks later, Hayden received a package from the railroad. It contained several photographs of a 1890s Pullman car that was currently unused in a railway roundhouse in Galesburg, Illinois. It was luxuriously built, featuring mahogany paneling inside, brass beds, and a galley. It was for sale and the railroad was asking $2,000 for it. Hayden couldn't resist; he immediately purchased the car.

Attached to a mile-and-a-quarter-long railroad train, Hayden and his friends Billy Pearson and Louis Vogler rode the car back from Galesburg to Oakland, California, the three of them drinking the entire time. From there the car was transported to Sausalito. For the next several years, Hayden would be using it as his office where he worked on his newest writing project: a novel.

The Hayden family had moved back east in 1965, renting a house in Redding, Connecticut, on the advice of Kitty's sister. Once again, Sterling was unhappy with it and roughly six months later, he uprooted the family and they moved back to the San Francisco area. Kitty bought them a house in the Pacific Heights section of the city. This, too, did not please her husband as he felt it was too high-scale for his tastes. By then, he was drinking heavily and spending most of his days writing in his railroad car.

Less than two years before his death, Hayden reflected on his railroad car. In a diary entry dated November 9, 1984, he wrote: "And it's coming back to me, just how it felt. 16 years & 7 months ago. That magical afternoon . . . in this old private railroad car: Burlington Northern No. 93.

Built in Burlington Yards-1890. For some forgotten wheel (A vice Pres. Or a Division superintendent). Oh the magic of that car! A schooner of the rails. Iron lined rail."[5]

In 1968, he gave his beloved railroad car to his daughter Gretchen but soon after it was confiscated by the Internal Revenue Service to pay off her father's federal tax debt.

CHAPTER TWENTY-ONE

Alcohol, Hashish, and River Barges

BY LATE 1967, HAYDEN'S DRINKING WAS ACCELERATING AND HE BECAME, in his own words, "detached." The wanderer in his soul was starting to again exert itself. After moving back to the Bay Area to their Pacific Heights home, Sterling would spend most of his days in the railroad car, writing and drinking. Kitty enrolled Andrew and David into the nearby Hillwood Academic Day School and also decided to take a job at the school. Sterling would soon react to what he perceived as the flashes of independence exhibited by Kitty in a somewhat jealous and possessive manner, one that would become repetitive and exaggerated as time went on. His pattern of behavior would almost become predictable as the years passed.

In December 1967, Sterling and Kitty, along with sons Andrew and David, traveled east via train to spend Christmas in New York City. While riding aboard the Burlington *Zephyr*, Sterling revealed to Kitty that he thought that they should separate. They had little in common, he explained. She was not much of a drinker, so he ended up drinking by himself. He was in many ways a "man's man" and liked to hang out with the guys and drink with his friends. Most important of all to him, he wanted to be free to travel, to wander whenever he wanted. Kitty was heartbroken and hid her tears from their children.[1] After spending Christmas in New York, Sterling headed back to Sausalito by himself. Kitty went on with the children to her sister Betty's house in Wilton, Connecticut. As always, Betty was a pillar of strength for Kitty to rely on.

A couple of weeks later, Sterling called Kitty from California. He missed her badly, he confessed. "I love you more than life itself. Please come back," he begged.[2] This was the beginning of another behavior pattern that Sterling Hayden would exhibit for the rest of his life. He would push away Kitty in a quest to be alone and free to wander whenever he pleased, and shortly after that, he would plead for her to come back to him. His desire to have her back would be especially pronounced if he perceived that she could get along without him and was able to build a life independent from him. Although she couldn't understand why he needed to wander off by himself, she did come back to him and always would. For all of his quirks, she loved him and missed him when they were apart. And Sterling missed her. She represented the strength and stability that held their family together. He needed her. And he loved her—beyond his ability to express it.

Hayden had been working on his novel for the past five years. Doubleday had provided him a $68,000 advance for the book, and he had already completed two 1,500-page manuscripts. As always, he was his own worst critic. He wasn't enthused about the drafts but submitted them anyway. More importantly, the editors at Doubleday were unhappy with his work and insisted on another rewrite. At that point, he simply walked away from the project. Hayden had taken the advance earnings he had just received from 20th Century Fox to star in an upcoming spy thriller called *Hard Contract* and deposited them in a European bank. Hence, it would have been futile for the publisher to sue him for the advance they had given him—he had no assets in America from which they could attempt to recoup their advance money. Hayden was aware of his increasing self-destructive tendencies. Reflecting on how his alcohol dependence had affected his work on his novel, he noted, "Tuesday (ten pages from 6:30—to now 9:30). Book could be done and gone but for the days (How many days in '67 alone) passed over hung [*sic*] on couch unable to even think of work . . . How many days?"[3]

He had been drinking more heavily than ever. The self-doubt that he experienced all of his life was starting to rear its head and eat away at his confidence. He began to realize that he could only write creatively when he was smoking and drinking to excess. He wryly noted the direct relationship, in his case, between cigarettes, booze, and writing. To him, there was something glorious about it; and also quite tragic and savage about it.[4] His diary entry of March 9, 1968, reflected his growing sense of creative and personal detachment when he wrote, "our 8th anniversary . . . Drift . . . Do nothing at all."[5]

He had been through one rehab program and the thought of what sobriety would cost him was frightening. "Does this mean I'll never be able to sit again in a café in Paris and watch the world go by, and drink and laugh, he thought out loud?" In 1977, he would confess that the dour-appearing lives that recovered alcoholics seemed to live scared him. He admired them for their accomplishment in giving up drinking, but he couldn't imagine himself living such a bland lifestyle.[6]

His growing self-loathing had much to do with the damage he knew he was doing to his relationship with Kitty. Hayden was aware that she was the best thing that ever happened to him and knew that he was driving a wedge between them with his erratic and self-destructive behavior. His diary notes from the spring of 1968 were especially poignant. "And last night you lay so still. Didn't dare touch her hand until three. Heard her breathe. Saw her head lift, and then turn away from you. And thousands of subtle and not so subtle instances of rejection come back so clearly now. Though all the while deep inside you knew how lucky you were. How unique she was. All this you knew. But you hurt her. You did all you could to destroy her and the relationship—simultaneously and for the 8 years destroying yourself through the boozing, the chain smoking, the ridiculous diet, the hours all hours up or half up."

In the next entry he continued his self-degradation over his treatment of his wife. "Worst time of life—bar none—so low last night thought of bridge—the utter unutterable desolation and faintness of heart. Thought she is gone forever—the best girl ever happened to you in 52 years. Bar none—the shit I now see with my own eyes. . . . ONE THING SURE—from now on either YOU GO DOWNWARD PERPENDICULARLY VIA THE BOOZE AND THE CIGGIES—or you stand reprieved on your own-maybe?? . . . Enough boy watch it. Shit."[7]

One gets the impression that Sterling Hayden found it easier to express the depth of his love for Kitty to his diary than to her. It is a sad irony that a man who proved so eloquent with words and could write bestselling books found it so difficult to say the words that expressed his true feelings to the woman he loved.

...

One day in 1968, a female acquaintance came by the railroad car to visit with Hayden. She pointed out the obvious to him, a truth he was well aware of—he was drinking himself to death. Why not try grass, she suggested? He declined her offer, but she left a pipe and a small supply of marijuana. Several weeks later, feeling particularly down, he decided to try it for the first time. Sitting alone in the railroad car, he pulled the curtains shut and pulled out the pipe, filled it, and proceeded to smoke several pipefuls. At first, he felt nothing and he got up to get a drink. To his astonishment, he had no urge to drink. For the first time, he felt he had discovered something that would help him control his alcoholism to a degree. At the age of fifty-two, he had discovered the world of pot and hashish.

The wanderer inside of him was getting the best of him. He felt he couldn't go on with life as he was living it and he needed to try something new. He wasn't certain exactly what, but one thing he did realize was that no matter the course he might take, he would need money. And for that he could fall back to the occupation that he detested to help him out of his financial straits. He would take another acting job.

...

After walking away from his book project, much to the annoyance of Doubleday Publishing, Sterling Hayden decided to give up on his novel, at least for the immediate future. Instead, he accepted his next screen role. Offered a co-starring role with James Coburn and Lee Remick in a spy thriller titled *Hard Contract*, Hayden traveled to Spain for the filming. On his first day in front of the camera, he was nervous and unsure, and he kept missing his lines. It seemed like déjà vu for him. However, two months earlier in Sausalito, he had made an interesting discovery. The first time he had smoked marijuana it not only relaxed him but it seemed to have a pacifying effect on his craving for alcohol. That evening, he decided to try it for the first time on a movie set.

In a later interview he would recall, "out of despair, I thought, maybe a toke or two." The effect was nothing short of astonishing to him. "The next day on the set, it went beautifully. I went backwards and forwards with the dialogue. For the first time in my life, I said to myself, 'I have confidence in what I'm doing. This is how an actor is supposed to feel.' Since then, I've enjoyed acting immensely."[8] From that point on, smoking pot and hashish would become a regular part of his life. By the time he finished filming in Spain, he was smoking grass every day and often kept a log on how it made him feel, "because I was so fascinated by the subtleties of it." He was always very candid about it, speaking freely about his hashish usage with talk show host Tom Snyder on national television several years later.[9] It would also lead to an arrest when he landed at Toronto International Airport on April 16, 1981, when he was charged with possession of hashish. "I had three and a half ounces of Lebanese hashish in my pocket," he explained. The Canadian judge presiding over the case dismissed it. Among the reasons cited were the fact that he was using it to control his alcoholism and that his only prior arrest was for a civil rights demonstration. Summarizing his decision, the judge declared: "The judgment is unusual because this is an unusual man."[10]

After completing the filming of *Hard Contract* in 1968, he decided that he had to do something different, something that he had never done before. But what? After some self-reflection, he decided to drift, to "go with the flow": "I was weary then, so I decided to drift through Europe."[11] Once again, he wanted to be by himself. He knew this would be very difficult for Kitty, and their two sons, Andrew, born in February 1961, and David, born in September 1962. He also knew that he wanted to return to writing eventually. But first he had to drift. "That's a lovely way to live . . . it appears to be selfish, but I believe that we've got to try to be true to ourselves."[12] He would later justify this seemingly selfish plan on his part by referencing the philosophy that he had absorbed from Ernest Becker's 1973 Pulitzer Prize-winning book, *Denial of Death*, which had a tremendous influence on him. We were not put on this earth, Hayden agreed, to make anybody else happy first. He believed we must make ourselves happy, after which we can then relate to someone else and make them happy.[13]

Hayden initially traveled to Paris, then decided to go to Rotterdam and spend a weekend with Jan de Hartog, the Dutch novelist whom he greatly admired. De Hartog had achieved success as both a novelist and a playwright. However, it was de Hartog's background that really tied him to Sterling Hayden as a kindred spirit. De Hartog, like Hayden, had gone to sea at an early age and had aspired to become a writer. Early in World War II, de Hartog published his book *Hollands Glorie*, which described the heroic lives of Dutch sailors on ocean-going tugboats. The book's portrayal of Dutch independence and self-pride made de Hartog a target for the occupying Nazi forces. He worked for the Dutch underground before escaping to England, where he continued his work for the Dutch underground. As a correspondent in the Netherlands Merchant Marine, he gained experiences that became the basis of his future works, most notably *The Captain*, published in 1967. An avid reader, Hayden was undoubtedly impressed with de Hartog's work.

De Hartog could recognize and identify with the proverbial wanderer in Hayden's soul. Hayden shared with his fellow sailor/author his newly developed interest in river barges. As he got older, Hayden had begun to realize that the allure of the open seas was no longer calling to him. He had accomplished much as a schooner captain, but he had now shifted his attention towards the inland rivers. He would recall in later years: "I just feel the progression of time—you don't have the strength; you don't have the ability to take hold; you don't want to go running around up the rigging. Everything I used to love. I've had that. Fortunately, I found a fascination on the rivers that matches the sea, matches the sea. It's different, of course."[14]

Hayden would come to explain this shift in his interest: "It was the charm. The charm of barges. When you get into the canals . . . you move very slowly, so slowly that you actually have to have an acute sense of what's going on. You can't relax the way you can on a schooner at sea, where you've got the whole world around you. But the river life is just as fascinating as the schooner life was when I was a kid . . . Another part of the charm is that the barges themselves are beautiful . . . Unlike in the Mississippi River, or any other American river, where all barges are pretty much the same, in Europe they have every size and shape, and are beautifully painted. To me it was like paradise."[15]

After listening to his visitor voice his thoughts on barges, de Hartog had a recommendation for him. As he was uncertain exactly what Hayden was looking for, he advised him to travel to a town that was twelve miles away. There, in Dordrecht, he would probably find what he was looking for. "In this town," de Hartog explained, "there is a hotel named Bellevue, and it may be the most magical hotel in the world for people who love ships, because three rivers meet in front of the hotel, and between eight and nine hundred working barges go by five days a week."[16]

Hayden took his friend's advice, traveled to Dordrecht, and found the Hotel Bellevue. It was just as de Hartog described it. Before Hayden went inside, he walked around in front of the hotel and selected the room he wanted based on the view from the windows looking out on the water. Finally going inside, the compliant desk clerk gave him the room that he requested. Piling up the mattresses from four of the five beds in the room until they were window height, Hayden began his search for his perfect barge. It didn't take long. "And out here," he told an interviewer years later, "a barge rolled by! All the time. And there I was! So I sat there and lived and studied the river and watched the ships. I knew the size I was looking for, about one hundred fifty tons, and I began to chase 'em up and down the river. I finally bought one in Rotterdam after six months of looking."[17]

...

While in Holland, Hayden received another film offer, one that would prove to be intensely personal and poignant to him and, to a degree, also to the man offering the film role. That man was an outspoken member of the Hollywood Ten, Dalton Trumbo. After his blacklisting in 1947, Trumbo continued to work, clandestinely producing award-winning screenplays. In 1953, his screenplay for *Roman Holiday* won an Oscar, although the award was presented to Ian McClellan Hunter and John Dighton, who acted as fronts for Trumbo. The Oscar for Best Screenplay in 1956 went to "Robert Rich" for *The Brave One*—a pseudonym that Trumbo used when he wrote *The Brave One*. His re-emergence into the Hollywood community finally occurred in 1960, when he received screenwriting credits for the movies *Spartacus* and *Exodus*. By that time, the blacklist was, for all intents and purposes, over.

The 1960s proved to be a highly productive time for Dalton Trumbo as he wrote screenplays for five more movies, including *Hawaii* and *The Sandpiper*. In the late 1960s, he began a project of great personal importance to him—a film adaption of his classic 1939 antiwar novel, *Johnny Got His Gun*. Not only was he writing the screenplay, but for the first time, he would also be directing a movie. He had a definite vision for this film, and that vision included Sterling Hayden.

On Sunday, October 6, 1968, Trumbo called Hayden in the Netherlands to offer him the important role of the protagonist Joe Bonham's father. An American soldier, Bonham is nearly killed by an artillery shell on the last day of World War I. He loses his arms, legs, face, eyes, ears, mouth, and nose. Only his mind is intact, so he relives his life through memories and dreams. Trumbo wrote to Hayden the next day to elaborate on why he wanted him to star in the movie.[18] He began his letter by humorously warning Hayden that the film would mark his debut as a director "at the age of 62, as the oldest new director in the history of motion pictures," and he warned Hayden that senility sometimes rubs off on innocent bystanders. Trumbo then began to passionately present a heartfelt case in support of Hayden starring in the role, begging him to accept the offer.

The project was intensely personal for Trumbo; he pointed out that a good deal of *Johnny Got His Gun* was autobiographical. All of the details of Joe Bonham's background were actually based on his own upbringing. "I know my characters because I have seen them physically and at close hand in real life . . . I know exactly what each of them looks like and what sort of character he is. I am going to cling to the reality of each character like a barnacle, and once I have found a person memory and intuition tell me is *right*, I am going to pursue him to the ends of the earth." Trumbo confided to Hayden that he was always his first choice to play Bonham's father. To support his case, Trumbo attached casting notes that showed that the studios were considering six actors for the role: Jason Robards Jr., Arthur Kennedy, Ralph Bellamy, George C. Scott, Karl Malden, and Sterling Hayden.

The casting notes detailed Trumbo's views about why all of the other actors would be wrong for the role, and why Sterling would be perfect as the character. Trumbo's arguments included that fact that Hayden was an excellent actor and had a certain look that Trumbo envisioned for the part. But it was Hayden's inner qualities that drove Trumbo to pursue the actor for the part. "I want a man of great reserve to play the part of Joe's Father [*sic*]. I want a man of few words. A man who would find it embarrassing to reveal too much of himself. A man whose inner sense of dignity gives him a certain quality of shyness, of reserve." In Trumbo's mind, none of the other actors could pull this off.

But there was another facet of Joe's father that Trumbo felt that Hayden could bring to the screen. "Joe's father is a *strong* man who is also a failure, but I do not want him to *act* like a failure . . . I want Joe's father to gain *not* the audience's sympathy, but its admiration; and *not* because he is a failure, but because he is strong. Strong in the face of failure. It takes strength to be a failure without verging on the maudlin, and that is the sort of strength which Hayden has always projected onto the screen." Noting that Joe's father is not a loquacious man but a proud man who keeps his emotions carefully concealed, Trumbo stated: "That is the sort of man which Hayden represents to me in his screen personality, and that is the sort of man my [Joe's] father was."

In the closing paragraph of his letter, Trumbo assured Hayden that they would make every effort to accommodate his schedule and promised that the shooting should require no more than two weeks of Hayden's time. "There's little more I can say beyond the fact that I beg you to count up to 800,000 before you reject it," he noted.

Hayden, of course, never accepted the role for which Trumbo so passionately pursued him. He was in the process of "drifting," and his interest was now consumed with finding a barge. But more significantly, at that time Hayden was in the doldrums, with worsening alcohol abuse and creative inertia. His self-esteem—never very high—was negligible, and his gnawing sense of failure was always near the surface of his emotions. Perhaps Trumbo's description of Joe's father was too close to home for Hayden—a man trying to be strong in the face of perceived failure. Perhaps, in his own mind, he would be playing himself.

Hayden's diary contains an undated draft of a response to Trumbo.[19] It is handwritten and only semi-legible, but it captures his angst with accepting the role. "My dear Dalton Trumbo . . . Your book, a classic, seems [undecipherable]. Which is why I can't do it. I can't do it, Dalton

Trumbo, because of my respect for you, and for the good you have set yourself [*sic*] with this production.

"My approach to acting again, is complex. I can only do it if I do not take either the role or the whole thing seriously. This [your film] is no charade. I would take it very seriously. If for no other reason than my esteem for you. So there is a clash here. So the answer comes off, No. I will not be able to join you. Perhaps someday we can talk this out."

Dalton Trumbo proceeded to direct *Johnny Got His Gun* without Sterling Hayden's participation and it was released in 1971. The role of Joe's father went to Jason Robards Jr. Although they didn't know each other at the time, Hayden and Robards's paths would cross in the future—but for reasons that had nothing to do with filmmaking.

• • •

Not long after settling in at the Hotel Bellevue, Hayden promptly squandered some of the money that he had earned for *Hard Contract*. In the course of his river-watching, he noticed an old tugboat named *Speculant* that somehow appealed to him. Although it was old and broken-down, he impulsively decided he had to have it. He made an offer of $11,000 to the owner who gladly accepted it. He never moved aboard the boat nor did he make any attempt to refurbish it. It did not take him long to realize he had made a mistake and, in a move that indicated both his lack of business sense and indifference to money, sold the boat to the Amsterdam Museum for $4,000.

After several more months, Hayden finally found what he was looking for. It was a ninety-four-foot-long barge that was built in 1930 and was named *Who Knows*, a name that appealed to him. He decided to keep the name; it was one of the only times that he didn't rename a boat he had bought. He purchased the barge in May of 1969. Shortly after, Kitty, sons David, Andrew, and Matthew, and the family dog Rover flew to Europe and moved into the Hotel Bellevue with Sterling. The family spent the next two months cleaning and refurbishing the barge as best they could and in July they began a three-week journey to Paris. It rained every day of the trip.[20]

The accommodations aboard *Who Knows* were very basic, almost primitive. There was a larger cabin in the back and just forward was a small room with two bunks that the children would sleep in when visiting. In the large center room, Sterling would sleep on three tatami mats. Fresh water could be stored in tanks built into the hull in the front of the barge. There were no shower facilities and there was no toilet—the bathroom consisted of a closet that contained a bucket. Despite Sterling's installation of a copper fireplace that proved to be nonfunctional, the barge had neither heat nor air conditioning. There were no tables and chairs at which to dine—the Haydens and any guests would eat simple meals off of their laps. Everyone would take frequent sponge baths, and during prolonged stays docked in Paris, Kitty would take the children at least once a week to a nearby hotel for a decent bath or shower.[21] Often secured to the deck over the ensuing years was Sterling's beloved motorcycle, his 1954 single cylinder R26 BMW.

Just as he had anticipated, Hayden would become both a people-watcher and a world-observer. So important was his time aboard *Who Knows* to him that for the rest of his life, he would spend several months every year aboard it, mostly tied up to the Quai de Conti in central Paris. The family would often travel out to France to spend time with Sterling on the barge, despite the primitive accommodations. Kitty would recall at least six trips to Paris during the warmer months.

Meanwhile, in 1968, the Hayden family once again moved cross-country back to Connecticut. Knowing that the family would be traveling to Europe to spend time with Sterling on his barge, Kitty wanted to make the trip to Europe easier by living on the East Coast. She found a new home under construction in the town of Wilton, fifty miles north of New York City. Using her own money, she purchased the home, which would become the family's permanent residence. As usual, Sterling claimed he didn't like the house, deeming that it represented typical suburbia.

Aboard the *Who Knows*, Sterling resumed his writing and eventually finished his book in Sausalito, accomplishing another literary milestone.

CHAPTER TWENTY-TWO

A Literary Triumph and Final Years

THE 1970S PROVED TO BE A PERIOD OF PRIDE AND PROFESSIONAL ACcomplishment for Sterling Hayden, but it was also a time of worsening depression and alcohol abuse. His diary entries for 1972 documented his growing depression and despair. "S drunk; crying all times. . . . this depression is deep." Later that year he wrote, "You've got to write . . . you look like a *WRECK*. You are a wreck." In another notation of self-degradation, he wrote, "This thought: if the true state of the Pothead is to be *detached* this means detached everywhere."[1] In spite of the demons pursuing him, he would soon achieve triumphs in both the film industry and in the literary world.

While working on his novel, Hayden was contacted by director Frances Ford Coppola, who would be directing the film version of the best-selling novel, *The Godfather*. Coppola wanted Hayden to play the role of the corrupt police officer, Capt. McCluskey. It was a short but powerful role that Hayden excelled in. His onscreen death is considered one of the most gruesome ever filmed in Hollywood.

Hayden turned in what many film critics consider possibly his finest performance in the 1973 film *The Long Goodbye*. Maverick director Robert Altman had originally selected Dan Blocker of *Bonanza* fame for the role of alcoholic writer Roger Wade opposite Elliott Gould as an updated version of Philip Marlowe. Starring as the female lead was Nina van Pallandt. When Blocker died suddenly before filming began, Altman hired Hayden for the role. It turned out to be a wise decision. Hayden's performance impressed the film critics. Altman himself was delighted with Hayden. "I originally wanted Dan Blocker for the role," he confessed, "but he died just before shooting began, and I was persuaded to meet Sterling, who was just perfect. He improvised a lot of the dialogue, and he was pretty well whacked out most of the time. He was an alcoholic, and when he smoked grass and had booze in him he was something else. But he was wonderful. I loved him."[2] Generally, Hayden had a remarkable ability to report to a movie set ready to go even after a night of heavy drinking. For this role, he continued drinking throughout the production, recalling, "You saw me up on the screen, I was as out of control as I appear to be."[3]

In the 1970s, Hayden also became known for the famous roles that he turned down. Among the many movie offers he declined during this time, two that stand out are the role of Quint in Steven Spielberg's classic film *Jaws*—a role he would have been perfect for—and the role eventually played by Peter Finch in the 1976 classic *Network*. It was a part that would bring Finch a posthumous Oscar for Best Actor.

...

On November 6, 1976, Warwick Tompkins passed away after a brief illness at the age of seventy-six. A memorial service was held at the Sausalito Yacht Club, and at the time, Sterling and Kitty were staying across the street from the yacht club at the Hotel Sausalito. Sterling started drinking heavily and would continue for two weeks. He was drunk on the day of Tompkins's memorial service. Tompkins's son, Warwick Tompkins Jr., known as "The Commodore," knew that Hayden was in town and across the street, and he came to the Haydens' room to ask Sterling to attend the service. He was too drunk. Instead, from the window of their second-story room, he watched the guests arriving at the yacht club for his old mentor's memorial service. "You could tell he was going through a terrible time," recalled Kitty.[4]

After Hayden had named Tompkins in the 1951 HUAC hearings, Tompkins was fired from his job making films for the Los Angeles Board of Education. Riddled with regret over his actions, Hayden began sending money to Tompkins and his wife on a monthly basis for the next several years. Despite this act of personal contrition, Hayden and Tompkins had no further personal contact after the HUAC hearings.[5]

...

Throughout the 1970s and into the 1980s, Hayden continued his wandering ways in a spiritual sense, always searching for new ideas and fads to try. All the while his drinking was increasing. He was impressed with the book *Fasting Can Save Your Life*, written by alternative health advocate Herbert M. Shelton. Feeling that he needed to lose weight and also intrigued by the challenge, he began a fast, ingesting only water and smoking marijuana. Thirty days later, he ended the experiment after losing forty pounds. He also became interested in the self-improvement philosophy of Werner Erhard, whose Erhard Seminars Training, or EST, sessions were popular throughout the decade. He enrolled in the self-development seminar, and at the first class he quickly became bored. In addition, after nearly an hour he had to use the bathroom. The EST seminars had highly regimented procedures, one of which was that participants could only use the bathroom during designated breaks that were separated by many hours.[6] When told by one of the seminar personnel that he couldn't go to the bathroom at that time, Sterling told him, "You know what you are? You are chickenshit!" and left the session after only an hour.[7] Other techniques he would try included Rolfing, a pseudoscience that attempts to better align muscles by breaking up surrounding connective tissue, and eventually he would experiment with acupuncture.[8]

Another passion he indulged in during the late 1960s and early 1970s was motorcycling. As previously noted, he always had his 1954 BMW R26 motorcycle aboard the barge, taking it to explore the countryside when he first began his trips to Europe. In Sausalito, he frequently rode around the Bay Area in his favorite bike, the powerful BMW R75. One night he and Kitty were invited to a party in the Valley of the Moon outside of Sonoma, and Sterling proposed that they motorcycle out to the festivities. Kitty made him promise first that he would not drink; this time, he kept his word. However, she would recall the ride out and back, roughly fifty miles in each direction, as "very scary," particularly when they were on the open US Highway 101 traveling at very high speed.[9]

...

During the 1970s, Hayden was relaxing aboard *Who Knows* when an elegant, elderly lady approached the vessel. Stopping at the gangway, she called out "Hi Sterling." Looking up, he saw Madeleine Carroll. It was a bittersweet reunion. Madeleine had lived in Paris since the end of World War II. The two had not seen each other in over thirty years. The once-beautiful leading lady was now in her seventies, while her ex-husband, formerly "the most beautiful man in Hollywood," was now in his sixties and showing the ravages of alcoholism. Nursing a thigh injury, he struggled to his feet. Attempting to walk without a telltale limp, he sauntered to the gangway and invited her aboard. With a gentle smile, Madeleine said, "No, no, I just wanted to say hello," and declined the invitation. Shortly thereafter, she turned and walked away. They would never see each other again.[10]

...

It was in 1976 that Hayden savored perhaps his proudest triumph. After many years of writing both aboard the *Who Knows* and in Sausalito, he completed his long-awaited novel, which was published by Putnam on December 29. Titled *Voyage: A Novel of 1896*, the 700-page opus was a critically acclaimed bestseller. Drawing on his vast knowledge of sailing, he created an unforgettable tale of life at sea to rival the writing of Joseph Conrad and Herman Melville. Telling the story of the maiden voyage of *Neptune's Car* from Maine, around the Horn, to San Francisco in the pivotal election year of 1896, Hayden created a work that would rival his only other published work, his critically acclaimed autobiography. In a sentiment echoed by virtually all critics, *Kirkus Reviews* noted: "Film actor Hayden, who broke into print with *Wanderer*, has written another elemental smash hit."[11]

Putnam had arranged for the author to go on a publicity tour to promote the book, but in typical Sterling Hayden style, he initially refused, preferring to see how the book would sell on its own merits. He soon changed his mind and agreed to go on talk show host Tom Snyder's popular show, *Tomorrow*. The episode aired on March 25, 1977, and Hayden, no doubt to the relief of his publisher, proved to be an affable, talkative guest. The chemistry between him and Snyder was genuine, and his candor and openness made the show a delight to watch. Among the topics they discussed were his admiration for the Yugoslav Partisans during the war and his brief flirtation with the Communist Party in 1946. Snyder deftly led the conversation into Hayden's alcohol abuse. Hayden was remarkably open about this, as well as his use of marijuana and hashish. He also discussed his insecurity as an actor, admitting that he only felt relaxed in front of the camera when he was smoking marijuana.

A keen observer of the human condition, Hayden expressed to Snyder his amazement as he described people going through the motions of life but not observing life. "I perpetually marvel at the fact that people don't see anything." Describing his attempt to live his life, he presented an interesting contrast: he was not the one seeking a life of escape. The average man, he felt, was an escapist—one who escapes into the security of his job, rather than truly living life to the fullest. Referencing his three marriages, Snyder asked him if he, as a result of his unorthodox lifestyle, was hard on his wives. "Certainly not intentionally," he candidly replied.

That particular interview would prove to be the most popular program that *Tomorrow* ever broadcast.[12] Tom Snyder would have the show rerun three times over the next three years.

• • •

On March 25, 1977—the day that his interview with Tom Snyder was broadcast—Sterling and Kitty traveled to New York City to do a television interview with Stanley Siegel, the daytime talk show host whose program *The Stanley Siegel Show* was broadcast live daily from the WABC studios at 9 a.m.[13] *Voyage* had just been released to stellar reviews and Siegel was going to interview Sterling the following morning on March 26, which happened to be his sixty-first birthday. The night before, after the Haydens had checked into the Plaza Hotel, Sterling proceeded to get drunk as Kitty went to sleep. When she awakened the following morning, she realized that he had been drinking all night and was in no condition to be interviewed. Despite his drunken state, he insisted on going to the studio, so she escorted him there.

It was quickly apparent to Siegel that Sterling was indeed in no condition to give a cogent interview. Speaking with Hayden's beautiful and articulate wife, Siegel came up with a new plan: he invited Kitty to appear on the show with them so that he could interview both of them. During the short interview, Sterling, looking disheveled and obviously intoxicated, sat on Siegel's right while Kitty, looking elegant and beautiful, sat on his left. After introducing them, Siegel initially directed his questions towards Kitty. "Why do you like Sterling?" he asked her. "What do you find interesting about him?"

She smiled and replied, "There's so many . . . it would be hard to say. He's interesting to live with. It's not dull. It's like being married to a hurricane."

"He's a drinking man," countered Siegel. "Does he ever frighten you at all?"

"No, not at all," she responded.

Sterling began to interrupt the conversation, singing Kitty's praises and revealing his obvious drunkenness. He often stammered and repeated words in almost a staccato fashion. Siegel asked Kitty what it was that attracted her to Sterling, as they seemed a bit like an odd couple—the hard-drinking former sailor and the sophisticated New York society girl. "He was very different," she explained. "I wanted something different. I wanted to change my life."

Sterling, by then boisterous and quite gregarious, interjected to explain his attraction when he first met his future wife, stammering as he said, "Somehow I had the feeling that she maybe, maybe, maybe, maybe, maybe, maybe had the desire to embrace a different kind of life." Motioning with his hand towards Kitty, he explained to his host that it had been difficult for "this crazy, beautiful girl," to be his wife. "My natural habitat is to be all fouled up. To be broke to me is natural," he boasted.

At the end of the short program, Siegel asked Sterling to read a passage from the first chapter of *Voyage*. Sterling refused, claiming, "I can't read it." In fact, he appeared too intoxicated to read it. Instead, Stanley Siegel read it out loud. As he read from the book, the camera zoomed in for a close-up of Sterling, who was listening intently to Siegel's recitation of his own elegantly written words. Tears can be seen forming in his eyes. When he finished his recitation, Siegel complimented his guest on his eloquent writing. He then asked Sterling what he would like for an epitaph on his tombstone. Hayden immediately replied, "He tried."

Siegel thanked his guests and turned to Kitty who, of course, never expected to be on television, saying, "See, it wasn't that bad, was it?"

Thirty-nine years later, she would humorously recall this as her first and last television appearance.[14]

• • •

In 1978, *Voyage* was published in Sweden. Sterling was invited to Stockholm where he would address the publisher's dinner and discuss his bestseller. Kitty and son David flew to Stockholm to be with him. The Haydens were put up at the luxurious Grand Hotel on the Stockholm waterfront. In his 1982 interview with author Dennis Brown, Hayden told a humorous anecdote about staying at the Grand Hotel, although he provided no context for his visit there. According to Brown, Hayden related that he and a friend were staying there and they ended up shattering the window of their room. They called down to order a sumptuous dinner and then added, "But what we really need up here is a little plywood."[15]

The reality was quite different. Sterling arrived at the hotel to meet his family the day before the scheduled dinner and he had been drinking. He drank all night, and the following morning he and David were talking about World War II. With increasing bitterness and anger, Sterling began recalling how Sweden had remained neutral during the war. To help calm him down and to encourage him to eat, Kitty brought him a plate with an English muffin, when he suddenly took the plate and in a fit of anger hurled it at the window, shattering it. Hotel security was called and the publisher arranged to have Sterling taken to a rehab facility for the day to undergo an evaluation. Returning late in the day, Hayden attended the publisher's dinner that night and gave a lucid, entertaining speech.[16]

• • •

Tom Snyder finally persuaded Hayden to return for his second guest appearance on May 29, 1980.[17] This time, Hayden showed up wearing a headband in addition to his forked goatee, looking like an overage love child out of the 1960s. Snyder began the show by telling the audience that Hayden's appearance had generated the most response of any of the over three thousand guests who had appeared on the show over the previous seven years.

As before, Hayden chain-smoked throughout the interview. He had just returned from Yugoslavia for the funeral of President Josef Broz Tito, who had died on May 4, 1980. Asked by *Rolling Stone* magazine to write a piece on the funeral, Hayden had traveled out there at his own expense. He had simply wanted to pay tribute to the wartime leader of the Partisans. "He was," he shared with Snyder, "an original, never mind the politics. A giant of a human being." To him, the most touching part of the funeral was the tribute paid by twenty-seven people—heroes of the Partisan First Brigade. These men and women had been tortured and maimed by the dreaded Ustasha. All were crying as the casket of their leader passed by them. How did he himself feel as the casket passed him? Snyder asked. "One of a kind was going out," he reflected with genuine emotion. "A giant among giants. Very heavy feelings." He never could get himself to write the article for *Rolling Stone*.

As in the previous interview, there was obvious chemistry between the host and the guest. Once again, Sterling Hayden displayed the total candor, honesty, and self-deprecation that were his trademarks. He admitted that since his last appearance, he had spent two months in alcohol rehab. He couldn't go the AA route, he stated, mainly because he really didn't want to stop drinking. He maintained his sobriety for four months before relapsing. At the time of his second appearance, he was taking the prescription medication Antabuse.

He again shared with Snyder his personal feelings and philosophies. The only way he could get along in life, he explained, was not to be like anybody else. This lifestyle, he opined, was not for everybody but it fit him like a glove. "I'm a professional irregular, and I admit it," he explained. He also admitted that he had been battling depression for the past few years. It had been a hard time and he had not been that productive. When Snyder expressed surprise at that statement, citing his recent success with *Voyage*, Hayden replied: "You can be too irresponsible, you can be too lucky, and I realize that all my life I've been lucky." He illustrated that luck by relating his love of the sea and ships and his improbable success in Hollywood. "But basically I've been slugging it out with this thing called depression." Describing the deleterious effect that his battle with depression had on his family, he reasoned that you have to read and learn about it and you just have to hang on and embrace people as much as you can. "You embrace people as much as you can passing by, strangers," he told Snyder. He concluded his thoughts for the evening by saying: "To me, the greatest delight in life is just to say hello to people going by."

• • •

Sterling's downhill spiral accelerated in 1981. While living in Wilton, one of their children had had surgery and that January was undergoing further therapy. While Kitty was managing all of these events, Sterling continued to drink heavily. Kitty had had enough. She forbade him from drinking in front of her or in their house, and he agreed to her demand. Instead, he rented a mobile home and parked it in their driveway. There he would continue his drinking and socializing with all the guests who had come to see the family.

Later that month, he had a nightmare and awoke from a deep sleep with a start, jolting his neck. Kitty insisted he get help, so he traveled to New York City to be admitted to New York University Hospital. Kitty checked into the Sheraton Russell Hotel nine blocks away to be able to visit him daily in the hospital. Placed in cervical traction, he quickly became frustrated with what he perceived as his lack of any significant pain relief. Claiming that he was not getting any better, he told Kitty that he was going to leave the hospital. The following morning, he did leave the hospital against medical advice, but in his typical impulsive style, he did so without even informing his doctors or nurses of his decision and simply strolled out of the hospital. He walked the nine blocks to the Sheraton Russell Hotel to be with Kitty. Ultimately the pain symptoms slowly improved, possibly aided by the addition of acupuncture treatments.

On February 1, in an ongoing state of depression, Sterling called his film agent, Johnny Planco. He had a simple request—he wanted his agent to purchase a .357 magnum handgun for him. He was considering killing himself. Needless to say, Planco wholeheartedly refused.[18]

By May, Hayden had been sober for over six weeks, but during this time his depression worsened. He had been prescribed lithium in the past by one of his psychiatrists but had discontinued it. Now he restarted it without medical supervision or monitoring of drug levels. Always searching for new remedies, he tried LSD in England on his way to the barge in France, but he found that it did not help him. By June, he was back on the barge, still taking his lithium without medical supervision. He wrote frequently to Kitty to relate how depressed he was. It was especially hot that month in Paris, and with no air conditioning aboard, it became quite uncomfortable on the barge. In addition, there was an infestation of spiders. Lonely and depressed, Sterling asked Kitty to join him in Paris. This was the typical pattern of behavior for Hayden. He always had to wander; he had to seek solitude and be alone. Yet when Kitty would appear to him to be fine without him, and would start to enlarge her own circle of friends and exert her independence, Sterling would become lonely and jealous and try to immediately draw her back to him. If he sensed her independence, he would always insist that she come out to be with him no matter where he was. This was the pattern that began in late 1967 and had repeated itself through the years. Given his wandering ways, and his wanting to be alone and yet wanting his wife near him, his insecurities and depression, and his alcohol abuse and his hashish indulgence, it would take a very strong woman to be the wife of Sterling Hayden—one who could balance her love for him with a tolerance of his myriad of issues and eccentricities. That woman was Kitty Hayden.

Sterling would explain this ambivalence and the inner turmoil that it created within him to an interviewer in 1980. "You try to have the best of both worlds. I've tried to have the best of both—my family, my wife; and I also want the road too. In a way it's a form of hell, a still form of hell. Because even when I get away. . . . I mean when I hit the road, I usually think, 'Well, fuck it. That's the end of the marriage, of that life. OK or not OK, but that's the way it's got to be.' In order for me to be free as a man I've got to go, go, go. And so I go."

He continued: "But! After a month . . . suddenly one night I'm in a little hotel. I start to think about my wife and what I've left behind. And then I'm gone. I'm just plain fucking dead gone. And then I fight as hard to get back as I fought earlier to leave. It's a duality of the soul, an incredible phenomenon."[19]

...

By July of 1981, he was drinking heavily again, and Kitty didn't hear much from her husband. He suddenly wrote her, telling her he was going to be filmed aboard the *Who Knows* by a German film crew making a documentary about him. In addition, he told her he needed $900 to take care of the problems aboard the barge; as usual, he was broke. As the fiscally responsible half of the couple, Kitty refused, leading to arguments.

Sterling then did an end run around his wife and asked a friend in New York who sent him the money. "We are all enablers," she would write in her diary, commenting on the situation.[20]

...

Sterling Hayden would appear one more time on the screen, this time in an independent art-house movie that was actually filmed two years before being released in 1983. For over a year, German filmmakers Wolf Eckert Buhler and Manfred Blank had been trying to meet up with Hayden to do a documentary film on his life. Hayden finally agreed to meet with the filmmakers in July of 1981 aboard *Who Knows*. For three days, they discussed their proposed project. Hayden was enthusiastic about their proposal and agreed to do the film. They returned four days later and filmed for a week. The resulting film, *Pharos of Chaos*, was not released until October of 1983.[21]

The film's title (*Lechtturm des Chaos* in German) was taken from the proposed name of Hayden's sequel to his autobiography *Wanderer*. Roughly translating to "lighthouse," Hayden liked to describe himself as a lighthouse in a world of chaos. The resulting 119-minute film was an uneven, somewhat bizarre production that reflected poorly on its subject. Other than an occasional voice-over by the director, the only speaker in the film was Sterling Hayden. The Hayden who is seen in *Pharos of Chaos* contrasts poorly with the Hayden who appeared in the interviews with Tom Snyder.

Shooting aboard Hayden's barge, the filmmakers let Hayden ramble on without interruption. In contrast to the *Tomorrow* interviews, in which he was sharp, focused, and highly engaging, here he appeared to be intoxicated in many scenes (he is seen drinking his booze directly from the bottle in several shots and smoking hashish in a long hash pipe) and would keep repeating phrases. While there is no doubt that Tom Snyder's skill as an interviewer and the personal chemistry he had with his guest made those interviews fast-paced and highly entertaining, the Sterling Hayden who appeared in *Pharos of Chaos* was nonetheless a changed man.

The heavy drinking and depression were beginning to wear him down. Throughout the film, he appeared to be hamming it up for the camera, exaggerating his gestures while trying a bit too hard to come across as an eccentric genius. Part of this was his display of a persistent, irritating habit of ending literally every sentence that he spoke with "eh?" "huh?" or "hmm?" On the other hand, he showed off his scholarly side by quoting great writers and reading from Robert Louis Stevenson's *An Inland Voyage*. In addition, he described his rebirth since discovering life on the rivers of Europe. He again explained his disdain for the conventional life, referring to eager college students who "died" the moment they got out of college and went to work for Xerox and then retired at the age of sixty. "They died at 22. Strange that you can't see," he concluded as he took another swig of booze straight from the bottle.

The reality was that he was creatively drained and depressed, and he freely admitted this in front of the camera. He blurted out: "I'm all fucked up because I'm alone. I don't want to be alone," but he also conceded that even if his wife Kitty was there with him, he'd still be drinking. Poignantly, he stated, "I'm confused. I have wonderful sons and a daughter. So why do I drink? I don't know. Nobody knows." To him, it was causing the ultimate chaos—the inability to write. Something, he admitted, was wrong. He looked into the camera and described his breakdown. "I find myself crying all the time." To the camera crew he added: "This is rough shit, eh?" He revealed that he considered suicide, but compared to all the horrible things in the world, "this," he said, gesturing to the boats and the dockside of France on the barge's side, "is paradise." Shortly after this scene, the narrator reported that Hayden had just received a telegram from Kitty and he cried when he received it.

A relatively short amount of screen time was spent on Hayden's interesting past. It was over an hour into the film before the HUAC hearings were mentioned; the voyage aboard *Wanderer* was only briefly touched upon. At that point, Hayden repeated some of the thoughts he had shared with Tom Snyder. Concerning his HUAC testimony, he stated: "I'd hurt a man named Warwick Tompkins, and *I* must live with it all my life." When the conversation shifted to President Ronald Reagan, he opined: "His heart ain't where it should be."

On August 27, Sterling had cabled Kitty that he was drunk the night before and fell off the narrow gangplank of his barge. Had his son Dana not witnessed it and fished him out of the river, he surely would have drowned. He nonchalantly described the near-catastrophe for the film crew to share with audiences worldwide.

Towards the end of the filming aboard the barge, the narrator noted that Hayden had stopped drinking and he became more formal and laconic. Six months after filming was completed, the German filmmakers received a message from Hayden. He told them that he had been though alcohol rehab again, had stopped drinking, and was writing again. He was "working on his book like crazy," and he invited them to come back for another filming session. As the narrator stated, they declined, because, in essence, that would be another whole movie.

In truth, he missed Kitty and wanted to come home in June, but he had no money. She admitted to missing him terribly, too. That summer, she and her brother Richard rented a house in the Hamptons on Long Island while Sterling was forced to remain on the barge in Paris. But by the end of the summer, he was no longer drinking (although he still smoked hashish regularly). He cabled Kitty with some good news—he had been offered the part of abolitionist John Brown in the miniseries *The Blue and the Gray.* He now had the money to come home. In September 1981, Sterling flew home to Connecticut where Kitty was waiting for him.

The book that he was "working on like crazy" was, of course, his follow-up autobiography to *Wanderer*. He would never complete it.

...

Having accepted the role of John Brown, the Haydens flew together in September to Fort Smith, Arkansas, for the filming of the miniseries. Sterling remained sober throughout the shooting, although he frequently smoked hashish. One night during the shooting, director Andrew V. McLaglen invited the Haydens to dine with him. Kitty accepted the invitation but Sterling declined as he knew he would likely start drinking again. Hayden delivered an outstanding performance as John Brown, in *The Blue and the Gray*, one that earned high praise from *New York Times* critic John J. O'Connor. After the miniseries debuted in November of 1982, O'Connor wrote: "Mr. Hayden makes an imposing John Brown, capturing the passion of a fanatic and the searing insight of a prophet. His scenes carry a special stamp of authenticity."[22]

...

Sterling Hayden made his final appearance on *Tomorrow* on October 7, 1981.[23] In his introduction, Tom Snyder again recounted to his guest and the audience the tremendous response generated by Hayden's prior appearances. Snyder pointed out that Hayden was the only guest he ever had who would not do a pre-interview before they went on air. The spontaneity, candor, and honesty of his guest would shine through to the audience. Hayden and Snyder's chemistry remained intact, and again Hayden chain-smoked throughout the interview. The headband was gone and he featured a single brush beard. As always, he had his cane with him, one that he freely admitted he didn't need but simply liked to carry.

The day before his third appearance on *Tomorrow*, President Anwar Sadat of Egypt had been assassinated by the Muslim Brotherhood. The host and guest reflected gloomily on the situation, noting that in that same year (1981), President Reagan had survived an attempt on his life, as had Pope John Paul II. Snyder brought up the subject of Reagan and his role in Hollywood as the president of the Screen Actors Guild during the HUAC hearings, and asked Hayden his thoughts now that Reagan was president of the United States. Hayden admitted to initially having very complicated feelings and a sense of being scared at the thought of Reagan as president. He went on to explain: "Now as I watch everything transpire, there are many extenuating factors. I, as a onetime would-be 'Red,' um, yeah, and I wanted to be, after Yugoslavia and the thing when I was in the [Communist] Party, part of me said, 'This is the way I believe.' And I equated it with social reform and making it a better world. I still, part of me is that way. But, I'm not an idiot enough not to know that the Soviet Union's armament thing required a response from somebody, didn't it? So in a way . . . but now I get lost. The thing with Reagan's . . . the whole mood of the country going, shall we say, to the old stars and stripes thing, I understand that. I can cry when I see the flag, yeah."

After offering up faint praise for the president, the old idealist within him flared as he attempted to explain his feelings to Snyder. He criticized Reagan for rendering support to "the conservative right, against the people" in places like El Salvador. "This distresses me," he explained, as he felt that the only way to contain or overturn communism was "for heaven's sakes, for people to have a fair deal in this world." He couldn't understand Reagan's actions in El Salvador, as he considered him a brilliant and articulate man.

At the beginning of the interview, Hayden reiterated that he still loved observing the world go by from his barge in Paris. He was working on another book during his months on *Who Knows*. It was another autobiography, one that picked up where *Wanderer* had left off in 1960. Asked by Snyder why he was writing a sequel to *Wanderer*, he spelled out his reasons. As life progresses for some of us, he noted, it becomes more intense. The book was to be the story of getting old, of feeling more passion, experiencing the glory of life and the agony. Hence, he would continue writing his life story from the vantage point of having experienced life over the past twenty-plus years. Once again, Snyder and Hayden discussed his drinking and usage of marijuana and hashish. But possibly the key exchange occurred near the end of the interview during a discussion on passion and drive. Hayden termed it a need for obsession. His obsession had been ships, and now it was writing. This, to him, was the key. "There must be an obsession, must there not, huh?" he opined. "That's where people can be happy doing damn near anything, can't they?"

• • •

By late 1981, Hayden's drinking and hashish indulgence had progressed to the point where even he acknowledged that he definitely needed professional help to deal with his addictions. Sterling had already made several attempts to treat his alcohol addiction in the 1970s. He had completed a thirty-day program at Silver Hill Hospital in New Canaan, Connecticut, not far from their Wilton home but promptly relapsed. On another occasion, he traveled to Chit Chat Farms, a rehabilitation facility near Reading, Pennsylvania. The admission had been arranged, but after speaking to the physician in charge, Sterling walked around the facility and decided he didn't like it. He left ten minutes after he had arrived.[24] He had once called his old friend Barnaby Conrad from France, seeking his counsel. Knowing that Conrad had himself given up drinking, he sought his advice. "Start by limiting yourself," Conrad advised. "Limit yourself to one bottle a day." In what Conrad described as a classic but serious response, Sterling asked, "But what would I do in the afternoon?"[25]

Late that fall, Kitty met with a lawyer to discuss a possible legal separation from Sterling. Acknowledging how difficult the situation had become for her, he told her, "You've extended yourself more than any other woman." She decided not to pursue the legal action although Sterling's drinking would continue to interfere with their lives. In December, he drank for five straight days, leading Kitty to record in her diary on December 11: "Now I dread all social encounters."[26]

On January 4, 1982, Sterling was again drunk and feeling particularly terrible. Acknowledging that he needed professional help, he admitted to Kitty that he was committing "liquid suicide."[27] He had read about actor Jason Robards, a resident of nearby Southport, Connecticut, who had spent his adult years battling alcoholism. In 1972, Robards nearly died in a horrendous car crash while driving drunk, requiring extensive facial surgery as a result. This proved to be Robards's wake-up call. He successfully underwent alcohol rehabilitation and became an activist and public advocate for alcoholism awareness and treatment. He became a familiar face on television with the Ad Council messages for alcoholism treatment where he would say: "I'm living proof you don't have to die for a drink." On that January morning, Hayden obtained Robards's phone number from the William Morris Agency and called him. He told Robards of his alcohol problem and asked if he knew anyone who could help him. Robards recommended Dr. Nicholas Pace, who was affiliated with the National Council on Alcoholism in New York City.

On January 8, 1982, Sterling went to be interviewed by Dr. Pace. He returned on the nineteenth with Kitty for a physical examination focused on detecting signs of alcoholic organ damage. The results had Dr. Pace very concerned about the condition of Sterling's liver. He recommended immediate inpatient treatment for a comprehensive approach to Sterling's alcoholism issues. Much to Kitty's delight, Sterling agreed to go to the Hazelden Clinic near Minneapolis, Minnesota.

Hayden traveled by train to Minneapolis. On the night before he was admitted to the Hazelden Clinic, he stayed at the Hyatt Regency where he placed a stash of hashish in a hotel safe deposit box. He had been told in advance by the Hazelden staff that he had to promise to refrain from marijuana and hashish for a year after discharge since indulging in the drugs would almost certainly result in a relapse into his drug of choice, alcohol. On January 24, he was admitted to the clinic and three days later called Kitty. Much to her delight, he told her he had decided to stay at Hazelden, stating, "I hope it works."[28] From February 1 through February 8, he dutifully called Kitty every night to report on his daily routine. On February 19, Kitty took part in a two-hour teleconference with Sterling's therapist, Dr. Fred Holmquist. During the conference, Dr. Holmquist again reminded Sterling of the need to remain abstinent from hashish for at least a year. Interestingly, Sterling had previously told Kitty of his plan to resume smoking hashish before he left for Hazelden. "He always told me everything," Kitty recalled.[29] Kitty did not mention to Sterling's therapist her husband's intentions during the two-hour session. Hayden remained at the Hazelden Clinic for the full thirty-day program and was discharged with his medallion signifying successful completion of his therapy course. At that point, Dr. Pace strongly recommended to Sterling and Kitty that Sterling begin to regularly attend Alcoholics Anonymous meetings. Knowing her husband only too well, she recorded in her diary, "Fat chance."[30]

Upon discharge, Hayden immediately returned to the Hyatt Regency and went to his safe deposit box to reclaim his hashish. Although he had pledged abstinence from the drug for a year, Hayden proved to be incorrigible and promptly resumed his self-destructive habits that very night in the hotel. He called Kitty that night, "stoned out of his head."[31] The following morning, he checked out of the hotel and boarded a train for Seattle, where he consulted with a psychologist that had been recommended to him in Minnesota. Following the consultation, Sterling departed for Sausalito. Surprisingly, he would abstain from alcohol for the next year and a half.

What Sterling Hayden really wanted to do was concentrate on his writing in solitude. In Sausalito, he found a studio apartment to rent with a patio that provided a panoramic view of San Francisco Bay. There he also resumed his hashish habit. In early March, Kitty and their son David came to Sausalito to visit him and stayed at the Hotel Sausalito. At that time, Sterling was not drinking but continued to smoke hashish regularly. He was lonely and he wanted Kitty and the family to move out to Sausalito. As always, he had no concept of how financially unfeasible his proposal was. He was perpetually broke, and Kitty couldn't afford to maintain two homes. As a result, they decided to commute across the country; Kitty and her husband would make regular trips between Sausalito and Wilton to be with each other.

After remaining on the wagon for over a year, Sterling relapsed into his drinking habit while on his barge during May of 1983. He had been fasting for nine days when a friend came by to visit him and he resumed his drinking. The following morning, he called Kitty to confess his transgression. Although she was disappointed with his actions, she did admire his honesty. This established a new behavioral pattern for him: generally, when old friends would come to visit him in Sausalito or on the barge, he would resume his excessive drinking. Interestingly, he would always call Kitty the following day after each drinking binge to confess that he had fallen off the wagon. She would recall at least nine occasions when he dutifully confessed to her on the phone that he had been dead drunk the day before.[32] But he would no longer drink in front of her—she would not allow it.

He was determined to make a final stab at writing. "The only thing important is to write again," he would claim to his wife as she grew increasingly angry over the whole situation. In May he proudly reported that he had not smoked hashish for eight days, claiming, "It's not good for me when I'm writing." His abstinence would be short-lived. Frustrated, Kitty turned to Dr. Pace for his thoughts and he offered a somber prognosis: under the best of circumstances, it would take Sterling Hayden years to be fully recovered from his alcoholism and its associated ramifications. But Kitty Hayden's growing frustration with her husband's habits was about to accelerate.

Throughout their marriage, Sterling had always been fiscally irresponsible. Kitty wisely kept her financial affairs separate from her husband's. Money never meant anything to Sterling, who didn't believe in investing money. In the past when he was broke (which was often), he could always accept a movie role and collect a paycheck for what he called "another crap picture." Even at the beginning of their marriage, the burden of leading the family always fell to Kitty. All of the cross-country moves, all of the child-raising responsibilities, and all of the financial affairs were always left to Kitty. In the words of their son David, "My mother was the glue that held the family together. Her responsibilities were much more extensive than most women."[33] In May of 1982, Sterling infuriated his wife with another spontaneous act of fiscal irresponsibility.

Sterling's attorney Joe Gelband had taken the money he had earned for his last three movie roles and established a pension fund that was intended to support Hayden in his later years. However, by May of that year Sterling was not only out of money, but he was also contributing nothing to the support of his family. A child of the Depression, he was also convinced that the banks were going to fail. Sterling approached a different attorney and had him collapse his pension fund and used it to buy gold Krugerrands. Obtaining $100,000 worth of Krugerrands, he took the gold and buried it near the Golden Gate Bridge. Thinking better of the plan, he dug it up and kept it in the closet of his Sausalito apartment. He would sell $33,000 worth at a time when he needed the money to live on to continue his writing. "I know I have to write or I have no future," he told Kitty.

Whenever he received a paycheck from making a movie, Sterling would contribute to family finances. As soon as the proceeds were exhausted, however, he returned to his usual state of insolvency. Now at last with a pension fund arranged, some future financial stability had been achieved for not only him but also for his family. His impulsive dismantling of the pension plan infuriated Kitty. Seeking legal counsel, she arranged to have Sterling contribute $800 a month for the next six months towards the family finances.

...

Hayden increasingly wanted to be alone so that he could concentrate on his writing. He had rented a studio apartment in Sausalito in 1982 after leaving the Hazelden Clinic and, as a result, he and Kitty made twelve cross-country trips to spend time with each other, while at the same time accommodating Sterling's desire for solitude. They fell into a regular schedule—they would be together for two weeks and then apart for ten days, all to allow Sterling to be alone with his writing. Perhaps he perceived that his creative powers were ebbing, or perhaps, as he was approaching the age of seventy, he sensed that his drinking and smoking were catching up to him. On July 24, 1983, he recorded in his diary: "Since March in 1916 I've been engaged in the honorable endeavor of trying to survive, or, better yet survive handsomely and best of all maybe even distinguish myself in this extraordinary life as it plays itself out . . . things seem to be slipping away: it's true."[34]

Over the next year and a half, Kitty became increasingly concerned about Sterling's escalating complaints of bone pain, for which he was taking Percodan; he attributed the symptom to the arthritis of aging. Hayden had a physical exam when he was at the Hazelden Clinic in 1982, but Kitty suspected it wasn't a complete examination. She insisted he get a comprehensive physical examination. Sterling knew Dr. John F. Catchpool, an excellent primary care physician, and scheduled an appointment. Catchpool, who was in practice in Sausalito, had a distinguished medical career, having worked in the past with both Dr. Albert Schweitzer and Dr. Linus Pauling.

On January 26, 1984, Dr. Catchpool performed a complete physical examination on Sterling. The following day, Kitty and Sterling met with the doctor to discuss his findings. Catchpool had discovered an enlarged, irregular prostate gland that was suspicious for malignancy. For months, Sterling had exhibited symptoms of an enlarging prostate, and coupled with his findings on the physical exam, Catchpool arranged for a consultation with Dr. Patrick McLin, a prominent Bay Area urologist. On February 14, Dr. McLin operated on Hayden and performed a transurethral resection of the prostate. The following day, he delivered the results of the pathology report on the resected tissue to Sterling and Kitty. The report confirmed that, in fact, Hayden had prostate cancer that had already metastasized to his bones. The postoperative plan of management consisted of estrogen therapy and radiation therapy to slow the progression of the cancer. In addition, a regimen of pain medications was prescribed to help Sterling cope with the increasing bone pain. When he informed his good friend columnist Herb Caen that he had terminal cancer, Caen recalled him saying in a booming voice, "Well, it's the next adventure, right?"[35]

Sterling's condition seemed to rally by that summer and he decided to go Europe and return to his barge. Kitty did not go with him; instead, his old friend Bill Pearson accompanied him. Sterling had stopped smoking before they left, but being with the chain-smoking Pearson, he was soon once again heavily smoking, much to Kitty's disappointment. Son David came for a short visit from Oxford, where he was studying, and Hayden and Pearson soon departed for Paris. It was there that Sterling's health took a turn for the worse and he felt so poorly that he flew back to the New York in May. What he really wanted to do was to return to his apartment in Sausalito so he could resume his writing.

He would never return to his beloved barge again.

Kitty would eventually arrange to have the barge sold to settle Sterling's $190,000 tax debt to the IRS.

...

Hayden returned to California, but by Christmastime 1985, his health had continued to worsen. Despite the fact that he decried the materialism and commercialism that he felt had become intertwined with the holiday season, he had often spent previous Christmas holidays together with his family in Wilton. Although increasingly frail, he announced to Kitty, "I'm coming east."[36] By this time, he was largely non-ambulatory and wheelchair-bound. Son Dana took him to the airport in San Francisco and Kitty met him with a limousine at the airport in New York. He arrived appearing quite ill and she immediately took him to a hospital in Norwalk, Connecticut, a short distance from Wilton. After being admitted to a private room, Sterling received intravenous fluids and morphine to control his pain, and general supportive care. In short order, he was rehydrated and his pain came under reasonable control, and he was discharged to their home. Sterling Hayden spent Christmas 1985 and New Year's Day 1986 with his family at their residence in Wilton. He would never return to their Connecticut home.

Hayden flew back to California on January 3, 1986. Six days later, Kitty flew to California to be with her husband at the small Sausalito apartment. She would be by his side the last four months of his life. As his cancer spread, Hayden was in increasing pain. Dr. Catchpool would often stop by to check on Sterling, and a hospice nurse made regular visits.

Friends such as John Huston paid visits to the Sausalito apartment to see Sterling, knowing that his condition was terminal and that he didn't have much longer to live. A week after Huston's visit, another old friend from Sterling's past came to visit him. Dennis Powers, who had been the youngest crewmember aboard *Wanderer* and was now a filmmaker, screenwriter, and producer, arrived in the Sausalito apartment to see his old mentor. Hayden was delighted to see his former shipmate and they had a meaningful reunion. Powers had written a screenplay for *Wanderer* that John Huston had expressed interest in filming. Hayden told Powers: "John Huston was just here a week ago and wants to do the book. But I don't want John to do it—I want someone who was there. You're that person."[37] Powers optioned the book and held the option for several years, but the movie was never made.

On March 26, Sterling's seventieth birthday, another old friend came to visit him. Barnaby Conrad and Sterling shared the same birthday, and Conrad flew up from Santa Barbara to be with the man he had been friends with since their days together in Tahiti. "He was brave as hell and though gaunt and moving painfully and slowly," recalled Conrad, "his voice was strong and optimistic."[38] Sterling reminisced about Tahiti and Gloucester when he suddenly began reminiscing about his wartime experiences, something he rarely did. It was then that Sterling told the story of how in 1945 when he returned to Paris he had telephoned Madeleine Carroll and Gen. Eisenhower had answered the phone.[39] Kitty had never heard that story before.

• • •

Despite his deteriorating condition, Sterling had been invited to be interviewed for the BBC's series *Talking Pictures*.[40] He agreed to give the interview on April 16, but as that date approached, his pain was intensifying to the point of becoming unbearable. The morning of the interview, Dr. Catchpool arranged to have a morphine pump inserted to control Sterling's pain. Since the BBC film crew was scheduled to arrive a little later that morning, Kitty asked him if he wanted to cancel the interview. "Absolutely not," he replied.[41] Just before the film crew arrived at the Sausalito apartment to begin the taping, Sterling put his jeans on over his nightgown and donned a brown jacket.

For the interview he appeared gaunt, his face noticeably thinner. He explained to the interviewer this was the result of having lost fifty pounds. He pointed out to the interviewer that the brown jacket he was wearing was the one he wore in his first movie, *Virginia*. As usual, he smoked cigarettes throughout the interview. Draped around his right shoulder was a green strap. In one scene, as the camera pulled back briefly, the strap could be seen draped around his neck and attached to a canvas bag on his lap. Unbeknownst to the BBC crew and viewers of the program, the bag contained the morphine pump for his infusion. The interviewer, crew, and subsequent viewing audiences were treated to Sterling Hayden at his best. Just as he appeared in the Tom Snyder interviews, he was sharp and focused the entire time, despite any pain he may have been experiencing.

The interviewer covered many topics from Hayden's past, with an emphasis on the HUAC hearings and his early film career. Of his testimony before the HUAC, Hayden unequivocally stated: "It's the only thing I've ever done in my life of which I'm ashamed." Asked if the HUAC hearings had an impact on the Hollywood community, perhaps resulting in less controversial topics and more "timid" films, Hayden initially stated, "I don't think they had too much of an impact." Upon further discussion, he conceded, "Well, perhaps they did." He also interestingly stated that he did not have a prepared script for his HUAC testimony. Rather, he recalled, he had his own prompter notes on cards with details he could refer to when answering the committee's questions.

He recalled for the BBC his journey from Gloucester fisherman to movie star virtually overnight and he discussed his discomfort in that role. Describing the majority of the films he appeared in, with the exception of *The Asphalt Jungle* and *Dr. Strangelove*, he used a descriptive word: "Excrement."

Overall, it was a solid interview and Sterling Hayden came across as intelligent, knowledgeable, and articulate. The crew loved interacting with him and stayed the entire day with the Haydens in the small apartment after Kitty made them lunch and coffee. It was an impressive showing for a man who had only thirty-seven days to live.

...

Kitty would reload the pump at the set dosages prescribed by Dr. Catchpool and managed by the visiting nurse. Soon after, Hayden began hallucinating on the morphine. During a prior hospitalization, he had the following hallucination: he thought he was back at sea on one of his beloved schooners and began barking out orders to his crew. Kitty couldn't help but notice he had a big smile on his face during his imaginary return to the sea that he loved. There, in Sausalito one night with Kitty asleep on the floor and Sterling in the small double bed, he awoke confused and agitated. Pulling out the morphine pump, he got out of bed while Kitty remained sound asleep on the floor and called his son who was staying nearby. He began ranting that Kitty was being duped by a drug cartel and was in trouble; he insisted his son call the police. By this time, Kitty had awakened and saw Sterling on the floor. The police arrived just as Sterling reached the door and was about to tumble down the stairs. The policemen each took one of Hayden's arms and gently assisted him back in bed. Shortly after that, Kitty reattached the morphine pump.

Not long after, a hospital bed was brought to the apartment and arranged so that Sterling could look out the windows at the panoramic view of the bay. One night he again began to hallucinate on the morphine and became agitated, screaming, "The ship's on fire! The ship's on fire," while struggling to get out of bed. Kitty tried to restrain him and grabbed his nightshirt, but he was able to free himself. As before, he was about to reach the door to the small apartment, while Kitty screamed for help. Two neighbors heard her screaming and ran up to their apartment as Sterling once again reached the entrance to their apartment. They both gently assisted him back into his hospital bed. Soon, Sterling was in excruciating pain. After his doctor had adequately sedated him, he remained virtually comatose for several days before regaining his senses. In one of his last semi-lucid moments, he said to Kitty: "I hope this flight of fancy never ends."[42]

The downhill course rapidly progressed. By early May, the high level of morphine was not enough to control the pain. With Dr. Catchpool and Kitty by his side, he suddenly boomed out, "Kill me!"[43] Stepping out to the patio, the doctor told his devoted wife what she already knew—the end was very near. He increased the morphine infusion and the groggy patient seemed calmer. On May 13, he slipped into a coma. During these final days, Kitty and the hospice nurse noticed a swelling pushing up Sterling's lip. They called Sterling's dentist, who was a longtime friend. He promptly came over to the apartment to check his old friend's mouth. Sterling had developed an abscess on his gums, but he was too far gone to attempt any procedure. After briefing Kitty on his findings, the dentist said goodbye to his beloved friend and expressed his sorrow to Kitty. She could see the tears forming in his eyes.

Several of the Hayden children had joined Kitty in the small studio apartment, sleeping on the floor near their father. His long journey finally came to an end at the end of May. With Kitty and several of his children by his side, he passed away peacefully at the age of seventy.

In the introduction of the 1977 rerelease of *Wanderer*, Sterling Hayden wrote that he still was "lost." His "wandering" was the means that would finally lead him to the freedom and adventure that he had always quested after. He quoted an unknown author: "He wanders east, he wanders west. Where will he ever come to rest?" It summed up Hayden's life perfectly.

Nine years after contemplating this question, on May 23, 1986, the handsome, unconventional individual known as Sterling Hayden finally found the unencumbered freedom that he had sought his entire life.

The wanderer had finally gone home.

• • •

A private memorial service was held for his family and friends. His remains were cremated. His family scattered his ashes off of Point Sausalito, into San Francisco Bay.

In a sense, his life had been a series of wars, wars that left him scarred and full of self-doubt. He had come though World War II and emerged a bona fide war hero, yet his idealism resulting from fighting with the Partisans against the Nazis (as well as the influence of Warwick Tompkins) led to a brief flirtation with the Communist Party. He was involved in the war between Hollywood and the House Un-American Activities Committee during the Red Scare, and his cooperation with the committee, while giving him the opportunity to make a living in the film industry that he so detested, would haunt him for the rest of his life. In his war with his second wife, he would ultimately prevail but would become a fugitive from justice in order to accomplish his goal. For his entire adult life, he battled alcoholism and later substance abuse. His life's struggles were perhaps best described by the narrator of *Pharos of Chaos* when he stated: "We knew of a different struggle, one with no end—Hayden's war with himself."

Columnist Herb Caen wrote an emotional obituary for his close friend. "We knew for months that Sterling was dying but, to borrow the excruciating last words of another great friend, Bill Saroyan, we thought an exception would be made in his case. Sterling had cancer, but he was bigger than life and would beat it, somehow, some way."[44]

Sterling Hayden had spent his life searching, wandering, seeking. And when his ashes were scattered and his long journey finally ended, the wanderer had, at last, managed to be with the only things that truly mattered to him and that he truly loved—his wife, his children, some close friends, . . . and the sea.

Epilogue

IT HAS BEEN NOTED BY FAMILY AND FRIENDS THAT NONE OF STERLING Hayden's many gifts ever really brought him any degree of satisfaction. Perhaps the only realistic observation to counter that assertion was offered by Dennis Powers, who sailed with Hayden to Tahiti on the voyage of the *Wanderer*. "You know where I saw this satisfaction? Behind the wheel [of *Wanderer*] and we were going like hell. And there he was, understand? You could really see that he would say in his thoughts, 'God damn, this is great!'"[1]

. . .

Several years after Sterling Hayden died, author Dennis Brown returned to Sausalito, where he had interviewed Hayden in 1982. Stopping into a delicatessen to order a sandwich, Brown asked the man preparing his sandwich if he remembered a man named Sterling Hayden who used to live nearby. "Do I remember Sterling Hayden?" the man replied incredulously. "I used to go up to his place all the time and hang out," he told Brown. "We were best friends. Do I remember Sterling Hayden?! No one who knew him would ever forget him."[2]

NOTES

INTRODUCTION

1. Hinkson, J. (2012, May 17). *Sterling Hayden: Film Noir's Nothing Man*. Retrieved November 21, 2015, http://www.criminalelement.com/blogs/2012/05/sterling-hayden-film-noirs-nothing-man-thriller-noir-wwii-the-godfather-jake-hinkson.
2. McConnell, S. (1988, January). "Leaving the Party: The Politics of Sterling Hayden." *New Criterion*, 1–12, 1.

CHAPTER ONE: BEGINNINGS

1. Hayden, S. (1963). *Wanderer*. New York: Alfred A. Knopf, 71.
2. Ibid.
3. Ibid., 83.
4. Ibid., 86.
5. Ibid., 86–87.
6. Ibid., 89.
7. Ibid., 97.
8. Ibid., 96.

CHAPTER TWO: THE LURE OF THE SEA

1. Hayden, S. (1963). *Wanderer*. New York: Alfred A. Knopf, 109.
2. Ibid., 113.
3. Ibid., 115.
4. Ibid., 121.
5. Ibid., 125.
6. Ibid., 128.
7. Ibid.
8. Ibid.

9. Ibid., 130.
10. Ibid., 131.
11. Ibid., 132.
12. Ibid., 136.
13. Ibid., 137.
14. Ibid., 138.
15. Ibid.
16. Ibid., 142.
17. Ibid., 144.
18. Ibid., 145.
19. Ibid., 165.
20. Ibid., 164.
21. Ibid., 166.
22. Ibid., 170.
23. Ibid., 171.
24. Ibid., 174.
25. Interview with Kitty Hayden, October 27, 2015.
26. Motavalli, J. (1980, February 27). "An American Odyssey." *Fairfield Advocate*, 14–16, 14.
27. Hayden, S., op. cit., 182.
28. Ibid., 183.
29. Ibid., 184.
30. Ibid.
31. Ibid., 189.
32. Ibid., 190.

CHAPTER THREE: MENTORS

1. Playfair, S. R. (2003). *Vanishing Species: Saving the Fish, Sacrificing the Fishermen*. Lebanon, NH: University Press of New England, 26.
2. Hayden, S. (1963). *Wanderer*. New York: Alfred A. Knopf, 191.
3. Ibid., 193.
4. Hatch, N. (2002, July/August). "Another OSS Marine." *Purple Heart Magazine*, 25–26, 26.
5. Interview with David Hayden, November 24, 2015.
6. Interview with Norman Hatch, November 23, 2015.
7. Hayden, S., op. cit., 197.
8. Ibid.
9. Oliver, M. (2004, December 4). "Electra Johnson, 95; With Husband, Told of Adventures Sailing Around Globe 7 Times." *Los Angeles Times*. Retrieved December 17, 2014, http://articleslatimes.com/2004/dec/04/local/me/-johnson4.
10. Hayden, S., op. cit., 197.
11. Ibid., 198.
12. Ibid., 205.
13. Ibid.
14. Ibid.

15. US Department of Labor. (1938, May 9). *List or Manifest of Aliens Employed on the Vessel as Members of Crew; Vessel "Yankee."* Retrieved November 15, 2014, http://www.ancestry.com.
16. Waller, D. (2011). *Wild Bill Donovan*. New York: Simon & Schuster, 46.
17. Hayden, S., op. cit., 207.
18. US Department of Labor., op. cit.
19. Johnson, I. (1939). *Sailing to See: Picture Cruise in the Schooner Yankee*. New York: W. W. Norton & Company, 205–206.
20. Mortland, D. F. (1983, September 1). "Lincoln Colcord: At Sea and at Home." *Colby Quarterly*, 125–43, 126.
21. Ibid., 128.
22. Ibid., 126.
23. Hayden, S., op. cit., 211.
24. Ibid., 212.
25. Ibid.
26. Ibid., 213.
27. Ibid.
28. Ibid., 214.

CHAPTER FOUR: YOUNGEST CAPTAIN

1. Letter from Julian Hatch to Captain John Foss, February 8, 2007, provided by Kitty Hayden.
2. McLaren, R. K. (2006). *A Race for Real Sailors: The Bluenose and the International Fishermen's Cup, 1920–1938*. Jaffrey, NH: David R. Godine, 200–201.
3. Hayden, S. (1963). *Wanderer*. New York: Alfred A. Knopf, 219.
4. McLaren, R. K., op. cit., 201; *The Bluenose, a True Canadian Champion*. (2008, May 29). Retrieved December 21, 2014, http://www.tourcanada.com/bluenose.htm.
5. Hayden, S., op. cit., 222.
6. McLaren, R. K., op. cit., 200.
7. Hayden, S., op. cit., 224.
8. Hayden, S., op. cit., 227.
9. Interview with Norman Hatcher, November 25, 2015.
10. Hayden, S., op. cit., 227–28.
11. Hayden, S., op. cit., 228–29.
12. Hayden, S., op. cit., 230.
13. Donald J. Langely Jr. and Holly J. Blake. (1998). *Tahiti Bound*. Stratham, NH: A. T. I. Publishing, 21.
14. Ross, L. (1946, June 22). "The Kaiser's Yacht." *New Yorker*, 66.
15. Hayden, S., op. cit., 233.
16. "New in News." (1939, February). *Boy's Life*, 25.
17. Donald J. Langley Jr. and Holly J. Blake, op. cit., 154–55.
18. Hayden, S., op. cit., 236.
19. Ibid., 239.
20. Ibid., 242.
21. Ibid.

CHAPTER FIVE: INVENTING A HOLLYWOOD STAR

1. Hayden, S. (1963). *Wanderer*. New York: Alfred A. Knopf, 242.
2. Ibid., 242–43.
3. Ibid., 262.
4. Ibid.
5. Ibid., 263.
6. Ibid., 265.
7. Ibid., 266.
8. Ibid., 271.
9. Ibid., 272.
10. Ibid., 276.
11. Ibid.
12. Ibid.
13. Ibid., 278.
14. Daniel. (2006, October 28). *Visit to Saudreville, Outside Paris*. Retrieved January 1, 2015, http://www.madeleinecarroll.com/visit-to-saudreville-outside-paris/.
15. Hayden, S., op. cit., 282.
16. Ibid.
17. Ibid., 284.
18. Crowther, B. (1941, January 29). "Virginia, a Highly Romantic Drama of the Old Dominion and Its Folks, at the Paramount." *New York Times*. Retrieved January 10, 2015, http://nytimes.com/movie/review?res=9E04E5DC173AE33BBC4151DFB766838A659EDE.

CHAPTER SIX: WALKING OUT ON HOLLYWOOD

1. Wilson, L. (1959, August 16). "The Man Who Got Away." *Corpus Christi Caller-Times*, 119.
2. Hayden, S. (1963). *Wanderer*. New York: Alfred A. Knopf, 288.
3. Ibid., 289.
4. Ibid.
5. Ibid., 290.
6. Ibid.
7. Ibid., 291.
8. Ibid., 292.
9. Ibid.
10. House of Representatives, Eighty-Second Congress. (1951). *Hearings before the Committee on Un-American Activities*. Washington, DC: United States Government Printing Office, 129.
11. Hayden, S., op. cit., 292.
12. Ibid.
13. Ibid., 293.
14. Ibid.
15. House of Representatives, Eighty-Second Congress, op. cit., 129.
16. Schwartz, S. (1996, July 26). "Soviet Spies Cast a Wide Net in S.F." *San Francisco Chronicle*, A4.

17. Hayden, S., op. cit., 293.
18. Ibid.
19. Ibid., 294.
20. Ibid.
21. House of Representatives, Eighty-Second Congress, op. cit., 130.
22. Hayden, S., op. cit., 295.
23. Ibid.
24. Ibid., 296.
25. Ibid.
26. Ibid., 297.
27. Ibid.
28. Ibid., 298.
29. Ibid.
30. Ibid., 299.
31. Smith, R. H. (2005). *OSS: The Secret History of America's First Central Intelligence Agency*. Guilford, CT: First Lyons Press, 24.
32. Office of the Assistant Secretary of War. (1976). *War Report of the OSS*. New York: Walker Publishing Company, 294.
33. Hayden, S., op. cit., 299.
34. Ibid.
35. Ibid., 300.
36. Narrative of Lt. John Hamilton, USMCR, 1, November 2, 1944, NARA RG 226, Records of the Office of Strategic Services, Entry 224: OSS Personnel Files, Boxes 308, 320.
37. Ibid., 300.
38. Ibid., 301.
39. Ross, B. (2011, February 17). *Training SOE Saboteurs in World War Two*. Retrieved July 24, 2014, http://www.bbc.co.uk/history/worldwars/wwtwo/soe_training_01.shtml.
40. Ibid.
41. Ibid.
42. Ibid.
43. Hayden, S., op. cit., 301.
44. Ibid.
45. Narrative of Lt. John Hamilton, USMCR, op. cit., 1.
46. Kershaw, R. (2010). *Sky Men: Always Expect the Unexpected—The Real Story of the Paras*. Great Britain: Hodder & Stoughton, 82.
47. Parachute Training Record, S. Hayden, January 4, 1942–January 11, 1942. NARA RG 226, Records of the Office of Strategic Services, Entry 224: OSS Personnel Files, Boxes 308, 320.
48. Ibid.
49. Ibid.
50. Robert E. Sherwood to Robert A. Solberg, memorandum, February 18, 1942. NARA RG 226, Records of the Office of Strategic Services, Entry 224: OSS Personnel Files, Boxes 308, 320.
51. Fisher Howe to William Whitney and Robert Solberg, memorandum no. 1, January 15, 1942. NARA RG 226, Records of the Office of Strategic Services, Entry 224: OSS Personnel Files, Boxes 308, 320.

52. Fisher Howe to Thomas G. Early, correspondence, January 26, 1942, NARA NARA RG 226, Records of the Office of Strategic Services, Entry 224: OSS Personnel Files, Boxes 308, 320.
53. Hayden, S., op. cit., 302.
54. Ibid.
55. Ibid.
56. Secretary to Colonel Solberg to Mr. Stirling Hayden, correspondence, February 21, 1942, NARA RG 226, Records of the Office of Strategic Services, Entry 224: OSS Personnel Files, Boxes 308, 320.
57. Hayden, S., op. cit., 303.
58. Ibid., 304.
59. Ibid.
60. House of Representatives, Eighty-Second Congress, op. cit., 130.
61. Hayden, S., op. cit., 304.
62. Ibid.
63. Ibid., 305.
64. Ibid.
65. Ibid., 306.
66. Ibid., 307.
67. Ibid.
68. Chamberlain, D. (2010). 39 *Steps to Stardom: The Life and Times of Madeleine Carroll.* Leicester, UK: Troubador Publishing, 182.
69. Ibid.
70. Ibid., 186.
71. Ibid., 199.

CHAPTER SEVEN: JOINING THE OSS

1. Hayden, S. (1963). *Wanderer*. New York: Alfred A. Knopf, 309.
2. Rehill, J. E. (1999). *Stars in the Corps: Movie Actors in the United States Marines.* Annapolis: US Naval Institute Press, 20.
3. Hayden, S., op. cit., 309.
4. Narrative of Lt. John Hamilton, USMCR, November 2, 1944, 2, NARA RG 226, Records of the Office of Strategic Services, Entry 224: OSS Personnel Files, Boxes 308, 320.
5. Rehill, J. E., op. cit., 20; Hayden, S., op. cit., 310.
6. Ibid., 309.
7. Brown, A. C. (1982). *Wild Bill Donovan: The Last Hero.* New York: Time Books, 301.
8. Ibid., 302, 308.
9. Ibid., 236.
10. Ibid.
11. Office of the Assistant Secretary of War. (1976). *The Overseas Targets: War Report of the OSS, Volume II.* New York: Walker and Company, 223, 225.
12. Office of Strategic Services (1944). *Operational Groups Field Manual–Strategic Services Manual No. 6.* Washington, DC: Office of Strategic Services, 7–10.

13. R. Davis Halliwell, “Memo to subject's file concerning Lt. Stirling Hayden, USMCR,” May 4, 1943, NARA RG 226, Records of the Office of Strategic Services, Entry 224: OSS Personnel Files, Boxes 308, 320.
14. Ellery C. Huntington to Mr. Mudge, “Memorandum: OSS Operational Groups—French Unit—Lt. Hayden and Major Fuller,” May 22, 1943, NARA RG 226, Records of the Office of Strategic Services, Entry 224: OSS Personnel Files, Boxes 308, 320.
15. Charles S. Cheston to William Mudge, “Request for Transfer—2nd Lt. Sterling Hayden,” May 24, 1943, NARA RG 226, Records of the Office of Strategic Services, Entry 224: OSS Personnel Files, Boxes 308, 320.
16. Ellery C. Huntington to Charles S. Cheston, “Operational Groups, OSS Personnel—2nd Lt. Sterling Hayden,” June 3, 1943, NARA RG 226, Records of the Office of Strategic Services, Entry 224: OSS Personnel Files, Boxes 308, 320.
17. Application for Employment and Personal History Statement for Sterling Hayden, undated, NARA RG 226, Records of the Office of Strategic Services, Entry 224: OSS Personnel Files, Boxes 308, 320.
18. Hayden, S., op. cit., 310.
19. Smith, R. H. (2005). *OSS: The Secret History of America's First Central Intelligence Agency.* Guilford, CT: First Lyons Press, 26.
20. Bradley, M. (2014). *A Very Principled Boy.* New York: Basic Books, 66.
21. Office of the Assistant Secretary of War, op. cit., 225.
22. G. R. Holden to Personnel Officer, SO, “Memorandum: Transfer of Lt. John Hamilton from OG to SO,” July 21, 1943, NARA RG 226, E 224.
23. Narrative of Lt. John Hamilton, op. cit., 2.
24. Smith, R. H., op, cit., 113.
25. Hayden, S., op. cit., 310.
26. Narrative of Lt. John Hamilton, op. cit., 3.
27. Hayden, S., op. cit., 310.
28. Ibid., 311.

CHAPTER EIGHT: YUGOSLAVIA

1. Kirk Ford Jr. (1992). *OSS and the Yugoslav Resistance, 1943–1945.* College Station: Texas A&M Press, 5.
2. Smith, R. H. (2005). *OSS: The Secret History of America's First Central Intelligence Agency.* Guilford, CT: First Lyons Press, 119.
3. Ford, K., op. cit., 7.
4. Smith, R. H., op. cit., 120.
5. Ibid.
6. Ibid., 121.
7. Ibid., 122.
8. Ford, K., op. cit., 10.
9. Ibid., 22.
10. Smith, R. H., op. cit., 125.
11. Ibid., 126.
12. Ibid.
13. Hayden, S. (1963). *Wanderer.* New York: Alfred A. Knopf, 311.

14. Narrative of Lt. John Hamilton, USMCR, November 2, 1944, NARA RG 226, Records of the Office of Strategic Services, Entry 224: OSS Personnel Files, Boxes 308, 320.
15. Hayden, S., op. cit., 313.
16. Brown, A. C. (1982). *Wild Bill Donovan: The Last Hero*. New York: Time Books, 444.
17. Smith, R. H., op. cit., 125.
18. Brown, A. C., op. cit., 444.
19. Ibid., 445.
20. Ford, K., op. cit., 24.
21. Brown, A. C., op. cit., 445.
22. Ibid., 447.
23. Ibid.
24. Ibid., 449.
25. Ford, K., op. cit., 26.
26. Narrative of Lt. John Hamilton, USMCR, November 2, 1944, 4, NARA RG 226, Records of the Office of Strategic Services, Entry 224: OSS Personnel Files, Boxes 308, 320.
27. Ibid.
28. Ibid.
29. Ford, K., op. cit., 28.
30. Gay, T. M. (2013). *Savage Will: The Daring Escape of Americans Trapped behind Nazi Lines*. New York: Penguin Group, 228.
31. Ibid.
32. Narrative of Lt. John Hamilton, USMCR, November 2, 1944, NARA RG 226, Records of the Office of Strategic Services, Entry 224: OSS Personnel Files, Boxes 308, 320.
33. Ibid., 5.
34. Hayden, S., op. cit., 314.
35. Ibid.
36. Ford, K., op. cit., 28.
37. Major Hans V. Tofte to Director, Strategic Services Unit, "Recommendation for Award of the Silver Star to Captain John Hamilton, USMCR," NARA RG 226, Records of the Office of Strategic Services, Entry 224: OSS Personnel Files, Boxes 308, 320.
38. Ibid.
39. House of Representatives, Eighty-Second Congress. (1951). *Hearings before the Committee on Un-American Activities*. Washington, DC: United States Government Printing Office, 131.
40. Brown, D. (1999). *Actors Talk*. New York: Proscenium Publishers, 123.
41. Ibid., 123–24.
42. Ibid.
43. Ibid., 124.
44. Ibid., 124–25.
45. Ibid., 125–26.

CHAPTER NINE: BRAVERY, CHAOS, AND A RESCUE MISSION

1. Ford, K. (1992). *OSS and the Yugoslav Resistance, 1943–1945*. College Station: Texas A&M Press, 61.

2. Ibid., 60.
3. Major Robert J. Koch to Colonel Toulmin, "Personnel-Shipping Business," January 3, 1944, 1 NARA RG226, E 224, B 120, F 458.
4. Ibid.
5. Major Hans V. Tofte to Director, Strategic Services Unit, "Recommendation for Award of the Silver Star to Captain John Hamilton, USMCR," February 28, 1946, page 1, NARA RG 226, Records of the Office of Strategic Services, Entry 224: OSS Personnel Files, Boxes, 308, 320.
6. Narrative of Lt. John Hamilton, USMCR, November 2, 1944, 5, NARA RG 226, Records of the Office of Strategic Services, Entry 224: OSS Personnel Files, Boxes 308, 320.
7. Major Hans V. Tofte to Director, Strategic Services Unit, op. cit., 2.
8. Narrative of Lt. John Hamilton, op. cit., 6.
9. Ibid.
10. Ibid.
11. Major Robert J. Koch to Colonel Toulmin, op. cit., 1.
12. Gay, T. M. (2013). *Savage Will: The Daring Escape of Americans Trapped behind Nazi Lines*. New York: Penguin Group, 4.
13. Turner H. McBaine to Director, OSS, ME. "Capt. Hans Tofte, Lt. Robert Thompson, Lt. John Hamilton," December 28, 1943, page 1, NARA RG 226, E 190, B 120, F 458.
14. Smith, R. H. (2005). *OSS: The Secret History of America's First Central Intelligence Agency*. Guilford, CT: First Lyons Press, 135.
15. Turner H. McBaine to Director, OSS, ME., op. cit., page 1.
16. In *Wanderer*, Hayden re-created this confrontation in the form of a four-page letter to Warwick Thompkins where he changed the name of Richard Weil to "Sam Golden—a credit manager for a chain of restaurants." Hayden, S. (1963). *Wanderer*. New York: Alfred A. Knopf, 315–18.
17. Turner H. McBaine to Director, OSS, ME., op. cit., page 1.
18. Ibid.
19. Ibid., 1–2.
20. Lt. Col. J. E. Toulmin to Major Robert Koch. "Memorandum," December 30, 1943, NARA RG 226, E 190, B 120, F 458.
21. Major Hans V. Tofte to Director, Strategic Services Unit, op. cit., page 3.
22. Major Robert J. Koch to Colonel Toulmin, op. cit., page 1.
23. Ibid.
24. Ibid., 2.
25. Ibid.
26. Ibid.
27. Ibid., 3.
28. Lt. Col. J. E. Toulmin to Major Robert Koch, "Memorandum," January 3, 1944, NARA RG 226, E 190, B 120, F 458.
29. Narrative of Lt. John Hamilton, op. cit., page 7.
30. Ibid.
31. Ibid.
32. HQ, SBS, OSS/I. "Final Report on Operation AUDREY, the SBS Shipping Line From Italy to Partisan Forces in Yugoslavia," May 16, 1944, page 8, NARA RG 226, E 99, B 36, F 137.

33. Ibid.
34. Ford, K., op, cit., 29.
35. Gay, T. M., op. cit., 235.
36. Hayden, S. (1963). *Wanderer*. New York: Alfred A. Knopf, 313.
37. House of Representatives, Eighty-Second Congress. (1951). *Hearings before the Committee on Un-American Activities.* Washington, DC: United States Government Printing Office, 132.
38. Ford, K., op. cit., 86.
39. House of Representatives, Eighty-Second Congress, op. cit., 132.
40. McConnell, S. (1988, January). "Leaving the Party: The Politics of Sterling Hayden." *New Criterion*, pp. 1–12, 6.

CHAPTER TEN: MISSIONS TO ALBANIA AND AN EFFORT IN FILMMAKING

1. Lucas, P. (2007). *The OSS in World War II Albania*. Jefferson, NC: McFarland & Company, 17.
2. Ibid., 29.
3. Ibid., 24.
4. Ibid., 19.
5. Ibid., 43.
6. Narrative of Lt. John Hamilton, USMCR, November 2, 1944, page 8, NARA, RG 226, Records of the Office of Strategic Services, Entry 224: OSS Personnel Files, Boxes 308, 320.
7. Ibid.
8. Hayden, S. (1963). *Wanderer*. New York: Alfred A. Knopf, 321.
9. Narrative of Lt. John Hamilton, op. cit., page 9.
10. Ibid.
11. Ibid.
12. Ibid., 11.
13. Ibid., 10.
14. Lucas, P., op. cit., 42.
15. Ibid., 43.
16. Ibid., 59.
17. Quayle, A. (1990) *A Time to Speak*. London: Barrie & Jenkins, 301.
18. Ibid.
19. Ibid.
20. Ibid.
21. Lucas, P., op. cit., 61.
22. Ibid.; Quayle, A., op, cit., 301.
23. Hayden, S., op. cit., 325.
24. Lucas, P., op. cit., 62.
25. Ibid.
26. Ibid.
27. Narrative of Lt. John Hamilton, op. cit., 10.
28. Freeman, M. P. (1997). *The Cinderella Front: Allied Air Operations in Yugoslavia during World War II.* Montgomery, AL: Air Command and Staff College, 36.

29. Lt. J. Hamilton to Commanding Officer, SBS, "Photographic Unit, Project for," undated, NARA RG 226, E 190, B 120, F 474.
30. Major Walter M. Ross to Capt. George Vujnovich, "Memorandum on Field Photographic Unit.," December 23, 1943, NARA RG 226, E 190, B 120, F 474.
31. Lt. J. Hamilton to Commanding Officer, SBS, op. cit.
32. Lt. Cdr. Edward J. Green to Lt. John Hamilton, "Field Photographic Project," May 19, 1944, NARA RG 226, E 190, B 120, F 474.
33. Lt. Cdr. Edward J. Green to CO/OSS, Italy, "Project for Field Photographic Unit," May 30, 1944, NARA RG 226, E 190, B 120, F 474.
34. Ibid.
35. CO, 2677th Regiment, OSS (Prov) to CO, OSS/Italy, "1st Endorsement," June 8, 1944, NARA RG 226, E 190, B 120, F 474.
36. 2nd Lieutenant John Hamilton, U.S. Marine Corps, (SO), screenplay entitled "The People Fight," NARA, RG 226, E 190, B 120, F 474.
37. Ibid., 1.
38. Ibid., 9.
39. Ibid., 8.
40. Hayden, S., op. cit., 320.

CHAPTER ELEVEN: AIR CREW RESCUE UNIT AND A LOSS OF FAITH

1. Ford, K. (1992). *OSS and the Yugoslav Resistance, 1943–1945*. College Station: Texas A&M Press, 99.
2. Leary, W. M. (1995). *Fueling the Fires of Resistance: Army Air Forces Special Operations in the Balkans during World War II*. Washington, DC: Air Force History and Museums Program, 29.
3. Hutchins, B. (2008). *General Nathan Twining and the Fifteenth Air Force in World War II*. Denton: University of North Texas, 58.
4. Ford, K., op. cit., 29.
5. Leary, W. M., op. cit., 30.
6. Ford, K., op. cit., 108.
7. Personnel Information Blank for 2nd Lt. John Hamilton, August 5, 1944, NARA, RG 226, Records of the Office of Strategic Services, Entry 224: OSS Personnel Files, Boxes 308, 320.
8. Narrative of Lt. John Hamilton, USMCR, November 2, 1944, page 12, NARA, RG 226, Records of the Office of Strategic Services, Entry 224: OSS Personnel Files, Boxes 308, 320.
9. Ibid.
10. Ibid.; 2nd Lt. John Hamilton to Chief, SO-Bari, "2nd Lt. John Hamilton; Report on the movements of the Hacienda Mission and observations as a result thereof, covering the period from 17 August 1944 to 24 September 1944," September 28, 1944, page 1, NARA RG 226, E 144, B 69, F 615-A.
11. Narrative of Lt. John Hamilton, op. cit., 12.
12. Ibid., 13.
13. Ibid.
14. 2nd Lt. John Hamilton to Chief, SO-Bari, op. cit., page 1.

15. Ibid., 2.
16. Narrative of Lt. John Hamilton, op. cit., pages 14–15.
17. 2nd Lt. John Hamilton to Chief, SO-Bari, op. cit., 2.
18. Ibid., 3.
19. Ibid.
20. Chief, SO-Bari to Chief, SO-Washington, "2nd Lt. John Hamilton; Report on the movements of the Hacienda Mission and observations as a result thereof, covering the period from 17 August 1944 to 24 September 1944," October 2, 1944, NARA RG 226, E 144, B 69, F 615-A.
21. Ibid., 2.
22. Ibid., 3.
23. Ford, K., op. cit., 82.
24. Hayden, S. (1963). *Wanderer*. New York: Alfred A. Knopf, 313.
25. House of Representatives, Eighty-Second Congress. (1951). *Hearings before the Committee on Un-American Activities*. Washington, DC: United States Government Printing Office, 132.
26. Ibid.
27. Chief, SO-Bari to Chief, SO-Washington, "Major Linn M. Farish's Observations in Yugoslavia for the period 19 September 1943–16 June 1944; Summary of Report of," July 4, 1944, NARA RG 226, E 136, B 35, F X-82.
28. Ibid., 3–4.
29. Ibid., 5–6.
30. Ibid., 6.
31. Ibid., 7.
32. Ibid., 8–9.
33. Ibid., 9.
34. Theater Service Record on 2nd Lt. John Hamilton, October 30, 1944, NARA, RG 226, Records of the Office of Strategic Services, Entry 224: OSS Personnel Files, Boxes 308, 320.
35. Hayden, S., op. cit., 323.
36. Ibid., 324.
37. Ibid., 325.
38. Ibid.
39. Ibid., 326.
40. Ibid.
41. House of Representatives, Eighty-Second Congress, op. cit., 133.
42. Ibid.
43. Hayden, S., op. cit., 326.
44. Ibid., 327.
45. House of Representatives, Eighty-Second Congress, op. cit., 136.

CHAPTER TWELVE: EUROPEAN THEATER

1. Student Training Record, 1st Lt. John Hamilton, January 13, 1945, RG 226, Records of the Office of Strategic Services, Entry 224: OSS Personnel Files, Boxes 308, 320.
2. Hayden, S. (1963). *Wanderer*. New York: Alfred A. Knopf, 328.

3. Lieutenant General John K. Cannon to Colonel Edward J. F. Glavin, "Commendation," April 25, 1945. RG 226, Records of the Office of Strategic Services, Entry 224: OSS Personnel Files, Boxes 308, 320.
4. Conrad, B. (1994). *Name Dropping: Tales from My Barbary Coast Saloon*. New York: HarperCollins, 165.
5. Madeleine Carroll to Dwight D. Eisenhower, January 30, 1945, Box 17, Carr to Carso (Misc.), Dwight D. Eisenhower: Papers, Pre-Presidential, 1916–52. Dwight D. Eisenhower Presidential Library; Dwight D. Eisenhower to Madeleine Carroll, February 8, 1945, Box 17, Carr to Carso (Misc.), Dwight D. Eisenhower: Papers, Pre-Presidential, 1916–52. Dwight D. Eisenhower Presidential Library.
6. Dwight D. Eisenhower to Madeleine Carroll, January 26, 1945, Box 17, Carr to Carso (Misc.), Dwight D. Eisenhower: Papers, Pre-Presidential, 1916–52. Dwight D. Eisenhower Presidential Library.
7. Hayden, S., op. cit., 329.
8. Muth, J. (2013). *Command Culture: Officer Education in the U.S. Army and the German Armed Forces, 1901–1940, and the Consequences for World War II*. Denton: University of North Texas Press, 247.
9. Hayden, S., op. cit., 329.
10. Ibid., 330.
11. Smith, R. H. (2005). *OSS: The Secret History of America's First Central Intelligence Agency*. Guilford, CT: First Lyons Press, 215.
12. Ibid., 330.
13. Chief of Branch Field Photographic Branches OSS to the Adjutant OSS, "HAMILTON, John J. Capt. 0–22085, U.S.M.C.R. request transfer of." May 24, 1945, RG 226, Records of the Office of Strategic Services, Entry 224: OSS Personnel Files, Boxes 308, 320.
14. Hayden, S., op. cit., 331.
15. Chamberlain, D. (2010). *39 Steps to Stardom: The Life and Times of Madeleine Carroll*. Leicester, UK: Troubadour Publishing, 217.
16. Hayden, S., op. cit., 332.
17. Ibid., 333.
18. Rehill, J. E. (1999). *Stars in the Corps: Movie Actors in the United States Marines*. Annapolis: US Naval Institute Press, 23.
19. Separation Process Form for Captain John Hamilton 0–22085, November 26, 1945, RG 226, Records of the Office of Strategic Services, Entry 224: OSS Personnel Files, Boxes 308, 320.
20. Commanding Officer, Naval Branch OSS to Chief, Personnel Branch, "Transfer of Personnel," November 26, 1945, RG 226, Records of the Office of Strategic Services, Entry 224: OSS Personnel Files, Boxes 308, 320.
21. Headquarters, Mediterranean Theater of Operations, U.S. Army, "General Orders Number 145," July 31, 1946, RG 226, Records of the Office of Strategic Services, Entry 224: OSS Personnel Files, Boxes 308, 320.

CHAPTER THIRTEEN: JOINING THE COMMUNIST PARTY IN HOLLYWOOD

1. House of Representatives, Eighty-Second Congress. (1951). *Hearings before the Committee on Un-American Activities.* Washington, DC: United States Government Printing Office, 137.
2. Hayden, S. (1963). *Wanderer.* New York: Alfred A. Knopf, 342.
3. Ibid., 341.
4. Ibid., 342.
5. Ibid., 343.
6. Ibid.
7. Ibid.
8. House of Representatives, Eighty-Second Congress, op. cit., 138.
9. McConnell, S. (1988, January). "Leaving the Party: The Politics of Sterling Hayden." *New Criterion*, 1–12, 8.
10. Brown, D. (1999). *Actors Talk.* New York: Proscenium Publishers, 116.
11. Hayden, S., op. cit., 344.
12. Ibid., 345.
13. Ibid., 346.
14. Ibid., 347.
15. House of Representatives, Eighty-Second Congress, op. cit., 139.
16. Hayden, S., op. cit., 348.
17. House of Representatives, Eighty-Second Congress, op. cit., 140.
18. Hayden, S., op. cit., 348.
19. Ibid., 349.
20. Ibid.
21. Ibid.
22. House of Representatives, Eighty-Second Congress, op. cit., 146.
23. Ibid., 142.
24. Crichlow, D. (2013). *When Hollywood Was Right.* Cambridge, UK: Cambridge University Press, 82.
25. Ibid., 83.
26. Hayden, S., op. cit., 353.
27. Peary, G. (undated). "Talking with Sterling Hayden." Retrieved August 29, 2014, http://www.geraldpeary.com/interviews/ghi/hayden.html.
28. Sterling Hayden interview with Tom Snyder on *Tomorrow*, broadcast March 25, 1977.
29. Hayden, S., op. cit., 353.
30. Ibid.
31. Ibid., 354.
32. Ibid., 355.
33. Ibid., 356.
34. Ibid.

CHAPTER FOURTEEN: SEARCHING FOR SUBVERSIVES IN HOLLYWOOD

1. Navasky, V. S. (1980). *Naming Names.* New York: Viking Press, 78.
2. Ibid., 79.

3. Ibid., 80.
4. Cogley, J. (1956). *Report of the Blacklisting, 1. Movies. New York: The Fund for the Republic,* 6.
5. Ibid., 7.
6. Ibid., 4–5.
7. Ibid., 7.
8. Ibid., 8.
9. Dick, B. F. (1989). *Radical Innocence: A Critical Study of the Hollywood Ten.* Lexington: University Press of Kentucky, 7.
10. Cogley, J., op. cit., 22.
11. Ibid., 12.
12. Feinberg, S. (2014, August 20). "Lauren Bacall, Political Activist: She Knew How to Whistle . . . and Speak Her Mind." *Hollywood Reporter.* Retrieved January 3, 2014, http://www.hollywoodreporter.com/race/lauren-bacall-political-activist-she-726095.
13. Cogley, J., op. cit., 8.
14. House of Representatives, Eighty-Second Congress. (1951). *Hearings before the Committee on Un-American Activities.* Washington, DC: United States Government Printing Office, 145.
15. Hayden, S. (1963). *Wanderer.* New York: Alfred A. Knopf, 361.
16. Ibid., 360.
17. Ibid., 361.
18. House of Representatives, Eighty-Second Congress, op. cit., 141.
19. Hayden, S., op. cit., 361.
20. Ibid.
21. Ibid., 362.
22. Ibid., 363.
23. Ibid.
24. Ibid., 364.
25. Navasky, V. S., op. cit., 134.
26. Gordon, B. (2004). *The Gordon File.* Austin: University of Texas Press, 89–90.
27. Ibid., 90.
28. Ibid., 92.
29. Hayden, S., op. cit., 361.
30. Ibid., 364.
31. Ibid., 365.
32. Ibid., 368.
33. Ibid.
34. Ibid., 371.
35. Ibid., 372.
36. Ceplair, L. (1983). *The Inquisition in Hollywood, Politics in the Film Community, 1930–1960.* Oakland: University of California Press, 390–91.
37. Ibid., 391.
38. Navasky, V. S., op. cit., 99.
39. Ibid.
40. Ibid., 104.
41. Ibid., 100.
42. Ibid., 141.

43. Ibid., 142.
44. Ibid.
45. Ibid., 135.
46. House of Representatives, Eighty-Second Congress, op. cit., 148.
47. Ibid., 149.
48. Hayden, S., op. cit., 375.
49. Ibid., 377.

CHAPTER FIFTEEN: NAMING NAMES

1. House of Representatives, Eighty-Second Congress. (1951). *Hearings before the Committee on Un-American Activities*. Washington, DC: United States Government Printing Office, 63.
2. Ibid., 81.
3. Ibid., 90.
4. Ibid., 92.
5. Ibid., 94.
6. Ceplair, L. (1983). *The Inquisition in Hollywood, Politics in the Film Community, 1930–1960*. Oakland: University of California Press, 372.
7. House of Representatives, Eighty-Second Congress, op. cit., 106.
8. Ibid., 107.
9. Ceplair, L., op. cit., 373.
10. House of Representatives, Eighty-Second Congress, op. cit., 114.
11. Hayden, S. (1963). *Wanderer*. New York: Alfred A. Knopf, 378.
12. Ibid., 382.
13. Ibid., 384.
14. Ibid., 385.
15. Ibid.
16. Ibid., 385–86.
17. Ibid., 388.
18. Telephone interview with Norman Hatch, November 23, 2015.
19. Navasky, V. S. (1980). *Naming Names*. New York: Viking Press, 101.
20. House of Representatives, Eighty-Second Congress, op. cit., 128.
21. Hayden, S., op. cit., 389.
22. House of Representatives, Eighty-Second Congress, op. cit., 129.
23. Ibid.
24. Ibid., 130.
25. Ibid.
26. Ibid., 132.
27. Ibid.
28. Ford, K. (1992). *OSS and the Yugoslav Resistance, 1943–1945*. College Station: Texas A&M Press, 86.
29. House of Representatives, Eighty-Second Congress, op. cit., 133.
30. Chief, SO-Bari to Chief, SO-Washington, "2nd Lt. John Hamilton; Report on the movements of the Hacienda Mission and observations as a result thereof, covering the period from 17 August 1944 to 24 September 1944," October 2, 1944, pages 2–3, NARA RG 226, E 144, B 69, F 615A.

31. House of Representatives, Eighty-Second Congress, op. cit., 136.
32. Ibid., 137.
33. Ibid., 138.
34. Ibid., 140.
35. Ibid., 143.
36. Ibid., 144.
37. Ibid., 145.
38. Ibid., 145–46.
39. Ibid., 147.
40. Ibid., 148–49.
41. Ibid., 149.
42. Ibid.
43. Ibid., 150–51.
44. Ibid., 151–54.
45. Ford, K., op. cit., 80.
46. Ibid., 60.
47. Jerome, F. (2003). *The Einstein File: J. Edgar Hoover's Secret War against the World's Most Famous Scientist.* New York: St. Martin's Press, 242.
48. House of Representatives, Eighty-Second Congress, op. cit., 154–58.
49. Ibid., 158–61.
50. Ford, K., op. cit., 82.
51. House of Representatives, Eighty-Second Congress, op. cit., 161–63.
52. Ibid., 163.
53. Ibid.
54. Ibid., 165–67.
55. Ibid., 167–71.
56. Hayden, S., op. cit., 389–90.
57. Ibid., 390.
58. Ibid.
59. British Broadcasting Corporation, *Talking Pictures: Sterling Hayden Interview*, filmed April 16, 1986.
60. Hayden, S., op. cit., 392.

CHAPTER SIXTEEN: DIVORCE AND ESCAPE

1.Hayden, S. (1963). *Wanderer*. New York: Alfred A. Knopf, 392.
2. Ibid., 393.
3. Ibid., 395.
4. Ibid.
5. "Sterling Hayden Accuses Ex-Wife." (1958, October 30). *Toledo Blade*, 38.
6. "Around the World Actor Sterling Hayden Wins Divorce from Former Model." (1955, August 28). *Daily (Provo, Utah) Herald*, 16.
7. "Actor Divorces Wife Who Looked Up, Down to Him." (1955, August 27). *Pittsburgh Post-Gazette*, 1.
8. Hayden, S., op. cit., 420.
9. Ibid., 421.

10. Ibid.
11. Interview with Norman Hatch, November 23, 2015.
12. Hayden, S., op. cit., 24.
13. Hayden, S., op. cit., 25.
14. Ibid., 30.
15. Ibid., 26.
16. Ibid., 27.
17. Interview with Dennis Powers, January 17, 2016.
18. Ibid.
19. Ibid.
20. Ibid.
21. Hayden, S., op. cit., 31.
22. Ibid., 6.
23. Ibid., 7.
24. Ibid., 14.
25. Brown, D. (1999). *Actors Talk*. New York: Proscenium Publishers, 117.
26. Hayden, S., op. cit., 11–12.
27. Ibid., 16.
28. Ibid., 32.
29. Hayden, S. (1959, July 26). "Why I Defied the Law." *Parade*, 2.
30. Hayden, S., op. cit., 34.
31. Ibid., 36.
32. Ibid., 37.
33. Interview with Norman Hatch, November 23, 2015.
34. Interview with Dennis Powers, January 17, 2015.
35. Hayden, S. (1959, July 26). "Why I Defied the Law." *Parade*, 2.

CHAPTER SEVENTEEN: *WANDERER* TO TAHITI AND BACK

1. Interview with Dennis Powers, January 17, 2015.
2. Ibid.
3. Hayden, S. (1963). *Wanderer*. New York: Alfred A. Knopf, 156.
4. Ibid., 158.
5. Ibid., 159.
6. Conrad, B. (1994). *Name Dropping: Tales from My Barbary Coast Saloon*. New York: HarperCollins, 160.
7. Hayden, S. (1959, July 26). "Why I Defied the Law." *Parade*, 2.
8. Interview with Dennis Powers, January 17, 2015.
9. Conrad, B., op. cit., 161.
10. Ibid., 162.
11. Hayden, S. (1959, July 26). "Why I Defied the Law." *Parade*, 2.
12. Ibid.
13. Ibid.
14. Wilson, L. (1959, August 16). "The Man Who Got Away." *Corpus Christi Caller-Times*, 119.
15. Hayden, S. (1963). *Wanderer*. New York: Alfred A. Knopf, 402.

16. Ibid., 403.
17. Ibid., 405.
18. Ibid.
19. Ibid., 410.
20. Ibid., 413.
21. Ibid., 414–15.
22. Ibid., 416.
23. Ibid.
24. Ibid., 417.
25. Ibid., 418.
26. Ibid., 426.
27. Ibid., 424.
28. Ibid., 425.
29. Ibid., 426.
30. Ibid., 431.
31. Ibid.
32. Ibid.
33. Ibid., 432.
34. Brown, D. (1999). *Actors Talk*. New York: Proscenium Publishers, 118.
35. Ibid.
36. "Film Actor Handed $49,518 Judgment." (1961, August 6). *Reading Eagle*, 12.

CHAPTER EIGHTEEN: A NEW BRIDE AND LITERARY ACCLAIM

1. Interview with Kitty Hayden, October 27, 2015.
2. Ibid.
3. Ibid.
4. Ibid.
5. Ibid.
6. Stern, H. (1960, February 14). "Miss Harris Stars in 'Ethan Frome.'" *Chicago Tribune*, 3.
7. Lowery, C. (1960, February 19). "Exciting Production Given in 'Ethan Frome' TV Show." *Ocala Star-Banner*, 7.
8. "Sterling Hayden to Marry New Yorker." (1960, Mar 3). *St. Petersburg Times*, 10a.
9. Interview with Kitty Hayden, October 27, 2015; McDonald, J. (1960, March 10). "All the World Loves Lovers—Hayden and Socialite Wed." *San Rafael California Daily Independent Journal*, 1.
10. Ibid.
11. Newquist, R. (1964). *Counterpoint*. Chicago: Rand McNally, 336.
12. Interview with Kitty Hayden, December 28, 2015.
13. Interview with Kitty Hayden, October 27, 2015.
14. Hayden, S. (1963). *Wanderer*. New York: Alfred A. Knopf, 151.
15. Brown, D. (1999). *Actors Talk*. New York: Proscenium Publishers, 118.
16. Osterburg, J. (1988, May 22). "The Wanderer Remembered." *San Francisco Chronicle*.
17. Ibid.
18. Ibid.

19. Ibid.
20. Letter from Sterling Hayden to Summerhill School, August 27, 1961. From the Sterling Hayden Collection, Howard Gotlieb Archival Research Center at Boston University.
21. Letter from Summerhill School to Sterling Hayden, September 4, 1961. From the Sterling Hayden Collection, Howard Gotlieb Archival Research Center at Boston University.
22. Interview with Kitty Hayden, October 27, 2015.
23. Letter from Sterling Hayden to George (no last name), February 12, 1962. From the Sterling Hayden Collection, Howard Gotlieb Archival Research Center at Boston University.
24. Sterling Hayden Collection. (n.d.). Retrieved May 15, 2014, http://hgar-srv3.bu.edu/collections/collection?id=122131.
25. Brown, D., op. cit., 118.
26. Review of *Wanderer* by Sterling Hayden. (1963, October 21). *Kirkus Reviews.*
27. Review of *Wanderer. Los Angeles Times.*
28. Newquist, R., op. cit., 332.

CHAPTER NINETEEN: RADICAL REDUX

1. McConnell, S. (1988, January). "Leaving the Party: The Politics of Sterling Hayden." *New Criterion,* 1–12, 1.
2. Ibid., 3.
3. Ibid., 5.
4. Ibid., 3.
5. Ibid., 5.
6. Ibid.
7. Ibid., 7.
8. Newquist, R. (1964). *Counterpoint.* Chicago: Rand McNally, 339.
9. Ibid., 375.
10. McConnell, S., op. cit., 9.
11. Ibid., 8.
12. Interview with Kitty Hayden, November 10, 2015.
13. Ibid.
14. "Rival Cuba Rallies—They Talk, Talk." (1962, October 28). *San Francisco Examiner,* p. 1.
15. Ibid.; McConnell, S., op. cit., 10.
16. Newquist, R., op. cit., 340.
17. Letter from Reverend Albert Colton to Sterling Hayden, January 22, 1964. From the Sterling Hayden Collection, Howard Gotlieb Archival Research Center at Boston University.
18. Nolte, C. (2014, March 1). "S.F. Palace Hotel Sit-in Helped Start the Revolution 50 Years Ago. *SFGate.*
19. "226 Arrested in S.F. Demonstrations." (1964, April 12). *Santa Cruz Sentinel,* 1.
20. McConnell, S., op. cit., 2.

CHAPTER TWENTY· RETURN TO FILM

1. LoBrutto, V. (1999). *Stanley Kubrick: A Biography*. Cambridge, MA: Da Capo Press, 113–20.
2. Interview with Kitty Hayden, October 27, 2015.
3. Brown, D. (1999). *Actors Talk*. New York: Proscenium Publishers, 115–16.
4. Crowther, B. (1964, January 31). "Review—Dr. Strangelove or: How I Learned to Stop Worrying and Love the Bomb." *New York Times*.
5. Sterling Hayden diary entry, November 9, 1984. From the Sterling Hayden Collection, Howard Gotlieb Archival Research Center at Boston University.

CHAPTER TWENTY-ONE: ALCOHOL, HASHISH, AND RIVER BARGES

1. Interview with Kitty Hayden, January 22, 2016.
2. Ibid.
3. Sterling Hayden diary entry, September 1968, provided by Kitty Hayden.
4. Sterling Hayden interview with Tom Snyder, *Tomorrow*, broadcast March 25, 1977.
5. Sterling Hayden diary entry, March 9, 1968. From the Sterling Hayden Collection, Howard Gotlieb Archival Research Center at Boston University.
6. Sterling Hayden interview with Tom Snyder, *Tomorrow*, broadcast March 25, 1977.
7. Sterling Hayden diary entries, September 1968, provided by Kitty Hayden.
8. Brown, D. (1999). *Actors Talk*. New York: Proscenium Publishers, 116.
9. Sterling Hayden interview with Tom Snyder, *Tomorrow*, broadcast March 25, 1977.
10. Peary, G. (undated). *Talking with Sterling Hayden*. Retrieved August 29, 2014, http://www.geraldpeary.com/interviews/ghi/hayden.html.
11. Interview with Tom Snyder, *Tomorrow*, broadcast March 25, 1977.
12. Ibid.
13. Ibid.
14. Brown, D., op. cit., 120.
15. Ibid.
16. Ibid., 120–21.
17. Ibid., 121.
18. Letter from Dalton Trumbo to Sterling Hayden, October 7, 1968. From the Sterling Hayden Collection, Howard Gotlieb Archival Research Center at Boston University.
19. Sterling Hayden diary entry, undated. From the Sterling Hayden Collection, Howard Gotlieb Archival Research Center at Boston University.
20. Interview with Kitty Hayden, November 19, 2015.
21. Interview with Kitty Hayden, October 27, 2015.

CHAPTER TWENTY-TWO: A LITERARY TRIUMPH AND FINAL YEARS

1. Sterling Hayden diary entries from notebook labeled August 28–October 7, 1972. Box 14, Folder A, "Weird Writing, Correspondence, Story." From the Sterling Hayden Collection, Howard Gotlieb Archival Research Center at Boston University.

2, Thompson, D. (2006). *Altman on Altman*. New York: Farrar, Straus, and Giroux, 32.
3, Motavalli, J. (1980, February 27). "An American Odyssey." *Fairfield Advocate*, 14.
4, Interview with Kitty Hayden, November 10, 2015.
5, Interview with Kitty and David Hayden, October 27, 2015.
6, Galanter, M. (1999). *Cults: Faith, Healing, and Coercion*. New York: Oxford University Press, 75.
7, Interview with David Hayden, December 28, 2015.
8, Interview with Kitty and David Hayden, October 27, 2015.
9, Interview with Kitty Hayden, November 19, 2015.
10, Interview with Kitty and David Hayden, October 27, 2015.
11, Review of *Voyage: A Novel of 1896*. (1976, December 1). *Kirkus Reviews*.
12. Sterling Hayden interview with Tom Snyder, *Tomorrow*, broadcast March 25, 1977.
13. Sterling Hayden interview with Stanley Siegel, *The Stanley Siegel Show*, filmed March 26, 1977.
14. Interview with Kitty Hayden, November 10, 2015.
15. Brown, D. (1999). *Actors Talk*. New York: Proscenium Publishers, 126.
16. Interview with Kitty and David Hayden, December 28, 2015.
17. Sterling Hayden interview with Tom Snyder, *Tomorrow*, broadcast May 29, 1980.
18. Interview with Kitty and David Hayden, November 2, 2015.
19. Avedon, B. (1980). *Ah, Men!: What Do Men Want?: A Panorama of the Male in Crisis, His Past Problems, Present Uncertainties, Future Goals*. New York: A & W Publishers, 99–100.
20. Interview with Kitty Hayden, November 10, 2015.
21. *Pharos of Chaos: A Profile of Sterling Hayden*. Red Harvest Films, October 1983.
22. O'Connor, J. (1982, November 14). "'The Blue and the Gray' Often Loses Sight of the Civil War." *New York Times*.
23. Sterling Hayden interview with Tom Snyder, *Tomorrow*, broadcast October 7, 1981.
24. Interview with Kitty Hayden, November 10, 2015.
25. Conrad, B. (1994). *Name Dropping: Tales from My Barbary Coast Saloon*. New York: HarperCollins, 164.
26. Interview with Kitty Hayden, November 10, 2015.
27. Ibid.
28. Ibid.
29. Ibid.
30. Ibid.
31. Ibid.
32. Interview with Kitty and David Hayden, October 27, 2015.
33. Interview with David Hayden, November 2, 2015.
34. Sterling Hayden diary entry, July 24, 1983. Box 14, Folder A, "Weird Writing, Correspondence, Story." From the Sterling Hayden Collection, Howard Gotlieb Archival Research Center at Boston University.
35. Conrad, B., op. cit., 165.
36. Interview with Kitty Hayden, October 27, 2015.
37. Interview with Dennis Powers, January 17, 2016.
38. Conrad, B., op. cit., 164.
39. Ibid., 165.
40. BBC series, *Talking Pictures: Interview with Sterling Hayden*, filmed April 16, 1986.
41. Interview with Kitty Hayden, November 10, 2015.

42. Ibid.
43. Ibid.
44. Conrad, B., op. cit., 164.

EPILOGUE

1. Interview with Dennis Powers, January 17, 2016.
2. Brown, D. (1999). *Actors Talk*. New York: Proscenium Publishers, 127.

BIBLIOGRAPHY AND SOURCES

NATION ARCHIVES AND RECORDS ADMINISTRATION: OFFICIAL OSS DOCUMENTS

The numerous declassified documents referenced in the endnotes concerning Sterling Hayden's World War II service were obtained from the National Archives and Records Administration (NARA) in College Park Maryland. All OSS records are located in Record Group (RG) 226. I have listed the documents in the endnotes by both document title and sender and recipient, as well as date and page number. I obtained Sterling Hayden's OSS personnel records, also located in RG 226, online from NARA as they were posted by the archives in 2008.

STERLING HAYDEN COLLECTION AT BOSTON UNIVERSITY

The Sterling Hayden Collection at the Howard Gotlieb Archival Research Center at Boston University contains a treasure trove of material that includes diaries, correspondence, drafts of his two books, and many photographs. The archive has always been closed to researchers, but I visited the facility in January of 2016. I am honored to be the only researcher ever granted access to the Sterling Hayden Collection.

DWIGHT D. EISENHOWER PRESIDENTIAL LIBRARY AND MUSEUM

The Dwight D. Eisenhower Presidential Museum and Library was the source of the correspondence between Gen. Eisenhower and Madeleine Carroll cited in this book.

BOOKS AND JOURNAL ARTICLES

Avedon, Burt. *Ah, Men!: What Do Men Want: A Panorama of the Male in Crises, His Past Problems, Present Uncertainties, Future Goals*. New York: A & W Publishers, 1980.

Baptiste, Fitzroy Andre. *War Cooperation and Conflict: The European Possessions in the Caribbean*. Westport, CT: Greenwood Press, 1988.

Bradley, Mark A. *A Very Principled Boy*. New York: Basic Books, 2014.

Brown, Anthony Cave. *Wild Bill Donovan: The Last Hero*. New York: Time Books, 1982.

Brown, Dennis. *Actors Talk*. New York: Proscenium Publishers, 1999.

Ceplair, Larry, and Steven Englund. *The Inquisition in Hollywood, Politics in the Film Community, 1930–1960*. Berkeley: University of California Press, 1983.

Chamberlain, Derek. *39 Steps to Stardom: The Life and Times of Madeleine Carroll*. Leicester, UK: Troubador Publishing, 2010.

Cogley, John. *Report on Blacklisting, I. Movies*. Washington, DC: Fund for the Republic, 1956.

Combined Wire Services. "14,124 Reservists Called Up." *Independent Press-Telegram (Long Beach, CA)*, October 28, 1962.

Conrad, Barnaby. *Name Dropping: Tales from My Barbary Coast Saloon*. New York: HarperCollins, 1994.

Critchlow, Donald T. *When Hollywood Was Right*. New York: Cambridge University Press, 2013.

Crowther, Bosley. "Movie Review—Dr. Strangelove or: How I Learned to Stop Worrying and Love the Bomb." *New York Times*, January 31, 1964.

———. "Movie Review—'Virginia,' A Highly Romantic Drama of the Old Dominion and Its Folks, at the Paramount." *New York Times*, January 29, 1941.

Deery, Phillip. *Red Apple: Communism and McCarthyism in Cold War New York*. New York: Fordham University Press, 2014.

Dick, Bernard F. *Radical Innocence: A Critical Study of the Hollywood Ten*. Lexington: University Press of Kentucky, 1989.

Ford, Kirk, Jr. *OSS and the Yugoslav Resistance, 1943–1945*. College Station: Texas A&M Press, 1992.

Foss, John. Letter to Julian Hatch, February 8, 2007, provided by Kitty Hayden.

Freeman, Gregory A. *The Forgotten 500: The Untold Story of the Men Who Risked All for the Greatest Rescue Mission of World War II*. New York: NAL Caliber, 2008.

Freeman, Maj. Paul. "The Cinderella Front: Allied Special Air Operations in Yugoslavia during World War II." *Air Command and Staff College*, March 1997.

Gaines, William C. "The United States Coast Artillery Command on Aruba and Curacao in World War II." *Coast Defense Study Group Journal* 11, no. 2 (May 1997).

Galanter, Mark. *Cults: Faith, Healing, and Coercion*. New York: Oxford University Press, 1999.

Gay, Timothy M. *Savage Will: The Daring Escape of Americans Trapped behind Nazi Lines*. New York: NAL Caliber, 2013.

Gordon, Bernard. *The Gordon File*. Austin: University of Texas Press, 2004.

Hatch, Norm. "Another OSS Marine." *Purple Heart Magazine* LXVII, no. 6 (July/August 2002).

Hayden, Sterling. *Voyage: A Novel of 1896*. New York: G. P. Putnam's Sons, 1976.

———. *Wanderer*. New York: Alfred A. Knopf, 1963.

———. "Why I Defied the Law." *Parade*, July 26, 1959.

Horne, Gerald. *Class Struggle in Hollywood, 1930–1950*. Austin: University of Texas Press, 2001.

House of Representatives, United States Congress. *Hearings before the Committee on Un-American Activities*. Eighty-Second Congress, First Session, March 8 and 21, April 10, 11, 12, and 13, 1951. Washington, DC: Government Printing Office, 1951.

Huot, Louis. *Guns for Tito*. New York: L. B. Fisher, 1945.

Hutchins, Brian. "General Twining and the Fifteenth Air Force in World War II." Master of Arts Thesis, University of North Texas, May 2008.

Jerome, Fred. *The Einstein File: J. Edgar Hoover's Secret War against the World's Most Famous Scientist*. New York: St. Martin's Press, 2003.

Johnson, Irving. *Sailing to See: Picture Cruise in the Schooner Yankee*. New York: W. W. Norton & Co., 1939.

Kershaw, Robert. *Sky Men*. London: Hodder and Stoughton, 2011.

Langley, Donald, Jr., and Holly J. Blake. *Tahiti Bound*. Stratham, New Hampshire: A. T. I. Publishing, 1998.

Leary, William M. "Fueling the Fires of Resistance: Army Air Forces Special Operations in the Balkans in World War II." US Army Air Forces in World War II series, 1995

LoBrutto, Vincent. *Stanley Kubrick: A Biography*. Cambridge, MA: Da Capo Press, 1999.

Lucas, Peter. *The OSS in World War II Albania*. Jefferson, NC: McFarland & Company, 2007.

Martin, Douglas. "Angus Cameron, 93, Editor Forced Out in McCarthy Era." *New York Times*, November 23, 2002.

McClaren, R. Keith. *A Race for Real Sailors: The Bluenose and the International Fisherman's Cup, 1920–1938*. Jaffrey, NH: David R. Goldine, 2006.

McConnell, Scott. "Leaving the Party: The Politics of Sterling Hayden." *New Criterion* 6, no 5 (January 1988).

Mortland, Donald F. "Lincoln Colcord: At Sea and at Home." *Colby Quarterly* 19, no. 3 (September 1, 1983).

Motavilli, Jim. "An American Odyssey." *Fairfield Advocate* II, no. 28 (February 27, 1980).

Muth, Jorg. *Command Culture: Officer Education in the U.S. Army and the German Armed Forces, 1901–1940, and the Consequences for World War II*. Denton: University of North Texas Press, 2011.

Navasky, Victor S. *Naming Names*. New York: Viking Press, 1980.

Newquist, Roy. *Counterpoint*. Chicago: Rand McNally, 1964.

Office of Strategic Services. "Operational Groups Field Manual, Strategic Services Field Manual No. 6." Washington, DC: OSS: April 25, 1944.

Osterberg, June. "The Wanderer Remembered." *San Francisco Chronicle*, May 22, 1988.

Playfair, Susan R. *Vanishing Species: Saving the Fish, Sacrificing the Fisherman*. Lebanon, NH: University Press of New England, 2003.

Quayle, Anthony. *A Time to Speak*. London: Barrie & Jenkins, 1990.

Roosevelt, Kermit. *The Overseas Targets: War Report of the OSS, Vol. II*. New York: Walker and Company, 1976.

———. *War Report on of the OSS, Volume I*. New York: Walker and Company, 1976.

Ross, Lillian. "The Kaiser's Yacht." *New Yorker*, June 22, 1946.

Smith, Richard Harris. *OSS: The Secret History of America's First Central Intelligence Agency*. Guilford, CT: First Lyons Press, 2005.

Thompson, David. *Altman on Altman*. London: Faber and Faber, 2006.

Tompkins, Warwick. *Fifty South to Fifty South: The Story of a Voyage West Around Cape Horn in the Schooner Wander Bird*. New York: W. W. Norton & Company, 1938.

Waller, Douglas. *Wild Bill Donovan*. New York: Simon & Schuster, 2011.

Weinberg, Gerhard L. *A World at Arms: A Global History of World War II*. New York: Cambridge University Press, 1994.

Wise, James E, Jr., and Anne Collier Rehill. *Stars in the Corps*. Annapolis, MD: US Naval Institute Press, 1999.

INTERNET SITES ACCESSED

"The Bluenose, a True Canadian Champion." Accessed December 21, 2014, http://www.tourcanada.com/luenose.htm.

Crew manifest of vessel *Yankee* arriving at Gloucester, Massachusetts, on May 9, 1938. Accessed November 15, 2014, http://www.ancestry.com.

"Electra Johnson Spread Her Love of Seafaring." *Seattle Times*, December 4, 2004. Accessed December 17, 2014, http://seattletimes.com/html/nationworld/2002109772_johnsonobit05.html.

"Lauren Bacall, Political Activist: She Knew How to Whistle . . . and Speak Her Mind." *Hollywood Reporter*. Accessed August 3, 2014. http://www.hollywoodreporter.com/race/lauren-bacall-political-activist-she-726095.

"Operational Groups of the O.S.S." Office of Strategic Services Operational Groups website. Accessed June 6, 2014, http://ossog.org/overview.html.

"1940s The Conference of Studio Unions—A Democratic Alternative to the IATSE (and Why Warner Brothers Threw Gas Grenades at the CSU): The Conference of Studio Unions." Accessed August 26, 2014, http://runawayproductionhistory.wordpress.com/2011/05/09/1940-the-conference-of-studio-unions-a-democratic-alternative-to-the-iatse-and -why-warner-brothers-threw-gas-grenades-at-the-csu/.

"Stanley Kubrick." Accessed November 15, 2014, http://en.wikipedia.org/wiki/Stanley_Kubrick.

"Sterling Hayden (1916–1986)." Howard Gotlieb Archival Research Center, Boston University. Accessed May 15, 2014, http://hgar-srv3.bu.edu/collections?id=122131.

"Sterling Hayden: Film Noir's Nothing Man." Accessed November 21, 2015, http://www.criminalelement.com/blogs/2012/05/sterling-hayden-film-noirs-nothing-man-thriller-noir-wwii-the-godfather-jake-hinkson.

"Talking with Sterling Hayden." Accessed November 1, 2014. http://geraldpeary.com/interviews/ghi/hayden.html.

"Training SOE Saboteurs in World War Two." BBC. Accessed July 24, 2014, http://bbc.co.uk/worldwars/wwtwo/soe_training_01.shtml.

"Visit to Saudreville, Outside Paris." Accessed January 1, 2015, http://medeleinecarroll.com/visit-to-saudreville-outside-paris/.

"The War for Warner Brothers." IATSE Local 728. Accessed August 26, 2014, http://iatse728.org/Strike.php.

"WW2 People's War." BBC Home. Accessed July 9, 2014, http://www.bbc.co.uk/history/ww2peopleswar/timeline/factfiles/nonflash/a1138376.shtml.

INDEX

SH refers to Sterling Hayden.

ACRU (Air Crew Rescue Unit), 131–33, 140, 151
Africa, Red, 245–46
Africa, Spike, 238, 240, 245–48, 253, 257
Albania, 117–18; American airmen in, 118–19; Grama Bay supply base, 119–20, 123–24; Italian POWs in, 118–24; nurses and medics, rescue of, 106–9, 114–15; Seaview supply base, 118–20, 123–24
Aldebaran (aka *Meteor III*) (yacht), 44–47
Alfred A. Knopf, 264, 267
Allen, Gordon, 135
Allenberg, Bert, 65, 162–63
Allin, J. B., 126–27
Altman, Robert, *The Long Goodbye*, 288–89
American Federation of Labor, 167
American League Against War and Fascism, 171
American Slav Congress, 219
American Youth Congress, 171
AMPP (Association of Motion Picture Producers), 172, 175
Animal Farm (Orwell), 269
Anti-Nazi Germans, 153
Argyll and Sutherland Highlanders, 70, 72
Arisaig House, 70–71
Arnold, H. H. "Hap," 84
Asphalt Jungle, The (Huston), 181–84
Astley, Phillip, 53
Bacall, Lauren, 174, 175, 211
Bahama Passage (Griffith), xii, 3, 55, 59–61
Bailey, S. W., 92
Balli Kombetar (Albania), 117–18
Barker, Lex, 197
Baroway, Leo, 219
Battle of the Bulge, 151–52
BBC, 93, 307–8
Becker, Ernest, *Denial of Death*, 282
Benson, Melvin, 93, 97–98, 104–5, 217–18
Bessie, Alvah, 174–77, 187, 192
Biberman, Herbert, 174–77, 187, 192, 196
Biddle, Francis, 171
Biddle List, 171–72
Blacklist, Hollywood, 175–76, 187–88, 195–96, 284
Blank, Manfred, *Pharos of Chaos*, 213, 297–99, 310
Blocker, Dan, 288
Blue Lagoon (schooner), 33–34
Bluenose, 40–41
Bogart, Humphrey, 174, 176, 211
Boothbay Harbor, 14–16
Boston Herald, 43, 45
Boston Post, 42
Bounty, HMS, 32, 35
Boys' Life, 45
Bransten, Louise, 220

Brave One, The (Trumbo), 284
Brecht, Bertolt, 173
Bridges, Harry, 269, 271
Bridges, Lloyd, 180
Brown, Anthony Cave, 96–97
Brown, Dennis, 101, 293, 311
Buhler, Wolf Eckert, *Pharos of Chaos*, 213, 297–99, 310
Bulkeley, John D., 76
Burdick, Eugene, 271

Caen, Herb, 256, 305, 310
Cagney, James, 167
Calhern, Louis, 184
Cameron, Angus, 264, 269–71
Cannon, John K., 151
Captain, The (de Hartog), 282
Carnovsky, Morris, 209
Carroll, Madeleine (SH's first wife): divorce from SH, 151, 154, 159–61; and Eisenhower, 151, 307; marriage to Phillip, 53; marriage to SH, 75, 77–78, 80–81, 129; name change to Hamilton, 83; publicity stunt in Monopoli, xii; in Red Cross, 102, 129, 151; reunion with SH, 290; SH's affair with, 53–54; SH's chemistry with, 59–62; SH's courtship of, 65, 67–68; war effort support, 81
Film career: *Bahama Passage*, 55; *The General Died at Dawn*, 53; *Lloyds of London*, 53; *My Favorite Blonde*, 80–81; *The Prisoner of Zenda*, 53; *The Southerner*, 50; *The 39 Steps*, 53, 80; *Virginia*, 52–55
Case, Allan, 149
Castro, Fidel, 261, 271
Catchpool, John F., 305–9
Ceplair, Larry, 194–95
CFA (Committee for the First Amendment), 173–77, 186–87, 210–11, 221
Charlotte A. Littlefield (sailing ship), 37
Chase, Allan, 206
Chateau de Saudreville, 53
Cheston, Charles S., 85
Chetniks, 90–93, 97, 115, 131–33, 137, 141, 223, 226–27
Chit Chat Farms, 301
Churchill, Winston, 92–93
CIA, 271
Civil rights movement, 272
Coburn, James, 281
Cohen, Ernest Philip: and HUAC, 188–89, 199; treatment of SH, 179–86, 197
Cohn, Harry, 175
COI (Office of Coordinator of Information). *See* OSS
Colcord, Frances, 38–39
Colcord, Lincoln: *The Drifting Diamond*, 37; as editor of *The Nation*, 37; friendship with SH, 37–39, 86, 116, 145–47, 149; on SH's politics, 146, 161; "The Stein Song," 37; at University of Maine, 37; *Vision of War*, 37; on *Yankee*, 36–38
Cole, Lester, 174–77, 187, 192
Communism: in California, 148; in Hawaii, 226; in Hollywood, 163–64, 166, 171; and individualism, 270; and psychoanalysis, 180; and Taft-Hartley Act, 167; in United States, 149. *See also* HUAC
Conrad, Barnaby, 250, 301, 307; *Matador*, 249; *Name Dropping: Tales from My Barbary Coast Saloon*, 249
Constitution (US), 173
Coon, Carlton, 96
Cooper, Grant, 242–43, 253–54, 256
Coppola, Frances Ford, *The Godfather*, 288
Cossacks, 135, 137
Cristofani, Al, 257
Croatia, 90–92, 133–35
Crowther, Bosley, 55, 275
CSU (Conference of Studio Unions), 166–67, 208–9, 214–15, 221–23
Cuban Missile Crisis (1962), 271–72

Daily People's World, 148
Da Silva, Howard, 196–97, 209
Davis, Bette, 231
Davis, Roger, 245
de Hartog, Jan, 283; *The Captain*, 282; *Hollands Glorie*, 282
Denial of Death (Becker), 282

De Noon, Betty Anne (SH's second wife): divorce from SH, 235–36; marriage to SH, 168; opposition to HUAC, 173; relationship with SH, 168–70, 177, 184, 197; and SH's HUAC testimony, 199–200; on SH's voyage with children, 240–43, 251; Tahiti movie incident, 169
Deranian, B. Nelson, 131–32, 137–38, 140–41
Devine, Robert, 261
Dickson, Benjamin A., 152–53
Dickstein, Samuel, 171
Dies, Martin, 171
Dighton, John, 283–84
Dmytryk, Edward, 174–77, 187, 192
Donen, Stanley, *Love is Better Than Ever*, 196
Donovan, David, 35
Donovan, William J. "Wild Bill," 35, 139, 203; on Chetniks, 91, 131; on guerrilla warfare, 69; on intelligence organizations, 68–69; and London Agreements, 92; and Operation AUDREY, 95–96; as OSS head, 68–69, 72, 84, 139; and SH's OSS career, 3, 74, 83–86; and SOE-Cairo mission, 92–93
Doubleday & Company, 263, 279, 281
Doyle, Bernadette, 220
Doyle, Clyde, 213–17, 225–26, 229, 231
Drifting Diamond, The (L. Colcord), 37
Dr. Strangelove (Kubrick), 274–76
Dunne, Phillip, 173, 211
DuPont Show of the Month, The (CBS), 259

Eaker, Ira, 132
Early, Thomas G., 74
Eisenhower, Dwight D., 96–97, 151, 307
Elco Boat Works, 76
Ellen, Ward, 94, 98, 112–14, 217–18
El Matador, 249
Englund, Steven, 194–95
Erhard, Werner, 290
Ethan Frome (Wharton), 259
Ethel B. Penney (schooner), 49
Executive Order 9835 (1947), 172
Fairbairn, William, 72
Farish, Linn, 93, 111–12, 131–32, 136, 140–44, 217–18
Fasting Can Save Your Life (Shelton), 289
Fath, Creekmore, 150
Faulkner, William, 48
FBI, 86–87, 172, 185, 189–91, 197–99, 212
Featherstone, George S., 82
Federal Employee Loyalty Program, 172
Fifteenth Air Force, 132
Fifty South to Fifty South (W. Tompkins), 62
Filene's Basement Department Store, 29
Finch, Peter, 289
Fishermen, 28, 30
Florence C. Robinson (brigantine), 42–45
Folkoff, Isaac "Pop," 63, 148, 202, 205, 219, 221
Fonda, Henry, 173
Foreign Information Service, 74
Freeman, Dwight and Pearl, 226
Freeman, Y. Frank, 60–61, 65–67, 231
Freud (Huston), 196
Fultz, Harry T., 118

Gang, Martin, 181, 185–87, 212; and HUAC, 187–90, 197–99, 201, 203, 209, 231
Gann, Ernest K., 178
Gardner, Ava, 173
Garfield, John, 180
Gelband, Joe, 304
General Motors, 273
George, Harrison, 148, 205
George, Peter, *Red Alert*, 274
Gershwin, Ira, 173, 211
Gertrude L. Thebaud (schooner), 30, 40–41
Giants in the Earth (Rolvaag), 37
Ginsberg, Henry, 65–66
Glavin, Edward, 128, 151
Gloucester, Massachusetts, 26–27, 40–41
Gloucester Daily Times, 42
Godfather, The (Coppola), 288
Goldwyn, Samuel, 175
Gordon, Bernard, 180–81
Goufrain, Harry, 49–50
Gough, Lloyd, 209

Gould, Elliott, 288
Green, Edward, 126–28, 133, 138, 140, 144
Griffith, Edward H., 49; *Bahama Passage*, xii, 3, 55, 59–61; and SH, 50–52, 55; *The Southerner*, 50; *Virginia*, xii, 3, 52–55
Grippo, Joe, 243–44, 251
Gumpert, Emil F., 242–43, 258

HACIENDA mission, 151, 167, 205; evacuation to Bari, 135–36; Partisans and, 134, 137, 139–40, 147, 205
Hackett, Jack, 30, 40
Hagen, Jean, 183–84
Haley, Harold J., 258
Hallinan, Vincent, 269
Halliwell, R. Davis, 85
Hallowell, Maine, 17
HALYARD mission, 132–33
Hamilton, John (*pseudonym*). *See* Hayden, Sterling
Hamilton, Madeleine. *See* Carroll, Madeleine
Harcourt, Lord, 97
Harnicker, John, 120, 133, 217–18
Harris, Julie, 259, 261
Hatch, Norman, 31–32, 43, 200, 237, 246
Hawaii (Trumbo), 284
Hawaiian Civil Liberties Committee, 226
Hawks, Virginia, 48
Hawks, William, 48
Hayden, Andrew (SH's son), 265–66, 278, 282, 286
Hayden, Catherine Devine "Kitty" (SH's third wife), 278, 296, 303–5; Belvedere homes, 262–63, 267; courtship and marriage to SH, 259–62; in Dordrecht, 286; Nantucket home of, 266; relationship with SH, 278–79, 280, 296, 301; on SH's drinking, 295, 303; on *Stanley Siegel Show*, 292–93; in Stockholm, 293; on *Who Knows*, 286–87; Wilton home of, 287, 295
Hayden, Christian (SH's son), 184, 266
Hayden, Dana (SH's son), 184, 266, 298, 306
Hayden, David (SH's son), 278, 282, 286, 293, 303–4
Hayden, Frances Walter (SH's mother), 9–12, 17–18, 21, 25–26, 144–45, 179
Hayden, Gretchen (SH's daughter), 184, 266, 277
Hayden, James "Jim" (SH's stepfather): marriage to Frances, 12–13, 21, 26; relationship with SH, 16–18, 21, 26
Hayden, Matthew (SH's son), 184, 266, 286
Hayden, Sterling: on acting and money, 3, 4, 52, 59, 64–67, 182–84, 237–38, 308; appearance of, 3, 21, 42, 55, 275–76; beginnings as writer, 161–62; on books, 15–16; childhood, 3, 9–13; children and fatherhood, 184, 235–37, 242, 250, 257, 265–66, 286; death, 309–10; drinking and smoking, 3, 38, 39, 145–47, 159–60, 162, 169, 177–78, 184, 275–76, 278, 279–80, 288–89, 291–93, 295–98, 301, 303, 305–6; drugs, 280–81, 288–89, 291, 302–3; education, 4, 10, 17–18; engagement to Marno, 45–46; financial troubles, 4, 241, 243–44, 253, 258–59, 304; Huston meeting at MGM, 181–82; individualism of, 4–5, 116, 250, 268, 270; kidnapping charges against, 249–50; on labor strikes, 208–9, 214–15, 221–23; mental health, 179–86, 197, 235, 295–96, 303; on Morley, 209, 211–12, 220, 225, 230; as naïve idealist, 215–17; name changes, 83, 101, 237; obsession with writing, 264–67; on Parks, 228; physical fitness, 71–72; prostate cancer, 305–9; in rehab, 294, 298, 301–2; relationship with father, 9–12; relationship with mother, 144–45, 179; relationship with stepfather, 16–18, 21, 26; restlessness, 9–10, 29, 202, 273; river life, 282–83, 286, 298; self-doubt and

self-hatred, 3, 35, 44–46, 65, 72, 75–76, 160, 177, 213, 230–32, 270, 279–80, 289; in Stockholm, 293; in Tahiti, 45; vs. Koch, 110–13, 136; *Walden*'s influence on, 116, 270; on Wallace rally, 228–29; at White House, 150; on *Who Knows*, 286–87, 290, 295–97, 305; on women, 160, 162, 250, 259–60

Film and television career: *The Asphalt Jungle*, 181–84; *Bahama Passage*, xii, 3, 55, 59–61; *Blaze of Noon*, 178; *The Blue and the Gray*, 299; *Dr. Strangelove*, 274–76; *El Paso*, 178; *Ethan Frome*, 259, 261; *The Godfather*, 288; *Hard Contract*, 279, 281; *Johnny Guitar*, 231; *Journey into Light*, 198–99, 231; *The Killing*, 231, 274; *The Long Goodbye*, 288–89; *Manhandled*, 178; *Pharos of Chaos*, 213, 297–99, 310; *The Stanley Siegel Show*, 292–93; *The Star*, 231; *Suddenly*, 231; *Talking Pictures* interview, 307–8; *Ten Days to Tulara*, 274; *Tomorrow* interviews, 291, 294–95, 297, 299–301; *Virginia*, xii, 3, 52–55

Life at sea: *Aldebaran* project, 44–47; *Blue Lagoon*, 33–34; in Boothbay Harbor, 14–15; at Elco Boat Works, 76; *Ethel B. Penney*, 49; *Florence C. Robinson*, 42–45; *Gertrude L. Thebaud*, 30, 40–41; *Horizon*, 30–33; *Oretha F. Spinney* project, 60–62, 77–80; *Puritan*, 23–25; *Quest/Wetona*, 162–63, 169; *Wander Bird*, 62–63; *Yankee*, 34–36

Military life: as intelligence officer, 150–53; as liaison to Partisans, 105–6, 111; in Marine Corps, 3, 80–83, 85, 155, 185; in OCS, 82–83; and Operation AUDREY, 113–14; in OSS, xi–xii, 3, 68, 83–86, 154–55; on OSS officers, 217–18, 222–23, 226–27; rescue missions, 101–2, 106–8, 114–15, 119–24; Silver Star, 100, 155, 160, 189, 200, 205; in Special Operations, 87–89, 92–103; vs. the British, 103, 119–21

Political life: CFA membership, 173–74, 176–77; on civil rights movement, 272; and communism, 115, 125, 139, 149, 159, 163–64, 166; Communist Party affiliation, 3, 163, 167–68, 178, 185–86, 189, 269–70; doubts vs. idealism, 143–44, 160; on joining the Party, 163, 203, 207–8; on leaving the Party, 210–14, 270; Stapp's meeting with, 164–66, 211; and Tompkins, 63–64, 70, 115, 139–40

Hazelden Clinic, 302, 305

Hepburn, Katharine, 173

Heyerdahl, Thor, 179; *Kon-Tiki*, 178

Hinkson, Jake, 4

Hitchcock, Alfred, *The 39 Steps*, 53, 80

Hoffman, Carl, 87

Holden, G. R., 87

Holden, William, 178, 231

Hollands Glorie (de Hartog), 282

Hollywood blacklist, 175–76, 187–88, 195–96, 284

Holman, Russell, 51, 159, 207

Holmquist, Fred, 302

Hood, R. B., 190–91

Hoover, J. Edgar, 84, 171, 189–90, 212

Horgan, Tom, 41, 43, 48–50

Horizon (sloop), 30–33

Horne, Frederick, 84

Horton, Howard T., 25

Hotel Bellevue (Netherlands), 283, 286

Howe, Fisher, 74

Howell, John, 16–17

Hoxha, Enver, 117

HUAC (House Un-American Activities Committee): and CFA delegation, 173–77, 210–11, 221; and Chetniks, 226–27; and Cohen, 188–89, 199; on communist meetings, 208, 214–15, 216, 223, 225, 228, 229; FBI interview with SH, 185, 189–91, 197, 212; and fear of Soviet espionage, 171; Hollywood Ten, 174–77, 187, 192; and naming names, 3, 194–95, 201, 205–6, 217–18, 229–30; Parks's testimony, 193–97, 201, 220, 228,

230; SH on ex-communists, 212–13, 226; Waldorf Statement, 175–76
Hudson, William, 91–92
Hunter, Ian McClellan, 283–84
Huntington, Ellery, 85–87
Huot, Louis, 88, 93, 95–98, 109, 113–14
Huston, John, 173, 211, 306–7; *The Asphalt Jungle*, 181–84; *Freud*, 196

IATSE (International Alliance of Theatrical Stage Employees), 166–67
International Fisherman's Cup, 40–42
International Longshoremen's Union, 63–64

Jackson, Donald L., 220–24
Jacobs, Stephen T., 114
Jaffe, Sam, 184
Jaws (Spielberg), 289
Jerome, Victor Jeremy, 149, 165, 171, 192–93, 206
John Harvey, SS, 99
Johnny Got His Gun (Trumbo), 284–86
John Paul II, Pope, 300
Johnson, Electra "Exy," 32–33, 35
Johnson, Irving, 32–39, 42, 86; *Sailing to See: Picture Cruise in the Schooner Yankee*, 36
Johnston, Eric, 174–75
Jolson Sings Again, 193
Jolson Story, The, 193

Kaye, Danny, 55, 174
Kearney, Bernard W., 220
Keep America Free, 219
Kelly, Gene, 55
Kennedy, John F., 271–72
Kent, Rockwell, *N by E*, 29
Khiefets, Gregory, 227
Killing, The (Kubrick), 231, 274
Kirkus Reviews, 267, 291
Kirsch, Robert, 267
Knox, Alexander, 173, 210
Koch, Robert, 94, 99–100, 109–13, 119, 136, 217–18
Kon-Tiki (Heyerdahl), 178
Korcula (Croatia), 105
Korean War, 185
Koshkin, 256
Kraigher, George, 132–33
Kubrick, Stanley: *Dr. Strangelove*, 274–76; *The Killing*, 231, 274; *Lolita*, 274; *Paths of Glory*, 274; *Spartacus*, 274
Kukich, Nick, 118–19, 121–22, 124

Land, Emory, 86
Langley, Donald J., Jr., 44–45
Lardner, Ring, Jr., 174–77, 187, 192
Lawrence, Stanley, 171
Lawson, John Howard, 171, 174–77, 187, 192
League of American Writers, 171
Lear, Edward, "The Owl and the Pussycat," 262
Lees, Robert, 208
Lesser, Sol, 197
Little, Brown and Company, 269
Lochaber (Scotland), 70
Lohan, Samuel, 97
Lolita (Kubrick), 274
London Agreements (1942), 84, 88, 92
Long Goodbye, The (Altman), 288–89
Los Angeles Times, 250
Love is Better Than Ever (Donen), 196
Loyalty Order (1947), 172
Lucas, Peter, *The OSS in World War II Albania*, 124
Lyman, Ellwood W., 148, 206, 219

MAAF (Mediterranean Allied Air Force), 132
MacArthur, Douglas, 76
MacDonald, Malcom, 54
Maclean, Fitzroy, 93, 97, 104
MacMurray, Fred, 50, 52, 54–55
Macrae, John, Jr., 266
MAES (Medical Air Evacuation Squadron), 106–7, 115
Maltz, Albert, 174–77, 187, 192
Mandel, Louis, 195
Mansfield, William, 92–93
Marine Corps, 85–86
Marshall, George, 84
Marx, Groucho, 174

Matador (Conrad), 249
Mayer, Louis B., 175
McBaine, Turner, 99–100, 105, 108–10, 113
McConnell, Catherine Devine. *See* Hayden, Catherine Devine
McConnell, Neil, 259–60
McConnell, Scott (SH's stepson), 4, 259–60, 269–70, 273
McEdward, Nelson, 126–27
McLaglen, Andrew V., 299
McLin, Patrick, 305
McNarney, Joseph, 84
Meersman, Marno, 45–46
Meersman, Scudder, 45
Mihailovich, Draza, 90–93, 97, 132, 139, 141
Monroe, Marilyn, 184
Moran, D. Perry, 101–3
Morley, Karen, 178, 209, 211–12, 220, 225, 230
Motion Picture Association of America, 175
Motor Torpedo Boat Squadron 3, 76
Moulder, Morgan M., 223, 230
Mouton, Cecil, 41
Murin, Steve, 226
Murphy, Robert, 223
Mussolini, Benito, 117
Musulin, George, 131–33, 141, 218, 226

Name Dropping: Tales from My Barbary Coast Saloon (Conrad), 249
Naming Names (Navasky), 188
Nation, The, 37
National Labor Relations Act (1935), 167
National Liberation Front (Albania), 117–18
National Negro Congress, 171
National Security Agency, 86–87
Navasky, Victor S., 187; *Naming Names*, 188
Nazis: in Albania, 117–18; German people's opposition to, 153; in Yugoslavia, 90–92
N by E (Kent), 29
Neill, A. S., 265
Nelson, Steve, 148–49, 205–6, 219
New York Times, 232
North, Joe, 206

O'Connor, John J., 299
Officer Candidate School (Quantico), 82–83
Operation AUDREY, 95–99, 104, 109–10, 112–15, 121, 139, 155
Operation Barbarossa, 91
Operation DRAVO, 125
Operation Herbstgewitter II, 105
Operation RATWEEK, 125, 130
Oretha F. Spinney (schooner), 60–62, 77–80
Ornitz, Sam, 174–77, 187, 192
Orwell, George, *Animal Farm*, 269
OSS (Office of Strategic Services) (COI): Albanian rescue mission, 106–9, 114–15, 118; communist influence on, 139, 218, 223; Dickson on, 152; under Marshall, 84; Operational Groups, 84–85, 87, 111, 127–28; Operation AUDREY, 95–99, 104, 109–10, 112–15, 121, 139, 155; and SOE, xii, 87, 92–93, 96–99, 104, 121–22; Soviet sources inside, 86–87; training schools, 69–72; under William Donovan, 68–69, 72, 84, 139;, Yugoslavia mission, xi–xii, 85, 92–103
OSS in World War II Albania, The (Lucas), 124
Osterberg, June, 264
O'Toole, Lawrence Patrick Joseph "Larry," 7, 41–43, 46, 48–49, 51, 54, 168–69, 231
"Owl and the Pussycat, The" (Lear), 262

Pace, Nicholas, 302–3
Palacios, Carlos and Agnes, 255
Paramount Pictures, 50–51, 54–55, 65–66, 80, 159
Parks, Larry, 193–97, 201, 220, 228, 230
Paths of Glory (Kubrick), 274
Pavelic, Ante, 90, 92. *See also* Ustasha
Pearson, Billy, 276, 305–6
Peck, Gregory, 173

"People Fight, The" (SH), 128–29
Peter, king of Yugoslavia, 90–91
Pharos of Chaos (Buhler and Blank), 213, 297–99, 310
Pickering, Betsy, 250, 259–60
Pine, Ben, 27, 40–42, 86
Planco, Johnny, 295
Polonsky, Abe, 166, 208
Pomeroy, William, 262
Popovich, Eli, 131–32, 136, 139, 141, 218, 223
Potter, Charles E., 222–23, 227–28
Powe, Ralph, 192
Power, Sir Arthur, 96
Powers, Albert, 19–20
Powers, Dennis, 239–40, 246–47, 250, 306–7, 311
Puritan (schooner), 23–25
Putnam, 291

Quayle, Sir Anthony, 118–24; *A Time to Speak*, 122, 124

Racial protests (1960s), 272–73
Rajacic, Joseph, 133
Rand, Ayn, 172
Rankin, John, 171
Reagan, Ronald, 167, 223, 231, 300
Red Alert (P. George), 274
Red Scare, 171, 219. *See also* HUAC
Remick, Lee, 281
Republic Pictures, 241, 244–46, 253–54, 258
Restless (schooner), 19–20
Ringway Field, 73
Robards, Jason, Jr., 286, 301–2
Robeson, Paul, 269
Robinson, Edward G., 211
Robinson, William A., 42
Rolfing, 290
Rolling Stone, 294
Rolvaag, Ole, *Giants in the Earth*, 37
Roman Holiday (Trumbo), 283–84
Roosevelt, Alice, 44
Roosevelt, Eleanor, 150
Roosevelt, Franklin D., 35, 38–39, 55, 68, 76, 84, 91, 97, 107
Ross, Walter M., 126
Russell, Bill, 52

Sadat, Anwar, 300
SAG (Screen Actors Guild), 165–67, 208–9, 214–15, 221–23, 300
Sailing to See: Picture Cruise in the Schooner Yankee (I. Johnson), 36
Sandpiper, The (Trumbo), 284
San Francisco Bay Area, protests in, 272–73
SBS (Special Bari Section), 89, 93, 98–99, 105; Albanian rescue mission, 108–9; under Koch, 94; movie about Partisans, 126–30, 133
Schary, Dore, 175
Schneiderman, William, 148, 205
Scott, George C., 274
Scott, Robert Adrian, 174–77, 187, 192
Scribner, Joseph, 110
Seaman's Service, 81
Seitz, Albert, 93
Selig, George, 134
Sellers, Peter, 274–75
Serbia, 90–92, 122, 135
Shelton, Herbert M., *Fasting Can Save Your Life*, 289
Sherwood, Robert E., 74
Siegel, Stanley, 292–93
Silver Hill Hospital, 301
Sinatra, Frank, 174
Smith, Lloyd, 107–8
Snyder, Tom, 168, 281, 291–92, 294–95, 297–300, 307–8
Society of Independent Motion Picture Producers, 175
SOE (Special Operations Executive): in Albania, 106–8, 118; Force 266, 114, 126; and OSS, xii, 87, 96–99, 104, 121–22; sphere of control, 84, 88, 92; training school, 70–71
Solborg, Robert, 68–70, 74
Sondergaard, Gale, 196–97
Sorrell, Herbert, 166–67, 221–22
Southern, Terry, 274
Southerner, The (Griffith), 50
Spartacus (Kubrick), 274

Special Committee on Un-American Activities, 171. *See also* HUAC
Special Intelligence Branch (SI), 68–69, 128, 150, 153
Special Operations Branch (SO), 68–70
Spielberg, Steven, *Jaws*, 289
Stalin, Joseph, 117
Stapp, John, 164–66, 211
"Stein Song, The" (L. Colcord), 37
Sterling, Mont (SH's uncle and godfather), 9, 17
Stevenson, Robert Louis, 250
Stone, Shepard, 153
Strong, George V., 84
Summerhill School, 265–66
Summer Place, A (Wilson), 243
Sykes, Eric Anthony, 72

Taft-Hartley Act (1947), 167
Talbot, Herb, 46–47
Tavenner, Frank S., Jr., 192, 194, 198, 200–214, 218, 229
Taylor, Elizabeth, 196
Taylor, Frances, 44
Taylor, Robert, 172
39 Steps, The (Hitchcock), 53, 80
Thomas, J. Parnell, 172, 174–75
Thompson, Dody Weston, 240, 252
Thompson, Robert: at Monopoli, 100; Operation AUDREY, 113–14; OSS Yugoslavia mission, 94–97; SH's HUAC testimony on, 217–18; vs. Koch, 110, 112–13
Thoreau, Henry David, *Walden*, 116, 270
Time to Speak, A (Quayle), 122, 124
Tito, Josef Broz, xi, 89, 91, 93, 97–98, 131, 294. *See also* Yugoslav Partisans
Tofte, Hans: Albanian rescue mission, 108–9; HACIENDA mission, 136; HUAC testimony on, 217–18; on Huot, 97; at Monopoli, 99–100; Operation AUDREY, 113–14; OSS Yugoslavia mission, 94–95, 98–99; Silver Star recommendation, 155; vs. Koch, 99, 110–13
Tompkins, Gwen, 62–63
Tompkins, Warwick: *Fifty South to Fifty South*, 62; friendship with SH, 21–22, 62–65, 70, 86, 115, 139–40, 147–49, 161; HUAC testimony on, 62, 115, 201–7, 217, 219–21, 224–27, 289; and Johnsons, 32; politics of, 62–63, 115; on SH biography, 161
Tompkins, Warwick, Jr., 289
Toulmin, John, 98, 109–10, 112–13, 125
Truman, Harry S., 167, 172
Trumbo, Dalton, 174–77, 187, 192; *The Brave One*, 284; *Hawaii*, 284; *Johnny Got His Gun*, 284–86; *Roman Holiday*, 283–84; *The Sandpiper*, 284
Tumbler Island, 15–16
Turner, Lana, 55
20th Century Fox, 279
Twining, Nathan, 132

Ustasha, 90, 92–93, 105, 135, 294

Vallee, Rudy, 37
van Pallandt, Nina, 288
Van Upp, Virginia, 55
Velde, Harold H., 192–93, 217–20, 222, 226–28
Virginia (Griffith), xii, 3, 52–55
Vis (Croatia), 106, 111, 126
Vision of War (L. Colcord), 37
Vogler, Louis, 276
Voyage: A Novel of 1896 (SH), 4, 279, 287–88, 291–92
Vujnovich, George, 126

Wainwright, Stuyvesant, II, 152–53
Walden (Thoreau), 116, 270
Waldorf Statement, 175–76
Walker, Flora, 237, 257
Walker, Turnley, 237, 257, 262
Wallace, Henry A., 228–29
Walter, Frances. *See* Hayden, Frances Walter
Walter, Francis E., 194, 213
Walter, George (SH's father), 9–12
Walters, Angus, 40
Wanamaker, Nita, 250

Wander Bird (schooner), 62–63
Wanderer (SH), 4, 16, 41, 124, 161, 186, 250–52, 263–64, 267–70
Wanderer voyage: and court order, 257–58; crew of, 239–40, 248–49; funding for, 238, 241, 244–46, 253–55; publicity surrounding, 250–51, 259, 263; return to US, 252–56; SH's children on, 238, 240–46, 249–51, 256; Tahiti, 246–49, 252
Warner, Jack, 172
Warner Bros., 243
Wassookeag School, 17–18
Weil, Richard, 94, 99–100, 108–14, 136, 320n16
Weissmuller, Johnny, 197
West, Paul, 88–89, 104
West Highland Line (Scotland), 72
Wharton, Edith, *Ethan Frome*, 259
Wheeler, William, 187–88, 199–201, 205
White, Wilfred, 22–23, 26
Whitmore, James, 184
Whitney, William, 74
"Why I Defied the Law" (SH), 250–51
Wilson, Sloan, *A Summer Place*, 243
Winters, Bea, 163–64, 208, 211, 216, 221, 227
Wood, John S., 192, 194–96, 213, 222, 228–30
World War II, 70, 154; in the Balkans, 87–88, 92; Battle of the Bulge, 151–52; German attack on Bari, 99; in North Africa, 92; Pearl Harbor, 69. *See also* Nazis
Wuchinich, George, 218–19, 222–23, 226
Wyler, William, 173–74, 176

Yankee (schooner), 32–36
Young, Edward G., 70–71
Yugoslavia: Allied failures in, 140–42; American airmen in, 131–33, 140, 151; Farish on, 142–44; Operation RATWEEK, 125, 130; OSS mission, xi–xii, 85, 92–103
Yugoslav Partisans: abuse by, 137, 139–40; Allied support of, 131; escape from Korcula, 105; Farish on, 141; movie about, 110, 125–30, 133; supplies to, xi, 88, 93–94, 100, 114; vs. Chetniks, 91–93, 137, 141–42, 223

Zog, Amhed, king of Albania, 117